Lawrence Tierney

Lawrence Tierney

Hollywood's Real-Life
Tough Guy

Burt Kearns

UNIVERSITY PRESS OF KENTUCKY

Published by The University Press of Kentucky

Scholarly publisher for the Commonwealth, serving Bellarmine University, Berea College, Centre College of Kentucky, Eastern Kentucky University, The Filson Historical Society, Georgetown College, Kentucky Historical Society, Kentucky State University, Morehead State University, Murray State University, Northern Kentucky University, Spalding University, Transylvania University, University of Kentucky, University of Louisville, University of Pikeville, and Western Kentucky University.
All rights reserved.

Editorial and Sales Offices: The University Press of Kentucky
663 South Limestone Street, Lexington, Kentucky 40508-4008
www.kentuckypress.com

Library of Congress Cataloging-in-Publication Data

Names: Kearns, Burt, author.
Title: Lawrence Tierney : Hollywood's real-life tough guy / Burt Kearns.
Description: Lexington, Kentucky : University Press of Kentucky, [2022] | Series: Screen
    classics | Includes bibliographical references and indexes.
Identifiers: LCCN 2022029990 | ISBN 9780813196503 (hardcover) |
    ISBN 9780813196510 (pdf) | ISBN 9780813196527 (epub)
Subjects: LCSH: Tierney, Lawrence, 1919-2002. | Motion picture actors and actresses—
    United States—Biography. | Motion pictures—History—20th century.
Classification: LCC PN2287.T483 K43 2022 | DDC 791.4302/8092 [B]—dc23/
    eng/20220805
LC record available at https://lccn.loc.gov/2022029990

This book is printed on acid-free paper meeting
the requirements of the American National Standard
for Permanence in Paper for Printed Library Materials.

Manufactured in the United States of America

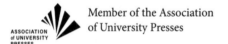
Member of the Association
of University Presses

ASSOCIATION
of UNIVERSITY
PRESSES

For Alison,
who had my back
in my one and only
Hollywood bar brawl.

If you've ever seen *The Devil Thumbs a Ride,* that could be called *The Lawrence Tierney Story,* because it's about some nice guy who's driving down the street and Lawrence Tierney's hitchhiking on the side of the road. And you stop to pick him up. You're having a good day and you're a nice guy, but because you bumped into Lawrence Tierney, he's gonna ruin your life. From that moment on, your day's gonna be fucked and your life is going to be ruined while he's in your presence.

Quentin Tarantino

I respected Lawrence. I was awed by him. After we were shooting *Reservoir Dogs,* I'd turn on the TV late at night and—"Holy shit, there he is! There's Lawrence Tierney. Oh, my God." And there he'd be with his handsome face in some black-and-white movie, usually playing some sort of a bad guy. That was back in the day. And I have tremendous respect for those guys, so I wasn't about to give Lawrence a hard time. I'm just a kid playing Mr. Blonde in a Tarantino movie. I didn't know what the hell I was doing, but I knew that he did. So even when he was throwing punches at me, I found it kind of endearing.

Michael Madsen

I think he had a mental illness that was deeper than alcoholism. He had some kind of manic depression. He needed to drink. He needed to fight. And he had this mania to him. But he could be very nice. My mom said, "Larry can be the most charming man in the world, and then he can turn on a dime and be an absolute bastard one second later."

Timothy Tierney, Lawrence Tierney's nephew

He could have had the same career as Robert Mitchum if he had played the Hollywood game. But he didn't—and of course alcohol didn't help. He used to sit in my room and say to me, "David, don't get involved in drinking, 'cause you'll wind up in one of two places: the hospital or jail."

David Del Valle, film historian and Tierney's friend

Contents

Photos follow page 232

Prologue

It was the most important week in Quentin Tarantino's life.

The former video store clerk was directing his first motion picture. *Reservoir Dogs* was based on his script about the aftermath of a botched diamond heist. The casting of Lawrence Tierney as the criminal mastermind was especially satisfying for Tarantino. Tierney was the real deal: Hollywood's coldest, most brutal "tough guy" actor, a star whose career was derailed in the 1940s and '50s by his offscreen boozing, brawling, and bouts with the law. Tarantino had dedicated the *Reservoir Dogs* script to him.

So it was an intense disappointment when the young director realized on Day One that his hero was "a complete lunatic" who "needed to be sedated." Tierney argued with and antagonized the other actors and crew. He'd walk away while Tarantino was giving direction. He didn't understand the script and he couldn't remember his lines.

"This fuckin' shit is too fuckin' convoluted!" he'd shout in front of the others. "This thing is so fuckin' repetitive! I'm just saying the same thing over again!"

By Friday afternoon, after days of putting up with Tierney's hostile antics, it seemed Tarantino had made it through his first week as a director. There were twenty minutes left before the crew wrapped for the weekend. Tierney needed only a few more shots to complete a scene. Tarantino was explaining to Tierney when, midsentence, the actor turned away. Instinctively, Tarantino grabbed his arm. "Lawrence," he snapped. "Stay here!"

"Get your fuckin' hands off me!" Tierney shook loose and thrust the heel of his hand into Tarantino's chest.

"Fuck you!" The twenty-eight-year-old rookie director charged toward the seventy-two-year-old actor. Fists flew. As the other cast members moved in to separate the pair, Tarantino was enraged. "Fuck you, you fat fuck! *You're fucking fired!*"

1

Violence, Chaos, and Drunkenness

When Lawrence Tierney walked onto the RKO Radio Pictures lot at the corner of Melrose Avenue and Gower Street in Hollywood in 1943, he was no twenty-four-year-old innocent squinting in the glare of the big city lights for the first time. He had acting experience, a street-savvy survival instinct that would allow him to support himself no matter how show business turned out, and all the elements that would lead to the trouble ahead. The anger, temper, weakness for alcohol, violence, and even the seeds of mental illness he'd carry through *Reservoir Dogs* and beyond, were part of his DNA when he entered the world on March 15, 1919.

Lawrence James Tierney was born in the Bedford-Stuyvesant neighborhood of Brooklyn, described at the time as "the second borough of importance of the boroughs that make up New York," into a home that had its share of love and pampering, but was also a hotbed of violence, chaos, and drunkenness. Tierney's official, often-repeated biography would not betray the darkness behind closed doors among the family in which he was the firstborn and, for the first five years of his life, only child of young, Brooklyn-born, Irish-American parents who married on October 12, 1916. His father, Lawrence Hugh Tierney ("Lawrence Sr."), was twenty-seven, a traveling salesman and would-be artist. The son of Irish immigrants James and Mary Laughlin Tierney, Lawrence Sr. was the youngest of a dozen children and the only son. His wife was the former Marion "Mary" Alice Crowley, the fiery, argumentative twenty-three-year-old daughter of Margaret Barry Crowley and Timothy Francis Crowley. Mary Alice's mother was born in Brooklyn. Her father, Tim Crowley, was forty-seven years old at the time of Lawrence's birth, an Irish immigrant, sailor, scrapper, and diehard drunk.

"I have a photo of Tim Crowley," says Timothy Tierney, Lawrence Tierney's nephew. "This guy just looks like someone you do not want to meet. He's in his navy uniform, and he's so muscular and huge, it's like his shirt is gonna split at the seams. He's like a no-neck! His neck is so thick, it just goes straight into his head! And he was just not a nice man. When he would come over, all the kids would run and hide in the laundry bin and in the closets because he was so terrifying. As intimidating as Larry could be in his prime, this guy strikes me as Larry times ten. Ten times bigger, nastier, crazier."

In his first five years, young Lawrence was tossed amid the maelstrom of two families and two worlds. He was doted on and "spoiled" by eleven aunties, but any trace of "sissyness" was knocked out of him by his father—and by his grandfather, who treated the child as a brawler-in-training. He was left flinching in the crossfire of marital combat, as his parents fought like animals and spat in the child's presence words far more forbidden in a Roman Catholic home than the four-letter ones—words like "divorce."

As faithful and fearful Catholics, Lawrence and Mary Alice Tierney did not separate (that split would come thirty years later), and the household had calmed to an uneasy truce by the time another child entered the picture. Gerard Kenneth Tierney (who was nicknamed "Roddy" and in adulthood would work under the name "Scott Brady") was born on September 13, 1924. A third boy, Edward Michael, followed on May 13, 1928, and the family was complete. All three sons were born in Brooklyn, although even before Gerard's birth, the Tierneys had moved to Queens, the largest, though one of the less populated, of the five boroughs, first to Richmond Hill, and ultimately to a house on the tree-shaded Sixtieth Place in the Ridgewood neighborhood. The three sons would grow strong and tall and share characteristics in looks and temperament. Lawrence, though, would be different. He was quieter, yet more easily angered and apt to fly off the handle. His future was shaped by the early years and influences that his younger brothers were spared.

"He told me, 'Everything we do goes back to our mother,'" Tierney's late-in-life friend, the film historian David Del Valle, says. "'Every single mistake we've made, however we feel about our true selves, is based on how our mothers treated us in the first seven years of life.'"

"I sometimes say that Scott and Eddie were more Tierneys and Larry was more of a Crowley," Lawrence's nephew (and Edward's son) Michael Tierney told Gary Sweeney on his *Midnight Palace* radio show in 2011. "Because it seems like the madness comes from the Crowley side: our grandmother, Mary Alice Crowley, the daughter of Timothy Crowley. A lot of the alcoholism seems to come from that side of the family, a lot of the violence, whereas I see that Lawrence Hugh Tierney, our grandfather, and Scott and Eddie seem to be a little more stable and consistent. Larry was very influenced by his grandfather, Timothy Crowley. He was a real tough guy who taught Larry how to fight."

Timothy Tierney says: "He said to seven-year-old Larry Tierney, 'Hey, you're growing up now. It's about time you learned how to fight, don't you think?' And Larry said, 'Yeah, show me how to fight, Grandpa.' And he backhanded Larry and sent him on a backwards somersault across the living room."

Timothy Crowley died on October 1, 1939. "He was killed in a bar fight," his great-grandson says.

"When the family was in New York during the Depression, times were hard," Timothy Tierney says. "My dad said, 'Imagine being a traveling salesman during the Depression, when no one had money.' But then Lawrence Sr. got the job as the aqueduct police chief."

A political connection allowed Lawrence Tierney Sr. to move the family to the city suburbs in the mid-1930s, into a two-story house in the more upscale environs of Yonkers in Westchester County. With no background in law or law enforcement, Lawrence Sr. was named chief of the New York Aqueduct Police. Known today as the New York City Department of Environmental Protection Police, the seven-hundred-man force was responsible for the safety of New York City's water supply, patrolling ninety-five miles of aqueduct, five hundred miles of canals, and key railroad bridges in the state. (In July 1941, Lawrence Sr. was cited in the *New York Times* after the arrest of a potential Russian saboteur, caught surveying the Catskill aqueduct. He held the chief's title through World War II.)

Lawrence the son attended Boys High School, a public yet highly competitive college preparatory school in Bedford-Stuyvesant. Boys High attracted elite students and taught in the classic tradition, including classes in Latin. Tierney's knowledge and appreciation of classic literature and poetry can be traced to these years. A voracious reader since childhood and a crossword puzzle expert in adulthood, he excelled in academics and was an award-winning star on the track team, specializing in the half-mile, 1,000-meter, and 600-meter races. When graduation neared, he juggled the choice of traveling to Michigan State University in East Lansing, known for its championship track and field and cross country programs, or staying close to home and accepting an athletic scholarship to Manhattan College. In the Boys High tradition, Tierney took the scholarship.

But weeks before his first college semester, his scholarship was suddenly in jeopardy, due to an incident that put Tierney in the headlines for the first time: "YOUTH INJURES HAND IN STAIRWAY TUMBLE." "Lawrence Tierney, eighteen, of 44 Cricklewood Road, found his reflexes acting properly yesterday afternoon and as a result required treatment for lacerations of the left hand."

According to the *Yonkers Herald Statesman* of August 18, 1937, teenage Tierney told police he tripped on the stairs to the basement of his home, and when he reached out for balance, ran his hand through a window. Of course, as a harbinger of many incidents to come, Tierney's account was not quite the entire story. Timothy Tierney says that "rotten older brother" Lawrence was chasing Gerard to "beat him up" when he ran his forearm through the glass window of a door that Gerard had slammed behind him. "My dad told me that Larry was a terror to have as an older brother, and that he really gave my dad some severe beatings."

Tierney was taken to St. John's Riverside Hospital and treated by his family physician. The injury didn't affect his sports scholarship, and he was in class when the Manhattan College School of Arts' fall term began on September 20. The nerve damage to his left arm would be serious enough, however, to disqualify him from military service during the Second World War.

Tierney was a standout on the Manhattan College cross country team, but quit school after his sophomore year. While he continued to run with the New York Athletic Club track team and competed in meets at venues including Madison Square Garden, he took advantage of his father's connections to land work as a sandhog: a construction worker toiling underground and underwater on the New York aqueduct system. "As a kid I did nothing but tough jobs," he told gossip columnist Sheilah Graham years later. "I was a sandhog during the building of the aqueduct, a locomotive builder, punch-press and jackhammer operator." A friend's suggestion led him to the John Robert Powers Modeling Agency in Manhattan, and less strenuous work as a catalog model. "At first I thought it was kinda sissy stuff," he told an interviewer a few years later, "but soon changed my opinion of the work."

When RKO Radio Pictures press agent Rutgers Nielson was tasked in 1947 with molding Tierney's official origin story, he located a specific place and moment at which Tierney turned to acting. It was New Rochelle, New York, an evening in the summer of 1942. Tierney stood outside a stage door, waiting for a girl he'd be taking on a date. "While waiting, young Tierney noticed an inscription on the door—The New Rochelle Players," the flack hammered out. "The door opened, an elderly gentleman invited him inside, and asked what experience he had had. 'Well,' replied the boy, 'I worked for a while as a sandhog on the New York Aqueduct, and then I was in a steel mill in Philadelphia.' The man wanted to know what acting experience he had had. The youth had never known an actor. The stranger, a dramatic coach, liked Tierney's voice and appearance and offered him a part in the amateur show. That night Tierney studied a script instead of dancing."

By Nielson's account, Tierney appeared onstage the very next evening, in a skit titled *Son of Naples* before an audience of soldiers at the nearby Fort Slocum military post. A few months and many acting classes later, he joined the Blackfriars, a theater group headed by Augustin Duncan, brother of acclaimed dancer Isadora Duncan. That led to work with the American-Irish Theatre and, in April 1943, his first real break in show business.

The theater group was presenting *War Wife* at the Malin Studio Theatre, an Off-Broadway showcase at 135 West Forty-Fourth Street, in the heart of the Broadway theater district. Described in its press release as "a thrilling comedy about the women who battle alone after their man has gone into service," the experimental work was the first (and only) play by the Rev. William Willard Whalen, a child actor turned Roman Catholic priest turned theater script doctor. Two days before the premiere on April 29, it was announced that leading man Ralph Kandel had dropped out of the production. Taking his place for the six-night run was Lawrence Tierney.

Tierney's debut in the small theater must have gone well. After the first performance, Whalen walked onstage and applauded the star.

"Tomorrow," he announced, "I want all movie scouts to come here. We have Errol Flynn, years younger and without a yacht!"

Weeks later, RKO Radio Pictures, one of Hollywood's original "Big Five" studios, signed Tierney to a seven-year option contract.

That signing was the result of an equally fortuitous circumstance. Tierney had accompanied a friend to a casting interview at RKO's talent department in Manhattan, when attention turned to him. The version that Nielson typed out for a Hollywood columnist was very similar to the story Tierney told to cable access talk show host Skip E. Lowe in 1985.

"I was working as a lifeguard at the time," Tierney recalled, "and I had been asked to do some modeling and I got into that with the John Robert Powers Agency. One day, we were set to go on an interview for a modeling commercial. . . . A guy named George Schaffer, real nice guy, said, 'We have about two hours to get there. Let's share a cab while we go downtown to the interview.' I said, 'Fine.' And then he said, 'By the way, since we have the time . . . would you mind coming over to RKO Studios with me?'—not the studios, but the offices—'I'm working on getting a film contract. . . . I have an appointment there.'

"So I went over with him and I sat in the outer office. Marion Robinson, who was a very nice woman who was one of their casting directors, came out to bring him into her office. While he was in there, she asked him who I was. And he told her I was another model. And so she asked to meet me. And I came in and she said, 'Are you an actor?' I said, 'Well, I think I could act.' I always did. I used to watch them in films and say, 'Why can't I do that as well as anyone else?' . . . I read for her. I've always had the ability to read cold very well, without a lot of preview study. And she liked my reading and had me read for Arthur Willi, who was her boss, and they liked me. And then Ben Piazza came out. He was at RKO, head of casting, and they signed me to a contract."

Lawrence Tierney recalled that he arrived in Hollywood on July 4, 1943. He was 175 pounds, a shade over six feet tall, with an athletic build, gray-green eyes, brown hair, and a distinctive flesh-colored mole on his chin. When he walked through the door of the RKO Radio Pictures studio building at 780 North Gower Street and onto the studio lot, he was another face in the RKO's contract player crowd. There was no need yet to feed image-burnishing items to the many gossip writers who happily filled columns and broadcasts with phony quotes and couplings. He merely had to keep his nose clean, look good, and learn how to act on camera.

RKO got its money's worth from the start, slotting Tierney in *Gildersleeve on Broadway,* the third feature based on the popular *Great Gildersleeve* radio comedy. In his screen debut, the twenty-four-year-old played a tough-looking cab driver. The uncredited role was followed by more unbilled appearances: an FBI man in *Government Girl,* a crewman in *Seven Days Ashore,* an orchestra leader in *The Falcon Out West,* and a seaman in *The Ghost Ship.* He was handed the role in *The Ghost Ship,* a colorful character with a memorable death scene in which he was crushed by the ship's anchor chain, after he struck up a friendship with the producer. Russian-born Val Lewton was head of RKO's horror unit, and the success of his low-budget horror-thrillers, *Cat People* and *I Walked with a Zombie,* made him a big man on the RKO lot.

"Val Lewton was a very wonderful, kind, talented and gentle man. And he was a real nice guy," Tierney told Michael and Cheryl Murphy in an interview for *Psychotronic Video* magazine in 1990. "He liked me. He got a kick out of me. When I first came here, I carried the Brooklyn accent and I'd say, 'Doity poiple boids' and all that stuff and I amused him very much.

"He kept telling me, 'Where do I know you from?' when I was introduced to him. And I said, 'Gee, I don't know, did you spend much time in New York? Have you ever been in jail in New Jersey?' And we had a laugh or two, but he couldn't figure out where he knew me from. So about two or three weeks later, I'm walking down the studio lot and from his office up on the third floor he hollered out, 'Lawrence, Lawrence!' and I said, 'Who is it?' and he said, 'It's Val Lewton, come on up!' So I went up and he said, 'Now I know where I know you from.' And he had two books in front of him. A Sears and Roebuck catalog and a Montgomery Ward catalog. I had done a lot of modeling before I got into the business, so there were old pictures of me in bathing suits, hats and jackets, suits. So that's where he said he saw my face many times. 'It's my hobby to buy things from the Sears and Roebuck catalog.'"

"Larry said to me one day, without any equivocation, 'David, the nicest man I ever met in Hollywood was Val Lewton,'" Del Valle says. "'Val Lewton was like a father to me.'"

"Larry spoke very highly of Val Lewton, always," recalls writer and director C. Courtney Joyner, a close friend to Tierney in his later years. "And I think that he's extremely important just because of the casting of *Ghost Ship*. It put Larry truly on film for someone to see, so that when he went in and muscled in on *Dillinger*, there was something to point to. And Larry always appreciated that."

Gildersleeve on Broadway and the wartime office comedy *Government Girl* were released a week apart, October 28 and November 5, 1943. Lawrence Tierney had made it to the big screen, though one might need to be a catalog aficionado to notice. Production on his first credited, costarring role began two days before *Government Girl* opened. Once again, he could thank Val Lewton for the break.

Youth Runs Wild was a B-movie about juvenile delinquency (which the US government had tagged as a major issue in wartime America), based on a *Look* magazine photo essay, "Are These Our Children? (Can We Keep Them Out of Trouble?)," from the issue of September 21, 1943. Lewton was assigned as producer, novelist John Fante brought on to write the script, and *The Ghost Ship* director Mark Robson to helm. The cast was headed by Bonita Granville, Kent Smith, Jean Brooks, and, in the role of Larry Duncan, Lawrence Tierney. Larry Duncan was a garage owner who runs a tire theft operation, corrupting young kids while their fathers are at war and mothers working in factories. The first time that moviegoers could read his name on the screen, Lawrence Tierney was the bad guy.

Notice of, and some acclaim for, the actor wouldn't occur for another nine months. In the meantime, Tierney supplemented his meager contract wage with various side jobs: on construction sites, in a slaughterhouse, in a lumberyard in Beverly Hills, and as a post hole digger for the advertising company Foster & Kleiser. "Where you see F, you see K," Tierney would wisecrack to his pals. The gag showed he could be as down-and-dirty as any blue collar worker, but also revealed the classical and literary education instilled at Boys High School. The coded reference (followed by an even more graphic one) was first published in 1920, in James Joyce's novel *Ulysses*, in a song by the Prison Gate Girls: "If you see Kay / Tell him he may / See you in tea . . ."

Attention was paid in the summer of 1944, when RKO's publicity department began anticipating the opening of *Youth Runs Wild*. The scoop on Lawrence Tierney was given to his hometown paper, the *Brooklyn Eagle*: "Lawrence Tierney, N. Y. A. C. athlete who ran against Glenn Cunningham and Gene Venske at various Madison Square Garden meets, will make his film debut in 'Youth Runs Wild,' RKO Radio's feature drama shortly to have its Broadway premiere at the Palace Theater. Tierney was previously on the Manhattan College track team. His father is chief of the New York City Aqueduct Police, now engaged in guarding the New York City water supply system covering several up-state counties." *Youth Runs Wild* opened on September 1, 1944. The *Deseret News,* reporting on its premiere in Salt Lake City, praised the film's "message of parental and civic responsibility for the emotional maturity of America's adolescents," though when the film opened in Boston, the *Globe* reviewer noted that if the behavior and reaction of adolescents in the theater was any indication, "one is forced to the conclusion that pictures like 'Youth Runs Wild' swell juvenile egos into believing that underage delinquency is a keen delight and a minor triumph."

The editors of *Look* weren't wild about the picture, either. They refused to promote it in the publication. They were only half as displeased as Val Lewton. Before the picture opened, RKO tested two versions. One cut was Lewton's. A second, edited by the studio, excised some edgy and violent scenes. When the studio decided to go with its own cut, Lewton demanded his name be removed from the credits. It was not. *Youth Runs Wild* didn't do well at the box office. In the end, the studio complained that it lost $45,000 on the picture.

On the bright side, Lawrence Tierney was on the Hollywood map. His photo, cheek-to-cheek with Bonita Granville, was printed in newspapers around the country, and the RKO publicity department got some editors to run brief features on the actor. "STAGE DOOR JOHNNY GETS BID TO ACT" recounted the story of how Tierney became an actor by chance, all because he was waiting for a gal at a stage door.

"If it hadn't been for that 'stage door Johnny' episode I never would've thought of acting," Tierney was quoted.

The brief item served several purposes. It established Tierney as a ladies' man and a man's man: a strong, down-to-earth working stiff who could romance a beautiful actress. It also put a spin on Tierney's teenage hand injury, claiming that he wasn't off fighting the war because he was "rejected by the army due to an injured left hand while working in a shipbuilding yard."

After more than a year in Hollywood, a picture of Lawrence Tierney was beginning to form in the eyes of the American public. The picture was not recognized by the executives at RKO Radio Pictures who, as was standard in Hollywood, held a very one-sided option contract with the young actor. Tierney was bound to the studio for seven years, but the studio could cancel the agreement every six months. In 1944, Tierney got word from his agent that RKO Radio Pictures was not planning to pick up his next six-month option.

"They dropped my option and Val Lewton was mad about it," he told the Murphys. "About a week later, they said they decided not to drop my option and my agent said, 'No, he's signed to do a test at MGM now, you'll have to wait.' So I went to MGM, then I went to Universal, then I went to 20th Century Fox, then I went to Warner Brothers. Warner Brothers did five screen tests of me. They finally decided they weren't going to sign me to the contract.

"During that time, I heard about a film in a headline in Hedda Hopper's column that said the King Brothers were looking for a new unknown to play Dillinger. So I went over there that day."

2

Poverty Row

What was most important for Lawrence Tierney, what changed the course of his life—what defined and possibly cursed it—took place in 1944 after he walked out the doors of RKO Radio Pictures at 780 Gower Street, turned right, and strolled almost three miles up the sidewalk to an office on Poverty Row.

Poverty Row wasn't a street or a location. It was a rank, the name given the small, independent "studios" that churned out B-movies on bare-bone budgets, even tighter schedules, and with D-list stars, and occasionally came up with a hit. Many of the Poverty Row production companies were clustered around Gower Street near Sunset and Hollywood Boulevards. The King Brothers were set up on the Monogram Pictures lot, a couple of miles east.

The King Brothers were a trio of big, fat, noisy, pushy *machers* who'd turned themselves into movie producers by necessity. Frank and Maurice Kozinsky (kid brother Hymie tagged along as "technical advisor" when he returned from the Marine Corps) were boys when their father, a Russian immigrant and fruit merchant, moved the family from New York City to Los Angeles in the 1920s. Over the years, the brothers rose from shining shoes and hawking newspapers to bootlegging and making a fortune owning slot machines (thousands of them). They "made a killing," Tom Treanor wrote in the *Los Angeles Times* in 1941. "They operated almost every kind of machine from the original one-armed bandits to elaborate pinball games. One time they had 19,000 machines out."

The Kozinskys moved into the motion picture business in a roundabout but perfectly logical manner. The brothers were developing "slot machine movies"—motion picture jukeboxes—and asked Cecil B. DeMille to provide them with footage to run on their slot machine projectors. In their opinion, DeMille didn't act quickly enough on their request, and when he did, offered them *dreck*. The brothers put their heads together, and after consulting a couple of guys they knew from the racetrack—Louis B. Mayer and Frank Capra—decided to do it themselves.

They shot their first picture in six days for less than $20,000. The picture made some money, so they made another one. They changed their name from Kozinsky to King in 1942 and got into business with Monogram, one of the most monied operations on Poverty Row. Monogram was known for Westerns and adventure movies. In 1944, the King Brothers proposed a gangster picture.

Gangster pictures were a problem for the major Hollywood studios, but a sure sell for Poverty Row. The heyday of gangster classics like *Public Enemy* and *Scarface* in the early 1930s crashed to a halt in 1934 when, faced with boycotts and possible government censorship, the Motion Picture Producers and Distributors of America, which represented the five major studios, began enforcing its Picture Production Code. The self-censoring set of moral guidelines laid out what was acceptable when it came to sex, violence, and politics, and applied to every film the majors released.

The rules didn't always apply to the low-budget independents. That's one reason the King Brothers didn't hesitate asking Monogram to finance a film about John Dillinger, the infamous midwestern gangster, bank robber, and cop killer whose spree ended on July 22, 1934, when he was shot down by federal agents as he stepped out of the Biograph Theater in Chicago. It didn't matter to the brothers that four months before Dillinger's demise, MPPDA president Will Hays decreed that "no picture based on the life or exploits of John Dillinger" was to be "produced, distributed or exhibited by any member company" because "such a picture would be detrimental to the best public interest."

Lawrence Tierney was at loose ends when he learned about the Dillinger picture. Caught in the middle of RKO's indecision and rejection elsewhere, living in a furnished room with little money, he was considering a way out. His friend Jack Gage, a dialogue director who was helping him control his "doity boids" Brooklyn accent, suggested that Tierney reboot his career by heading back to New York, getting more experience as a stage actor, and returning to Hollywood with some solid credits. Tierney took the advice. He bought a ticket on the streamliner, a sleek train that would pull out of Union Station and chug him on his way home. He was four days from the "all aboard" when he read the item in Hedda Hopper's column.

"I just walked into the King Brothers' office without an agent or even an introduction," he told Patricia Clary of the United Press the following year.

"Morrie and Frank interviewed me. But when they learned I had never played a role in the movies they said 'no'—politely, but 'no.'"

Clary wrote that Tierney was so desperate for the part that he waited until the King Brothers' secretary wasn't looking and swiped a copy of the *Dillinger* script. He went home and practiced the scene in which Dillinger is betrayed by the Lady in Red (who lured him to his death).

"I barged into the King offices the next day, breezed right by the secretary and went into the scene without wasting time on formalities. It was lucky for me they didn't toss me out right away. Instead, they listened, liked my reading and signed me for the role even though I had no name value."

That was how it happened—but not quite. Looking back forty-five years later, Tierney recalled that when he first stepped into the King Brothers' office, "they were out to lunch," so he grabbed a *Dillinger* script from a pile and slipped it under his coat. He studied the script at a nearby diner and returned that afternoon to face a "very gruff" Morrie and Frank King and their production manager, Clarence Bricker. The role, they told him, had already been cast. Anthony Quinn had the part.

Before Tierney could board the train to New York, he got a call from his agent. RKO was picking up his option, after all. He'd be making a hundred dollars a week.

"The week after that, I'm walking around the studio lot and I pick up a newspaper and there's a banner headline in the column: 'King Brothers still looking for unknown to play Dillinger,'" Tierney told the Murphys. "My agent got my screen tests from Warners, showed them to the King Brothers, so they brought me in and talked and talked and talked. I said, 'Gee, you guys are funny, I was in here two weeks ago and I didn't have an agent. I wasn't signed with anyone. All I had was a ticket to New York and I stopped in and you told me it's all cast.' They said, 'You're full of shit.' They wouldn't believe me. I went home, brought the script, threw it on their desk and said, 'There's your script, I'm the guy to play it!' I think that convinced them. They thought, 'This guy's a crook, he should play Dillinger!' So that's how I got the part."

That's exactly how it happened—only not exactly. There was another person in the room when Tierney first auditioned for the King Brothers. Philip Yordan was convinced that Tierney, the unknown with the doity boids accent, was the only man for the role.

Yordan had written the script that Lawrence Tierney "borrowed" for his impromptu audition. He had come up with the idea of focusing on John Dillinger after the Kings turned to him to write a gangster picture (their first choice for a writer, George Beck, wanted too much money). Yordan had received his first writing credit in 1942 on a film called *Syncopation* that starred Adolphe Menjou, and he'd written the mystery movie *The Unknown Guest* for the King Brothers in 1943. His latest work was a play, *Anna Lucasta*, set to open in August on Broadway at the Mansfield Theatre, with an all-Black cast.

Yordan said he got help writing *Dillinger* from producer and director William Castle (later known for his innovative B-movie promotion gimmicks, and as producer of *Rosemary's Baby*). "I had a secretary and I dictated the whole script to her. William Castle was supposed to direct it. He was sitting with me as I dictated," Yordan told Patrick McGilligan in 1987, in an interview that would appear in McGilligan's book *Backstory 2: Interviews with Screenwriters of the 1940s and 1950s*.

When Yordan showed the finished work to the King Brothers, he said "they liked it," but that Steve Broidy, president of Monogram Pictures, thought it was too expensive to lens. "Broidy says, 'Are you crazy? . . . This picture looks like it's going to cost over $50,000. The one I made before cost $26,000. We have got to protect our investment, so Chester Morris has to play Dillinger.' I said, 'Chester is fifty years old and he can't play Dillinger.' He says, 'Well, I'm not going to put up the money unless . . .'

"There was a kid that came in the office by the name of Larry Tierney," Yordan recollected. "Boy, he looked like Dillinger, and he was mean, and I wouldn't sell the script until they agreed to put him in it."

The King Brothers were faced with a double dilemma: a studio that rejected the budget, and a writer who had the nerve to withhold the script unless he had casting approval. Chester Morris was only forty-three years old, not fifty—*and who the hell was Lawrence Tierney?* They put the gangster picture aside for a moment. Frank King suggested that Yordan write them something "simple"—meaning cheaper to produce. In short order, he gave them two more scripts. After *Johnny Doesn't Live Here Anymore* and *When Strangers Marry* were produced (both featuring rising star Robert Mitchum, recently under contract with RKO) and promised to turn a profit, Broidy decided that Monogram would ante up something substantial by Poverty Row standards—$65,000—for their gangster picture.

(The MPPDA got wind of the plans, and on June 28 Will Hays's successor, chief censor Joseph I. Breen, sent a letter to Frank King, reminding him that the Production Code Administration would approve the Dillinger picture only if "numerous violations of the Special Regulations Re Crime in Motion Pictures" were cut from the script. According to the American Film Institute archives, Breen also warned that "political censor boards everywhere" would be "critical" of the film.)

Mitchum lobbied for the Dillinger role, but RKO nixed it as wrong for his image (and $350, the weekly fee RKO would charge to loan out the actor, may have been more than the Kings could stomach). Yordan, meanwhile, stuck to his guns about his choice for the lead. Monogram caved and moved to "borrow" the unknown Lawrence Tierney (and the blonde Anne Jeffreys to play Dillinger's moll, the Lady in Red) from RKO Radio Pictures.

RKO didn't blink. They rented Tierney to Monogram for a hundred dollars a week.

Monogram Studios made the announcement on October 4, 1944. John Dillinger, shot dead in front of a Chicago movie theater, was coming back to life and Lawrence Tierney would inhabit his body. The newspapers made note of the fact that the studio had chosen a twenty-five-year-old who'd appeared only in minor roles in *The Ghost Ship, The Falcon Out West,* and *Youth Runs Wild.* Seasoned actors Edmund Lowe, Elisha Cook Jr., Eduardo Ciannelli, and Marc Lawrence had also signed on. The veteran filmmaker Max Nosseck would direct, the respected Dimitri Tiomkin was composing the score—but again, the star was an *unknown.*

"Well, now here's one for the books. Lawrence Tierney, the newcomer who will play John Dillinger in the Monogram movie, is the son of a New York police captain!" Curiosity about the jackpot winner, supposedly selected after a six-week search, was satisfied by Louella Parsons and the other Hollywood columnists, who filled in the blanks with RKO's press materials. "Six feet tall, 25 years old and considerably better looking than the late Dillinger," Parsons wrote. The King Brothers and Monogram weren't cheaping out when they settled on their hundred-dollar-a-week Dillinger, she contended. "Established actors 'spoiled the illusion.'"

Production on *Dillinger* got under way the following Tuesday, October 10. Filming was completed in twenty-one days. There was some location shooting out of town in Simi Valley, at Big Bear Lake, and in the San Bernardino National Forest, but the King Brothers saved money by using archival footage. One holdup scene was borrowed from Fritz Lang's 1937 film, *You Only Live Once.*

Lawrence Tierney appeared to have carried out his first starring role without a problem. It was years later—seventy years after the final shot setup—that costar Anne Jeffreys revealed that Tierney's future issues were already emerging. "The only actor I had a problem with was Lawrence Tierney in *Dillinger,*" she told film noir scholar and critic Jason A. Ney in the Spring 2015 issue of *Noir City* magazine. "He threatened to push me off a flight of stairs at the top of a set. We were standing at the top waiting to make an entrance, and he whispered in my ear, 'I'm gonna push you down the stairs.' And he meant it, too!"

Jeffreys says she was saved by a gaffer working with the lights. "A voice from up in the rafters said, 'You do and I'll smash you!' That took care of that, because he meant it." Tierney, she said, "was all right sober, but if he had one drink—wow. He was a wild man."

When filming wrapped, Tierney walked back down Gower Street to RKO Radio Pictures studios, where he was slotted into more no-name roles. He had a small part as Lt. Cmdr. Waite in *Back to Bataan,* a rousing war movie starring John Wayne and costarring Anthony Quinn. Tierney portrayed an air force lieutenant in *Those Endearing Young Charms,* Lew Allen's wartime romantic comedy starring Robert Young and Laraine Day.

A hundred dollars a week wasn't movie star money. Tierney regretted that he'd quit his job digging post holes, erecting billboards for Foster & Kleiser. He regretted the decision until the day he looked up at one of the billboards he'd built and saw his picture on it.

3

Public Enemy No. 1

Ha! Lawrence Tierney, who plays the title role in "Dillinger," once lost a job because he wasn't hard-boiled enough to make bill collections.

ERSKINE JOHNSON, IN HOLLYWOOD
MARCH 16, 1945

The executives at RKO Radio Pictures didn't pay much attention to their contract player's work at Monogram Studios and continued to waste Tierney in small supporting roles in early 1945. He was credited as "Larry Tierney" in *Birthday Blues,* a comedy short starring vaudeville comic Leon Errol and directed by Hal Yates, another vaudeville veteran who'd directed early Laurel & Hardy comedies. The film was released on February 16.

Dillinger was scheduled to open exclusively in Cincinnati, Ohio, on April 6. As the date neared, Monogram's publicity department began offering "news" items to increase excitement over the film and its star. The main couriers who'd turn out to be chroniclers of the future adventures of Lawrence Tierney were the syndicated newspaper gossip columnists, some of whom had their own influential radio broadcasts. Chief among them were Hedda Hopper, Louella O. Parsons, Sheilah Graham, Harrison Carroll, and Jimmie Fidler. Though all had the power to destroy careers—especially the three women whom Graham dubbed "the unholy trio"—it would be Fidler who wielded the most moral authority and took the least pleasure in what was ahead.

Fidler was first to give notice that *Dillinger* might be something special when, two weeks before the premiere, he named it "Pic of the Week . . . entertainment for thrill-lovers." Six days later, before anyone had seen a frame of the picture, Sheilah Graham broke the news that Tierney was so good in *Dillinger* that the King Brothers already had him lined up for a second picture at Monogram. "Lawrence is under contract to RKO," she wrote. "But they

17

haven't used him yet." The movie was called *Payment Due,* a title that would prove somewhat ironic in light of what would transpire in the weeks to come.

Dillinger's world premiere took place on April 6, 1945, at the Strand Theatre on Walnut Street in Cincinnati. The following day's *Cincinnati Enquirer* featured E. B. Radcliffe's review: "'Dillinger,' at the Strand, is an o.k. gangster picture, which can lay its principal claim to distinction on the introduction of Lawrence Tierney, a tall, husky, and hard-faced handsome gentleman whose capacity for registering fierceness and cruelty makes him worthy of consideration as a possible important trespasser in the Bogart tough guy domain." Radcliffe paid lip service to the fears that gangster films encouraged juvenile delinquency. He noted that "the ease with which Dillinger outwits the law and succeeds in his early endeavors give him a sort of admirable cast," but offered "hope the grim ending registers with as forceful impact on the impressionable and adventuresome as the thrills of its early wild life."

That was beside the point. The point was not only that Lawrence Tierney was hailed as a rising star but also that the contract player whom RKO was sticking into generic bit parts was being touted as a rival to Humphrey Bogart. Somebody saw what the RKO Radio executives did not.

Dillinger opened in New York City on April 25 at the Victoria Theatre, the grand movie palace in Times Square at Broadway and Forty-Sixth Street. The *New York Times* was not overly enthusiastic, calling the film "a rip-roaring gangster melodrama reminiscent of the 'Public Enemy' school": "The scenarist obviously made no attempt to analyze the character and in his portrayal of Dillinger Lawrence Tierney merely snarls his way through the picture. Mr. Tierney, a newcomer, is tough and menacing, but his is strictly a physical characterization and contains no suggestion of the cunning, warped mentality of the real Dillinger." Wanda Hale in the *Daily News* was more charitable: "The acting is uniformly good, with Lawrence Tierney giving a sincere job of portraying the robber and killer."

The reviews didn't matter. *Dillinger*'s New York City premiere made Hollywood history, as the independent gangster film machine-gunned box office records at the Victoria and beyond. From the first screening at 8:30 a.m. through the continuous showings that followed, the twenty-four hundred seat theater was sold out, with an extra eleven hundred standees filling every available space. *Dillinger* was a hit, and as the picture rolled out across the country, the success would be repeated. Literally overnight, Lawrence Tierney was a movie star.

More than that, he *was* Dillinger.

Now, the suits at RKO noticed. A week after the New York City opening, the studio announced that their discovery Lawrence Tierney would star in the mystery melodrama *Step by Step*. Anne Jeffreys, RKO's other loan-out to Monogram's *Dillinger,* would costar. RKO also agreed to the King Brothers' request to borrow Tierney for Monogram's *Payment Due*. There was a slight catch. This time, the price would not be $100 a week, but $35,000.

Jimmie Fidler, who broke the story, observed, "It seems to me that Tierney's bosses might have shown a bit more gratitude to the independents who had made them a valuable property."

Five days later, the Allies accepted Germany's unconditional surrender of its armed forces, ending the war in Europe. The following day, May 8, 1945, there were spontaneous VE Day celebrations throughout the United States. Actress Shelley Winters related her memories of the day in her 1980 autobiography, *Shelley: Also Known as Shirley*. This was the day the twenty-four-year-old Jewish starlet, born Shirley Schrift, met Lawrence Tierney. Winters's memories and insights not only paint a picture of Tierney in his first weeks of stardom but also indicate the issues that would complicate his future.

Winters wrote that she attended a party that day at the home of Lawrence Tibbett, the Metropolitan Opera star and Academy Award–nominated actor (for *The Rogue Song* in 1930). After drinking one too many rum and Cokes, she began to sing "The Cuban Love Song" from Tibbett's 1931 movie of that name. Winters was singing and dancing alone when suddenly "a very strong hand across my mouth cut off my music and my breathing. A formidable husky voice whispered, 'You're making my headache worse.'" When she responded by pouring what remained of her Cuba Libre onto the man's shoes, he backed off and whispered, "You won't sing anymore, will you?"

"The tone of his voice made me look down to see if he had a gun pointed at my ribs," Winters wrote. "He didn't, but there was something so terrifyingly gentle about his manner and voice, despite his huge height and width, that I was sure he was a real gangster."

Lawrence Tierney was, he revealed quickly, only a movie gangster, and a sensitive one at that. When Winters began to cry, he dried her tears and quipped, "I didn't think the party was that bad." When she explained that she was crying with relief that the war was ended, and for her relatives who were in concentration camps, he told her that he felt like crying, as well.

"I have a brother who's in the Navy," Tierney said, "and he's decided that if it's so easy for me to become a movie star, he's going to take a crack at it, too. Our father is a New York cop, and he thinks I'm a pimp glorifying gangsters and that I'm going to teach my brother to be a pimp, too."

The pair were interrupted by a "quite drunk . . . slight" actor whom Winters referred to as "Jonathan Baker," who suggested they all leave the party for the Cock n' Bull, a British-themed tavern at the corner of Doheny Drive on the Sunset Strip. The trio drove off, and upon arrival at the pub, Winters's search for the ladies' room led to a memorable moment in her own legendary life. She opened the wrong door and was confronted with a large, framed picture of Adolph Hitler on the wall. "So I peed right under Hitler's picture," she wrote, "because I couldn't pee on it."

Winters found Baker and Tierney at the bar, in a heated, drunken political debate. Baker, who bragged of his friendship with the owners of the Cock n' Bull, began spewing pro-Nazi, anti-Semitic, and racist statements: "Tierney took one look at my anguished face; then he casually picked up Mr. Baker and threw him down the length of the bar, crashing into all the glasses and beer bottles, just like in a western. Then he grabbed me, and we got out fast, into the parking lot, and got in the car and drove away."

Winters and Tierney stopped for hamburgers and coffee at the Dolores Drive-In restaurant on Wilshire Boulevard. There was some awkward small talk. He brushed off her questions about having acted in New York and claimed to have been a cop in Brooklyn and served a six-month stretch on an honor farm. Then "he smiled at me for the first time, one of the sweetest and most naïve smiles I've ever seen," and asked, "'Would you like to go to a motel with me?' The only answer I could think of: 'Would it take long?' And he replied, 'With any luck it shouldn't take too long.' And it didn't. So I spent the night of VE Day after the long war with a strange sad actor sleeping at my side and staring into darkness."

Although it wasn't reported at the time, on May 22, 1945, two weeks after his VE Day escapades with Shelley Winters, and eight days after he was officially dubbed a "star" by leading Hollywood gossip columnist and radio personality Jimmie Fidler, Lawrence Tierney made a public appearance in Beverly Hills. The venue was justice court. He was playing to an audience of one. Judge Cecil D. Holland had more than a decade's experience of looking down from the bench on Hollywood celebrities. Now, he looked down on Lawrence Tierney, who was charged with public drunkenness. Tierney was fined twenty-five dollars.

RKO Radio Pictures unleashed *Back to Bataan* on May 31. On June 19, movie fans caught Tierney in another small role, the one in *Those Endearing Young Charms*, burned off in the first months of the year, before *Dillinger's* release.

A second Tierney appearance that passed under the radar was a return engagement before Judge Holland on June 5. Again, the charge was drunkenness. For the second time, the newly branded movie star was let off with a twenty-five dollar fine.

While Tierney embarked on a drunken binge, *Dillinger* was on a criminal spree across the nation. The film was banned in Chicago and Memphis. The United States War Department "disapproved" of the picture because of the "lawlessness" it depicted. In South Bend, Indiana, about 150 miles down Highway 31 from Indianapolis, where the real Dillinger was born, cops rounded up seven teenage boys who admitted to committing scores of robberies over the past year. The kids told the cops they pulled off the heists "in a more professional manner" and learned to "case jobs before pulling them" after watching and studying *Dillinger.*

A lawsuit was filed on July 7 seeking to stop Monogram from exhibiting the picture anywhere. The suit was filed in John Dillinger's hometown, in Indianapolis Circuit Court, by Audrey Hancock—Dillinger's sister. The suit charged that the "picture is detrimental to the youth of the country and will cause a wave of juvenile delinquency."

Hancock had raised her younger brother John after the death of their mother when he was three years old. Since Dillinger's last stand on July 22, 1934, she'd defended him as an All-American boy whose misdeeds had been exaggerated. Her lawsuit against Monogram made similar claims: "Said picture shows John Dillinger shooting and killing various and divers persons, which said defendant Monogram Pictures, Inc., well know are false and untrue and are shown for the sole reason of making said picture exciting, threatening, violent and bloodthirsty to entice persons of juvenile age to see the film." The suit demanded that the film be "seized and destroyed" and $500,000 in damages be paid to Audrey Hancock, for the humiliation, embarrassment, pain, and mental anguish she endured while viewing the film at the Lyric Theater. This was the same Lyric Theater where, eleven years earlier—and eight days after Dillinger's death—she and her family had starred in a Dillinger-themed vaudeville show that presented the outlaw's life story in a most favorable light (launched, according to Dillinger Sr., to help pay his son's burial expenses).

Audrey Hancock declined to comment on her role in the Dillinger family tour (or others that followed). "I haven't got anything to say except that the motion picture about my brother is all a bunch of lies!" she told the *Star*.

The film continued to play in cities across the country. In Cincinnati, columnist E. B. Radcliffe reported that Tierney's success with the film was leading to more offers, including the featured role in a Clifford Odets adaptation of Cornell Woolrich's mystery novel *Deadline at Dawn*. "Which makes us wonder what he's been doing all this time in Hollywood and how come no bigger parts up to now despite a photogenic personality of some potency. Maybe some studio press experts will enlighten us."

The role in *Deadline at Dawn* would ultimately go to Bill Williams, another athletic RKO contract player. "Studio press experts" already had their hands full with their new star, Lawrence Tierney.

Two and a half million dollars. That was the projected gross for *Dillinger,* an independent picture produced for $65,000—less than a tenth the budget of the average studio feature. Harrison Carroll reported on July 27 that the execs at Monogram, a studio known for seven-day quickies, were "completely confounded—but in a hysterically happy way" over their unexpected windfall. And Lawrence Tierney? He was Cinderella, who six months earlier was moonlighting as a post hole digger. Carroll quoted a publicity man: "Tierney now walks up Sunset Boulevard and looks at a huge 24-sheet sign bearing his name as the star of 'Dillinger.' He looks down and sees the posts which hold up the signboard. He dug the post holes himself!"

It was another kind of hole Lawrence Tierney was digging for himself on Sunset Boulevard on the day that story ran in newspapers. The Los Angeles Police Department in Hollywood got an early morning call about a disturbance near the Hollywood Palladium and Sunset Gower Studios. Officers arrived to find Tierney, not far from his apartment at 1611 Vista Del Mar Avenue, in "a strangling condition." Whether he was being strangled, in the process of strangling another person, or strangling himself was unclear. In any case, he was once again intoxicated, and again booked for public drunkenness.

As the *Los Angeles Times* reported the following day, "the 'third time's a charm' saying didn't work out so well for film actor Lawrence Tierney, new Hollywood star." When he shuffled into Beverly Hills Justice Court, Tierney found himself facing the bench of Judge Cecil D. Holland for the third time in sixty-six days. This time, the judge had had enough. Tierney wouldn't walk away after peeling off cash to pay a twenty-five dollar fine. *Strangling condition?* The judge said he was sick and tired of dispensing mere fines to "repeaters."

At wit's end, Holland read the actor the riot act. Then the judge sentenced Lawrence Tierney—or as the *Los Angeles Times* and other outlets reported, sentenced "the star of *Dillinger*"—to ten days in the Los Angeles County Jail. Tierney was led off to serve his sentence.

RKO Radio Pictures released another Leon Errol comedy, *Mama Loves Papa*, on August 8, two days after Tierney was released from jail. Directed by Frank R. Strayer, the movie featured Tierney in another small, pre-*Dillinger* role, when studio bosses didn't know the star, and trouble, they had on their hands.

One hundred and ten days had passed since *Dillinger*'s New York City premiere. Three additional films featuring Lawrence Tierney, all shot before his breakout role, had been released in this period. Tierney himself had been arrested three times and had just completed a ten-day jail sentence.

On this day, Jimmie Fidler, the Hollywood columnist who was the first to point out that RKO Pictures hadn't recognized the star it had in Lawrence Tierney, claimed to have noticed something else: a vivid image that would provide the shorthand for reporters to follow in the decades to come. The item that appeared in his column of August 13, 1945, was clever, and possibly even true: "The showmanship displayed by newsboys is something uncanny. For instance, a few evenings ago, Hollywood's evening papers headlined the news that Lawrence Tierney, the star of the picture, 'Dillinger,' had been handed a ten-day jail sentence for being drunk and disorderly. Happening to pass the theater where 'Dillinger' is playing I noticed that one teenaged newsboy had taken his stance in the lobby to shout 'Extra! Lawrence Tierney jailed.' Just back of him was a life-sized poster showing Tierney, as Dillinger, peering through bars!"

Fidler's colorful juxtaposition of movie star and public enemy solidified the connection between Lawrence Tierney and his screen role as a criminal. From then on, the Dillinger connection would haunt Tierney's every misstep, and lead to ridicule and scorn at times when compassion or medical attention was needed. There would be no sympathy, no tears for "Lawrence Tierney aka Dillinger."

In years to come, Jimmie Fidler would be the only Hollywood authority to express concern and outrage at Tierney's behavior on a regular basis. Fidler, credited as the originator of the Hollywood gossip column (at the *Hollywood News* in 1920), and host of an influential syndicated radio show, had reason to be horrified by Tierney's antics. He was a survivor of an assault by another actor whose offscreen misbehavior was often seen as an extension of his film persona. Early on Sunday morning, September 21, 1941, Fidler had been attacked by Errol Flynn.

It happened at the Mocambo, the celebrity hotspot on the Sunset Strip—the nightclub with the Pan American decor, aviary of live exotic birds behind three-inch-thick plates of glass, big bands, and conga lines weaving through the room till dawn. Fidler was seated at a prime four-top with his wife Bobbie and another couple, celebrating his recent testimony in Washington in which he accused studio bosses of trying to censor his column and radio show. The Fidler party was starting on dessert when Flynn walked in.

Fueled by a night of club-hopping with fellow actor Bruce Cabot, the thirty-two-year-old movie star, swashbuckler, and cocksman snapped when he saw the gossip columnist. Flynn charged toward Fidler, crashed into him, and lifted the smaller man by a fistful of shirt.

"You're lousy and no good!" Flynn shouted. "You told the Senate one lie too many!" As if on cue, Phil Ohman's band stopped playing and everyone went silent as Flynn held Jimmie Fidler. Suddenly, Bobbie Fidler grabbed a dessert fork, lunged forward, and stabbed Flynn in the ear. Blood spurted and dripped onto the tablecloth, but the actor didn't seem to notice.

"A slap is more insulting than a punch!" he declared theatrically, and backhanded the comparatively little man across the face. Fidler shook free. The table was upended. Men rushed in to break up the melee in a scene that United Press reporter Frederick C. Othman wrote "resembled the riot of stunt men in a night club sequence of many a Flynn movie."

Nothing could have made the scene more cinematic—except what happened next. In the middle of the fighting, shouting, and breaking of dishes, bandleader Ohman struck up another number: "The Star-Spangled Banner." Within seconds, all action stopped as everyone stepped back, and stood at attention, hands over hearts—in Othman's prose, "dribbling blood, sweat and rosebuds from the overturned vases of one of Hollywood's most expensive drinkeries."

Fidler demanded that Flynn be charged with battery. Judge Cecil D. Holland—the same Judge Holland who called Tierney "out" on his third strike—adjudicated a solution. Flynn promised he'd never slap Jimmie Fidler again. Fidler's attorney promised he'd never again mention Flynn on his radio show.

After two atomic bombs were dropped upon its people, the Japanese government surrendered to the Allies in August and announced a formal surrender on September 2, 1945. World War II was over. On September 15, the *New York Times* reported that production of *Step by Step*, the RKO feature that would reunite Lawrence Tierney and his *Dillinger* moll Anne Jeffreys, would be postponed. So would production on *Deadlier Than the Male*, RKO's noir murder mystery in which Tierney was to star with Claire Trevor.

The reason for the delays had nothing to do with Tierney's latest arrest and jail term. RKO was making hay with the success of *Dillinger* and decided to cast their new star in *Badman's Territory*, a big budget ($600,000) Western, starring Randolph Scott, Anne Richards, and George "Gabby" Hayes. Tierney would play another noted outlaw, Jesse James. The bank, train, and stagecoach robber of the late nineteenth century was, in the producers' and public's imaginations, the perfect fit. Portrayed by Tyrone Power in the 1939 film *Jesse James*, the bad man was the first in a series of big, dynamic roles RKO was planning for its accidental star. The story was reported on Saturday. Already acquainted with a tommy gun, Tierney would need a crash course in looking good with a .45 revolver. He was going before the cameras on Monday.

"And all the time with a Brooklyn accent: 'All right, I'll meet you guys at the foist of the month! Split up!'" Tierney told the Murphys. "The horse that I had . . . he started jumping and leaping and I couldn't get ahold of him. . . . I couldn't get on. He'd run away. . . . I was so determined to get on, I leaped up and my right foot got on the stirrup instead of the left and I swung on and was riding backwards! That's a Brooklyn cowboy!"

Before the year was out, eagle-eyed moviegoers could catch Lawrence Tierney as a reporter in the Jack Haley musical, *Sing Your Way Home*. The film was released on November 14, 1945, but filmed the previous December, before Tierney's breakthrough—and publicized arrests.

Cameras rolled on *Step by Step* in December and production would continue into the new year. Tierney played an ex-marine who flirts with a US senator's secretary played by Jeffreys, and winds up running from police and chasing Nazi spies around the beach at Malibu. The film made use of more than sixty sets and locations and, it was reported, required many retakes of the beach scenes, because Tierney was displaying too much "enthusiasm" for Jeffreys in his tight swim trunks.

The public might have assumed that he was on a sober health kick, when it was reported on the day before New Year's Eve that Tierney's regimen of winter cold prevention on the Malibu set of *Step by Step* included stripping to his shorts, racing up and down the beach, and "going into a series of tumbling stunts," before "a shower, a brisk rub-down and his departure."

A more accurate assessment had been published the day before the end of November 1945. A day after Harrison Carroll reported that Tierney, seen at the Trocadero, was "no longer a problem boy for RKO," Jimmie Fidler made reference to Billy Wilder's current film about an alcoholic writer on a four-day binge: "We hear that Lawrence Tierney's pals are urging him to see 'The Lost Weekend'—and think about its moral."

"The drinking started out as a celebratory thing," David Del Valle says. "But because of the nature of alcoholism, the celebratory phase quickly ended and was replaced by 'You don't deserve this.' Alcohol took control of him. Any time Larry achieved success—and this is true with Errol Flynn and the rest— he'd immediately feel he wasn't worthy of it. And actors, macho, heterosexual actors, feel that acting is a sissy's job. It's an effeminate way to make a living. So they turn to alcohol to prove they're men."

4

The Battle of Decker's Lawn

Errol Flynn, for all his cinematic accomplishments, is remembered as much for his offscreen antics, fights, scenes, courtroom appearances—and membership in an informal club of Hollywood creatives that included figures even more lecherous, licentious, debased, and debauched than he. The "Bundy Drive Boys" were intellectually superior predecessors to the Rat Pack, with a floating celebrity membership that included the great actors Johns Carradine and Barrymore, comedian W. C. Fields, scribes Gene Fowler and Ben Hecht, bohemian poet and critic Sadakichi Hartmann, junior member Anthony Quinn, and, at its center, John Decker.

Decker, born Leopold von der Decken in Berlin in 1895, was a portrait artist, caricaturist (his painting of Fields as Queen Victoria hung in Chasen's restaurant for decades, until the place was shuttered in 1995), set designer, art forger, and scoundrel. Decker's cozy Tudor house at 419 Bundy Drive, in the sylvan hills north of Sunset Boulevard in the Brentwood neighborhood, was headquarters for the gang's all-night drunken benders, revelry, and Shakespearean monology.

The group had its heyday in the late 1930s. Staggering into the new decade, members dropped off or dropped dead, one by one. Decker left Bundy Drive in 1944 and moved into a studio and home at 1215 Alta Loma Road in the heart of West Hollywood, a block downhill from the Sunset Strip, behind the Mocambo. Errol Flynn paid the rent, and the studio was named the Decker-Flynn Galleries. Hollywood notables lined up to have their portraits painted in a room with walls displaying invaluable artwork from the greats that were probably forgeries created by Decker.

So where does Lawrence Tierney come in? According to *Hollywood's Hellfire Club*, the book by Gregory William Mank with Charles Heard and Bill Nelson, it began with a dame. Errol Flynn was driving John Decker in his convertible through downtown Los Angeles when they spied her in a shop window, nude but for a strawberry blonde wig. It didn't take much convincing for the two drinkers to hustle the damsel into the back of Flynn's car. The duo raced her across town to the gallery, she standing straight up behind them. She was quite a sight.

She was a mannequin, but the artist Decker saw her as something more. Once he had her inside his studio, he dressed and began to style the figure into a living work of art. The dressing dummy became, in his eyes, a woman. He named her Mona.

In the first weeks of 1946, John Decker announced he was hosting a party for the unveiling of a new statue. The shindig would be more accurately described, Mank wrote, as "rather a coming-out party" for Mona. Guests arrived at the studio-home on Alta Loma Road on Thursday, January 17, among them Bundy Drive survivors Quinn, Hecht, Mowbray, and Flynn, with his second wife, socialite Nora Eddington (they'd met in 1943, when she was nineteen and working at the courthouse snack counter when he was on trial for statutory rape—Flynn was acquitted). Other notables included Burgess Meredith and wife Paulette Goddard, Ida Lupino, Raoul Walsh, Merle Oberon, Jennifer Jones, David O. Selznick, Lon Chaney Jr., Harpo Marx, and a man who was new to the A-list but already gaining a reputation as an unpredictable character: the screen's *Dillinger*, Lawrence Tierney.

It was a typical Decker party. It was loud. Alcohol flowed copiously. Tempers flared. Arguments and rowdiness ensued. The revelry went late into the night and the following day. By early morning, approaching dawn, the majority of guests, including Errol Flynn, were long gone. Those who remained were sitting around the bar area, talking and drinking. No one paid much attention to Lawrence Tierney. He'd apparently had his fill and was sitting alone in a corner, stewing, when suddenly, there was a clatter. Sammy Colt, twenty-five-year-old son of John Barrymore's sister Ethel, was moving toward the bar for another drink when he stumbled and fell into Mona. As he flailed and descended, she tumbled with him. Colt hit the floor with a crash, smashing a hundred dollars' worth of liquor glasses on the way down. Mona landed on her face, chipping her right cheek and dislocating her right arm. Her head rolled across the studio floor, leaving her wig behind.

Diana Barrymore was a witness. The twenty-four-year-old, troubled sometime actress was the daughter of the late Bundy Drive Boy Barrymore—and Sammy's cousin. She and ghostwriter Gerold Frank recounted what happened next in her autobiography, *Too Much, Too Soon*: "Decker uttered an anguished cry, swooped down and picked up the headless figure, and hugged it to him. Lawrence Tierney, who had made a success of playing bad man Dillinger on the screen, accused Sammy Colt of stumbling and knocking it over. He took a punch at Sammy." Up and out of his self-loathing funk, Tierney had rushed over and socked Sammy in the jaw. He then stormed toward the door, had a word with William Kent, stepson of Mocambo owner Charlie Morrison, and punched him. The two men knocked each other around inside the studio before spilling out of the doorway onto the lawn on Alta Loma Road. Kent pounced and pinned Tierney to the ground. Anthony Quinn ran over and pulled Kent off. Tierney leaped up. His shirt torn to shreds, he began fighting anyone and everyone within reach.

Jack La Rue, another movie tough guy, attempted to play peacemaker. "Come on! Don't fight, don't fight!" he shouted, but when he stepped into the fray, Tierney belted him in the nose, which spurted blood as La Rue was launched backward into a parked car. He slammed into the vehicle and bounced off, smacking the back of his head, hard, on the concrete driveway.

By now, others were drawn into the violence. There were fights across the lawn when a woman stepped onto the battlefield. Diana Barrymore strode toward Tierney and got right in his face: "When I saw blood on Sammy and Jack, I exploded. I rushed up to Tierney—he'd ripped off his shirt and stood like a belligerent Tarzan—'You dreary, dreadful actor!' I cried. 'If you want to fight, hit me! You're punching everyone else, so why don't you hit a woman?' I slapped him with all my might, half a dozen times. I was wearing two rings and they must have hurt."

A woman egged her on. "Hit him, Diana!" she screamed. "That's the girl! Tell him where to get off!"

Tierney did not take Diana up on her offer. The air sputtered out of the fight balloon. Someone had called the law, but by the time the deputies from the West Hollywood Sheriff's Department arrived, Diana and her date had run out through the garden to their car. Most of the crowd had dispersed as well. Nobody, not even Jack La Rue, wanted to press charges against anyone else. The Hollywood people called it all a "misunderstanding." The deputies took La Rue to West Hollywood Emergency Hospital for X-rays. Alan Mowbray went along and later gave La Rue a ride home.

The following day, the events of John Decker's party, and Diana Barrymore's slaps—the papers counted eight of them—made headlines across the country. Tierney had already spun the story for Saturday's morning editions. "This talk of my being unsocial is ridiculous," he told Julian Hartt of the

International News Service. Tierney explained that he was leaving the party when William Kent started the trouble by taunting him. "I wasn't nasty to this fellow Kent," he claimed, "but on our way out he made a lot of cracks to me that anyone who liked Errol Flynn was no good anyway."

Determined to defend Flynn, Tierney said he invited Kent to step outside to settle the matter like men. Kent declined. "Tony Quinn came up," Tierney said. "I asked him to get this fellow out of the way or I was going to hurt him. Then Kent jumped me and we went to the ground."

"Tierney insulted a girlfriend of mine," Kent countered to the United Press reporter. "I guess he thinks he's Dillinger off the screen, too. He waited for me outside and then jumped *me*."

Tierney denied punching Jack La Rue. "I pushed him away and he fell and hit his head," he lamented, though La Rue wound up in West Hollywood emergency hospital with a busted-up nose and lip and head lacerations from Tierney's haymaker.

Diana Barrymore told a different story. She said it began when Sammy Colt fell against the Mona mannequin, and Tierney responded by punching him.

"I don't know what she's talking about," Tierney replied.

The sheriff's deputies who arrived afterward to take a report classified the melee as a "scuffle," though witnesses would never forget the free-for-all brawl, with as many as six simultaneous fistfights. Host John Decker had seen worse. "It was just another party and another fight; there are always fights around here. There are fights around here all the time, almost every night," Decker told the papers. "Certainly there was drinking. What would a party be like without drinking? We had a nice party."

In a sad coda to the incident, the wire service photo that accompanied the articles showed Decker in the aftermath, on his knees at Mona's feet, holding her severed arm in his hands and gazing up at her face. Mona looks away.

On January 27, Jean Hersholt, president of the Academy of Motion Picture Arts and Sciences, announced the Academy Award nominations for achievements in 1945. Among the nominees for Best Original Screenplay was Philip Yordan for *Dillinger*. *Los Angeles Times* drama critic Edwin Schallert labeled the nomination a "super surprise." Nine thousand Academy voters would have until February 11 to turn in their ballots. The awards show was scheduled for March 7.

⌒

It didn't take much longer than three weeks after the "Battle of Decker's Lawn"—twenty-three days, to be exact—for Lawrence Tierney to get himself into trouble with his fists again. This time it wasn't over a mannequin or Errol Flynn. It was a woman, a flaming red-haired bundle of trouble from Budapest named Hella Crossley. The papers described Hella as an "actress." Her first (and, according to IMDb, only) credited screen role was in Republic Pictures' lesbian-tinged women's prison melodrama, *Girls of the Big House,* which snuck into movie houses the previous November. Hella was said to be twenty-four, though as early as January 1941, she'd shown up in Walter Winchell's column, on the town in Manhattan: "the Hungarian rhapsody" who at the time was a "symphony" with Norman Anthony, the fifty-one-year-old magazine editor and author of *The Drunk's Blue Book.*

Lawrence Tierney, boozed up and looking for more, laid eyes on Hella at 3 a.m. that Sunday, February 10, as she was exiting a club called Vetry's Den at the corner of La Cienega and Santa Monica Boulevards in West Hollywood (about a two-minute drive from John Decker's place). The only complication was that Hella was on the arm of a Frenchman. Paul de Loqueyssie was a thirty-six-year-old writer and bit actor married to, but estranged from, Frances Ramsden, a willowy former Harry Conover model and aspiring actress from New England. De Loqueyssie was leading Hella to a car in the parking lot. He was four minutes away from getting her to his pad at 853 North Clark Street when Tierney charged over in pursuit of Hella's phone number and address. De Loqueyssie realized he was no match for this raging bull, especially one with a buddy hanging back, watching. He played it cool and tried to humor the lug as Hella refused to give him what he was after.

Once Hella managed to get into the car, Tierney hung onto the door, not giving up, asking over and over. De Loqueyssie was as tactful as could be. "Come on, mon ami . . . the lady is not interested." Frustrated, he gave Tierney a push. That was a mistake. Tierney responded by giving de Loqueyssie a beatdown, before stomping away with bruised knuckles, but neither address nor phone number.

The incident outside Vetry's Den remained a private matter until later in the year, when de Loqueyssie decided to sue.

The Hella Crossley incident didn't make the papers at the time, but word got around town. On February 12, Jimmie Fidler made "the case of Lawrence Tierney" the lead item in his In Hollywood column. Recounting the fairy tale trajectory that RKO's Rutgers Nielson had conjured for the columns, Fidler reduced big bad Lawrence Tierney to a boy who "practically tumbled into the acting profession" expecting a "sensational success" that he was not prepared to handle. No one told Tierney that moviemaking is a serious business, and that the glamour is only part of the marketing. "He had no way of knowing that a movie star is just another citizen, with responsibilities equal to any other American."

The "unfortunate" Tierney had "paid dearly" once his escapades went public, Fidler wrote. "Hollywood is more at fault than he. Hollywood should take the blame for not preparing him for sudden fame and wealth."

On Thursday night, March 7, 1946, Hollywood celebrated itself with the eighteenth Academy Awards ceremony. This was the first Oscars night since the end of the war, so there was substantially more Hollywood glamour than in recent years. The Oscar statuettes, made of plaster during the war years, were now solid brass with gold plating. Bob Hope and James Stewart hosted the show at Grauman's Chinese Theatre on Hollywood Boulevard—and Lawrence Tierney's breakout film was up for an award.

Philip Yordan and *Dillinger* lost in the Best Original Screenplay category to Richard Schweizer for the Swiss film, *Marie-Louise.* Written in French and German, *Marie-Louise* was the first foreign language film to win this or any other Oscar. Yordan, who'd be nominated again in 1951 for *Detective Story* and take home a statuette three years later for *Broken Lance,* took the loss in stride. He knew he never had a chance.

"In the 1940s the studios, all the majors, had signed a consent agreement not to make gangster pictures," he told Patrick McGilligan in that 1987 interview, "but Monogram was not a signatory, so when they made *Dillinger* based on my original screenplay, Louis B. Mayer was so indignant. He called up Frank King and says, 'Frank, you gotta destroy the negative for the good of the industry.' Frank says, 'Sure, what'll you pay me?' Louis B. Mayer says, 'I'll pay you nothing.' Hell, the picture went out, the picture cost $65,000, and it made $4 million. I had a third of it.

"I was leaving my seat to pick up the Oscar because I had pull with a lot of the writers, all the nominators, when they announced that *Marie Louise,* some picture made in Switzerland that nobody had ever seen, had won. I can't prove it, but at that time Walter Wanger was high up in the Academy, and later he told me, 'Look, we couldn't give it to *Dillinger.* We pulled a switch.' What the hell!"

Robert Mitchum, the RKO contract player who'd wanted the Dillinger role, had received a Best Supporting Actor nomination—the only Oscar nomination he'd receive in his career—for his role in *The Story of G. I. Joe*. He lost to James Dunn from *A Tree Grows in Brooklyn*.

Lawrence Tierney stayed out of trouble and the headlines on Oscar night, but not through the entire Oscar weekend. On Saturday night, March 9, the actor was drinking at the Mocambo, the club owned by the stepfather of William Kent, his opponent in January's John Decker fistfight.

Just after midnight, the bell in his head rang for round two. Tierney saw Kent, then saw red, then attacked. An off-duty cop moonlighting as a bouncer stepped in and manhandled Tierney out to the sidewalk, where the two of them slugged it out.

Deputy sheriffs confronted the—as the United Press described Tierney—"movie portrayer of Gangster John Dillinger," across the street from the club. Tierney told the lawmen he was "quietly enjoying a drink" at the Mocambo when Kent "began making abusive remarks to me."

The cops arrested Tierney on another drunk charge and took him to county jail. He was released on fifty dollars bail.

"I'd gotten things settled properly if the cops hadn't come," Tierney told reporters on Monday. "It was just a beef with the same guy who started the fight at artist John Decker's home."

Kent denied going after Tierney. "I'm awfully bored with that man," he told the *Los Angeles Times*.

The Mocambo commotion landed Tierney in Beverly Hills Police Court on Wednesday, March 27. Found guilty for the fourth time in less than a year, he learned that the stakes were raised beyond the ten-day jail sentence he'd received in his third go-round with Judge Cecil D. Holland. Judge Charles R. Griffin not only imposed a one-hundred-dollar fine but also handed Tierney a ninety-day suspended jail sentence and placed him on two years' probation. The actor would be required to check in with a probation officer once a month. Should he be arrested at any time in the next twenty-four months, he'd have to serve the ninety days, at least.

Tierney told the court he'd seen the error of his ways. He said he'd begun attending meetings of Alcoholics Anonymous, and insisted he'd already put his drinking days behind him.

"I'm on the wagon forever," Tierney announced. "When a man traverses the Hollywood jungles, he can't allow his wits to be fouled by alcohol. From now on, my characterizations of trouble will strictly be on the screen."

Tierney's involvement with Alcoholics Anonymous seemed promising, but may have been a factor in his future troubles. The AA program was founded in 1935 by an alcoholic named Bill Wilson (Bill W.) as a faith-based fellowship promoting "Twelve Steps" to sobriety. The "steps" call for the alcoholic to admit being powerless over alcohol, turn over his will and life to a Higher Power ("God as we understood him"), make amends to those he has harmed, pray—and to take a "fearless moral inventory" of the character defects and moral failings at the root of the problem. AA also promotes the belief that the only treatment for alcoholism is total abstinence. No matter how long one has maintained sobriety, the sip of one drink takes the alcoholic back to square one. Tierney's belief in and repeated "failures" at the Alcoholics Anonymous "cure" would lead to weeks, sometimes months, of white-knuckle abstinence and sobriety, followed by uncontrolled binges. The very program that the courts demanded he join would help guarantee his return to the drunk tank.

RKO executives let it be known that the Mocambo incident had cost Tierney the lead in *Deadlier Than the Male,* while they also moved to get him back on the straight and narrow. There were face-saving, optimistic gossip items like the one tossed to Harrison Carroll on April 9. Tierney, "riding the water wagon, actually tried to stop a fight at a spot the other night," rescuing actor Art Foster from "half a dozen assailants" (there was no mention of why Tierney was still showing up at "spots" that served alcohol). The studio also paid to bring Tierney's father, and later his mother, to Hollywood in an effort to keep him under watchful eyes.

Others were enlisted, as well. When Tierney arrived in Salt Lake City on April 17, 1946, to appear onstage with the premiere of *Badman's Territory* the following day, he was accompanied by Anne Jeffreys. Jeffreys had become famous for her role as Tess Trueheart in RKO's *Dick Tracy* movie series (Tierney had tested for the Tracy role that went to Morgan Conway). She was not cast in *Badman's Territory,* but *Step by Step* was set for release later in the year. Despite her past problems with Tierney, she was, at RKO's insistence, at his side for all four appearances at the Uptown Theater. Tierney's father also came along. Lawrence H. Tierney admitted to the local paper that he'd quit his job after his son made such a splash in *Dillinger.*

As *Badman's Territory* opened across the country in May, RKO rolled the dice and put Tierney to work in *Deadlier Than the Male,* after all. Director Robert Wise said he was "sold" on the promise that Tierney would behave. Wise may have been encouraged by Val Lewton. Wise had been with RKO since 1934, when he was apprenticed to a sound effects editor, and picked up an Academy Award nomination eight years later, for editing Orson Welles's *Citizen Kane*. He also worked with Welles on *The Magnificent Ambersons* (and against Welles when, on RKO orders, he reshot the ending), but it was Lewton who in 1943 gave Wise the opportunity to direct his first feature, *The Curse of the Cat People*. *Deadlier Than the Male*, which also starred Claire Trevor, Walter Slezak, and Elisha Cook Jr., would be released a year later as *Born to Kill*.

On the Fourth of July weekend, shortly after production wrapped in Hollywood, San Francisco, and Reno, newspapers around the country picked up a brief wire story that Tierney's younger brother Gerard had visited Tierney on the set of *Deadlier Than the Male*: "The result: An immediate offer of a screen test." What Lawrence Tierney confided to Shelley Winters had come to pass. Tierney's younger brother Gerard "Roddy" Tierney had only been in Hollywood for weeks since his discharge from the US Navy, and already there would be another Tierney for Lawrence to measure up against: five years younger, an inch or two taller, and ten times more sober. Jimmie Fidler broke the story that Lawrence, his brother, and father were living together in a hotel, sharing a single room. Fidler also made use of the one-liners submitted by gag writers: "Lawrence Tierney will be a big star if he scores as many hits on the screen as he has in night club fights" and "Add men I never expect to see wearing a monocle: Lawrence Tierney, always dissatisfied with a single glass."

RKO Radio Pictures' publicity department worked hard in July to get some positive ink for Tierney, slipping items to the gossips that didn't involve drunkenness or violence. Ed Sullivan, in his Little Old New York column, claimed that actress Jacqueline Dalya had "switched from Van Johnson to Lawrence Tierney." Bob Thomas found some irony in the news that Tierney was refused admittance to the Mocambo—because he wasn't wearing a tie. Hearst columnist Erskine Johnson raved about Tierney's "most phenomenal memory": "He asked me to name thirty objects, and I wrote them down as he repeated them—once. He remembered every object and in the right order. If acting fails him, he can always get a job in vaudeville as a trick memorist." There was also serious economic news. The King Brothers had attempted to borrow Tierney from RKO for the picture *Suspense* (also written by Philip Yordan). When Tierney asked for a bonus of $10,000, the brothers blew him off and hired Barry Sullivan instead. "They promised me a bonus when I made *Dillinger* for them," Tierney groused to Sheilah Graham. "And I didn't ever get it." For his work in the surprise hit, Graham revealed, Tierney had been paid "exactly $350—at the rate of $100 a week."

As soon as Tierney completed work on *Deadlier Than the Male,* he jumped into another film noir. In *The Devil Thumbs a Ride,* he was bad man Steve Morgan, a cold-blooded killer who holes up in a vacant beach house with two women and a married lingerie salesman. When *Devil* wrapped, the studio planned to get Tierney into cowboy duds to lens *Trail Street,* a Western with Randolph Scott, Robert Ryan, and Barbara Hale.

Step by Step arrived on screens on August 23. The film was reviewed in the *New York Times* the following day, coupled with Bosley Crowther's verdict on Howard Hawks's take on Raymond Chandler's novel, *The Big Sleep,* starring Humphrey Bogart and Lauren Bacall. *Times* movie reviewer "T.M.P." was not impressed with *Step by Step,* "a strong candidate for the title of the year's dullest and most fantastic melodrama." Tierney and Anne Jeffreys, he added, "move through the film like two bewildered innocents in search of a director."

Then again, Crowther didn't think highly of *The Big Sleep,* "one of those pictures in which so many cryptic things occur amid so much involved and devious plotting that the mind becomes utterly confused." The influential critic was also confused by the film's title and added that "Miss Bacall is a dangerous looking female, but she still hasn't learned to act."

In August 1946, Tierney moved on to another RKO picture, this time as a good guy—at least a bad guy who went straight—in *A Prison Story* (retitled *San Quentin* upon its release a week before Christmas). Tierney played a reformed ex-con and World War II hero, chasing down an escaped convict who's put San Quentin's rehabilitation program at risk. Offscreen, five months into a two-year probation, "on the wagon forever," and focused on acting, Tierney seemed in a position to shake off his offscreen "Dillinger" reputation.

And then, three weeks into August, Tierney fell off a table, fell off the wagon, and fell through the doors of the Hollywood Receiving Hospital, cut up, covered in blood, drunk, and itching for a fight.

5

Falling Off the Table

Hollywood Receiving Hospital was an infirmary attached to the Hollywood Police Station on Wilcox Avenue, just south of DeLongpre Boulevard. It was less than a mile from Lawrence Tierney's latest address at 1738 North Las Palmas Avenue, around the corner from the Musso & Frank Grill on Hollywood Boulevard. Saturday, August 17, 1946, had darkened down from a quiet, hot night into Sunday morning when the square-jawed twenty-seven-year-old staggered into the clinic. He was loud, demanding treatment, reeking of booze—and covered in blood. Cuts were visible on his hands and face. Blood gushed from the wide gash in his neck onto his shirt and pants, and poured from his right index finger.

By all appearances, Tierney had been slashed in a fight, the cut on his finger a defensive wound. Sweating and angry, he wasn't making much sense under questioning from the medics. He'd had it with the Hollywood hospital system! The nurses told him to quiet down. He only got louder. He pushed them aside. *Lemme outta here!* The doctors tried to restrain him. He bolted for the doors—and just as he made his getaway, several cops from the adjoining precinct charged in from the opposite direction and swarmed the bloody patient. Tierney fought back, wounds pumping, cops slipping in blood. It took a few of them to flatten Tierney onto a gurney and strap him down, flailing, so a surgeon could move in and quickly sew fifteen stitches to close up the gaping hole in his neck and another four to plug up his blood-spouting digit.

The cops ascertained that the suspect was visibly intoxicated, "belligerent," and causing a public disturbance. As soon as Tierney was sewn up and bandaged, the police brought him to their station next door. When they charged him with drunkenness, Tierney gave his name as "Francis Moran" and said he was an architect who lived on North Vista Street. The cops corrected him and locked him up.

Tierney was sprung before dawn Sunday after posting $100 bail. The bail was forfeited when he missed a 9:30 a.m. arraignment before municipal court Judge Louis W. Kaufman. When the judge was informed that Tierney was already on probation for another drunk conviction, he issued a bench warrant for the suspect's arrest. Bail was reinstated when Tierney showed up for the afternoon session. He was given until 9:30 a.m. Monday to enter a plea.

When Tierney turned up in court that morning, his throat and hand bandaged, he insisted it was all a misunderstanding. What happened? Tierney claimed he'd been at a girlfriend's house, sober as a, well, *judge,* when he stepped up onto a glass coffee table in order to change a lightbulb. He slipped, fell, crashed through the glass, and landed on the floor, cut, slashed, and gushing blood. Tierney claimed he'd visited two private hospitals whose staff refused to treat him before making it to Hollywood Receiving. Between the stops, his friend fed him some brandy to ease the pain.

Facing a potential revocation of his probation and a ninety-day jail sentence, Tierney pleaded "not guilty." He requested a jury trial.

Tierney returned to work at RKO on *San Quentin.* The makeup artists put a long thin plaster on his neck wound and covered it with makeup so the Frankenstein stitches didn't show on camera.

On Monday, September 23, the case of Lawrence Tierney was back in Los Angeles County Municipal Court. Tierney did not get his jury trial. Judge John J. Ford heard the defendant's side of the story but, relying on the arresting officer's report, found him guilty. The judge ruled that Tierney may have been sober when he fell through and shattered a glass table, but was most definitely drunk when he arrived at the hospital for treatment.

Bail was once again set at $100. A probation hearing was scheduled for October 8.

With a jail term looming, Lawrence Tierney still had Hollywood rooting for him. In her Hollywood Today column, Sheilah Graham sent a message to her readers—and the judge—that "Lawrence Tierney swears by earth and high heaven that now he really will sign the pledge or join Alcoholics Anonymous"—which he'd claimed to have done back in March after the Mocambo brouhaha. "Give him a break, Judge," Graham begged. "Just this once."

By the time of Tierney's probation hearing, Judge Eugene P. Fay may have missed Graham's column, but had studied Tierney's probation report. The jurist assessed the history of a strong, handsome young actor who worked regularly in motion pictures, was taking in at least $1,000 a month—and had been convicted five times for public drunkenness in the seventeen months since his star-making turn in *Dillinger*. The latest conviction was a violation of his existing parole set by a court in Beverly Hills. The judge could have thrown the book at Tierney. Instead, he doled out several chapters, including one that was unusual, but appropriate for an actor.

As Tierney stood nervously before the bench, shifting his weight from one foot to the other, Judge Fay sentenced him to sixty days in the Lincoln Heights jail, with all but five days suspended. Lawrence Tierney would spend one day in jail, the judge said, for each time he'd been convicted of drunkenness.

Judge Fay wasn't finished. The United Press reported from the courtroom: "Tierney, who in the last year has spent more time in police court than before cameras, listened pale-faced and silent as the judge fined him $50, forbade him to drive his car or drink anything stronger than ice cream soda for a year and delivered a twenty-minute lecture on the evils of drink."

"You are one of those individuals who can't handle liquor," Judge Fay told the actor. "Someone has to jolt you to your senses. You just can't handle the stuff."

Tierney interrupted. "It's not that, your honor. After I take it, I just have no control over myself."

"That's what I meant," the judge replied. "You and liquor don't get along and you might as well make up your mind to give it up or you will end up as one of the many derelicts you'll see in Lincoln Heights Jail."

Judge Fay then gave Tierney an acting assignment. Tierney would spend the five days in lockup observing his fellow prisoners. "Remember, most of those men you are going to meet were once as good-looking, as square-shouldered, and as healthy as you are today. You're headed for the same fate that has overtaken them.

"You're a nice-looking fellow," said the judge. "I don't want to see a man with your potentialities start on a long road of jail sentences."

Lawrence Tierney began serving his jail sentence the following day and was released on Monday, October 14. The day after Tierney walked into sunlight, Jimmie Fidler chimed in with an item in his column that was syndicated across the country and read in the *Los Angeles Times* by every player in the industry. By sending Tierney "to the county Bastille for five days," suspending the rest of his sentence and placing him on probation, Fidler wrote, Judge Fay "dished out punishment so light, in view of the offender's past record, that it seems at first thought like a mere slap on the wrist": "On second thought, however, it's evident that there's going to be a great deal of inconvenience in Tierney's future existence. With 60 days hanging over his head in Los Angeles and a 90-day suspended sentence threatening him in Beverly Hills, as the result of a previous rap, it looks like he's going to have to drive a long way to do his serious drinking with anything like safety." Fidler's column made clear that Hollywood was willing to give Tierney another chance, while keeping a close eye on his behavior.

Tierney's response was heard loud and clear two nights later.

The first call was received by the California Highway Patrol. Alan Gordon, a colorful press agent who fed equally colorful fictional stories and quotes to the columns, was on the horn from Ciro's, a swank nightclub located at 8433 Sunset Boulevard (two blocks east and across the Strip from the Mocambo). Lawrence Tierney, he said excitedly, had slugged him and was going wild in the place.

By the time police arrived, Tierney had scrammed. The highway patrolmen were taking Gordon's statement and putting out a call to be on the lookout when the LAPD got the alarm from Ella Campbell's cafe, a block east of Ciro's at 8351 Sunset. Lawrence Tierney, the caller said, had barged in and was involved in a violent argument with one of the customers. Police officers rushed to the scene—but too late! Like an angry, unpredictable tornado, Tierney had touched down, done his damage, and moved on. Where would he show up next?

The sheriff's department picked up the ball from there, after a distress call from The Players, Preston Sturges's multistory celebrity playground, two blocks farther east at 8225 Sunset Boulevard. There, in the shadow of the Chateau Marmont hotel, the law finally caught up with "the screen's 'Dillinger.'" Once again, police reported that the actor was "acting belligerently." Had he been drinking despite his promises and double probation? The encounter never got that far. While the highway patrolmen were wrapping up their visit at Ciro's, as the LAPD cop finalized a report from Ella Campbell's, the sheriffs were firm. They told Lawrence Tierney to go home. *Straight home!*

The headline on the International News Service story the following day told it all: "TIERNEY WINS BRUSH WITH LAW, DILLINGER GETS OFF WITH SCOLDING."

The lead paragraph reflected incredulity. "Lawrence Tierney, who became a star with his portrayal of John Dillinger on the screen, was chased by three law-enforcement agencies yesterday and went home with nothing more than a mild reprimand."

~❖~

The Hella Crossley incident led to Los Angeles Superior Court on November 20, when Judge Harold B. Jeffery heard Paul de Loqueyssie's lawsuit over the humiliating punches he'd received from Lawrence Tierney in the parking lot of Vetry's Den. De Loqueyssie accused Tierney of assault and battery and asked for $7,600 in damages.

Under questioning by his lawyer, David Matlin, de Loqueyssie told the court that when his date refused to give Tierney her phone number or address, the man became aggressive. "I tried to humor him, like one does a lunatic," he said. When Tierney held onto the car door and refused to let go, "I started pushing him away, but gently." That's when Tierney used his fists.

The alleged victim brought along two witnesses. Walter Halle, a writer from Beverly Hills, testified that he saw Tierney punch de Loqueyssie in the face. Hella Crossley was the second witness. She testified that after Tierney struck the French writer, he reached into the car, and did something that in the twenty-first century would have ended his career for good, and possibly landed him in prison. *He hit her dog.*

"That did not endear him to me," she said.

Lawrence Tierney was not in court to respond. His attorney, C. Richard Maddox, said he was away on a personal engagement in New York City. Maddox claimed his client had acted in self-defense and that the incident was "a misunderstanding in a clash of many temperaments . . . a comedy of errors."

The judge awarded de Loqueyssie $600.

For the moment, Tierney was back in New York City, preparing for the world premiere of *San Quentin* in Boston, followed by openings in theaters in New England the first week of December. Tierney was scheduled to travel with the picture through February, appearing onstage at showings in cities including Dayton, Lexington, Indianapolis, and Chicago. The prospect of Tierney taking his volatile offscreen act on the road prompted columnist Hazel Flynn, writing in the *Valley Times* over the hill from Hollywood, to issue a gentle warning: "Somebody should tell Mr. Tierney about Boston. It's no town for him to get tough in."

While he stayed out of obvious trouble in Manhattan, Tierney didn't keep his distance from the gin joints. The *New York Post*'s Earl Wilson wrote that he was seen at the Versailles, "sporting a new scar." Dorothy Kilgallen at the *Daily News* revealed that "local glamor girls . . . breathlessly report" that on their dates with Tierney he quoted "poetry, Shakespeare and the Scriptures during most of the evening." Not to be outdone, Ed Sullivan claimed that "cinema's

Dillinger" did a double take at Reuben's Restaurant on West Fifty-Seventh Street, "when he meets hat check girl, Mrs. John Dillinger!"

A verifiable claim came from Sheilah Graham, back in Hollywood. She met younger brother Gerard Tierney on the RKO lot. He told her that Larry was on the wagon, living with his father at the New York Athletic Club on Central Park South, and "really in training."

The premiere week gave RKO Radio Pictures an opportunity to rehabilitate Tierney's image. Tierney was on his best behavior when he arrived in Boston with *San Quentin* costar Barton MacLane and Lewis E. Lawes, the former warden of Sing Sing penitentiary and a prison reformer whose spoken introduction to the film gave it a veneer of gravitas. At a press reception in the Ritz-Carlton hotel on December 3, Tierney worked the room and charmed the critics.

Lawrence H. Tierney, former chief of police of the Aqueduct Service of Greater New York, added the icing. "Watching his broad-shouldered, blue-eyed, six-foot son move around among his admirers" at the Ritz-Carlton soiree, the senior Tierney took credit for making him a tough guy. "When Larry Tierney wanted a job, his father put him to work as a sandhog with his organization," Marjory Adams wrote in the *Boston Globe*. "And it was no job for a sissy." The elder Tierney insisted that Junior was nothing like the thug people read about. "He's a mamma's boy and worships his mother," he told the reporter. Of his three sons, he bragged, Larry was the "runt." Gerard, his twenty-two-year-old who'd been overseas in Japan, was six-foot-two and had two inches on Larry. Eddie, eighteen and six-three, was sought by the college football programs at Notre Dame, Holy Cross, and Brown.

Lawrence Tierney was onstage on Thursday before showings of the picture at the RKO Theatre on Washington Street. Marjory Adams noted that "the Dillinger of a past picture turns hero" in a film that would "appeal primarily to men" if "the numbers of unaccompanied males in the audience at the first show" were any indication: "They showed much enthusiasm for Larry Tierney when he gave a brief and good-natured talk to them—and Larry obligingly impersonated Humphrey Bogart and Edward G. Robinson for his admirers." Tierney's routine was only about five minutes long, but a crowd pleaser: a conversation among Bogie, Robinson, and himself, all agreeing that Hollywood wasn't big enough for all three tough guys. One of them had to go. That would be Tierney. The imitations and punchlines went over well. Then he told a little about life in Hollywood.

Tierney took the stage in other theaters around New England, without incident. The time away from Hollywood and with his family, some hoped, had soothed the beast inside.

6

Not So Tough— and Not Gene Tierney

With *San Quentin* opening strong on the East Coast, *Step by Step* still in theaters, and two more pictures in the can and soon to be released, 1947 promised to be a bright year for Lawrence Tierney.

Accompanied by his father on his personal appearance tours, he kept his confrontations to the screen, and RKO's publicity department kept the focus on his work. A glaring example appeared alongside Hedda Hopper's column in the Sunday papers on January 12. "NEW FACES BRIGHTEN FILM FARE" by the fictitious Melrose Gower (name of the street corner in Hollywood where RKO Radio Pictures was located) focused on four "fresh young faces on the screen these days": RKO players Robert Mitchum, Jane Greer, Anne Jeffreys, and Lawrence Tierney.

"Lawrence Tierney landed on the RKO lot just another husky young actor who might, with time, make good. Loaned to Monogram for the title role in 'Dillinger,' Tierney turned in a gunman characterization that stopped the critics cold—and RKO snapped him back in a hurry, gave him the lead in 'Step by Step,' then starred him successively in 'San Quentin' and 'Born to Kill.'"

Melrose Gower laid out the formula: keep Tierney working and maybe he'd stay out of trouble. Folks who awakened that Sunday morning would find the newspaper on their doorstep, open to the entertainment section, and perhaps believe that Lawrence Tierney's wild days were behind him.

They couldn't know that in the dead of night, at 3:30 that morning, while they slept, Tierney was in the middle of another fracas, one that would do him more damage than the shattered glass table. This time, far from Hollywood, Tierney picked the wrong person to spar with.

෴

As Henry Sturman told it, he just wanted to get a decent night's sleep. His apartment at 2460 University Avenue in the Bronx was full of relatives and too many babies—not his babies, the relatives' babies—so on Saturday, January 11, he escaped to Manhattan for some uninterrupted shut-eye. He booked himself a room at the Empire, the fifteen-story hotel at the corner of Sixty-Third and Broadway on the Upper West Side, a classy hideaway, and discreet, if not for the giant red neon "Hotel Empire" sign on the roof.

If Henry was looking for a night's sleep, someone might ask why he was walking the halls of the Empire Hotel around 3:30 in the morning, but that aside, as Henry Sturman told it, he'd been given a key to Room 431, and when he couldn't find the room, took the stairs back to the front desk in the lobby. He'd stepped onto the second floor when the elevator door opened, and a big, wide lug came charging out, right at him.

It was Lawrence Tierney. "I'm the house detective!" he shouted. "Where's the girl?" Tierney bowled into Sturman, knocking him down and kicking and punching him in a brawl that tumbled down into the lobby.

The desk clerk ducked for cover and called the police. When the cops arrived, Tierney had his own story. He said he'd entered the elevator in the lobby, expecting a ride to the eighth floor, where he and his father had a suite. Along with the elevator operator, there were two men—one of them Sturman—and a young woman in the elevator. The woman was "very drunk," he said, and protesting too much to be ignored by a gentleman. Tierney asked if there was any trouble.

The answer came when the elevator operator opened the door on the second floor. The two fellas pushed him out and Sturman began pummeling him with rights and lefts. The fight slammed back into the elevator and when the door opened again, into the lobby, the other guy and the girl vamoosed, leaving Tierney and Sturman to roll around on the carpet.

The cops were stuck with two combatants, each blaming the other, so they charged both men with assault and hauled them to the lockup on Fifty-Fourth Street, where they'd spend what was left of the night before appearing in weekend court later that morning.

Standing before Magistrate Julius Isaacs, Henry Sturman didn't exhibit any obvious battle scars. He had a lump behind his left ear, but you'd have to look closely to see it. Lawrence Tierney, on the other hand, was, in the words of a wire reporter in the courtroom, "a sorry sight." His right ear was torn. He had two obvious black eyes. His face was covered in cuts and bruises. "The film Dillinger" had, as the *Daily News* would trumpet in Monday's paper, "dropped another real-life decision." The explanation that followed explained why no other outcome could have been expected.

This time it wasn't a Hollywood swell or one-punch tomato can with whom Lawrence Tierney had scrapped. This time his opponent was, as the *News* reported, "a former collegiate middleweight champion." Twenty-five-year-old Henry Sturman had fought his way to an intercollegiate boxing title at the University of Miami in Florida. During the war, he was an army boxing instructor at Camp Sea Girt, New Jersey. After this bout, a headline in the paper in faraway Moline, Illinois, made it clear: "MOVIE DILLINGER FINDS HE ISN'T REALLY SO TOUGH."

Frank Ross and James Desmond, who covered the court appearance for the *Daily News,* had a fine time making fun of the "tough guy" actor, describing the courtroom scene as if it were a prizefight. The two fighters were "pretty evenly matched up. Tierney is just under 6 feet and broad enough in the shoulders to warrant his screen impersonation of John Dillinger. Sturman is a little shorter and was giving away some reach, but he carried enough weight to make his punches count." Tierney had more "extra-curricular brawling experience, having thrown or caught punches in a half dozen Hollywood one-punchers," but he'd also "dropped five decisions to John Barleycorn within a year." Faced with two competing stories by two men, the magistrate fired questions at both. Sturman said he'd seen another man and a woman at the elevator, but he didn't know them. He couldn't explain how Tierney was so badly beaten, and feinted by offering the court some gossip. He claimed that when he and Tierney spent those hours in jail (which the *Daily News* guys noted was "a familiar 'location' to Tierney in reel life, considering his next picture, San Quentin, is due on Broadway shortly"), Tierney whispered through the bars that "it was worth $300 to him to have the matter dropped."

Tierney and his attorney, Saul Price, denied that strongly. On probation, and ordered not to drink, as the *Daily News* wiseacres put it, "nothing stronger than malted milk," Tierney also denied that he was impaired earlier that morning. "I was not drunk by any chance, Your Honor," he said, before admitting to having "three or four drinks."

The magistrate threw his hands up. He set a hearing for later in the week in Mid-Manhattan Court and told the fighters to be there. Sturman headed home to the Bronx. Lawrence Tierney and his old man set out to find another place to the spend the night. After the fight, management had kicked them out of the Empire Hotel.

When the case resumed, most observers expected that the most sensational aspects of the story had already been aired. Rosaleen Doherty had the *Daily News* press credentials on Tuesday, and picked up the plot twist in the next act of a real-life B-movie that was turning into a farce: "The fisty little real-life drama presenting Lawrence J. Tierney, 27, and Henry Sturman, 25, ex-college boxing champ, in an absorbing meller entitled 'When Strong Men Meet' brightened considerably yesterday in Mid-Manhattan Court. A character got into the act." The "character" was thirty-one-year-old Silvio Domenico. He said he was a "salesman" who bought and sold just about anything. He listed his residence as the Midtown Hotel at Sixty-First and Broadway, two blocks south of the Empire. Domenico was sworn in as a witness to the Tierney v. Sturman matchup. From the witness stand, he testified that he saw Lawrence Tierney kick Henry Sturman. Was that a gasp from the gallery? Tierney's attorney Saul Price waited a dramatic beat before approaching the witness.

"Didn't you approach my client and offer to, quote, 'say anything you want me to?' Didn't you say, 'If you want to do the right thing by me, I can have someone from the hotel testify that Sturman offered a bribe to a hotel employee for a pass key to a hotel room?'"

Suddenly in a role that could have been played by Elisha Cook Jr., Domenico denied it.

Price dug in. "Didn't you offer to sell your testimony to my client for quote, 'a couple of hundred dollars?'"

"No. I did not!"

The gavel came down. "This is serious," said Magistrate Isaacs. He instructed Price to file a perjury complaint against the witness. The salesman who bought and sold anything bought himself a perjury charge. He was ordered held on $10,000 bail. The Tierney–Sturman bout was adjourned until January 21.

Silvio Domenico's true identity and game were revealed in April 1951 when ex-convict Pete Lombardo traded a rambling confession in return for a reduced sentence on burglary charges in Pittsburgh. Domenico—aka "Slugs" Domenico—was a member of the La Rocca crime family's East Liberty rackets mob. "Slugs told me he had to appear as a witness for this movie actor, Lawrence Tierney, which is true because he showed me pictures," Lombardo ratted. "Lawrence Tierney was staying at the same hotel with him and he had some trouble there and they were holding Lawrence Tierney for assault and battery and Slugs was to be a witness for him, and when he went there he shook Lawrence Tierney down. He told me this. He said if he came through, he would witness for him, or else go talk to the prosecution."

Lawrence Tierney continued to provide great entertainment in his hometown, making the columns for his wild life—and social life. The *Daily News's* On Broadway columnist Danton Walker quipped on January 15 that "Joe Marr of 'The Iceman Cometh' thinks it's too bad Dillinger is dead, as he'd be so good in a movie called 'The Life of Lawrence Tierney.'" Dorothy Kilgallen revealed a few days later that socialite Vivi Stokes was seen on the town "handholding" Tierney. "Vivi Stokes" was Vivian Stokes Stillman Taylor—*Mrs.* Henry Stillman Taylor. A beautiful, witty, and sharp society girl, she'd grown up in Newport, Rhode Island, part of a debutante crowd that included Jacqueline Bouvier. Vivi had made romantic scandal headlines in 1941, when Jakie Webb, son of millionaire W. Seward Webb and great-great-grandson of shipping and railroad magnate "Commodore" Cornelius Vanderbilt, left her at the altar, hopped a plane, and eloped with society playgirl Lenore Lemmon (Jakie, a problem drinker, was court-martialed by the US Army in 1943 after his arrest for impersonating an air force captain while on an AWOL bender). Vivi was two weeks short of twenty years old when she married Taylor, son of the president of Standard Oil, in October 1943. She was twenty-three and still married, at least on paper, when she was seen with Tierney. Louella Parsons reported some days later that "'Mr. Dillinger' has fallen madly in love with Mrs. Stillman Taylor. . . . Through her, Lawrence was invited to all the most exclusive New York parties—and furthermore, I hear he behaved himself." Parsons also hinted that marriage was in the cards: "When next you hear from Lawrence Tierney, the bets are it will be from Sun Valley"—Sun Valley being Sun Valley, Idaho, the winter getaway for Hollywood celebrities and the rich and famous. Vivi was heading to Sun Valley for her winter jaunt—and to finalize her divorce.

During the week leading to the next court hearing, and in light of the unsettling appearance by Slugs Domenico, Tierney and Sturman decided it was in both their best interests to call it a draw. They dropped their charges against each other. The case did not resume in court on January 21, but another judge, in another court, did issue a ruling on that day.

Judge Jimmie Fidler insisted in the Court of Public Opinion that Tierney's record of five arrests in Los Angeles, combined with "another alcoholic adventure" in New York, "should—but probably won't—spur his studio bosses to take some positive action in his case.

"The first two or three times that Tierney was involved in scandals, it may have been reasonable for them to shrug the matter aside on the excuse that his escapades were his own business," Fidler columnized. "But it's no longer reasonable to take that attitude. By continuing to excuse and pamper him, his studio is assuming a full share of responsibility for his actions."

Fidler made it clear: Lawrence Tierney's problems were Hollywood's problems, and it was up to those in power to do something about them.

Tierney, meanwhile, carried on with his *San Quentin* tour. The week of January 26, he was in Chicago for the film's Midwest premiere, and according to *Showmen's Trade Review,* did yeoman's work: "In addition to being photographed for the *Chicago Tribune* color cover, Tierney was guest on the 'Tommy Bartlett Show' aired over 226 ABC network stations. He also recorded a 15-minute interview with Easter Straker for a playback over WIND. . . . A noon luncheon for the Chicago press was also part of the crowded day's schedule." Over a twelve-hour period on Wednesday, opening day, Tierney made six brief appearances onstage before showings at the RKO Palace Theatre. He got a good response from his Bogart and Robinson routine, and seemed to be back on track. But the following day, there were indications in Hollywood that if studio bosses were not paying attention to Jimmie Fidler's warnings, Fidler's colleagues were.

In a column bemoaning the fact that bad behavior by movie stars "only increased the stars' value," Erskine Johnson used Tierney as the prime example. "The screen's Dillinger keeps a scrapbook, no doubt, after a series of fistic encounters. But he goes right on appearing in pictures. . . . Every Hollywood contract carries a morality clause. But not one has ever been used to break a contract."

A more ominous signal appeared the following day. When Tierney made four appearances onstage at her city's Circle Theatre, Martha Hatton noted in her *Indianapolis News* radio column that "there seems to have been considerable confusion concerning the fact that Lawrence Tierney, and not Gene Tierney, has been appearing at the Circle Theater in connection with his picture, 'San Quentin.'"

In days to come, several stories would point out that Lawrence Tierney was not related to the twenty-six-year-old Academy Award–nominated actress. This disclaimer had not appeared in print since the fall of 1944, when Louella Parsons made the clarification after newcomer Lawrence Tierney won the *Dillinger* role. Gene Tierney, the beauty with the "enchanting overbite," may have been born in Brooklyn, but 20th Century Fox, which had her under contract, wanted as much distance as possible from the other Tierney.

❧

The RKO Radio Pictures team took advantage of Tierney's time on the road for interviews with reporters and columnists who lived and worked far from the Hollywood bubble. This helped present the actor as a well-dressed, respectable artist, as opposed to an out-of-control and possibly bipolar drunk.

In Dayton, Ohio, where Tierney was onstage at the Colonial Theatre on February 1, 1947, Arthur S. Kany uncovered a deep secret: "He wants to play opposite Ingrid Bergman on the screen. As who wouldn't!" Tierney revealed other hidden desires to the *Dayton Herald* columnist: "I'd like to take a fling at playing on the legitimate stage," he said. "I think that would be fun. And then I'd like to make one horror picture to outdo anything Karloff has ever done."

The light column ended on a surprise twist: news that when the personal engagement tour ended in New York several weeks later, Tierney's parents were joining Gerard and moving to Hollywood permanently. Youngest brother, US Army private Edward Tierney, planned to join the family when he returned from his tour of duty in Korea. "According to one of the Hollywood radio columnists Sunday night," Kany wrote, "a 'warm' welcome is awaiting Tierney out there. He stated that a warrant has been sworn out by the Beverly Hills police for Tierney's arrest on a charge of violating his parole."

Tierney was in St. Louis two weeks later, to walk onstage at the Fox Theatre, and be trotted out to meet the local press. After a breakfast at the opulent Coronado Hotel, he sat, weary and unguarded, with Myles Standish, drama and movie critic for the *St. Louis Post-Dispatch*. Standish turned the talk into an article that was a shock from its opening line: "Yeah," said Lawrence Tierney, "I've been arrested a few times for getting cockeyed drunk."

The piece was a deep-dive pocket profile of the actor in which Standish pegged Tierney as someone who "isn't at all embarrassed by" but "not particularly proud of his several courtroom appearances and the bouts that led up to them, but on the other hand he doesn't put on an act claiming it's all one continuous mistake." Standish's description and insights revealed the value— and danger—in allowing a Hollywood outsider to inspect the product in the flesh: "He's tall and broad-shouldered, with hard straight features and light blue eyes that looked as if he hadn't rested too well the night before. He has a New York accent and a fairly subdued manner. He doesn't seem to be too sure of himself, and is still far from smooth. His hands and wrists are surprisingly small for such a big man. He dresses conservatively, especially for an actor—he was wearing a dark blue suit, plain dark red tie, and striped blue shirt, and his black shoes were unshined."

Standish, a veteran newspaperman and former crime and courtroom reporter, got Tierney to open up about his recent legal-, combat-, and booze-related troubles, revealing details about skirmishes that in many ways contradicted what had been sworn to in court.

Of his arrest in August, after he took a spill while allegedly changing a lightbulb: "I just fell into a coffee table at a party at a friend's house. The glass cuts a long gash in my neck—look, you can still see the scars—and cuts an artery in my right forefinger. They take me out to find an emergency hospital. The first one is being painted and the painters are all horrified to see me covered with blood. They don't like it, see, so we go into another emergency hospital. There are only two nurses there, and they are horrified, too. 'Oh my,' they say. 'There isn't any doctor here. You're too badly hurt for us to do anything.' So out we go, still looking for a doctor, me spouting blood like a fountain. All the time, I am taking nips out of a bottle, sort of medicine, see. So I'm pretty plastered when we get to a first-aid clinic at a police station."

Most surprisingly, Tierney, "with a reminiscent glint in his eye," went into detail about his fight with Henry Sturman. This recollection rang a bit truer than what was reported by the New York press.

"It was just one of those things," he told Standish. "I come back to my hotel early in the morning pretty looped, and I see two guys getting off the elevator on the second floor with a girl between them, so stiff she could hardly walk. They sort of dragged her to a room. I said to myself, 'Geez, what's going on here, I better help her.' So I get off there too, though my room was on the fifth floor.

"One of the guys comes out of the room and says, 'What do you want, buddy?' I say, 'What are you doing to that girl?' He says, 'Who are you, a hotel dick or something?' Real tough. I say, 'Yes.' He looks me over and sees by my tuxedo I'm not a hotel dick. So he takes a swing at me.

"We fight all over the hall. Then the elevator man opens the elevator door to see what all the noise is about, and we rassle into the elevator. 'Going down,' says the elevator man, and shuts the door. We're banging each other's brains out in the elevator, see? Down it goes to the first floor. The elevator man pulls open the door. 'First floor,' he says. 'All out!' So we knock each other out into the lobby and continue the go there.

"Suddenly the other guy stops fighting and says, 'I'm going to have you bumped off before the morning. I know the guys who can do it, too.' He goes to a phone. I say to myself, 'Geez, this is bad. He looks like he really means it.'

I don't want anybody pumping me full of bullets. That bullet stuff is all right in pictures. But not for me in real life. So I go up to a friend's room on the seventh floor to hide. The police come and get me there."

"Pretty plastered" and *"pretty looped"*: Tierney was under a court's order to abstain from alcohol. In two separate court cases, he'd testified under oath that he had not violated that prohibition—with the exception of a pain-killing shot of brandy offered after an innocent fall from a coffee table. Now, he confessed to the newspaper audience that in reality, he continued to drink to the point of intoxication and violence.

To the relief of the RKO Radio Pictures publicists, Standish's article was an aberration. The majority of press coverage Tierney received on the road contained material regurgitated from the studio's press office. In fact, on February 18, Wood Soanes, the *Oakland Tribune*'s drama editor, opened his feature on the actor's life by attributing the information to press release copy churned out by RKO's Rutgers Nielson. It was only at the end of the article that Soanes got down to the nitty gritty. "As far as his studio is concerned, however, Tierney is a major headache. Scarcely a month goes by without him being involved in some public brawl or being tossed in the jug for drunk and disorderly."

After mapping out Tierney's greatest hits and kicks since the John Decker free-for-all, Soanes ended on what was becoming a common disclaimer: "Incidentally, Tierney is no relation of Gene Tierney."

7

The Drunk Farm

Lawrence Tierney arrived in Baltimore on Saturday, February 22, 1947, and checked into a suite at the majestic Lord Baltimore Hotel. He'd make several appearances on Sunday at showings of *San Quentin* at the Hippodrome Theatre, a grand old vaudeville house that, like so many others, had made way for the movies. Tierney was a special addition to a lineup that included musical comedy star Bill Johnson and comedian Artie Dann. The stay in Baltimore seemed to go without a hitch, and Tierney moved on to wind down his participation in the promotional tour. By mid-March, the film would be represented onstage by the mysterious Mr. X, an ex-con delivering a five-minute spiel about life behind prison walls.

The stay, however, did not go on without a hitch. On March 3, Dorothy Kilgallen revealed that Tierney not only came close to missing the Hippodrome shows, but almost did not make it out of Baltimore at all—because he was in jail, after another early-morning fight in a hotel hallway.

While Tierney was allegedly impersonating the house detective in his bout at the Empire Hotel in New York, he was mixing it up with the real deal at the Lord Baltimore. The hotel's security man had responded in the early morning hours to a complaint about loud noise from Tierney's suite. A fight followed. Tierney was arrested and tossed in the police station lockup. Fortunately for him, he had the right phone number in his pocket. "Because he was making a personal appearance in a local theater . . . the theater manager had him booked under another name and arranged bail immediately. . . . It was done so skillfully that even the Baltimore police didn't know the gent in question was Lawrence Tierney."

The Devil Thumbs a Ride was rolled out on February 20, 1947. Second-billed in double features, the melodrama was not a film for critics to love, but a dark, over-the-top thrill ride for fans, with Tierney rebounding into the bad guy mode he was born for. Bosley Crowther of the *New York Times* gave the film a thumbs-down on March 22. "It is pictures like this which give the movies a black eye and give us a pain in the neck," he wrote. "In the role of the thug, Lawrence Tierney, who played Dillinger a couple of years back, behaves with the customary arrogance of all gunmen in cheap Hollywood films."

The role as Steve Morgan, even more than that of John Dillinger, was the one that cemented Tierney's image for the rest of his career. "Lawrence Tierney is at his most vicious and amoral here," poet and novelist Barry Gifford wrote in his film noir appreciation, *The Devil Thumbs a Ride & Other Unforgettable Films*. "The wickedest looking big lug in B movie history. . . . Tierney invests this basically stupid plot with such genuine virulence that *Devil* must be ranked in the upper echelon of indelibly American *noir*."

Tierney was not so appreciative. He realized the character of Steve Morgan was so powerfully evil that it would limit his acting opportunities. "I didn't like it at all," he told Broadway historian and documentary filmmaker Rick McKay in *Scarlet Street* magazine in 1998. "See, I resented all those pictures that they put me in. I never thought of myself as that kind of guy. I thought of myself as a nice guy who wouldn't do rotten things. But obviously that miserable son of a bitch in the film would! I hated that character so much, but I had to do it for the picture."

Lawrence Tierney took his time making his way back to Hollywood. The *Salt Lake Tribune* reported on his "in again out again" visit to the city on March 21, including a stay at the city's Temple Square Hotel and an afternoon spent driving through the canyons. The *Tribune* story clarified that Tierney "is no relation to Gene Tierney, incidentally."

Louella Parsons reported on April 4 that Tierney was back in Hollywood and ready to work on his next RKO picture, *Bodyguard*. "It's a meat racket expose and the setting is Kansas City." Parsons retracted her earlier scoop that Tierney was on the verge of marrying socialite Vivi Stokes. "Larry says she's a swell girl but they are not tuning up the wedding bells."

Tierney meandered up to the Monterey Peninsula on the central California coast on April 10 for the premiere of the RKO Radio comedy, *The Farmer's Daughter,* and the grand opening of the Alisal Theatre. The $350,000 state-of-the-art movie house was a first-class cinema in the second-class but rapidly growing city of Salinas. The event was a flashy, Hollywood-style spectacle with klieg lights sweeping the skies, booming music in the air, and red carpet interviews with industry heavyweights and stars including Van Johnson,

Kay Kyser, Georgia Carroll, and Vera Allen. Tierney made the scene without making a scene.

He may have been keeping a low profile because of a legal matter hanging over his head. In the wake of his clash with the glass coffee table in September 1946, his probation in Beverly Hills was on the verge of being revoked, and a ninety-day prison sentence loomed. Tierney had since spent five days in jail and been busted once more on a drunk rap—twice, counting the false identity arrest in Baltimore.

Tierney was back in Beverly Hills Justice Court on April 16, back where his troubles began in 1945, standing before Judge Cecil D. Holland. At this juncture, Tierney's transgressions were too numerous and too public to overlook. Judge Holland had no choice but to send Tierney to county jail—but he did give him a break. The judge allowed the sentence to be served over the next four weekends—Saturdays through Mondays. Tierney could keep working and avoid trouble.

The following Sunday, while Tierney was serving out his first weekend, he received national attention, courtesy of syndicated columnist Jack Lait Jr., a prominent newspaperman and screenwriter with an affinity for the seamy side of Hollywood. Lait had a genre-crossing connection to Lawrence Tierney. As a young reporter for the *Chicago Tribune,* he'd made his bones on July 22, 1934, when he got the scoop on the killing of John Dillinger: "John Dillinger, ace bad man of the world, got his last night—two slugs through his heart and one through his head. He was tough and he was shrewd, but he wasn't as tough and shrewd as the Federals, who never close a case until the end. It took 27 of them to end Dillinger's career, and their strength came out of his weakness—a woman."

Lait took on the "screen Dillinger" in his column with a lead that was slightly less impressive than the one conjured for the end of Public Enemy No. 1: "'He's not really a bad boy—he's just a little wild.' Since time immemorial, doting maiden aunts have used that line to explain and excuse the escapades of wayward youths. And for the past three years, Hollywood has been shaking its collective head and quoting that familiar old line about Brooklyn's Lawrence Tierney."

Lait's column, which included the disclaimer that Tierney was "no relation to Gene Tierney, also of Brooklyn," was a laundry list, colorfully written, of the offscreen antics "which have landed him, at one time or another, in (1) the newspapers, (2) the clink, and (3) the bad graces of his studio bosses. . . . The odd—and rather sad—part of it is that Larry is ordinarily a swell guy, modest, friendly, likeable, as nice a kid as you could hope to meet. Nobody knows what takes him over periodically and makes a Brooklyn Comanche out of him.

"Hollywood likes Larry," Lait concluded, "and is pulling for him—not only as a good guy but as a talented actor, of which there are none too many hereabouts. The town is keeping its fingers crossed, hoping he'll get himself straightened out—before it's too late."

As the calendar page turned to a new month, fingers crossed, Lawrence Tierney was on his way to overcoming his issues. His parents were with him in Hollywood for support. Brother Gerard Tierney was finding his away around town, hacking, taking day labor jobs, working on losing his Brooklyn accent, and, thanks to the GI Bill, attending acting classes with Lela Bliss and Harry Hayden at their Bliss-Hayden drama school on South Robertson Boulevard in Beverly Hills. Completing the family circle was Private Edward M. Tierney, US Army. Eighteen years old and at least two inches taller than his oldest brother, he'd soon be civilian Edward M. Tierney, perhaps ready to try his own luck in Hollywood.

Born to Kill, the first film noir directed by Val Lewton's protégé Robert Wise, was released on the last day of April. After its opening at the Palace, Crowther of the *New York Times* described the picture memorably, as "an hour and a half of ostentatious vice . . . morally disgusting . . . an offense to a normal intellect . . . malignant . . . cheap . . . unsavory" and "a smeary tabloid fable." Tierney, he wrote, was "given outrageous license to demonstrate the histrionics of nastiness." To Kate Cameron in the *Daily News, Born to Kill* was "as lurid a collection of low-lives as ever appeared at one and the same time in a film"; Tierney's character Sam Wilde, an "atavistic killer . . . a tough and terrible . . . megalomaniac who kills anyone getting in his way or crossing him ever so lightly." Cameron wrote that Tierney played "the role with too much realistic effect for the comfort of the audience." (Barry Gifford wrote in 1988 that "Tierney's menacing presence is . . . a brute fantasy come alive in all of his horrifying glory. . . . There's no decency at all in Lawrence Tierney's face, the most cruelly handsome visage on film. Unlike Mitchum's face there's no relief in sight, a man incapable of compromise.")

There would be similar reaction to *Born to Kill* from critics and censors across the country who saw the film squeezing nihilistically against the restrictions of the Motion Picture Production Code. Various communities cited Tierney as a bad influence, and enough reason to stop the film from being screened. *Born to Kill* was banned from theaters in Tennessee and Ohio.

There was more trouble ahead. Even before the stacks of the *Times* and *Daily News* that contained the *Born to Kill* reviews were tossed from delivery trucks onto the sidewalks in front of New York City newsstands, an incident on the opposite side of the country, in the middle of a street in Beverly Hills, would portend bad news for *Born to Kill* and RKO Radio Pictures, and even worse news for Lawrence Tierney.

The calls came in to the Beverly Hills Police Department in the early morning of Thursday, May 1, 1947. More than one resident of the ordinarily quiet—especially at that hour—100 block of South Spalding Drive complained of men fighting, shouting, and "using loud and profane language" in the middle of the street. Radio officers Tom Taylor and Robert Huff made the turn off Wilshire Boulevard and encountered two men, one shirtless, both bloodied, battling like a couple of bare-knuckle boxers, trading punches, haymakers, and hooks—cursing each other out as they duked it out. The men looked very much alike, though one was noticeably older than the other.

The older man, the one who was stripped to the waist, his eyes in a mad dog frenzy, was Lawrence Tierney. His opponent—huskier, a little taller, had removed his jacket. He was eighteen-year-old Edward Tierney, who'd returned from duty in the US Army a week earlier.

The cops watched a moment, amazed at the intensity of conflict and the way the punches were landing. Then they moved in and separated the pair. Lawrence told them everything was fine. He and his brother were only settling a debate over a girl named Betty.

"We were visiting a girl named Betty and got into an argument," Police Chief C. H. Anderson later quoted Edward. "So we went out in the street to finish it . . . to decide this thing like gentlemen," the cops quoted Lawrence.

According to the arresting officers, the brothers brawled in the street because Betty's apartment was too cramped for the rumble. Both Tierneys were booked for drunkenness and disturbing the peace. Edward was released on $100 bail. Lawrence Tierney's bail was $250. The case was set to be heard before Judge Charles Griffin in Beverly Hills Police Court on Monday at 2 p.m., but the arrest meant that Lawrence Tierney had to first make a stop in Beverly Hills Justice Court. That Friday morning, he was back before Judge Cecil D. Holland, who was allowing him to serve his probation violation sentence on weekends. Tierney had spent the past two weekends in county jail. He had two weekends to go.

Waiting outside court, the Tierney brothers joked with reporters who'd gathered around them.

"We were just having a friendly quarrel, eh, Eddie?" big brother prompted.

"That's right, Larry," Edward replied.

Tierney explained the misunderstanding to the newsmen. He'd met Eddie at a bowling alley and later went to a friend's apartment to talk. The argument erupted when he insisted that Edward go home to see their mother. He left Betty out of it. He also denied that the fight was fueled by alcohol. "I haven't been drunk nor have I had a drink since last October," Tierney insisted—forgetting what he'd told Myles Standish in St. Louis. "I leave the liquor store alone because it is hard on me."

It was a sad scene in court. Tierney's fifty-five-year-old father, a real-life lawman and new Angeleno, pleaded on his son's behalf. Tierney himself was described as "crestfallen" as he stood before the judge, who clearly was exasperated.

"We have given this boy all the breaks," Judge Holland announced. "He has ruined the reputation of the entire motion picture industry. He has shown no respect for anyone and must be taught a lesson."

He peered down at Lawrence Tierney. "Your family and friends seem to suffer more than you do, and you place an undue load on the motion picture industry by the way you act up. Your family has suffered a lot and when I gave you four weekends to spend in jail recently, I took pity on your family, not you.

"You have had four or five chances to straighten yourself out. Now I think you'd better spend about ninety days with a pick and shovel in a county road camp and see if that won't do you some good."

Tierney was led out to begin his sentence at the Los Angeles County Jail. The structure held 2,647 male prisoners but was supplied with only 1,815 bunks. Tierney had no seniority among the jail population, so he was forced to sleep on a mattress on the floor in a corridor.

He was due to appear in court with Edward on Monday to face Judge Griffin on the latest drunk and disturbing the peace charges. The judge said he wouldn't insist that Tierney show up as long as he was at work with the road gang. Edward and the brothers' attorney, Richard Maddox, made the date. Maddox asked for a week's continuance so he could prepare a plea. The judge compromised; Maddox had until Friday at 2 p.m.

After the newspapers ran photographs of Tierney lying on a mattress on the floor of a jailhouse hallway, cigarette in hand, celebrity apparently led to some privileges—and trouble. By Tuesday night, Tierney was bunking alone in a two-man cell, but when the 6:30 alarm rang the next morning, he failed to rise. Deputy Floyd R. Huston walked by the cell at 7:05 a.m. and saw that Tierney was still sleeping. He reported the prisoner to Lt. A. E. Hirsch, and Tierney was thrown into solitary for the rest of the day. That meant no candy, no mail, no visitors—and no cigarettes. The jailers warned Tierney that if he slept in again, he just might find himself locked in solitary for the remainder of his sentence, with no time off for good behavior.

On Friday, May 9, Tierney was transported from the county jail to Beverly Hills Justice Court to face the music for the May 1 street fight. He pleaded not guilty to drunkenness and disturbing the peace. Judge Griffin found him guilty on both counts. On the drunk charge, the judge gave Tierney a choice of an extra five days in jail or a twenty-five-dollar fine. Tierney chose to pay the quarter. For disturbing the peace, the judge handed Tierney an additional ninety days in jail, but suspended the sentence, on the condition that the actor abstain from all alcohol during his probation.

Edward was convicted of being drunk. He was fined ten dollars.

So how did the news media handle the story? Most fell back on the usual angle that "the screen's Dillinger," the "movie tough guy," "28-year-old bad boy on and off the screen," was in trouble again, as would be expected from such a convincing movie bad man. Tierney's past clashes were rehashed, while cinema and real life were blurred further by that wire photo of Tierney, in jailhouse fatigues and holding a cigarette, resting on a mattress in the Los Angeles County Jail, "waiting to be shifted to a county road camp."

The latest headlines competed with and overshadowed the publicity for *Born to Kill*, and damaged the prospects of a film that had been expected to do well. RKO Radio's production boss Dore Schary cited *Born to Kill* days after its release when he announced that his studio would no longer produce pictures that depict arbitrary violence. "I think this kind of picture is . . . doomed," he told the *Showmen's Trade Review*. "I think it is a reflection of what you saw years ago when there were gangster pictures. They (the public) wanted them . . . and then they got tired of them." Schary attributed the current cycle of movie violence to the war. Audiences, he said, now wanted "sweetness and light."

The day after Schary made his comments in New York, Danton Walker wrote in his *Daily News* Broadway column on May 6: "John Golden hopes to star Gene Tierney on Broadway this Fall. . . . Lawrence Tierney (no relation) supposed to have been canceled out by his studio because of his numerous scrapes." The Lawrence Tierney report was not confirmed, and was quite possibly conjecture, coming as newspapers were picking up RKO's latest press release, revealing that Tierney would not be playing a criminal in *Bodyguard,* but a "good guy."

Hedda Hopper wrote that the decision to cast Tierney as "a hero, not a heel" was a deliberate move by the studio, the first step in a longer-term, if unusual, rehabilitation strategy. "Studio officials say he'll be given no more heavy roles," she reported. "They think that if 'Dillinger' could make a problem boy out of Tierney, heroic roles can, by the same token, turn him into a good citizen in private as well as professional life."

Only one Hollywood journalist looked beyond the sordid surface thrills of Tierney's fight and jailing. Jimmie Fidler had been commenting on Tierney's misdeeds from the start. This time, he'd seen enough, spelling it out in his May 12 column, "SCREEN DRUNK NEEDS DISCIPLINE." Fidler thundered that Tierney's brawl was no surprise, because the actor had already been revealed as "an incorrigible" whose "craving for alcohol and fisticuffs seemingly has become pathological and irresistible."

Fidler placed much of the blame for Tierney's scandals on the bosses at RKO Radio Pictures, who he claimed "have been pampering Tierney for two years. Never once have they enforced their weak-as-dishwater threats to discipline him if he failed to behave. On the contrary, they have made every effort to soft pedal his misconduct. They boosted his pay, gave him better roles, and, in short, gave him a pat on the back when the situation demanded a lusty kick in the pants." Had the studio taken action a couple of years earlier, Fidler argued, Tierney might have been set straight, and served as a warning to other actors "inclined to mistake position for license." Now, not even another jail term would change his ways.

"The proper place for Lawrence Tierney," Jimmie Fidler concluded, "is a sanatorium, not a carefully propped-up pedestal."

Lawrence Tierney was slotted into the corrections system but not lost to the Hollywood press. A week after Tierney's most recent court appearance, Los Angeles chief jailer Clem Peoples announced on May 16 that Tierney would be transferred to the Sheriff's Honor Farm in Castaic to finish out his sentence. The correctional facility, a former dairy farm in bucolic northern Los Angeles County, was an all-male, minimum-security detention center in which inmates worked in a farm setting, tasked with farm chores. The institution was also known as the Wayside Jail, and more commonly as the Wayside Drunk Farm, because so many inmates were there for alcohol-related crimes.

Lawrence Tierney had several alcohol-related crimes clouding his future, not the least of which was the bloody, drunken escapade the previous summer that began when he crashed through a glass coffee table and ended with him strapped down by police while a doctor stitched him up. Judge Eugene P. Fay had handed Tierney a sixty-day jail term, but suspended all but five days. The sentence was contingent on Tierney staying out of trouble and off the sauce for a year. His conviction for the Beverly Hills street fight meant that he might have to serve another fifty-five days.

Tierney was driven back to municipal court in Los Angeles to face Judge Fay on May 21. In Tierney's earlier appearance, the judge lectured him about his drinking, and called him "one of those individuals who can't handle liquor." This time, as the judge decided whether he had violated probation, Tierney was prepared. He told Judge Fay that his latest incarceration got him thinking seriously about his situation and led him to join Alcoholics Anonymous. Tierney said he truly believed he'd conquered his addiction to alcohol.

"No organization is going to do you any good until you make up your own mind that you're through with liquor," Judge Fay lectured. He reminded Tierney that his jail sentence had been suspended because he'd promised to remain sober and out of trouble. Additional jail time seemed inevitable, but Judge Fay once again proved to be, if not an "old softie," at least a jurist who was sympathetic to an alcoholic's plight.

The judge ruled that Tierney would remain on probation, but must report to a county parole officer thirty days after his release from the honor farm.

The good news on Thursday was followed by devastating news on Saturday, relayed by Jimmie Fidler: "Lawrence Tierney, serving a 90-day rap for his latest brawl, is suspended from the RKO payroll, and insiders say his contract will definitely be dropped next option time."

8

The Milk Wagon

Cut loose from his Hollywood lifeline with his RKO contract in limbo, Lawrence Tierney would seem to have reached his lowest ebb in June 1947. He had no choice but to settle into the routine, and accept the downside of his celebrity status, at the Wayside Drunk Farm. "He told me the guards would razz him by calling him 'Dillinger,'" says nephew Timothy Tierney. "As in, 'Shovel this shit, *Dillinger!*'"

Tierney had a bunk in a barracks, and spent his days working in the dairy, milking cows, gathering crops—and attending meetings of Alcoholics Anonymous. His claims to Judge Fay that the fellowship had turned his life around appeared to have some basis in fact. On June 17, forty-seven days into his incarceration, word of his progress had spread all the way to New York City. Dorothy Kilgallen showed off the depth of her sources when she offered what she called one of those "stories-I-find-hard-to-believe" in her On Broadway column. The jailed Lawrence Tierney, she'd been told, "is reported in the throes of a reformation that inspires him to lecture other Hollywood tipplers on the evils of demon rum. He is supposed to have said he'll never take another drink." She added parenthetically and wickedly, "Was that with water or soda, Larry?"

As eye-rolling as the story seemed, Lawrence Tierney had indeed gained a reputation throughout the Drunk Farm for his AA talks, attracting many fellow inmates to meetings to hear stories in which he used himself as a pathetic example of how alcohol can ruin a career and life.

That same day in downtown Los Angeles, two humbled men were sitting across from Los Angeles Assistant Chief of Police Joseph Reed, Sheriff's Captain M. F. Nurenberg, and Deputy District Attorney Kenneth Lynch—otherwise known as the county parole board. Lawrence H. Tierney and an anonymous member of Alcoholics Anonymous had been given a hearing during which they both pleaded for Tierney's early release.

After listening to the father and hearing the glowing and inspirational testimony from the AA man, the board members agreed that Lawrence Tierney should receive early parole and be set free the following morning.

On July 18, having served a little more than half his ninety-day sentence, Tierney walked out of the prison farm, whistling.

"I feel fine, and life at the farm agreed with me," he told reporters. "I realize most of my troubles have been due to drink, but that's all going to be changed now."

One thing that had definitely changed was RKO Radio Pictures' attitude and fortitude. Upon Tierney's walk to freedom (albeit under two years' probation), the jail farm warden sent a letter to *Bodyguard* producer Sid Rogell and RKO. He confirmed that Tierney had been a model prisoner, an example and real help to others, and had made such a good impression during his stay that he earned his early release. The corrections official asked that Tierney be given yet another chance, a chance to get that role in *Bodyguard* and play the good guy.

While the RKO suits held their cards close to their chests, Tierney showed his hand, announcing plans for a nationwide lecture tour, as Hollywood's foremost non-anonymous member of Alcoholics Anonymous.

"There's just one thing," Louella Parsons pointed out when she broke the news of the warden's letter to RKO. "It's wonderful that Tierney is reformed and is taken to lecturing to other alcoholics, but I want to say one thing to Mr. Lawrence Tierney. If he falls off the water-wagon now and gets into a night club brawl, he will really be washed up. He's already had more chances than anyone has a right to expect."

At least one of Hollywood's moral arbiters was not so impressed by Tierney's evangelical zeal. Jimmie Fidler titled his column "TIERNEY'S PROPOSAL RIDICULOUS" and claimed he was left "gasping" by Tierney's planned temperance tour. "For sheer effrontery and bad taste, that one takes the proverbial cake."

Fidler reminded his readers that Tierney had "reformed" before, only to turn up a few weeks later, "tighter than a tick, in another jam." Fidler wrote that Tierney could quit drinking "if he's man enough to put everything he has in the fight." He hoped that Tierney would, because "sober, he's an alright guy and a good actor. But this proposed lecture tour of his smacks a devil of a lot more of publicity than it does of honest reform. The one way for Lawrence Tierney to reestablish himself with his employers and with his fans is to buckle down, keep his mouth shut, his nose to the grindstone—and PROVE by his everyday life that he's cured himself of a persistent weakness."

Tierney heard it over and over again. Alcoholism was a "weakness."

A more sympathetic and counterintuitive assessment of Tierney's plight came in an overview from someone far removed from Hollywood, stylistically and intellectually. The veteran journalist, editor, and literary critic Burton Rascoe was a contributor to *American Weekly*, the Hearst papers' Sunday supplement. On the second Sunday of August, his featured essay, "Lawrence Tierney's Big Problem," attributed Tierney's troubles not to alcohol, rage, or some psychological imbalance, but to the public's reaction to his role as John Dillinger.

Rascoe compared Tierney's situation to that of prizefighters and established movie tough guys who find themselves taunted by "any drunken stumblebum or smart aleck who wants to insult him or push him around." These professionals learn that they must swallow their pride, surround themselves with bodyguards, or retreat at the first sign of aggression. Retaliation would lead to serious consequences, from lawsuits to manslaughter charges. Rascoe suggested that Tierney, who "had a fine record" before *Dillinger* made him a star, was aware of that, and was releasing his anger and frustration by striking out at those close to him—his brother, for instance, or fellow members of the movie colony.

"The psychiatrists call that 'vicarious compensation for emotional frustration,'" Rascoe wrote. "All it means is that Tierney hit somebody he was fond of when he couldn't hit somebody he didn't like."

Waiting for word on his future from RKO, Lawrence Tierney set out to prove himself as a sober actor and citizen in good standing, not through volunteer work or temperance lectures, but by showing up at Hollywood's top nightspots and drinking milk, conspicuously. There was no shortage of beautiful women to help him along. Prominent among them was Vivi Stokes. Tierney may have brushed off suggestions of marriage back in April, but the socialite had been with him in Los Angeles since he left the Drunk Farm. The low-key relationship was revealed by Hedda Hopper around the time of Rascoe's piece. She reported that Lili Damita, the French actress and ex-wife of Errol Flynn, was "pretty angry" that her name had been linked with "Lawrence (Dillinger) Tierney." It was Lili's houseguest, Vivi Stokes, Hopper clarified, not Lili, who'd been helping Tierney through the difficult weeks of sobriety. Why was Damita upset? The Tierney gossip "caused her real New York heartbeat to tear his hair, and he can't spare any."

By September, Tierney still had not embarked on his national speaking tour, and there was still no official word on whether RKO would drop him from its roster. His suspension, official or not, was evident, because the studio had not called him to do any work. An SOS item was planted in more than one column, in almost exactly the same words: "Lawrence Tierney's wondering when RKO will trust him with another picture. He hasn't touched a drop of the stuff since he left the hoosegow and would like another chance to prove he can be a good boy." "Good boy" had become a term shared by gossip writers when describing the sober Tierney. The drinking, fighting Tierney? Bad man.

The first version of the "good boy" item ran in Hugh Dixon's Hollywood column on September 9, 1947. That evening, Lawrence Tierney was back at the Mocambo nightclub on the Sunset Strip, site of one of his more publicized punch-ups. Gossip tipsters raised an eyebrow when they saw Tierney socializing as the night slid into the morning of September 10 and the carousing reached a fever pitch. The eyes of the press also noticed the presence of another big screen bad guy, Bruce Cabot, a forty-three-year-old actor known for villainous screen roles (and Errol Flynn's wingman when Flynn bitch-slapped Jimmie Fidler at the club in 1941). Tierney and Cabot were at separate tables, but the pair's presence in the nitery would be worth a couple of bucks from one of the many competing Hollywood column writers.

Then, suddenly, there was a commotion at the bar. Voices were raised. A confrontation became a conflict. A barstool was hurled; cocktail glasses thrown and shattered as the two partiers pummeled each other. One fist connected with the wrong face. A bystander's shoulder was struck by a thrown chair, and then it was an anything-goes fightfest. No one thought of striking up the national anthem. The jaded crowd, accustomed to catching a too-late glance at a one-punch tiff that was over as soon as it started, actually cheered! A flying wedge of waiters and bouncers charged through the room and pushed the two fighters out onto the sidewalk. The doors slammed shut behind them and the brawl carried on into the street until sheriff's deputies pulled up to pull the two men off each other and wheel them to the station.

The incident made the papers later that day. Lawrence Tierney and Bruce Cabot were the first, and only, celebrity names mentioned in the Associated Press story that was first to hit the streets. The two movie stars were not, however, cited as participants, but as "film persons present (who) withdrew at the outbreak of hostilities and were not involved." The fighters were a couple of former college football heroes, a University of Southern California Trojan and a Ramblin' Wreck from Georgia Tech, both in their twenties.

As more facts came in, the United Press reported that Tierney "sipped milk and beamed as he watched the battle."

While Lawrence Tierney cooled his heels in Hollywood's penalty box in September, another Tierney was making his motion picture debut. Brother Gerard, who'd spent the past months taking day jobs and acting classes, was at Poverty Row's Nassour Studios at Sunset Boulevard and Van Ness Avenue, filming a role in *The Counterfeiters*. The movie starred John Sutton, Doris Merrick, Hugh Beaumont, and Lon Chaney Jr. Sam Newfield directed under the pseudonym Peter Stewart, because he was churning out too many cheap pictures under his own name. Gerard Tierney would receive his first screen credit as Gerard Gilbert, either a conscious effort to not ride on his older brother's coattails or to avoid any association with Hollywood's exiled bad man.

All the while, Lawrence Tierney remained in the public eye, on the big screen. With *The Devil Thumbs a Ride, Born to Kill,* and *San Quentin* in theaters across the country, his "live" appearances seemed to be restricted to celebrity nightspots. Tierney's public abstinence was so blatant that Sugie's Original Tropics, the Polynesian-themed restaurant and lounge on Rodeo Drive, added Tierney to the list of stars with drinks named in their honor. Alongside concoctions like "Mickey Rooney's Snowball" and "Dorothy Lamour's Sarong" was "The Tierney Teetotaler"—fruit punch, no alcohol. Tierney was seen with his glass of milk on the town with actresses including Nell King, Rita Johnson, and Shirley Ballard—though, after making the columns with Tierney at Ciro's, Shirley told Harrison Carroll that "her heart belongs to Michael North" (the recently divorced actor who played the salesman in *The Devil Thumbs a Ride*).

Tierney's relationship with Vivi Stokes was definitely on-again, off-again. While he was out and about, Vivi was being squired by Kurt Kreuger, a tall, dashing, blond German-born actor frustrated by the town's insistence on typecasting him as Nazis in war movies. Vivi had met Kreuger skiing in Sun Valley.

Louella Parsons kept the Vivi Stokes items alive, noting that the usually pugnacious Tierney, on his "milk routine," kept his cool when twice encountering Vivi and Kreuger in public: when he was solo in a Hollywood eatery and at the theater. Parsons reported in early October that Tierney and Vivi were on again, dining and making up at L'Aiglon. ("The night before, Tierney waited one and a half hours at the Chanteclair for Vivi, who failed to appear.")

By the end of the very turbulent year, Tierney and Vivi Stokes had what would seem to be the last of their blowouts. She packed up, left Los Angeles, and returned to the East Coast, with plans to fly back to Sun Valley in January—with Kurt Kreuger.

Tierney's most noticeable appearance of the fall season wasn't with Vivi Stokes or a starlet stand-in. Women screamed when he and kid brother Edward arrived at the Hollywood Press Photographers' Costume Ball at Ciro's. The third annual bash in late October was emceed by Bob Hope and attended by many of Hollywood's biggest stars, in costume. There was ventriloquist Edgar Bergen and his wife, Frances, dressed as Edgar's dummies Mortimer Snerd and Charlie McCarthy, Lana Turner with black hair, and Keenan Wynn . . . in blackface. "I thought Wynn was representing Iago in 'Othello,'" Hedda Hopper reported. "But he said, 'No, I'm a disappointed producer.' Keenan was five shades darker than the maharaja of Coochbehar, who impersonated baseball player Jackie Robinson."

No one made an entrance quite like Lawrence Tierney. He barged in wearing a gorilla costume. He was, it was announced, Gargantua, the lowlands gorilla who was star attraction of the Ringling Brothers circus. Eddie was dressed as his keeper. It was quite a self-aware, if not provocative, choice of costume. Eighteen months earlier, when Tierney was stripped to the waist and roaring to fight at John Decker's party, one guest had referred to him as "Tarzan." Now, enclosed in a Crash Corrigan–style monkey suit, Hollywood's scary bad guy had assumed the identity of a dangerous beast—the gorilla billed as the largest in captivity, with a fierce hatred for humans, and a menacing scowl, the result of acid thrown in its face by a drunk.

Wrote Hopper: "Even Orson Welles' mouth flew open at the sight."

In November 1947, mothers and anti–juvenile delinquency groups launched a nationwide protest when it was revealed that the widow of gangster Al "Scarface" Capone was pitching a movie based on his life. Capone had died at his Miami Beach mansion the previous January of ailments related to advanced syphilis. Columnist Erskine Johnson noted that the movie *Dillinger* had already grossed close to $2 million and that a Capone biopic was projected to break $10 million. The downside was that no matter how it was handled, the film would glorify the subject, and "make 10,000 more juvenile delinquents."

Johnson found one Hollywood star who was firm in his belief that another movie about another Public Enemy was a bad idea. "The kids and young people who see such pictures, I learned sadly enough, do not stop to analyze the criminal character of the man but see only the adventure and excitement. I'm convinced that such pictures do great harm to impressionable minds."

That quote came from Lawrence Tierney. Johnson wrote: "I admired his stand." Yes, Lawrence Tierney was being a very good boy. The first week of November, a new columnist joined the on-the-wagon bandwagon. Edith Gwynn, the Rambling Reporter for the *Hollywood Reporter* trade paper, jumped from seventy-five hundred potential readers to millions that very week with a new syndicated column, Edith Gwynn's Hollywood. The "oddest sight" of Gwynn's first week was at the Polo Lounge of the Beverly Hills Hotel: nightclub regular Johnny Meyer and Lawrence "Dillinger" Tierney at opposite ends of the bar. "Tierney had no drink—and Johnny had no girl."

Four days later, Hugh Dixon picked up the trail with some very good news: "RKO must be convinced that Lawrence Tierney has really reformed. The studio just picked up his option." Jimmie Fidler would smirk that RKO renewed Tierney's contract at a "reduced wage," but Tierney's weeks on the "milk wagon" appeared to have paid off. Now the studio only needed to cast him in a film.

Nothing was certain. Despite items slipped to the gossips, there was evidence that Tierney was downing something stronger than milk. There was the all-star junket in September to Panamint, California, a ghost town near Death Valley, 150 miles from Hollywood. The American Silver Corporation flew, bused, and trucked a hundred celebrities to the hellspot in order to dedicate a new silver mine, whose investors included Greta Garbo, Lana Turner, and Dore Schary. Hopper reported that during a journey under the blazing sun, comedian Ben Blue had left the truck and hiked to the mine—an incredible feat, considering that only weeks earlier Blue was reported to be dead (Ben Blue, attorney, died at Cedars of Lebanon Hospital on September 11, and a nurse mistakenly identified him as the sad-eyed comic). Tierney, Hopper wrote, remained on the truck with Jean Crain, Marilyn Maxwell, Vanessa Brown, and Sonny Tufts, but "ended up shirtless and off the wagon," and, according to another report, went off with heavy drinker Tufts, "arm in arm . . . last heard singing something sounding like 'Silver Threads Among the Gold.'"

The second, more disturbing item came to light the day after RKO announced it had picked up Tierney's option.

The scene was "a big drinking party," according to Edith Gwynn, at which Tierney had "STOPPED drinking milk!" and pressed his luck with one of America's good guys, a bona fide, if troubled, war hero. Audie Murphy, the Medal of Honor winner and most decorated American soldier of World War II, had been brought to Hollywood by James Cagney for a career as an actor. Murphy was deep in conversation with his girlfriend and future ex-wife, actress Wanda Hendrix, when Tierney interrupted and nosed in on the beauty. Murphy gave him the hint to make himself scarce. Tierney didn't get the message. Murphy, who suffered post-traumatic stress and blackout flashbacks from the war (and as a result often carried a pistol), stood, all five feet five inches of him, clenched his fists, and gave the big man a death stare. "Get out of my sight," he ordered. "If you don't get away from here, you'll be sorry."

Even in his tipsy state, Tierney could tell that the little hero meant business. He retreated.

"And stay out!"

Years later, looking back on the incident, Audie Murphy told an interviewer, "If somebody hadn't stopped me, I would very happily have killed him."

9

"Hello, sucker."

*What has happened to Lawrence Tierney's career at R.K.O.? I thought
they were going to give him another chance if he stayed on the wagon.*

SHEILAH GRAHAM, HOLLYWOOD TODAY, JANUARY 14, 1948

As 1948 rolled in, it was clear that Lawrence Tierney was no Errol Flynn. If
Tierney had any doubts, Hedda Hopper was there to remind him that Hollywood's hard-drinking, brawling, statutory-raping lothario had "settled down
to become a model family man and was given the story of Don Juan on the
screen." Tierney had served his jail sentence, "signed the pledge" of Alcoholics
Anonymous, and "made no more headlines, and now it seems he can't get a
job. He also lost his girl."

Well, it was true—sort of. Flynn wasn't simply handed *The Adventures of
Don Juan.* He'd been attached to various versions of the project since 1939, and
when he finally began shooting the swashbuckling role on the Warner Brothers
lot in October 1947, he was in shaky health with a problem ticker, bouts with
hepatitis, and periodic drinking binges that affected the production schedule.

Lawrence Tierney may have been on the outs with Vivi Stokes Taylor, and
she might be sliding around Sun Valley slopes with her new Hun, Kurt Kreuger,
but he was, officially at least, on the milk and water wagon and making the
columns with a new girlfriend. Actress Rita Johnson was thirty-four, twice
divorced, and once seen as successor to Jean Harlow. After Harlow, the original blonde bombshell, died during the filming of *Saratoga* in 1937, producers
planned for Rita to stand in for her in the scenes left to shoot. Rita had a screen
test with Clark Gable that made all the papers, but she didn't get the job. She
carried on in B-movies.

RKO had picked up Tierney's contract, after all. The only problem, and it was a big one, was that RKO wasn't using him. Tierney hadn't been on a film set since the summer of 1946 with *Born to Kill*. It was up to the gossip columnists to keep his name out there.

Harrison Carroll reported Tierney was on the town with model Barbara Bonnet. On paper, Barbara was a good match. Back in October, she'd wound up with a black eye at her boyfriend Charley Foy's supper club in Sherman Oaks. Charley's ex-wife, nightclub owner Grace Hayes, had socked her in the face. Charley said the punch stemmed from "bad blood" between him and Grace, and that everyone "should just forget it."

The night after Tierney's date with black-eyed Barbara, Louella Parsons placed him at the Mocambo with socialite and racehorse owner Liz Whitney, ex-wife of Jock Whitney of the New York Whitneys.

Tierney kept his head down in the following weeks until early on the morning of February 24. He had been sighted at a café called Barney's Beanery. When sheriff's deputies arrived, Tierney was standing. The man who had sighted him was on the floor, on his back, out cold.

Barney's Beanery wasn't one of those fancy Hollywood dress-up joints that defined the high times of the Golden Age. It was a hash house and bar that had opened in 1920 on Santa Monica Boulevard in West Hollywood, down the hill from the Sunset Strip. With license plates nailed to the walls and ceiling, hours from 5 p.m. to 5 a.m., and a menu labeled "Poison Chart," Barney's was a working man's eatery, but its hours, chili con carne, and French onion soup happened to attract a lot of Hollywood celebrities.

In the early hours of February 24, 1948, sheriff's deputies arrived at the Beanery in response to a call about two men fighting. They walked in to encounter a body on the floor and Lawrence Tierney and his brother Gerard waiting nearby. Before any preliminaries, Tierney made it clear that he hadn't been drinking. He said he'd been on the wagon since he walked out of the Drunk Farm the previous summer. Anyway, see, he and Jerry were sitting at a table over bowls of chili—Larry's accompanied of course, by a cold glass of milk—when he got up to get a pack of cigarettes. He was making his way across the restaurant when the guy who was now on the floor walked by and uttered two words. Fighting words: "*Hello, sucker.*"

The guy took a swing and hit Tierney in the left side of his face.

"I hit him back, just once," Tierney told the cops, "and down he went."

"Hello, sucker."

Did Tierney know this fellow? As a matter of fact, Tierney was acquainted with the man on the floor. He'd been part of a group of fellows that had taunted Tierney about *Dillinger* in a bar about a year earlier. One of the men tried to push Tierney's lit cigar into his eye.

When the man came to, he was identified as William Goldy, a plug-ugly tough guy in his late thirties who was a bartender at the Continental Café, farther east on Santa Monica Boulevard. That raised eyebrows on the lawmen. The Continental was a mob joint, owned by gangster Mickey Cohen. Goldy's story conflicted with Tierney's. He said he'd entered the Beanery with a waitress friend and was looking for a table when Tierney approached from out of nowhere, "hit me in the face four or five times and down I go."

The deputies determined that neither Tierney nor Goldy was drunk or disorderly, and so they prepared to leave without charging anyone. That was a welcome outcome for the actor, who was on probation. Another drunk conviction would send him back to the work farm to serve the remaining forty-two days of his sentence.

Goldy, his face bruised from Tierney's fist, wasn't satisfied. He wanted Tierney charged with assault and battery. He swore out a complaint in Beverly Hills Justice Court, and Justice of the Peace Henry H. Draeger issued a warrant for Tierney's arrest. When Tierney heard he was a wanted man, he posted $250 bail the next day. Arraignment was set for the following Tuesday, March 2, at 9:30 a.m.

"I was just sitting in the Beanery with my brother Jerry, eating something," Tierney told reporters. "I got up to get some cigarettes when this man Goldy comes at me with a crack: 'Hello, sucker!' and hits me on the left side of my face. He took a swipe at me. I hit him back, just once, and down he went. That's all I know. After that, somebody called the cops."

Goldy repeated his version, in which Tierney came up to him, "hit me in the face four or five times and down I go."

When someone asked why Tierney would attack him, Goldy removed his dark glasses and revealed a shiner. "I don't know," he said. "Unless it's on account of a year and a half ago I pushed Tierney's cigar in his face when he tangled with me in a Hollywood bar after telling me he's Dillinger."

Whatever the truth, Lawrence Tierney was back in the news for a public brawl. When he appeared in Justice Draeger's court on March 2, he pleaded innocent. The judge set the trial for May 18, and let Tierney remain free on that $250 bail.

Four days later, the situation became more complicated when Goldy sued Tierney for $100,000 in damages.

In the days between arraignment and trial, Tierney continued to be fodder for the gossip press on both coasts. Dorothy Kilgallen reported from New York that Vivi Stokes Taylor had ventured to Palm Beach—without Kurt Kreuger—and had taken up again with Jakie Webb, the wild card, problem-drinking rich kid who'd left her at the altar all those years ago. A week later, Kilgallen had Vivi with another "L.T."—Lawrence Tibbett Jr., actor son of the Tibbetts who'd hosted the VE Day party, where Tierney had met Shelley Winters.

Tierney might laugh off the planted dating items, but he was bound to have mixed feelings about other Hollywood news. Erskine Johnson reported on March 15 that Tierney's brother Gerard had signed a contract with Eagle-Lion Films. Eagle-Lion was a British company, owned by UK movie mogul J. Arthur Rank. Eagle-Lion had recently acquired the Poverty Row production company Producers Releasing Corporation, to crank out B-movies to be released along with its British imports. This time, the middle Tierney brother wasn't hiding his identity by calling himself Gerard Gilbert. He'd go by a different label, the name of a fictional boxing hero that he told *Modern Screen* his older brother found "in a novel he was reading." Now, and for the rest of his life, he'd be known as Scott Brady.

Scott Brady was signed to star in *Canon City,* a film based on a recent prison break in Colorado. While Edith Gwynn said he was a "smart feller" for not trading on his brother's name, within a week, that name was back on the board. RKO called Lawrence Tierney off the bench three days after the Academy Awards to star in not one, but two motion pictures. Production would begin in April on *Bodyguard.* In the fall, it would be *The Clay Pigeon,* a film noir about a World War II veteran accused of murder, based on a recent news story about a former GI who recognized his Japanese prison guard in Los Angeles.

The night they were handing out statuettes at the twentieth Academy Awards ceremony at the Shrine Auditorium in Los Angeles, Lawrence Tierney was in New York City, listening in with an A-list crowd at El Morocco, the glamorous nightclub with the zebra-striped banquettes on East Fifty-Fourth Street. Stars in the rooms included Jennifer Jones with David O. Selznick; Clark Gable with Dolly O'Brien Dorelis; Douglas Fairbanks Jr. and his wife, Mary Lee; Jimmy Stewart; and Adolph Menjou. Tierney's date? Vivi Stokes Taylor. When Charles Ventura, society editor of the *New York World-Telegram,* took notice, Vivi surprised him by getting up and pleading, "Please don't make a mountain out of a Morocco date with Larry Tierney, now will you?"

Tierney's time in New York City, coinciding with his return to the RKO fold, was full of contradictions. Before returning to Hollywood in April, he was seen at Billy Reed's Little Club at 70 East Fifty-Fifth Street, looking mean and scowling at customers. He showed up at the Harem Club, on Broadway and Forty-Ninth Street, where Desi Arnaz and "Latin American Bombshell" Diosa Costello were headlining and Lucille Ball was ringside, acting as unofficial hostess. "Filmdom's bad boy" sat alone in the back, "far back . . . just wanting be alone." There were reports of a fistfight at a bar on Third Avenue (Third Avenue and its bars were a location for *The Lost Weekend*), and Tierney accompanying Vivi Stokes Taylor at the Colony, the café society restaurant at Madison and East Sixty-First Street. In April, it was reported that he'd spent two weeks training at a resort in the mountains, and was working out at the New York Athletic Club, getting in shape for *Bodyguard.* Yet Earl Wilson claimed that "RKO had 3 men canvassing the 3rd Ave. bars for Lawrence Tierney, wanted back on the Coast." RKO's search party apparently found their man. Charles Ventura, the society editor who'd surprised the couple at the El Morocco, reported on April 14 that Vivi bade Tierney a "not too cheerful goodbye" at the airport, as he headed west to begin filming *Bodyguard* at the end of the month.

RKO was able to drum up anticipation for *Bodyguard* as a comeback vehicle for its two stars. Priscilla Lane, the youngest, and according to Louella Parsons, prettiest of the singing and acting Lane sisters, had starred in Alfred Hitchcock's *Saboteur* and Frank Capra's *Arsenic and Old Lace* before retreating from Hollywood to raise a son. Tierney, back in action after more than a year and a half, was potentially an even more newsworthy subject. When he returned to work on April 29, Bob Thomas reported that "Lawrence Tierney, looking nervous but determined, is working in the movies again and the eyes of Hollywood are on him."

Jimmie Fidler displayed his wit, and perhaps his cynicism, when he wrote that casting Tierney as a lieutenant of detectives was a sign that Hollywood's economy drive was under way: "With Tierney's experience of police methods to draw upon, it's obvious that for this one picture at least the studio should be able to dispense with a technical adviser."

The RKO press office, meanwhile, went into overdrive supplying columnists and editors with positive stories. When Tierney wasn't getting into fistfights in New York, he was convincing members of the New York Athletic Club to establish a gymnasium and sports center for underprivileged boys in his old neighborhood in Brooklyn. Tierney's father was supposedly searching for a location. Bob Thomas and others claimed that Tierney was taking his job very seriously, with a new attitude. If Tierney behaved, Hugh Dixon wrote, RKO would allow him to graduate to bigger-budget pictures. Sheilah Graham reported from the *Bodyguard* set that Tierney had dropped ten pounds for the role and was planning to marry his society girl, Vivi Stokes Taylor. "She is coming out here," Tierney admitted.

Yet, reality intruded. Hedda Hopper sent up the first warning flare, or took the first shot, on May 29, when she reported on how Tierney allegedly celebrated after *Bodyguard* wrapped: "He went to a restaurant and felt so good when he left that he picked a guy up off the pavement and slapped him down. The story of how he was eased out of New York after an escapade has never been printed. It's a lulu." "If Lawrence Tierney is drinking again, as reported by a columnist," Sheilah Graham shot back two days later, "the news is certainly news to his bosses at RKO. I saw Larry yesterday and he seemed perfectly sober. Why don't they leave this boy alone and give him a chance when he really is trying to overcome a craving?"

It's unlikely that the RKO executives were unaware of the gossip about Tierney's drinking. Some of the most harmful stories came directly from the *Bodyguard* set. "Larry told me that Priscilla Lane complained that he had liquor on his breath," Joyner says. "And he said never in a million years did he drink while he was making that movie. He said that really got him upset."

Earl Wilson traveled to Hollywood in early June to see for himself. He met a "reformed" Lawrence Tierney over breakfast at the Beverly Hills Hotel. "The handsome 29-year-old actor . . . who never gets in trouble in New York but who, for a time, was playing 'The Lost Weekend' all week out here in Saloon Society," stuck with coffee, and stuck by the script, claiming that he hadn't had a drink in seven months. "I decided it was a pretty good idea after that last beef I had," Tierney told the journalist. "The sore point is how they exaggerated. Now I've never been arrested for drunken driving, but a lot of people think I have and ask me about it.

"Because I play tough guy parts, it's worse for me," he complained. "People see you with a few drinks and they think they can take liberties. Some of them realize they have a nuisance value. They think if they can get you to take a pop at them they can slap a suit at you. A guy walked in a restaurant where I was about a week ago. He was a son-of-a-gun. He probably could've knocked me all over the place. He said, 'Are you as tough as you act in pictures?' I said, 'Yeah.' Well, he was taken aback, and walked away."

Wilson asked Tierney if he was planning to lead a prohibition movement in Hollywood. "Oh, hell, no," he replied. "Drinking's fine for people who can handle it. But so many people drink too much. You see people staggering on the streets out here.

"I was in a place the other night when the bartender's girl got mad at him. She was a very nice-looking girl but pretty tight. You know these ashtrays that have points on them? And these thick-bottomed bar glasses? She picked those up and started whacking him with them. Some people!" exclaimed Tierney. "Why, you never know what they're going to do when they're drinking.

"And I'm one of them. That's why I'm drinking this coffee."

William Goldy dropped his $100,000 lawsuit against Tierney on June 11, the day after Wilson's interview landed at the newsstands. Goldy offered no explanation for his change of heart, and when Tierney appeared in Beverly Hills Justice Court five days later to answer the battery charge that Goldy had filed, the accuser was nowhere to be found. Angered that Goldy had failed to appear, Judge Draeger dismissed the charge and issued a bench warrant for Goldy's arrest.

With that matter taken care of so quickly and cleanly, one would suspect that studio enforcers may have had a hand in it. In early June, RKO bosses pulled Tierney from the cast of *The Clay Pigeon*, which was scheduled to shoot in September, so he could walk immediately into the starring role in *Follow Me Quietly*, as an obsessed cop tracking a serial-killing strangler. RKO player Bill Williams would star in *Pigeon*, along with his real-life wife, Barbara Hale.

A month after production wrapped on *Bodyguard*, one last story from the set was handed to Jimmie Fidler. Tierney was performing a scene on the platform of a railway station, in which his character was smacked on the head with a blackjack and knocked out. The blackjack, of course, was a prop, down-filled and feather-light. Director Richard Fleischer called "Action." The blackjack came down, and Tierney crumpled. While falling, he struck his head on the sharp corner of a baggage truck. When he hit the platform, Tierney was out as cold as William Goldy, knocked out for real.

The item coincided with breaking news from RKO Radio Pictures. The studio had dropped Lawrence Tierney's contract. There would be no *Follow Me Quietly*. (That role would eventually go to William Lundigan.) He was again out in the cold, for real.

10

The Anti-Tierney

The first word of Lawrence Tierney's firing by RKO Radio Pictures came in a roundabout way from the East Coast on July 2, 1948. Dorothy Kilgallen reported that he had "quit RKO" and was "yearning for a Broadway play so he can get back to his Gotham gal, Vivi Stokes Taylor."

Jimmie Fidler presented a clearer, but still confusing, picture when he reported the following Tuesday that RKO had dropped Tierney's contract. His "lost weekends" had caused problems for the studio, but Fidler was "puzzled" by the timing: "Why is it that Tierney got only salary boosts when he was continually making the headlines, and now, when he is valiantly striving to keep out of scrapes, the best he can get is the boot?" After months on what seemed to be the comeback trail, Tierney may not have been surprised that RKO would not extend his contract in September. He knew he wasn't as clean as the stories had presented, and that Kilgallen's earlier item about his Third Avenue hijinks was far more accurate than the Carrie Nation imitation Tierney presented over coffee to Earl Wilson at the Beverly Hills Hotel. RKO's new production chief Sid Rogell would spell out the reasons to Hedda Hopper months later, when he professed to be as appalled as she was by rumors that RKO was planning a film about Benjamin "Bugsy" Siegel, the gangster who'd been rubbed out on June 20, 1947, in his girlfriend's home on North Linden Drive in Beverly Hills. "Anybody who makes that should be put out of the business," he said. "Why, we even threw Lawrence Tierney out after he had made a success in 'Dillinger.' We couldn't straighten him out—so we let him out."

Adding to the humiliation, and complicating matters within the Tierney clan, was another case of unfortunate timing: Lawrence Tierney's firing coincided with the release of *Canon City*, a picture based on the sensational escape of a dozen inmates from Colorado State Penitentiary on December 30, 1947—not seven months earlier. Gerard Tierney starred as the inmate who led the breakout. It was his first leading role, and his first billed as Scott Brady.

The week that Tierney was fired with a shrug, Eagle-Lion Pictures' origin story for their discovery Scott Brady was received, repeated by, and elaborated upon by columnists, broadcasters, and editors across the country:

Twenty-three years old. Six feet two inches tall. Born in Brooklyn, moved to Westchester when his father was named chief of the Aqueduct Police of New York. Attended high school in Yonkers where he was a star athlete. Served in the U. S. Navy and was light-heavyweight boxing champ at his Naval base. Attended Bliss-Hayden Dramatic School in Beverly Hills on the G. I. Bill. Thought acting was for "sissies," until older brother Lawrence took it up and he saw it as an easy way to make a living. Unmarried. Two more films in the can. Plays a boxer in *In This Corner;* a private eye in *29 Clues.*

Scott Brady was being pitched by Eagle-Lion as Lawrence Tierney–plus, or more to the point, the anti-Tierney. "I predict that, after *Canon City,* Scott will be as big a star as Larry," Sheilah Graham blurbed. "Scott looks quite different from his more famous brother—and he is quite different."

Gerard "Scott Brady" Tierney was sent to the East Coast on his first publicity tour, to make stage appearances along with the film, meet the press, glad-hand columnists, and sign autographs for fans. The studio also laid down the law: Scott Brady was banned from all bars, pubs, speakeasies, and bistros. He was to display model behavior—or, as Dorothy Manners put it, "super-model behavior."

Being a "good boy" was not a problem for the former Gerard "Roddy" Tierney. When he arrived in Boston, a profile in the *Globe* announced that Scott Brady was "a lot less tough to handle than his brother Lawrence. . . . The 23-year-old youngster is as nice a young man as you could hope to meet in a month of Sundays."

"Staunch Catholic" Brady told the paper he believed he got the role as real-life cop killer Jerry Sherbondy in *Canon City* "because of a prayer to St. Jude, the patron saint of lost causes." His grandmother, Maggie Crowley, gave him the prayer, he said, and he in turn passed it on to Sherbondy. "If St. Jude can get me into pictures," Brady told the lifer nicknamed Mad Dog, "maybe he can get you out of prison."

If that wasn't enough of a contrast with his older brother, Brady said he wasn't interested in the beautiful young women Hollywood had to offer.

"I want a girl I'll stay married to for ninety years," he said. "And I'd like her to be Irish, Catholic and very much the sort of girl my grandmother Maggie Crowley was like in her youth. She's still the kind of woman I admire most. She has fifteen grandchildren and five great-grandchildren and wears a hat that must be fifteen years old. But she's more of a woman than a lot of the stars you see in the studios. Give me a gal like Grandma was."

Quotes like that might be enough to drive a man to drink—and perhaps they did. Back in Los Angeles, Lawrence Tierney had supposedly taken Burton Rascoe's advice and hired a personal bodyguard to keep him out of trouble. That didn't work out so well, Jimmie Fidler reported. "We hear that he and the bodyguard had such a run-in the other night, in Tierney's apartment, that he's now in the bad graces of his landlord."

Fidler's gossip item ran on Thursday, July 29. By the weekend, Lawrence Tierney was back in jail.

This time it wasn't in Hollywood, but ninety miles up the coast, in Santa Barbara. According to the manager of a resort hotel there, Tierney had been "acting tough" and causing a disturbance in front of some of the other guests. The manager called police, who determined that Tierney was not only acting tough, but acting drunk. They arrested him and dropped him in the Santa Barbara jail.

A judge set bail at ten dollars. Tierney paid it on the spot. He threw in another ten dollars to pay the bail of his seventy-year-old cellmate, who was also in the tank, sleeping off a drunk arrest.

Tierney was told to appear in Santa Barbara Police Court on Monday, August 2. When he didn't show that afternoon, his ten-dollar bail was forfeited.

This arrest didn't make the front page, but even buried on page twenty-six of the *Los Angeles Times,* the latest bust had gossips and columnists alike writing the obituary for Tierney's career.

In far-off Miami, Florida, the pulp men's magazine writer Jack Kofoed declared in his *Miami Herald* column that Tierney had joined a line of great show business tragedies that included "fine performers (who) found an appetite for alcohol or dope was more than they could handle."

"Tierney might have gone places in the films, but old King Bourbon had him beaten from the start," Kofoed eulogized. Like hundreds of ordinary folk in the Miami community, he wrote, Tierney was a "weakling." "When will people learn that moderation is the only answer to health and happiness?"

The Anti-Tierney

Jimmie Fidler was sitting in the café on the RKO studio lot, notebook out, working up a column, when he caught wind of a conversation between two set workers at a nearby table. They were talking about recently banished RKO star Lawrence Tierney. One of them spoke in Tierney's defense. He said that because of all the publicity surrounding his fights, the actor had become a target. Tierney, he argued, was very much in the same position as a gunman back in pioneer days. Anyone who wanted to make a name for himself would take a shot at him.

"With his reputation," the man said, "Tierney should have his hands full any time he steps into a public place."

"Maybe," his colleague replied. "But a man who has his hands full doesn't help matters by keeping his fists clenched!"

Jimmie Fidler's recounting of that episode may have read as if he was at the table next to Confucius, but when it came to Lawrence Tierney, what could he say that he hadn't said before, and more than once? So he said it again, in many of the same words he'd used in May 1947, and repeated the following July. Tierney was "incorrigible," and "time after time he's landed in limbo, shed crocodile tears of repentance, promised to be good and then got out, forthwith, to get in another jam." Fidler pointed out that the Santa Barbara arrest story was running at the same time the trades were hinting that Tierney was being considered for a starring role in an independent feature. "The two stories make poor teammates," Fidler wrote with an almost audible sigh. "Producers, by continuing to forgive him and give him work, are obviously doing him no kindness, and certainly they're doing the movie industry no favors when they support and abet a man of Tierney's character."

As the final days of August, his RKO contract, and his $750 weekly salary ticked away, Lawrence Tierney was in the same spot he'd been in a year earlier. Sheilah Graham wondered, on a practical note, what he'd do next, whether he'd try to sign with some other studio "or save a lot of time by making an all-out effort to rehabilitate himself." She expressed sympathy for Tierney's parents, who had moved to Los Angeles "to live with him in the belief they could help him.

"Tierney is the only one who can do that."

And then, two events shook Hollywood with such force that everyone forgot about Lawrence Tierney's predicament until the next time he found a way to lurch into the headlines.

The arrest was front-page news across the country: "FILM STAR NABBED IN DRUG RAID." In this case, the RKO movie star known for his film noir and Western roles wasn't Lawrence Tierney but Robert Mitchum. Early on the first day of September 1948, the thirty-one-year-old, Oscar-nominated, $3,000-a-week box office favorite was arrested along with three blondes (one male, two female) in a raid on a secluded bungalow in Laurel Canyon.

The police bust netted nineteen marijuana cigarettes, valued at one dollar each, and six "roaches," which according to the *Los Angeles Times* was "underworld parlance for partly smoked marijuana cigarettes."

When he was arrested, Mitchum muttered, "I'm all washed up. This is the bitter end of everything."

Before high-profile attorney Jerry Giesler showed up to muzzle his talkative new client, Mitchum admitted to police and reporters during his fingerprinting at the central jail that he'd been a regular marijuana user for the past two years. One of the cops interrupted to ask, "Who's gonna bail you out, Bob? It's only a thousand dollars."

"Who knows?" Mitchum replied. "I've got two bosses, David O. Selznick and RKO studios. Have you ever listened to Selznick or RKO studios when they're peeved? I think I'd just as soon stay in jail. Anyway, if Selznick calls up, I'll hang up on him. The man can't do a thing. My career is washed up for good."

The cop asked Mitchum what he wanted to list as his occupation.

"Former actor."

"Don't worry," one cop supposedly said. "*We're keeping Lawrence Tierney's cell warm for you.*"

Mitchum and the others were charged with conspiracy to violate state and federal narcotics laws, jailed, and later released on $1,000 bail each. The arrest of their star led to a change in plans at RKO Pictures, but not in a way that Mitchum and others expected. The studio had been taken over that year by business tycoon, aviator, and eccentric Howard Hughes. Hughes had been producing, and occasionally directing, movies since 1926, and equated controversy with box office. As producer, he defied Will Hays's censorship of *Scarface*, Howard Hawks's 1932 gangster picture inspired by the crimes of Al Capone. As director and producer of *The Outlaw*, he generated much ink from his battle with the Motion Picture Association over "countless shots" of star Jane Russell, "in which her breasts" were not "fully covered." Hughes ordered that Mitchum's latest film, *Rachel and the Stranger*, be rush-released to cash in on the heavily publicized arrest. *Variety* reported later that month that the low-budget Western was No. 1 at the box office.

Mitchum's marijuana habit made Lawrence Tierney's alcoholic exploits seem almost quaint in comparison, but the events that unfolded the following Monday, September 6, at the Chateau Marmont Hotel on Sunset Boulevard were uncomfortably, and dangerously, sensational.

Tierney's occasional date and sometime girlfriend, Rita Johnson, the woman whose name in the papers always seemed to be followed by a comma and the phrase "once considered as a successor to the late Jean Harlow," received serious, and mysterious, head injuries in her apartment that afternoon. She was treated there by her personal physician for three days before she was accepted as a patient at St. Vincent's Hospital and underwent brain surgery. With Rita listed in very critical condition, the only clue to what happened was her incoherent mumbling that "the hairdryer fell on me." Police detectives from the division involved in the Mitchum case investigated. A maid showed them the bulky hairdryer in Rita's apartment. She said it had slipped in the past and might have slipped again while Rita was under it drying her hair, causing the forty-pound metal hood to smack the top of her head. The detectives didn't buy the theory. They suspected that Rita may have been the victim of a beating. Her current boyfriend, a writer named Mike McCausland, had an alibi that checked out, but Rita had two ex-husbands and more than a few old tough-guy boyfriends.

Walter Winchell seconded the suspicion about a week later, reporting the rumor that Rita's concussion was caused "by a former flame (screen actor-tough guy; not a writer), famed for knocking his darlings cold." Most insiders assumed Winchell was pointing to Rita's former fiancé, Broderick Crawford. It wasn't until the end of October that Edith Gwynn passed along the "local scuttle-butt" that "Rita Johnson and Lawrence Tierney were seeing a lot of each other before her accident." No one else made the Tierney connection.

The detectives kept digging. They couldn't interrogate the hairdryer, and they couldn't talk to Rita. She remained in a coma.

With September marking the end of Lawrence Tierney's time at RKO, it wasn't fun anymore for Harrison Carroll. "Tierney's case is one of the saddest on Hollywood record," he lamented on September 9. "Real talent being wasted there." Carroll offered no solution, but in Hollywood, there will always be someone looking to swoop in, and cash in, when the opportunity presents itself.

John Shelton, an actor who'd most recently been featured in *Joe Palooka in Winner Take All* (Joe Kirkwood Jr. played Joe Palooka), had secured the rights to *The Floyds of Oklahoma,* a book about brothers Charles and E. W. Floyd. Charles, aka "Pretty Boy Floyd," was the bank robber whom the FBI named "Public Enemy No. 1" the day after John Dillinger was shot dead. Charles was gunned down by police and FBI agents exactly three months later. E. W. Floyd was Charles's younger brother, a grocery clerk who was about to be elected sheriff of Sequoyah County, Oklahoma (he'd hold the job for twenty-one years).

Shelton and producer Leo Popkin hoped to turn the book into a movie that would show how Charles's death led E. W. to the right side of the law. Shelton said he wanted Scott Brady to star as E. W. Floyd, and as his older brother, in his second role as a Public Enemy No. 1, Hollywood's Public Enemy No. 1, Lawrence Tierney.

A few days later, Brady said there were no plans for him and his brother to costar in any film. "I'd like it very much," he told a reporter for Hearst's International News Service. "But Larry has other commitments."

The reporter added a helpful tagline to the story: "Incidentally, Scott doesn't drink."

Rita Johnson emerged from a coma on September 22. Five days later, her mother said that Rita spoke a few words. Nothing was said, or asked, about the incident that put her there.

Robert Mitchum and two of his codefendants pleaded innocent to charges of marijuana possession on September 29. Vickie Evans, the dancer who'd opened the door to the cops—and the only one not caught holding a reefer during the raid—didn't enter a plea. Her lawyer wanted time to have her case dismissed because of insufficient evidence.

Lawrence Tierney returned to the spotlight on October 7 at a party celebrating the opening of popular florist Jack Hirsch's new shop in Bel Air. Tierney's date was actress Shelley Winters—a surprise to many, considering that Winters's star was on the rise, thanks to her performance in George Cukor's *A Double Life,* which opened on Christmas Day 1947. Most guests were unaware of her assignation with Tierney on VE Day.

Louella Parsons reported that Tierney stuck to water. Hedda Hopper said his drink of choice was ginger ale.

On October 11, Lawrence Tierney attended a party on a boat, and sailed back into the headlines with an arrest so bizarre that it almost pushed Robert Mitchum and poor Rita Johnson off the front page.

11

In Like Dillinger

After pulling off a string of bank robberies, jailbreaks, and murders, John Dillinger and three members of his gang hightailed it to Tucson, Arizona, in January 1934. The criminals rented a house on Second Avenue to hole up in, but because the floors had just been waxed, spent a night downtown, at the Hotel Congress. When a fire at the hotel forced an evacuation on January 23, a fireman moving guests' luggage onto the street recognized two of the gangsters from photos in a detective magazine.

Two days later, police were waiting outside and inside the house on Second Avenue. Dillinger walked in, and when he encountered unexpected company, reached for the gun in his shoulder holster. He lowered his hand carefully and slowly when the muzzle of a submachine gun was pressed into his back.

"Well, I guess you win," said Public Enemy No. 1.

Dillinger, his men, and three women who accompanied them were arraigned and moved to the Pima County Jail. Well aware that Dillinger had previously broken out of jail in Lima, Ohio, and engineered the escape of his accomplices from the prison in Michigan City, Indiana, Pima County jailer Andy Dobek took extra precautions to make his jailhouse escape-proof. The building was turned into a fortress, surrounded by a cordon of armed officers. Machine gun barrels poked out of every window. The prisoners were placed in separate cells, each guarded with machine guns seized in the raid. All jail personnel were ordered to wear sidearms. Dobek knew he would most likely never guard someone so famous ever again. There was no way he would allow John Dillinger to escape under his watch.

Dillinger was ultimately extradited from Pima County back to Indiana, where he was held at the "escape proof" county jail in Crown Point, facing robbery and murder charges. On March 3, 1934, he escaped.

Dillinger's life and the events leading to his final appearance outside the Biograph Theater in Chicago that July have been well documented. But what

83

of Andy Dobek, the jailer who held America's most wanted criminal and his gang in his humble jail at the height of Dillinger's crime wave? Dobek lived with his wife, Theresa, and two children at 5456 Lazy Heart Street in Tucson. He continued his work as jailer and deputy sheriff, and in 1935 was elected Pima County constable. He served in that position until 1940, when he ran for sheriff, unsuccessfully, against incumbent Ed Echols. A veteran of World War I, Dobek joined the US Merchant Marine in 1942 and saw action in the Second World War. He returned home, and in 1944, again attempted to unseat Sheriff Echols. He ran "as the first veteran of this war to request employment as your sheriff." Echols won a fifth term.

The Dobeks' son became a chief master sergeant in the US Air Force. Their daughter married and moved to Santa Catalina Island, a twenty-two-mile-long, eight-mile-wide, largely uninhabited strip off the coast of Long Beach, California.

The island was known as the spring training site for the Chicago Cubs baseball team, whose owner, chewing gum mogul William Wrigley Jr., owned much of the land. Most of its population lived in the resort town of Avalon on the southeast end of the island. Avalon's harbor was where most visitors to the island docked their boats. The town's most prominent landmark was the Catalina Casino. Twelve stories tall, the building was never used for gambling, but contained a ballroom, art gallery, and state-of-the-art movie theater. Popular big bands and singers played the ballroom; studio bosses and producers often arrived on yachts to preview their latest features in the theater.

Andy and Theresa Dobek joined their daughter in Avalon on Santa Catalina Island, and in 1948, Andy took a job as a police officer in the town. It was a peaceful, quiet occupation for a semiretired lawman. There was no chance of a John Dillinger causing trouble here.

Not until October 10, when a yacht sailed into Avalon harbor. The boat carried a group of Hollywood types who partied on into the early hours of October 11. Around 2 a.m., the partiers disembarked, not to sleep the rest of the night in a local hotel, but to continue the party onshore. The group made its way, noisily, off the boat and onto Crescent Avenue, the strip of restaurants and shops facing the harbor. They found an all-night café at 106 Catalina Avenue and carried on where they'd left off on the yacht. Soon, one member of the party became unruly. Dottie Harns, the café manager, warned him to settle down. He didn't. He caused more trouble. He threw a raw onion across the room. Dottie Harns called the police.

When Officer Kern McDavid arrived, he was confronted with a big man, "drunk and throwing things." The officer managed to cuff the visitor and walked him to police headquarters a couple of blocks away. McDavid signed a complaint charging Lawrence Tierney with intoxication. Dottie Harns signed another complaint, accusing the actor of disturbing the peace.

It was in the Avalon lockup, with Tierney's eleventh arrest since his first starring role, that his art and life collided, and where the history of Hollywood and annals of American crime collided at an unlikely intersection. As Lawrence Tierney was led through the Avalon jail, the deputy who booked him in and turned the key that locked the screen's John Dillinger in a cell for the night was none other than Andrew "Andy" Dobek, the deputy and jailer who did the same for the real John Dillinger in Tucson in 1934.

Lawrence Tierney paid $200 to be freed. He forfeited the bail when he escaped from the island, skipping a 2 p.m. hearing before Justice Ernest Windle.

The press got wind of the coincidence the following day. When they tracked down Andy Dobek and asked him to compare "the reel and real Dillingers," he responded with a grunt, and refused to play along.

When was enough too much? Tierney's Catalina hijinks were not as serious as the trouble his hero Errol Flynn sailed into in 1941, when he took friends on a weekend yacht cruise to the island and allegedly raped teenage Peggy LaRue Satterlee on the return trip. The ensuing publicity was enough, however, to lead RKO to issue an official reminder that Lawrence Tierney had been stricken from its roster. "That doesn't surprise Hollywood too much," Louella Parsons commented.

The news led Jimmie Fidler to remark that for the first time, after nine arrests in the past two years, Tierney's "previously vociferous cheering section" was quiet.

"It's amazing how greatly Filmville's sympathies in such cases are swayed by financial considerations," Fidler wrote. "And even more amazing that the studio gentry haven't discovered that the best time to lop off a 'bad boy' is when he first proves himself incorrigibly bad."

Edith Gwynn's October 28 column exclusive linking Lawrence Tierney to Rita Johnson at the time of her injury did not lead to investigation (Rita never did recall what smashed her head), and there were signs that despite the latest arrest, Tierney might manage a comeback, despite RKO.

Hedda Hopper reported on October 30 that producer "Seymour Nebenzal wants to remake 'M,' the picture in which Peter Lorre made his American debut, with—you won't believe this—Lawrence Tierney." Harrison Carroll had more solid news ten days later: Tierney was signed to star in the independent feature, *I Shot Jesse James,* portraying Robert Ford, the "dirty little coward" who killed the outlaw leader of the James–Younger Gang in 1882. The eight-day shoot at Republic Pictures would pay Tierney $25,000. When producer Robert Lippert expressed doubts about hiring him, Tierney offered to post a $5,000 bond—and defer his salary—to prove he could be depended upon to get through filming without any lost weekends or one-punchers.

Most other Tierney-related gossip items were along the lines of Gwynn's gag: "Extra, extra! Lawrence Tierney hasn't had a drink for twenty minutes!" By December, even Jimmie Fidler was using him as a punch line. He wrote of two young women whose house on a hillside above Hollywood Boulevard was often damaged by runaway cars owned by people living higher on the hill. When new tenants had moved into the house directly above theirs, they hoped it would be an elderly couple who'd drive with care. "Then they learned the identity of the new neighbor. His name? Lawrence Tierney!"

In truth, Tierney's parents had moved back East and he was living in a hotel.

Cast adrift, Lawrence Tierney was at least reunited with his fellow Hollywood stars in print as 1948 came to an end. Bob Thomas looked back on "the year that has been (Hollywood's) worst in public relations: . . . Robert Mitchum was pinched with three others at an alleged marijuana party. . . . British actor Rex Harrison discovered the body of Carole Landis, apparently a suicide. . . . Robert Walker, boyish ex-husband of Jennifer Jones, has several scrapes with the law on drunk charges. . . . Errol Flynn got his usual share of newspaper space, this year by kicking a New York cop in the shins," and "Lawrence Tierney was involved in yet another café brawl."

Jimmie Fidler had the final word on the year. "Every once in a while," he wrote on December 28, "a real-life situation develops in Hollywood to support the old-fashioned theory that virtue pays." In this case, it was a tale of two brothers on the Republic Pictures studio lot. One was Scott Brady, a newcomer who "tended to his knitting, studied his profession and kept out of jams," and was costarring in one of the studio's most ambitious Class "A" offerings, *Montana Belle.*

The other was Hollywood veteran Lawrence Tierney. "He's had chances such as few actors ever get and anyone who reads the newspapers knows what he's done with them. He's working on an eight-day quickie."

Fidler's parable was only partially correct. Samuel Fuller, a writer taking on his first directing assignment on *I Shot Jesse James,* had no problem taking a chance on Lawrence Tierney, but despite Tierney's promises and offer to post a $5,000 bond, producer Lippert refused to bet on the bad man. Tierney lost the role to John Ireland.

12

Taxicab Confessions

New Year's Day 1949 fell on a Saturday, and for many in Hollywood, New Year's Eve festivities that began on Friday continued through the weekend, before everyone got back to business and focused on the latest developments in the saga of its most scandalized actor.

Robert Mitchum, Lawrence Tierney's former RKO stablemate, continued to dominate the Hollywood headlines. Mitchum's latest picture, *Blood on the Moon,* had opened in five theaters in Los Angeles on New Year's Eve, the second of his movies whose release had been hastened to take advantage of the publicity surrounding his marijuana arrest. With Mitchum and his codefendants scheduled to stand trial on January 10, Lawrence Tierney could take advantage of the cover and keep a low profile. Perhaps his most recent arrest would be forgotten—and it might have been, if only he hadn't hailed a taxi.

Cabbie William F. Crankshaw was enjoying a comparatively quiet shift on Monday evening, January 3, when a figure flagged him down. Crankshaw slowed to a stop, and a well-dressed man slid into the backseat and slurred an address in West Hollywood. A glance in the rearview mirror confirmed to Crankshaw that the fare had apparently not finished celebrating the dawn of 1949. It wasn't so unusual. What was very unexpected occurred once the twenty-five-year-old hack was racing toward his destination. Suddenly, without warning, the customer began climbing over the front seat. The car swerved as the man pulled his husky six-foot frame over the top and tumbled into the dashboard.

"Gimme the wheel!" he ordered, scrambling up and grabbing for the steering wheel.

"*What the*—?!" Crankshaw hardly had time to react when the stranger began pushing him aside. Drunk, out of control, and shouting all kinds of threats, the man was reaching past him to grab the handle on the driver's side door. He was attempting to open the door and shove the taxi driver into the street!

When the taxi ride ended, William Crankshaw was still behind the wheel, but the address of the stop was not the original destination. It was the L.A. County Sheriff's substation in Hollywood. The passenger was slumped in the front seat, out cold.

Crankshaw explained to the officers on duty that the unconscious man in the front seat had "threatened me and pushed me around," and had tried to commandeer his taxi and perhaps kill him by throwing him out of the moving vehicle. The cops looked into the cab. One nudged the other. They recognized the guy right away. They yanked his body out the passenger door, got him on his feet, slapped him around a bit until he came to, and as soon as the man was able to stagger, led him off to the drunk tank. They did not ask William H. Crankshaw how the man came to be knocked out.

By the following morning, the press had been alerted to Lawrence Tierney's latest arrest for drunkenness, and reporters and photographers were gathered at the sheriff's Hollywood substation to view the transfer of Tierney and other drunks and criminals to the sheriff's office for booking. Flashbulbs popped. The hungover gent seated next to Tierney in the back of the police wagon covered his face with his left hand, in shame. Tierney, slumped by the window on the passenger side, wore the sport coat and bleary expression from the night before. He looked to the photographers, raised his right hand, which was manacled at the wrist to his left, and gave them the "OK" sign. The photo was transmitted to newspapers across the country.

After his arrival at the sheriff's office, Tierney was released on fifty dollars bond, pending a court appearance on Wednesday. By then, he'd already made headlines:

LAWRENCE TIERNEY ARRESTED AGAIN

FILM DILLINGER PINCHED AGAIN

TIERNEY AGAIN, SAME OLD THING

JOHN BARLEYCORN HANGS UMPTEENTH KO ON TIERNEY

They were, of course, the worst headlines Tierney could face at the worst time. Four of his films—*Bodyguard, Dillinger, The Devil Thumbs a Ride,* and *San Quentin*—were in theaters, and the typical movie fan might assume that Tierney was working on his next picture. Worse yet, another picture had been shaping into a possibility. After weeks of embarrassing rejection, Tierney had finally roped in a producer willing to hire him. Harry Popkin, whose brother Leo had sought to team Tierney and Scott Brady as the Floyd brothers of Oklahoma, had met with Tierney that Monday, hours before the taxicab incident, and offered to cast him as the star of *Inside Alcatraz*, a movie set in the infamous island penitentiary. Tierney was so desperate to work that he again offered to put up a $5,000 bond to ensure he'd make it through production. No need, said Popkin, we know you can do it.

Barely sobered up, Tierney was back in Beverly Hills Justice Court on Wednesday, once again standing before Justice of the Peace Henry H. Draeger. He'd faced Draeger the previous February after knocking out William Goldy. That case had been dismissed. On this day, most everyone expected the jurist would throw the book at "Hollywood's gift to the barroom." All in the courtroom hung on Draeger's words as he began to speak.

"You've come a long way in motion pictures," the justice told Tierney. "The public still maintains faith in you because of your portrayals in pictures."

That faith obviously abused, Tierney awaited his punishment.

"I am going to give you," Draeger declaimed, "one more chance to demonstrate the faith of the public in you is not misplaced."

One more chance. Draeger sentenced Tierney to ninety days in jail for drunkenness, but suspended the sentence for a year, on the condition that Tierney stay away from old Mr. Barleycorn. Tierney was also fined $150 and, bringing to a close what reporters tabulated as his ninth arrest for drunkenness in three years, walked out of the courthouse, a free man.

Well, not quite free. The fallout was immediate. Louella Parsons reported that the Harry Popkin deal was off. With one evening at a local saloon and an unfortunate taxi ride, Tierney had managed to snatch defeat from the jaws of a comeback. Once again, he was an outcast in Hollywood. There was no one willing to take up his offer of a $5,000 surety bond. Yet, no matter the disgraces that Lawrence Tierney brought upon himself, his family, and his industry, there would always be someone willing to take advantage of his talents when he was at his lowest point.

In this case, it would not only mean leaving Hollywood. It would mean leaving the country.

Five days after Tierney's appearance in Beverly Hills Justice Court, Robert Mitchum and his reefer gang went on trial in downtown Los Angeles, on charges of possessing and conspiring to possess marijuana, which the

Associated Press explained was "a drug weed usually sold in the form of cigarettes."

The stage was set for a circus of a trial, and a long-running circus at that. Mitchum's attorney Jerry Giesler was the Johnny Cochran of his day, a celebrity himself, who'd managed a "not guilty" verdict in Errol Flynn's statutory rape trial, and in 1944 won an acquittal for Charlie Chaplin on Mann Act charges. Jury selection in the latest trial was expected to take up much of the first week, and after that, Giesler was bound to pull out the heavy artillery on behalf of his client. He even had Mitchum's mother on standby, ready to testify about her son's difficult life before Hollywood, including a stretch on a Georgia chain gang for a crime he swore he didn't commit.

Judge Clement D. Nye's courtroom was packed, with hundreds more gawkers in the hallways and clustered outside the courthouse, when he banged the gavel on Monday morning. After a series of legal maneuvers by the defense, it was agreed that Judge Nye alone could decide the conspiracy count, based on a reading of the thirty-two-page grand jury transcripts. The reading of the grand jury testimony, and the trial, took mere hours. The judge then found Mitchum, Lila Leeds, and realtor Robin Ford guilty of criminal conspiracy to violate state health laws by possessing marijuana. Vickie Evans was a no-show. Judge Nye issued a bench warrant for her arrest and set bail at $2,500. (Evans would be acquitted in March.)

Mitchum and his pals were to be sentenced on February 9. They faced from ninety days in county jail to six years in state prison. Once again, they were freed on $1,000 bail each. When he left the courtroom, the actor was mobbed by the fans in the hallway.

Erskine Johnson's column that day focused on New Year's resolutions that Hollywood stars "should have made." Robert Mitchum and Lawrence Tierney shared a single resolution: "To stay on the beam." The expression was generally accepted to mean to stay on the right path, the straight and narrow, not the modern, slang usage of "on the beam," which is to be high on marijuana.

In his columns that week, Jimmie Fidler directed his moral judgment at his favorite bad man. Ever more frustrated that no one in power in Hollywood was dealing with the threat posed by Tierney, Fidler made a suggestion that could have been contributed by a gag writer, but made some sense: "Wouldn't it be practical for the L. A. Police to assign a special cell to Lawrence Tierney?" (According to a cop at the time of Mitchum's arrest, that cell had already been reserved.)

Fidler also broke the news of Tierney's backup plan: to leave Hollywood to star in a picture being filmed in Italy: "If that's true, may heaven help the Italians. They may still refuse to release United States coin, but after that picture is finished, I'll predict that they'll be mighty anxious to release Lawrence Tierney." As is the case with so many movie projects, Tierney's Italian shoot was canceled before he could board a plane to Rome. That news may have pleased Jimmie Fidler, but the item he was fed a week later definitely did not. Harry Popkin, inspired by the wisdom of Judge Draeger, was considering giving Lawrence Tierney "another chance" by casting him in the Alcatraz picture, after all.

Fidler may have preferred that Tierney spend time in the actual prison in San Francisco Bay. The columnist restated his lack of sympathy for the actor on January 18, 1949, decreeing that anyone, be it Harry Popkin or Judge Draeger, who'd give Lawrence Tierney more "chances" was creating "a public menace.

"Seemingly, he can't get crocked without also getting belligerent, smashing things, insulting people and wanting to fight. If he's given enough chances," Fidler warned, "it will probably be some innocent bystander who will suffer."

But who was listening?

Robert Mitchum and Lila Leeds were sentenced on February 9 to sixty days in Los Angeles County Jail. (Robin Ford got a continuance because he'd since been arrested on another narcotics charge.) Mitchum's movie career appeared to have immunity. RKO Studios announced that it would not abandon plans to complete the film noir, *The Big Steal,* which Mitchum had already begun filming. Just as he'd rush-released *Rachel and the Stranger* and *Blood on the Moon* to make hay out of the Mitchum headlines, RKO's new boss Howard Hughes was certain the publicity would sell tickets. Producer Selznick, who along with RKO had Mitchum under contract, predicted that the jail term would make the actor a better man and even bigger star. Selznick hailed Mitchum as a "superb artist and an intelligent man who can be counted on to do his best from this point on for his wife, his children, for himself, for his employers, and the entertainment of those millions of fans who have demonstrated their eagerness that he should have a second chance."

Nobody was talking about Lawrence Tierney in those terms.

Broadway columnist Dorothy Kilgallen pretended she'd found the source of Tierney's latest crash. It was, she wrote, socialite Vivi Stokes Taylor. According to Kilgallen, Tierney never got over the loss of his socialite sweetheart, and now Vivi was returning to Hollywood in February "just to straighten him out." That was not quite Vivi's intention. When she met with Tierney, it was to tell him that she planned to marry a wealthy Brazilian. Count Marco Fabio Crespi was the brother of Count Rudi Crespi, who in January 1948 had married Consuelo O'Connor, the influential high-fashion model who, with her sister Gloria, composed high society's glamorous "O'Connor Twins."

After Vivi returned east, Tierney left the country after all, destination Lisbon, Portugal, where he was getting "another chance" from Juno Productions. *Dillinger* director Max Nosseck had cowritten a film about a man wrongly accused of murder, hiding out in the South American jungle. Tentative title: *Jungle Storm.* The cast included British actor George Coulouris, who'd appeared in *Citizen Kane* and *Joan of Arc,* and Marissa Flores, aunt of child star Margaret O'Brien. Flores, once the lead flamenco dancer for Xavier Cugat's orchestra, would be billed as Marissa O'Brien.

Hedda Hopper commented that Tierney had no choice but to seek work abroad, because he "wore out his welcome" in Hollywood. "After this is finished, Tierney is wanted for pictures in Paris and Italy. I guess if we don't want him, they do." Louella Parsons agreed that Tierney "couldn't beg or borrow another chance in Hollywood." The Portugal shoot would be a test of whether he could prove "he can be a good boy . . . behave," and get "another chance." Sheilah Graham confirmed that Tierney hoped to convince Hollywood it was safe to "take another picture chance on him.

"I hope it works," she wrote. "By the way, did you know Larry had never touched a drop in his life—until he came to Hollywood at the age of 24?"

Another chance? Wheels were barely up on Tierney's flight to Lisbon when Jimmie Fidler claimed he'd made good on his warning that Tierney would wind up hurting someone. "Lawrence Tierney's latest drunken brawl could've ended in tragedy had it not been for the interference of bystanders," he reported on February 27. "Tierney had his opponent down and was choking him when they were separated."

Two days later, Fidler tripled down on his attack while his target was too far away to give him a slap at the Mocambo. "During the month which preceded his departure for Portugal, he was involved in three brawls, one of which might have ended in serious injury for his opponent if bystanders hadn't interfered." Tierney was, he wrote, "a public menace" and the public needed to be protected from his "berserk, alcoholic rages.

"Tierney, with one drink under his belt, immediately becomes incorrigible. With two drinks down the hatches, he wants to fight." Arrest, fines, even jail terms had failed to stop his drinking. "He's virtually lost his chance for screen success," Fidler wrote. "And still he drinks."

Despite the harsh critique, Fidler remained one of the few in the industry who wanted to help. He acknowledged that Tierney was "remarkably likeable" when sober, and a better than average actor who could have been a star and a useful citizen, if not for his "chronic alcoholism": "To my way of thinking, Tierney is, and should be treated as a sick man. I think we should have laws which would recognize and intelligently try to cure this kind of sickness. It should be possible for a judge to sentence Lawrence Tierney to a stay of indeterminate length in a sanitorium and to scientific treatment designed to rehabilitate him as a useful member of society."

Made sense.

Scott Brady was taking in $1,000 a week in March 1949, shooting *The Western Story* (also known as *The Gal Who Took the West*) opposite Yvonne De Carlo, at Universal-International. U-I boss William Goetz was so pleased with Brady's work on the picture that he signed him to a seven-year contract (in addition to the deal Brady already had with Eagle-Lion). Younger brother Edward Tierney was working as Brady's stand-in—though, Brady noted, Eddie aspired to be a writer. "He hates actors."

Trumpeting the scoop that Brady, at six feet, two and half inches tall, had to wear lifts in his boots because John Russell, who played his brother, was six-foot-four, Sheilah Graham added that he was "a heck of a swell person." She noted that Brady's studio biography mentioned that he owed a lot to his older brother, Lawrence Tierney. In the wake of Tierney's latest scrape, the studio had given Brady the option of removing that paragraph.

"His answer was 'No.'"

Sporting a pinstriped suit instead of the denim he'd been wearing the past fifty days, Robert Mitchum walked out of the county honor farm with ten days sheared from his sixty-day sentence for good behavior. Mitchum had been transferred from the county jail on February 16, and had been a model prisoner the entire time. "I'll go back to making pictures Monday after a few days at home with my wife and two children," he told reporters before stepping into a taxi. "This has been a milestone in my life—a real experience."

All was quiet on the Tierney front in the weeks to follow. Jimmie Fidler decreed that no matter Lawrence's fate, the family name would carry on in Hollywood.

Along with Scott Brady's rise to stardom and Edward's writing ambitions, the patriarch, former police chief Lawrence H. Tierney, had also gotten into the act, having rubbed on the greasepaint for a role in *Montana Belle,* alongside son Scott Brady, George Brent, Forrest Tucker, Andy Devine, and as Belle Starr, Jane Russell.

Scott Brady was "having a kind of career that brother Lawrence did his best to throw down the drain," Sheilah Graham remarked when she announced he was about to sign for his biggest role yet, opposite Ginger Rogers in the crime and prison drama, *The Story of Molly X.* (When cameras rolled on *Molly X,* June Havoc and John Russell were the leads.)

In Lisbon, Portugal, and environs, Lawrence Tierney was far enough from gossips and tipsters to stay out of the headlines, if not trouble. If he was drinking, fighting, or in jail, he wasn't slowing production. Max Nosseck's movie, now titled *Kill or Be Killed,* wrapped on schedule. Scott Brady spread word of his brother's success, telling people that Lawrence had indeed been offered films in England, France, and Italy.

In May, a vacationing Hedda Hopper reached colleague Dorothy Manners over "transAtlantic telephone" from Paris. "Got a story for you," she said. "Errol Flynn is all over Paris with the beautiful Romanian Princess Irene Ghica." Hopper's confirmation that Flynn turned up in France while Tierney was in Europe provides a time frame to a story that Tierney told his friend Derek Bell many years later. "He said that he was in France with Errol Flynn," Bell says. "They were drinking at a sidewalk café. Larry said they'd been drinking for three days straight. And all of a sudden, Flynn jumped up and started running. Larry didn't know what to do, so he jumped up and ran out after Flynn. After a while, he caught up with him and said, 'Why are you running?' Flynn said, 'If I stop, I'll die.' He was probably just that close to dying of alcohol poisoning and maybe his body was trying to tell him something."

The weekend after Hopper's dispatch, Edith Gwynn confirmed reports from Europe that Tierney's work and behavior were "very good" and that he might remain there "indefinitely and appear in several more" pictures. She and others indicated that Tierney may have turned a corner in his struggles, and might even find fulfillment, and peace, as an expatriate.

Then, suddenly, without warning, he was in New York City.

Earl Wilson started the rumor on May 28, with an item claiming that Lawrence Tierney was "making the rounds" with a hatcheck girl from Tony's Trouville on East Fifty-Second Street. Days later, Ed Sullivan paired Tierney with actress Florence Wesson, a "Riviera lovely." Danton Walker reported the first verified sighting on June 7. Tierney had been spied at the Trouville with agent Patricia Harris. The pair were not canoodling. They were discussing a play: a "straw-hat revival of *The Last Mile*"—"straw-hat" referring to the summer theater circuit. *The Last Mile* was a play, written by John Wexley and set in the death house of an Oklahoma state prison, that ran for 289 performances on Broadway in 1930. Spencer Tracy was in the lead role of John "Killer" Mears. Clark Gable played Mears on the stage tour. *The Last Mile* had been made into a movie in 1932, starring Preston Foster (and would be remade in 1959, with Mickey Rooney).

Dorothy Manners confirmed that Tierney had returned to New York City "to discuss a summer stock 'deal', presenting himself all nice and shined up ready for another chance in native movies or on the stage." (Manners also mentioned that Tierney had been linked with Lady Iris Mountbatten, the twice-divorced, twenty-nine-year-old model and actress—and youngest great-grandchild of Queen Victoria. The Lady did protest, however, saying she'd only been on one date with the man.)

Two days later, Tierney was arrested after another drunken brawl.

13

Again

The Weehawken, New Jersey, police department logged the first call shortly before six a.m. on Thursday, June 9, 1949. It was a report of "mayhem being committed wholesale," a loud and violent riot outside a house at 755 Hudson Boulevard East. The sun was still on the rise when three radio cars skidded to a halt in front of the residence—only to encounter a young man sitting on the curb, alone.

He told the officers his name was Myles De Russy. He was twenty-five years old, a photographer who lived on West Seventy-First Street in Manhattan. The cops didn't ask what eye he used to look through the camera lens, but did ask how he got that big, fresh mouse under one of his eyes. Swollen and bloodshot, De Russy said he'd received it in the slugfest that somebody called the cops about, courtesy of one Lawrence Tierney.

Where was Tierney now? He was inside the house with the two other guys.

The cops walked up to the door, got everybody outside, and untangled the story. Bart Lauricella, who lived in the house, had hosted a party the night before. The party went into the morning. Shortly before dawn, Tierney, De Russy, and two other Manhattanites, a forty-five-year-old commercial artist named John Morris, and antique dealer Edward Corti, twenty-four, were about to make their way home across the river when punches began to be thrown.

Tierney admitted banging De Russy in the eye, but claimed the shutter-bug had tagged him first. De Russy refused to sign an assault charge against Tierney or anyone else, but the Weehawken cops, not happy about speeding off to a riot call before six in the morning, decided to charge all four men with disorderly conduct. The group had been processed and behind bars for about an hour when Lauricella showed up and paid Tierney's fifty-dollar bail. He let the other three stew. In what *Daily News* reporter Arthur Smith would call "a gallant touch," Tierney told his fellow arrestees he'd be back—and about three hours later, around noon, he was, with a fresh roll of bills. He peeled off fifty dollars for each of the three men, including the photographer whose eye he'd blackened.

The quartet would be reunited Monday evening at Weehawken Town Hall, where Magistrate Abraham Lieberman held court.

Were anyone looking for a bright side, this latest situation did have interesting parallels. Like Dillinger, Tierney had broken his gang out of jail. On paper, the Hudson Boulevard Boys could have been an East Coast version of the Bundy Drive Boys. The "Battle of Lauricella's Front Yard" could be an updated version of the Battle of Decker's Lawn. Only this time, there was no pretty scion of an acting dynasty to slap some sense into Tierney's head. Instead of eight slaps, there would be countless headlines: "FILM BAD BOY IN BAD AGAIN" . . . "L. (DILLINGER) TIERNEY STRIKES AGAIN" . . . "ACTOR LAWRENCE TIERNEY APES DILLINGER AGAIN." The operative word was "again." Again. Lawrence Tierney did it again. His past arrests were dredged up and listed, again. Monday couldn't come soon enough.

When Lawrence Tierney returned to Weehawken to face Judge Lieberman in police court, there were fans waiting for him outside town hall. The appearance was very much like Robert Mitchum's quick trial—more like a movie premiere than a criminal proceeding. The judge heard the evidence and delivered his verdict. Myles De Russy Jr., who'd already been gifted with a black eye from Tierney, was found guilty of disorderly conduct and fined fifty dollars. John Morris was also convicted of being a disorderly person. His fine was fifteen dollars. Edward Corti was found not guilty. Then it was down to Lawrence Tierney, the thirty-year-old actor whose future was again on the line.

Judge Lieberman shook his head. Citing a lack of evidence, he dismissed the charge. Not guilty.

The courtroom erupted. Dozens of "bobby sox fans" whooped and cheered, and then mobbed Tierney for autographs.

Acquitted or not, the Weehawken brawl was another mark against Lawrence Tierney at a time he was attempting to rush-release a stateside comeback—and when the differences between him and his good-guy younger brother were becoming clearer by the day. Scott Brady would soon arrive in Gotham to film *Port of New York*. He'd star as a US Customs agent chasing down opium smugglers in New York Harbor—a lawman guarding the water, just as his father did (Yul Brynner, in his first screen role, played the bad guy, with a full head of hair). Lawrence could be found in Manhattan—in the bars on

Third Avenue when he wasn't escorting another date in a midtown gossip bowl. "What a contrast between Lawrence Tierney, currently involved in still another bar room brawl back East, and Tierney's brother, Scott Brady, who will spend most of the summer acting as counselor at a YMCA camp in the California mountains!" Jimmie Fidler crowed, three days after Tierney walked out of court.

"Scott Brady called his brother, Lawrence Tierney, in New York after his latest shenanigans in Weehawken, N.J., and tried to pump some sense into him, long distance," Sheilah Graham claimed. "I'm ready to believe now it's hopeless."

Learning he'd lost the lead role in a remake of *Numbered Woman* even before the picture itself fell through, Tierney looked to the straw-hat circuit for redemption. He had his agent post a $3,000 bond to assure theater owners he'd show up on time and sober for every performance. A sobriety clause was also attached to a surprise offer from Hollywood. Producer Seymour Nebenzal was now planning to shoot his remake of Fritz Lang's *M* in Mexico, and wanted Tierney in the lead role of the compulsive killer of children. Neither option seemed likely, and in the weeks ahead, Tierney starred only in the columns, in remakes of what he'd played in the past. "Lawrence Tierney, while in a N. Y. bar," claimed Earl Wilson, "beat up a guy who sneered, 'I don't think you're so tough.'" With so many joints in which to drink and spar in anonymity, more of Tierney's drunken displays went unreported—until the day he received news that sent him into a tailspin: "Announcements are reaching here of the marriage in Mexico City on July 12th of Mrs. Vivian Stokes Taylor to Count Marco Fabio Crespi of Sao Paulo, Brazil and Rome. . . . The ceremony was performed in the United States Consulate."

Announcements soon reached newspaper readers of Lawrence Tierney's volatile reaction to the news that his former flame had tied the knot. Tierney repaired to P. J. Clarke's saloon on the northeast corner of Third Avenue and Fifty-Fifth Street and ordered a stiff drink. Then he ordered another. And another.

Then he stuck his head into an electric fan.

Cholly Knickerbocker (pseudonym of Igor Cassini) reported in the *Journal-American* that the stunt "resulted in his being scalped pretty badly." When other drinkers came to his aid, the bloodied Tierney was more concerned with repairing the fan than the cuts on his head.

Days later, when he showed up in a restaurant with a bandaged hand, the official explanation was that "he injured it in a water cooler." Jimmie Fidler got a laugh out of that one, crediting the excuse to a press agent's gift "to extract the last possible grain of sensation from anything concerning one of his clients." The story of Tierney being injured in a household accident and not a bar brawl was outlandish enough, but the addition of a water cooler made it "one of the few yarns fit to stand comparison with the classic about the man biting the dog."

Tierney bounced back quickly from the loss of Vivi Stokes. Days after the electric fan incident, Dorothy Kilgallen reported that his "big new romance" was Mary Rogers, the thirty-six-year-old Broadway actress and daughter of the late humorist and performer Will Rogers. The couple would prove to be an inflammable mix, making boisterous and contentious public scenes throughout the summer and into the fall.

Amid the stories of drinks and brawls and electric fans, *Bodyguard, Dillinger,* and *Devil Thumbs a Ride* remained in theaters, showing off Tierney's skills at playing guys bad and good. The Hollywood press agents who gave Jimmie Fidler a rueful laugh continued to polish Tierney's reputation. Marissa O'Brien, Tierney's costar, and Roy Hunt, the cameraman on *Kill or Be Killed,* were brought forward to attest that Tierney "couldn't have behaved better" during the shoot in Portugal. It was claimed that several more Hollywood producers were interested in hiring him. So were producers of a Broadway hit.

Sidney Kingsley's *Detective Story* had opened at the Hudson Theatre on March 23. The three-act drama was set in a New York City detective squad room and starred Meg Mundy, Maureen Stapleton, and as Det. Jim McLeod, Ralph Bellamy. Producers were considering casting Tierney as McLeod in the Chicago production.

Could any of it be believed? Sheilah Graham reported on August 3 that Tierney was poised to start a movie in New York, and then go on the road with Arthur Miller's play, *Death of a Salesman,* which had opened on Broadway in February. He did neither, but it was a throwaway line that led off Graham's column item that was cause for a doubletake: "Lawrence Tierney seems to have decided against a stay at that Kansas clinic." The "Kansas clinic" was obviously the Menninger Clinic in Topeka, a psychiatric facility and sanitorium whose doctors had treated a number of Hollywood celebrities. At the time, its most famous patient was movie star Robert Walker, who'd gained fame during World War II in boy-next-door roles, but was also a severe alcoholic with a number of drunk and disorderly arrests. Five months Tierney's elder, Walker received sympathy and support from the industry not afforded Tierney, in part because of his image (a "shy guy" as opposed to "tough guy") and industry status (his ex-wife Jennifer Jones had married David O. Selznick in July), but mainly because he suffered from mental illness.

Tierney split with Mary Rogers at the end of August and spent some time in Hollywood (allegedly followed there by actress Jacqueline Parker), but when he returned to the city in September, he hadn't completely dimmed his torch for Will Rogers's daughter. Managers of East Side restaurants were reportedly nervous whenever Mary showed up with a date. Tierney, Kilgallen wrote, "seems to have a sixth sense about finding her, and he's almost sure to show up sooner or later and have noisy 'words' with her current escort." (The coupling, and Tierney's reputation, were so toxic that in December, when Rogers was seen around town with a "banged-up leg and using a cane," Edith Gwynn actually asked, "Is she seeing Lawrence Tierney again?")

The following eight weeks were summed up in the columns:

Edith Gwynn, September 14: "Mary Rogers, dotter of Will, and Lawrence Tierney are reported battling their way all over Manhattan now—after cooing at each other for a while."

Dorothy Kilgallen, September 22: "The Lawrence Tierney-Mary Rogers romance is on again."

Ed Sullivan, October 1: "Lawrence Tierney and Mary Rogers a China Doll twosome."

Erskine Johnson, October 11: "Lawrence Tierney is back to Will Rogers' daughter, Mary."

Sheilah Graham, October 19: "I'm told Lawrence Tierney is talking a picture deal at Metro. I doubt that there could be a contract unless Larry cures himself of what ails him."

Earl Wilson, October 20: "Lawrence Tierney, showing up for a date covered with soot, explained, 'I don't know what happened to me; I woke up in a coal bin.'"

Louella Parsons scored an interview with ex-con Robert Mitchum that was published on October 30. Reflecting on his sixty days in county custody, the actor said he was set on making a movie that advocated prison reform. "My weeks in jail did much for me," he said. "They made me have an understanding of my fellow men and their problems. I believe that most of these men need a psychiatrist to help them go right."

This led Parsons to ask the next, obvious, question: "What about Lawrence Tierney?"

"I am convinced that Lawrence Tierney is very sick and that he needs a doctor's care more than anything else," Mitchum replied. "But I don't want to get into a discussion about that. I'd rather talk about the picture I am going to make."

The day after the Mitchum exclusive, Parsons expressed regrets that Tierney and actor Sonny Tufts had been "acting up" and making "spectacles of themselves" in New York City nightspots "in a manner that won't help either of them or good Hollywood public relations." Tierney, she reported, showed up for a reading of the lead role in the Chicago production of *Detective Story*, "leaning too far to portside. P. S. He didn't get the part."

With the drunken fumble of *Detective Story*, it appeared that barrooms and courtrooms would be the only venues in which to catch a Lawrence Tierney performance. Earl Wilson reported in November: "When a drunk accosted him, Tierney flattened him, then took him to the hospital." Wilson followed with: "Lawrence Tierney wants to do a B'way show. In fact, he's pouring over scripts." The spelling of "pouring" was key to the punchline.

Who could have predicted that by the end of the month, Tierney would be back onstage, in a starring role? On the day it was reported that baby brother Eddie, the would-be writer, had not only enrolled in acting school but been signed by Universal-International as an actor ("I won't blame him if he changed his name as Scott did," Louella Parsons sniffed), the *Montclair Times* of New Jersey reported that Lawrence Tierney would return to the stage on November 28, "as star of John Wexley's gripping epic drama, *The Last Mile*." Tierney would have the role once owned by Spencer Tracy and Clark Gable, but not on Broadway or even the straw-hat circuit. The show would go on in Newark.

And when the show did go on, when Tierney took the stage as "Killer" Mears, the tables turned once again. Word reached Manhattan literally overnight. Lawrence Tierney was powerful in *The Last Mile*. Across the Hudson River, where the Battle of Lauricella's Front Yard had raged six months earlier, he began attracting theatergoers from New York City to the Newark Opera House for what was heralded as an unexpected triumph.

Even Dorothy Kilgallen changed her tune. Two days after opening night, her usual column item about a Tierney disruption had a twist: "The screen's bad boy, Lawrence Tierney, pulled a switch in a Third Avenue bar the other night—summoned the police patrol cars because a woman was bothering HIM!" Scott Brady telephoned Louella Parsons to rave that his big brother was so good in the role that the producers were planning to bring the show to New York. Seymour Nebenzal, who for months had touted the idea of starring Tierney in a remake of *M,* said Tierney's success in *The Last Mile* proved he'd "turned over a new leaf," and wired the actor a solid offer.

Parsons also reported an enthusiastic call from Joe Rock, an old-timer who in the 1920s had produced silent shorts featuring Stan Laurel. Old Joe said he'd purchased rights to a story about the state prison in Huntsville, Texas, that he planned to film there. He claimed to have a releasing deal with Eagle-Lion, and he, too, wanted Lawrence Tierney.

"Nothing makes me so happy," Louella Parsons wrote, "as to report that a really fine actor, who once stumbled into a pitfall of temptation, is trying to regain his footing and win a new lease on life."

The biggest and most newsworthy offer was announced three days before Christmas. This time, Lawrence Tierney gave Parsons the tip: he was going to make a picture at United-International, and his costar would be Scott Brady. "I also had an offer to go to RKO," Tierney told the columnist, "and I want you to be the first to know it. I read what you said and I want to say I never am going to let you down."

"Larry," Parsons typed in reply, "we're forgetting everything that happened yesterday. We're all standing looking ahead, after all, it soon will be 1950."

What could go wrong?

14

The Payoff

Suggest Stars Start '50 with Good Resolutions
LAWRENCE TIERNEY—*I'll try, once again, to stop looking
at the world through old-fashioned glasses.*

HAROLD HEFFERNAN, NORTH AMERICAN NEWSPAPER ALLIANCE

Lawrence Tierney began 1950 in a different kind of fight: a behind-the-scenes battle for top billing in *The Payoff*, the film in which he'd share the screen with younger brother Scott Brady.

Brady had starred in five movies in the year and a half since his first major marquee role in *Canon City*. The film noir *Undertow*, the latest production featuring "Hollywood's first star to be produced by the G. I. Bill of Rights," had been released in December. Lawrence Tierney had not been in a Hollywood picture in almost two years. *Kill or Be Killed*, the movie he'd shot in Portugal, had been picked up for release by Eagle-Lion, but he was still struggling to revive his career. So it was odd that he was taking such a hardball stance when he was signed to a precarious, one-picture deal with Universal-International at the lowball fee of $7,500. Tierney's recalcitrance did not go unnoticed by the man who'd tracked his career and antics since he first went astray. Tierney was taking, in Jimmie Fidler's view, the "wrong pose."

"Lawrence Tierney, back in Hollywood again for picture work after a reportedly sober stay in the east," Fidler wrote on January 17, "instead of holding out for top billing, should be down on his 'hunkers,' thanking his lucky stars that he's getting another chance."

Amid rumors of a brotherly feud, Tierney was given yet another chance in January when U-I cast him in *Winchester '73*, a big-budget Western topped by James Stewart, Shelley Winters, and Dan Duryea. Tierney would play the

Kansas Kid—the bad man. According to Hedda Hopper, Tierney got the role, and a shot at a long-term contract, because he'd "been a good boy."

"Maybe I am gullible," Hopper's rival Louella Parsons enthused, "but after I talked with Tierney, I had the feeling that he is going to do everything he can to be a good boy, and I am glad he is being given this chance."

"Good boy" or not, Tierney was out of *Winchester '73* within two weeks, and production outside Tucson, Arizona, was delayed. Universal-International blamed the move on script revisions that cut Duryea's part from the picture. The studio needed to fulfill a contract commitment with Duryea, so he was placed in Tierney's role. Tierney, it was promised, would be cast in a meaty role in another picture. (An alternative explanation was voiced by Sheilah Graham: "No one seems to know why Larry broke three studio appointments for wardrobe tests, etc. which is why he is out of *Winchester 73*.")

Days later, U-I kept its word and shifted Tierney to the Western *Saddle Tramp,* starring Joel McRae. The studio held out hope that *The Payoff* would follow. Scott Brady, who'd gone out of his way to praise his brother and shoot down any notions of rivalry, said, "The pay-off is that Larry will be the hero. I'll be the heel."

Just as quickly, Tierney was out of *Saddle Tramp.* "Tierney has not been acting up," Universal producer Leonard Goldstein told reporters. "We took him out of *Saddle Tramp* because the part was too heavy. He only has one commitment with Universal, and it will probably be *Tomahawk* with Van Heflin, and he'll play a good man."

The shuffling came to a stop at the end of March, when U-I cast Tierney in *The Magnificent Heel.* He'd put the spurs and cowboy hat aside for a modern-day film noir starring Howard Duff as a press photographer who gets tied up with the Mob. Tierney would be back as a bad man, in the role of a gangster. This picture went into production in early April. It would be released as *Shakedown.*

While all the offscreen wrangling was taking place, Tierney was doing his usual wrestling on the social scene. He'd left Mary Rogers in New York ("quiet as the proverbial church mouse . . . staying home reading historical novels," according to Kilgallen), and was seen with a number of women: sipping soft drinks at Sugie's Tropics with Posey Judge, former girlfriend of FDR's son, Elliott; on the town with former Goldwyn girl Selene Walters, recently courted by the Shah of Iran; and spending time with the blonde Spanish-American B-movie starlet Adele Mara, another veteran of Xavier Cugat's troupe.

With the recent marriages of Jimmy Stewart, Clark Gable, and Cary Grant, Lawrence Tierney was even included on Sheilah Graham's list of Hollywood's most eligible bachelors. Howard Hughes, who "rates above any movie star in the matter of millions and glamour," topped the list. "Lawrence Tierney is available for girls with a mission. So is his brother, Scott Brady, less colorful, more reliable."

Attractive to the ladies he may have been, but Tierney still managed to instill a sense of danger and fear whenever he was in any place where alcohol was served. Leonard Lyons recounted a story on January 31 about a party in Beverly Hills. A guest had stepped away from his date to fetch cocktails, and returned to find Tierney attempting to put his arms around the woman. "When Tierney left to get a drink," Lyons wrote, "the man whispered to the lady: 'Look, if that guy insults you, you're strictly on your own.'"

The warning signs were there. Jimmie Fidler laid them out once again in March, when he presented Tierney's "unique explanation" for his latest relapse. Tierney said that no one took him seriously when he tried to reform, and that a nightclub (where, Fidler wrote, "he was involved in a half-dozen brawls") refused to admit him, even after he promised not to drink alcohol. "And so, he reasoned, why stay sober if no one's willing to give you the benefit of the doubt?

"What a pity it is that a man with Tierney's great ability has so little common sense. Hollywood has been remarkably patient with him. . . . A man who has spent years in tearing down the confidence of his associates ought to be willing to spend a reasonable time in rebuilding it. Tierney will have to do just that if he wants to recapture his wasted success."

Perhaps because of stories like that, April was a month of physical and reputation rehab. Jack Lait Jr. of the *Brooklyn Eagle* bumped into Tierney at the Mocambo and asked if he really was at odds with his brother. "Of course not," Tierney replied. "Scott's a good kid. What would we be fighting about?" Erskine Johnson said he got quotes from Tierney while the actor was "working hard on a de-blubber program at Terry Hunt's gym." What about all those bad man stories? "I don't mind anything that is printed about me as long as it is the truth," Tierney said. "I've got nothing to hide and I got nothing to be ashamed of—except getting drunk a few times."

On April 27, Bob Thomas of the Associated Press wrote that the *Shakedown* shoot was a success and that U-I had an option to sign Tierney to a long-term contract. "It looks as though they will pick it up," Tierney said. Was he afraid of being typecast with all the gangster roles?

"Many stars have made a mint by being typed," he reasoned.

Lawrence Tierney was prepared to begin filming *Tomahawk*. Everything was falling into place. He made it 128 days into the new year before he was in trouble again.

Monday night fights at the Ocean Park Arena in Santa Monica were known to attract a rowdy crowd. Tierney was ringside with a blonde on May 8, 1950, eyeing the preliminary bouts leading to the ten-round main event between lightweight boxers Lou Williams (a sparring partner of charismatic "Golden Boy" Art Aragon) and Frank Muche. There was excitement in the twenty-four-hundred-seat arena when lightweight Sammy Figueroa flattened Chuck Edwards in the third round. Tierney perked up even more when a beer vendor came down the aisle, handing out bottles and snatching bills and pocketing coins along the way. Tierney had already polished off a few. This time, he reached out and swiped a bottle from the bucket, and when the peddler asked for his money, Tierney laughed and waved him off. The peddler stood his ground. Husky Tierney stood up. There was an exchange. The cops were called over.

The beer seller gave the cops the lowdown. Tierney acted as if it were all a big joke. He pointed the neck of the beer bottle at the officers.

"Stick 'em up!" he said.

He thought that was pretty funny. The cops had seen enough. They led Tierney up the aisle and out of the arena. They left the blonde to fend for herself.

The two fighters in the main event were pretty evenly matched until the third round, when Williams opened a cut under Muche's left eye. So much blood poured from the gash in the fourth round that referee Reggie Gilmore stopped the fight.

Tierney, meanwhile, was booked on another drunk charge at Santa Monica Jail. He posted ten dollars bail and was scheduled to face municipal judge Thurlow Taft in the morning.

When he appeared in court, Tierney pleaded innocent.

"I plead guilty to friskiness but not drunkenness," the actor told Judge Taft. "I did a lot of kidding. It might have been mistaken for drunkenness."

When the judge said he didn't buy the excuse, Tierney said he wanted to talk to an attorney. The judge granted him a continuance. Tierney was allowed to remain free on ten dollars bail, to stand trial on May 24.

Frisky or not, the incident led to familiar headlines—"LAWRENCE TIERNEY IN CLINK AGAIN" . . . "LAWRENCE TIERNEY AGAIN IS BOOKED AS DRUNK"—while in New York, top-rated broadcaster and gossip columnist Walter Winchell took notice of the latest arrest and turned it into something of a tabloid poem: "'Nancy Sinatra Files for Separation' . . . 'Rita and Aly Reported Tiffing' . . . 'Sonny Tufts Arrested' . . . 'Lawrence Tierney in Another Fight.' Hollywood back to normal."

Jimmie Fidler was sure to take notice. He repeated the mantra he'd chanted since 1947. Tierney was "an incorrigible dipsomaniac . . . of the dangerous type who, once in his cups, manages to get involved in a fight." Fidler had said before that "only the whims of Lady Luck have kept him from being involved in a tragedy, with someone else, in all probability, being the principal victim one day. I charge that the men who condone and continue to employ a public menace of his caliber are irresponsible. If, as seems likely, his career does end in tragedy, how can they be considered as anything but accessories before the fact?"

Lawrence Tierney returned to face Judge Taft on Wednesday, May 24. He dropped his request for a jury trial and pleaded guilty to the drunk and disorderly charge. The judge fined him fifty dollars and placed him on probation for two years.

After the guilty plea in Santa Monica, Tierney was chopped from *Tomahawk*. His U-I deal was axed. Howard Hughes wouldn't be signing him to a new contract at RKO any time soon. He would not get a second shot at *Wyoming Mail*, which Tierney's agent made him turn down because the part was "too small," and despite Louella Parsons's excitement over the casting coup, Allied Artists would not produce *Police Story*. The picture was to star "the whole Tierney family, Scott Brady, Larry Tierney, their young brother Eddie Tierney, and their father, Lawrence H. Tierney.

"Larry will need some money when he finishes paying his fine for reckless driving," Parsons wrote, referencing yet another encounter with the law. "With his father to watch him you can bet he will keep in line."

The repercussions hit with unfortunate timing. Lawrence Tierney had already been trotted out for one-on-one interviews to promote *Shakedown*. Profiled as "the meanest man in the movies" by Frank Neill of the International News Service, Tierney gulped conspicuously from a big glass of milk and complained that his bad guy roles gave the audience the wrong idea. "You've got to be a rugged individualist to accept roles like these. No real movie fan ever likes you as a result of them, either. When the picture is over, and they're out of the theater, as far as they are concerned, I'm still a no-good so-and-so. And if you don't believe me, I'll let you look at some of my fan letters."

Sheilah Graham amped up the "poor little tough guy" angle a few days later for a column with a mouthful of a title: "The Bottle Has Kept Larry 'Dillinger' Tierney in Trouble, But Now He's Trying To Be a Good Boy."

"'I've got to be more careful than anyone else in town,' he tells me with a troubled frown. 'I'm trying to get started again, and I can't afford to let the word get around that I drink anything stronger than carrot juice.' A week later Tierney was arrested on a drunk charge. 'I was sober,' he insists—'just acting playful.' Playful or drunk, Larry has probably washed out his last remaining chance to be a Hollywood movie star. But you never can tell."

Tierney was "dead sober at lunch" when he told Graham his role as a racketeer in *Shakedown* was "the only kind of part they'll ever give me now. But . . . I typed myself. . . . I guess my name is synonymous with murder, so I've got to make the best of it."

As Graham described it, Tierney spent his nights on the town with "dozens" of "pretty girls around Hollywood," but was serious about none, because "he had and is still having such a bad time in Hollywood that he doesn't know what tomorrow may bring or where he's going from here.

"When you talk to Larry, it's impossible to believe he's been such an alcoholic," Graham observed. "He's very quiet, very intelligent, can quote good poetry by the hour. He's very charming and seems quite sincere in his desire to be a good boy. I hope he's able to cure what ails him. It's a shame to drown a good career in a bottle."

Heading into that summer of 1950, Lawrence Tierney was living in a small house in Beverly Hills with his father, mother, and youngest brother, Edward. Middle brother Gerard—Hollywood's Scott Brady—had distanced himself a bit further from the family name by moving into an apartment of his own. Tierney owned four suits and a tuxedo that, due to his alcohol-expanding frame, no longer fit. He drove a fancy Cadillac and spent many nights escorting pretty women to restaurants or clubs where he'd be seen—preferably with a glass of milk—and get his name in the columns. If he didn't shack up with a date, he'd return home and read in bed for hours. He got by on very little sleep. He was always restless, always on edge. Reasons for self-medication were obvious, but not addressed.

Tierney remained a ubiquitous presence onscreen. Each week, *Kill or Be Killed* opened in another part of the country, in most cities second-billed on a double feature. When the picture opened in New York City, paired with the Rex Allen Western, *Hills of Oklahoma,* the cowboy movie got two and a half (out of four) stars from Wanda Hale in the *Daily News. Kill or Be Killed* received two. Hale said the film "has no mystery but suspense is worked in generously throughout the story."

Tierney's life was playing out the same way. There was no mystery of what would happen next. There was suspense, however, about when and where he'd slip, and how the stumble would affect his fortunes. There was little concern in Hollywood about the "why." Tierney continued to frequent establishments and venues that would be prone to trouble, and because he was seen in such places, continued to maintain a starring role in newspaper columns.

The United States entered the war in Korea on June 27, 1950. Louella Parsons launched something equally historic on June 29—a rare retraction. She admitted a mistake in announcing Tierney's "romance" with Beverly Michaels, a B-movie actress and former Broadway showgirl. Parsons had confused the young woman with Kay Crespi (no relation to the Count), another showgirl who'd worked, played, and made her way to Hollywood with Beverly. "Beverly and Kay look very much alike, hence the mistaken identity," Parsons wrote. "That's all today. See you tomorrow!"

There was no retracting the bad news in July. Edith Gwynn said Tierney was "moaning aloud" because he hadn't seen a penny of his deferred salary or percentage of profits from *Kill or Be Killed.* Later that month, Scott Brady confirmed to Sheilah Graham that *The Payoff* was not going to happen.

"What's cooking with Lawrence Tierney?" she asked him.

"Your guess is as good as mine," Brady replied. Graham said he replied "somberly."

But once again, when the future looked the bleakest, the tables turned. Tierney was hired back at RKO, where it all began, and where everything began to go downhill. *Best of the Badmen* was a Technicolor Western starring Robert Ryan and Claire Trevor. Tierney strapped on the six-guns as Jesse James, the same outlaw he'd played in *Badman's Territory* in 1945. He'd be billed eighth on the poster, but he was back in the game.

"If he comes through this one without any more scandal," Graham claimed, "Howard Hughes will sign him to a term contract. Larry's recent trouble in a nightclub is expected to end in only a fine. He still insists he wasn't imbibing."

This was quite a break, but when a writer for one of the trades said Tierney "rated" one, a prominent colleague disagreed. "I can't think of anyone who rates a 'break' less than a guy who's consistently proven, via some thirteen arrests for drunkenness and brawling in the last four years, that he's an incorrigible misbehaver," Jimmie Fidler fumed. "Such misplaced sympathy is enough to convince any young movie hopeful that a bottle in one hand and a bag of newspaper clippings in the other would be more apt to get him a 'break' than any amount of sincerity or hard work."

Tierney went to work on *Best of the Badmen*. He kept out of trouble. Seen at Café Gala with actress Joan Whitney, he was guzzling orange juice. Approached by Sheilah Graham, he boasted about younger brother Eddie, who like Scott Brady took acting courses at Bliss-Hayden and was starring in the school's stage production of *Light Up the Sky*. "Larry, I am assured by Scott, isn't even looking at the bottle, let alone sampling the contents," Graham wrote. "I hope he's right."

Shakedown opened on September 1. Tierney was fourth-billed, but he got good notices as a gangster.

A week later, on Monday, September 8, he returned to Ocean Park Arena on Pico Boulevard in Santa Monica. The colorful fight card featured boxers including "New Orleans bobber-and-weaver" welterweight Bobcat Terrance, middleweight Flash Gordon, and, in the ten-round main event, lightweight local hero Alfredo Escobar, who won a split decision against Chuck "The Chocolate Soldier" Wilkerson.

At ringside, Lawrence Tierney survived a split decision, as well. He received much attention, and even made the papers the following day, after he poured the contents of a bottle over a man's head. The decision was split because it was decided that the liquid was not alcohol but Coca-Cola, and Tierney, though frisky, was not arrested.

Production on *Best of the Badmen* wrapped at the Iverson Movie Ranch on September 20. *Shakedown* opened in five theaters in Los Angeles the following week. The *Los Angeles Times* said the picture was "such a lively, engrossing opus that we can, despite the scallions tossed at our profession, heartily recommend it for entertainment." Reviewer G. K. wrote that "Howard Duff as the photographer does a good job, and so do the other players," including Lawrence Tierney.

❧

Saturday, October 14, 1950, four a.m.: The Los Angeles Police Department received an urgent call. A man was assaulting a woman inside a car parked in the middle of the intersection of Normandie Avenue and Jefferson Boulevard in South L.A.

A radio car sped to the scene. The officers found a Cadillac parked in the street. A woman was in the front seat. Wandering in the street, around the car, was Lawrence Tierney.

15

The Respectful Prostitute

More than one neighbor phoned in the complaint. A man and woman were shouting loudly in a parked car. A woman was being assaulted in a parked car. A man was molesting a woman in a parked car in the middle of Normandie Avenue at the corner of Jefferson Boulevard. When the police car pulled up to the Cadillac, the cops were ready for anything. They found Jean Wallace in the front passenger seat.

Wallace was a hard luck platinum blonde actress who'd celebrated her twenty-seventh birthday two days earlier. The second ex-wife of forty-five-year-old actor Franchot Tone (his first was Joan Crawford), and mother of his two sons, Wallace had, in recent years, survived two suicide attempts, and been arrested for drunk driving, wearing only a red coat and blue lace panties, in West Hollywood on Christmas Day. Now, she looked frightened, but unmolested.

Lawrence Tierney was in the street, staggering and circling the scene. When the officers approached, he shouted, "I demand a sobriety test! *I want a sobriety test now!*" He was wild enough that the cops cuffed him before stuffing him into the back of a patrol car for the drive to University station.

Tierney flunked the sobriety test and became, in the words of the cops, "belligerent." When he went after a newspaper photographer and attempted to punch a reporter, he was handcuffed again. The cops affixed him with another drunk charge, fingerprinted him, and put him in a cell. Jean Wallace, meanwhile, denied she'd been assaulted in any way. She did not want to file any complaint against Lawrence Tierney. The police sent her on her way.

Tierney paid the twenty dollars bail and was released, as well. Many papers later that day reported that this was Tierney's twelfth drunk arrest. The INS reporter was more accurate when he wrote that Tierney had been arrested on the familiar charge for the "umpteenth" time.

"Larry called and asked if I would be interested in playing with him in a play, *The Respectful Prostitute*." Jean Wallace sat with Louella Parsons the following day, as sincere as could be. "We talked about the part and then I offered to drive him home. Suddenly he became wild and started to scream."

It was unfortunate that the title of the play—actually a French existential take on American racism that was written by philosopher Jean-Paul Sartre and had run on Broadway in 1948—only added to assumptions about the illicit nature of the incident. Parsons summarized the situation as "a bad break." After all her scandals, Wallace had been "making a wonderful comeback, and everyone in Hollywood knows that she has given up all intoxicants." She also had much at stake. Jerry Giesler was representing her request to annul her recent, impulsive Tijuana marriage to a young army sergeant. Wallace would also be in court, attempting to regain custody of her sons from Franchot Tone.

"I don't think Franchot will oppose this move—or even care," Jean Wallace said. "He is so taken up with Barbara Payton. Everyone says they will be married." Barbara Payton was four years younger than Jean Wallace and, as Franchot Tone would find, four times the trouble.

After the initial headlines, including the memorable "TIERNEY ONCE MORE GETS HIS SNOOT WET," interest in Tierney's alcoholic antics waned considerably. When Jimmie Fidler got around to addressing the all-too-familiar issue, he offered a solution: Tierney's longest sober stretches "were in response to ultimatums from producers who have put him on probation. This time, in the interest of public safety and for his own good, he should be ruled out—not for a month or two, but for a sufficient length of time to effect a real cure. And he shouldn't be taken back until doctors offer certificates attesting the cure."

Fidler expressed sympathy for Scott Brady the following week. It seems a female columnist (Fidler wasn't naming names) had confronted Brady after Tierney's latest arrest and asked, "What gives with your brother again?" Fidler wrote that Brady responded graciously, while probably wishing he could drop through the floor.

"It just so happens that Brady has conducted himself as admirably as Tierney has conducted himself otherwise, and it strikes me as extremely unfair to put Scott on the spot every time his brother steps out of line."

Lawrence Tierney stayed out of sight for weeks. In early November, Louella Parsons had to settle for a sighting of Scott Brady and his mother at the

Encore club. "The whole family feel so badly over Lawrence Tierney." When Hedda Hopper logged the first verified Tierney sighting, on November 30 at the Kings Restaurant ("Food Fit for a King") on Santa Monica Boulevard, the actor was "sticking strictly to buttermilk," and "told friends he'd joined Alcoholics Anonymous."

"I finally discovered that alcohol can whip me," Tierney told Sheilah Graham in December. The Jean Wallace drunk arrest had been settled. He'd avoided jail but remained Hollywood's most identifiable member of Alcoholics Anonymous. Days later, when Graham ran into Tierney at Ciro's nightclub, a leading dispenser of alcoholic beverages, he told her that Academy Award–nominated screenwriter Fred Finklehoffe (*Meet Me in St. Louis*) had offered him the lead in his World War II stage play, *Mike McCauley*. "I told Larry to grab it," Graham wrote. "Apart from re-establishing himself in his career, he'll appear with Isa Miranda, a fine actress."

Danton Walker reported on December 15 that Tierney was planning a lecture tour on behalf of Alcoholics Anonymous, like the one he'd announced after his release from the county drunk farm in 1947.

Many columnists closed out 1950 with traditional holiday columns. Erskine Johnson composed a letter to Santa Claus, warning of the new rooftop danger that was also leading to a revolution in Hollywood: "Television. Drive carefully, Nick, or you and your reindeer will get all tangled up on somebody's roof. Now gifts for the kids. . . . Lawrence Tierney: An AA diploma." Louella Parsons wrote: "May Lawrence Tierney keep on the same straight path he's trodden the past two months." While the sentiments were very much in the holiday spirit, Dorothy Kilgallen offered the most accurate reading of Lawrence Tierney as he headed into 1951: "Lawrence Tierney punched a drunk at a party for introducing him as 'Scott Brady's brother.'"

Tierney didn't take the starring role in *Mike McCauley*. He didn't lose the part because of his troubles with the law, or the distraction of his twice-weekly meetings of Alcoholics Anonymous (which were widely publicized by him and his flacks). Three days into the new year, it was announced that Tierney had been signed to another movie.

Eagle-Lion, the pride of Poverty Row, was taking a chance by signing him to star as a criminal psychopath in a low-budget gangster flick titled *The Hoodlum*. Director Max Nosseck was back on board, and so was another Tierney. Lawrence was responsible for casting his youngest brother Eddie in a costarring role—as his own character's brother. Edward Tierney's only other film appearance had arrived on screens the previous November: an uncredited role as a policeman in *Undercover Girl*, Universal's film noir starring brother Scott Brady and Alexis Smith. Eddie could use the break. His writing career was not exactly thriving. "Rejection slips! It would be wonderful if Eddie could get them," Lawrence told Erskine Johnson. "All he gets from editors are notes saying, 'Are you kidding?'"

Scott Brady had turned down the lead role in *The Hoodlum* before it was offered to his older brother. Brady was signed to Eagle-Lion, but had sued the studio the previous September for interfering with his career. He claimed his contract allowed him to be loaned out only to major filmmakers. When the studio loaned him to independent producer Jack Schwarz, he balked—and was suspended. *The Hoodlum* was a Jack Schwarz production.

Week by week, Lawrence Tierney worked at proving himself to Hollywood. The misunderstanding of alcoholism, its causes and effects on the brain, had lulled many powerful people who should have known better to believe that the troubled actor had somehow turned over a new leaf with the turn of the calendar page. The most astounding change of opinion was Jimmie Fidler's. It was one thing to write on February 26, 1951, about a sight "I never expected to see": Tierney in the Hollywood Athletic Club swimming pool, and not at the bar. His column of March 6 was quite another. For years, Fidler had insisted that producers who hired Tierney were abetting a "public menace."

Now, when it came to Tierney's latest chance, Fidler declared: "*He's earned it.* According to friends who have had plenty of opportunity to observe his actions of late, he's now seated firmly on the water wagon. They think he's there to stay. Evidently the producer who is entrusting to him a top role in a half-million dollar picture thinks so, too."

Five months after his drunk arrest with Jean Wallace, less than three months after Tierney allegedly punched out someone at a party for referring to him as "Scott Brady's brother," Jimmie Fidler was comfortable stating that Tierney had reformed, thanks to "an enormous exercise of willpower." Fidler gave credit to Alcoholics Anonymous and Tierney's friends, but declared that the main factor in Tierney's reformation was "fear." For that, Fidler took credit.

"It was when he lost his employment that he began to face facts."

Cameras rolled on what would be a two-week shoot for *The Hoodlum* on March 15, 1951, Tierney's birthday. Tierney telephoned Louella Parsons that day to celebrate not himself, but Edward. "You already know my other brother,

Scott Brady, and me—and now I want you to meet the latest member of the Tierney family to become an actor," he told her. "I, of course, play the villain and Eddie plays the good boy." The "good boy"? Parsons said Tierney was "making his mother and all his friends happy by being a very good boy"—a "very good boy" at age thirty-two.

With the "third of the Tierney brothers of Brooklyn getting into the Hollywood swim," wrote Al Salerno at the *Brooklyn Daily Eagle*, "that gives boro four Tierneys in all, last being Gene, no relation."

"The three Brooklyn lads are, if I'm not mistaken, unique in the history of Hollywood," Jack Lait Jr. columnized in the same paper. "I've searched my memory, and I can't recall any instance of three brothers being film stars at the same time. Oops—maybe I'm being a bit previous. Ed, after all, isn't a star yet. But he's getting off to a good start."

When *The Hoodlum* wrapped, Jack Schwarz announced that Lawrence Tierney had appeared in almost every scene, and that the shoot ran smoothly. "Larry knows now what it means to be a good boy," Parsons repeated—such a good boy that director Ida Lupino was talking to him about playing an escaped killer in *They Spoke to God*. At the Lobero Theatre in Santa Barbara—where *Mike McCauley* flopped—Tierney was scheduled to star in another revival of *The Last Mile*. If all went as planned, the play would open on April 30, tour the West Coast, and then head to Chicago and a possible revival on Broadway.

Then, plans again changed dramatically. After slugging away on Poverty Row, where Robert Mitchum would later say "we lit our sets with cigarette butts," Tierney was suddenly and somehow elevated to a role in a "Class A" Technicolor production at Paramount. He'd be a villain in *The Greatest Show on Earth*, producer and director Cecil B. DeMille's all-star epic about life, love, and betrayal behind the scenes of the Ringling Bros. and Barnum & Bailey Circus.

"I was brought in to meet Cecil B. DeMille. I looked at him straight in the eye and he liked my manner," Tierney told the Murphys in 1989. "I got along with DeMille very well. He liked me a lot."

Louella Parsons broke the story on April 21, the day after the deal was signed, "with the greatest happiness because it proves what can be done if a man or woman is strong enough to overcome obstacles." Not only did the signing promise Tierney a possible Paramount contract, but within hours of the signing, Ida Lupino took up the option for him to star in her escaped killer picture.

"His mother's prayers, his brothers' and friends' encouragement have made all this possible," Parsons wrote about her good boy. "And of course, Larry's own intestinal fortitude."

Good news for Lawrence Tierney always seemed to be followed by bad. When he next made the gossip pages on May 8, he was accompanied by actress and Texas beauty Pat Buckner at the Gourmet Beverly Restaurant on North Canon Drive in the heart of Beverly Hills. He was in good form and said to be twenty pounds lighter.

A week later, he was punching a Texas oilman. It was a one-puncher at The Doll House nightclub in Palm Springs, the celebrity getaway in the desert, a hundred miles east of Los Angeles. In Tierney's defense, witnesses confirmed that he'd done everything possible to avoid an altercation.

"I've been on the wagon for nine months and I have been trying very hard to stay out of trouble," Tierney told a reporter. "I was sitting at the bar drinking a Coke with Terry McGuire, a friend of mine, and a couple of girls. This stranger came up and pushed his way between the two girls. He offered to buy them a drink and butted into our conversation. It is very important to me to avoid trouble, so I leaned over and asked the bartender who the man was. The fellow heard me and told me not to be a wise guy. He grabbed my coat collar and forced me back over the bar. I asked him not to start anything, but he cocked his other hand back as if he were going to hit me. I expect to start work soon and I didn't want my face damaged, so I let him have one left to the mouth," he said. "Then people separated us."

The Hoodlum's official release date was July 5, 1951, but Jimmie Fidler was among those who attended an advance screening in June. In a column that rated recent films as "good," "fair," and "questionable," *The Hoodlum* was "Questionable: A well-played but distasteful story about a completely despicable character." Tierney had apparently played the character despicably well enough that Danton Walker reported that he, "of all people," was soon to begin filming *The Life of Moses*—in the title role.

Lawrence Tierney as Judaism's most important prophet? The *Moses* item, which was tagged in more than one column as "wild gossip," was in fact a million-dollar picture proposed by a company called Crusader Films. Jack Eisenbach, head of production, was a New Yorker who specialized in biblical pictures and promotional reels for California desert communities. The technical adviser was Shimon-Leib Schwartz, a Los Angeles mohel who'd circumcised Eisenbach's son. Tierney's name had been floated after Eisenbach asked readers of the *B'nai B'rith Messenger of Los Angeles* newspaper to write in the name of "a tremendous actor" who could portray the dynamic leader. Wrote Shimon Wincelberg in the *Indianapolis Jewish Post*: "At least it won't be Mickey Rooney."

Alas, Tierney as Moses was not to be. The film, with the third act excised, was released in 1952 as *The Boyhood of Moses*. Young Moses was played by Joseph Campanizzi.

Amid all the activity, questions about the Palm Springs incident lingered. Tierney's agent, Bill Shiffrin, who'd negotiated the deal with Paramount, stood up for his client once again. "Larry begged the guy to leave him alone," he told Erskine Johnson. "But the guy kept on. Larry thought of his career and everybody who believed in him for five minutes. Then he couldn't take it any longer and swung. I say that it's a good thing that not all Hollywood stars are cream puffs."

For Lawrence Tierney, the darkest hour always seemed to be just before the dawn. The five o'clock hour on June 21, 1951, was dark in more ways than one. The waning crescent moon shed no illumination onto what was transpiring outside the two-story apartment house at 117 West Channel Road in Santa Monica. The building was across the road from a row of restaurants and bars, including the S. S. Friendship, a pioneering gay bar with the bow of a boat jutting out over the entrance, and a structure or two away from the Pacific Coast Highway and Will Rogers State Beach, named for the late father of Lawrence Tierney's former galpal Mary Rogers. Will Rogers Beach, with access through a pedestrian tunnel under the PCH, was known to the habitués of the S. S. Friendship and other homosexuals as "*Ginger* Rogers Beach," the unofficial gay beach of Los Angeles.

Lawrence Tierney and his pal Bob Crockett arrived at 117 West Channel Road to meet women. Nancy Ulvand was twenty-three, her sister Liz a year older. The Ulvands were commercial artists, attractive blondes from Minnesota, rooming in one of the building's five apartments. Tierney had met one of the sisters, and knowing there was another to spare, dragged Crockett down to the beach on June 20. The girls had company when Tierney and Crockett arrived, so the two men sauntered across the road to one of the bars. Around 5:30 a.m., with the ocean air a comfortable sixty degrees, the pair were back outside the apartment house. The place was battened down, lights out. *Throw some pebbles at their window?* The two galoots, having had enough to drink that their drunkenness had progressed to a stage of sobriety, were laughing—Tierney in the front yard and Crockett on the sidewalk, making a bit too much noise, perhaps.

From inside the house, a dog was barking. A light switched on. The front door opened, and Tierney's eyes widened in drunken alarm. A large dog, snarling and growling, burst from the porch and charged straight at him!

Tierney jumped back onto a ledge, and just as the collie was about to take a bite, gave it a kick that sent the animal flying back, then running away, squealing. *What the hell?* He looked to Crockett standing nearby, ready for whatever came next, when a figure appeared at the door. "Hey, your dog—" Before Tierney could get the words out, a man, mid-twenties, not so big at all, was off the porch, rushing him. Up on the ledge, Tierney let go with another kick. This time, there was an audible crack as his shoe connected with the man's face. John Naylor groaned as he fell onto his back. He covered his face with his hands and stumbled back to the house. Tierney took a deep breath. *Time to make like tree and leave*—but now Naylor was back, wielding a twelve-inch butcher knife! His face bloodied, eyes rolling, he was swinging wildly as if he were blind. This time, Tierney gave him a sock in the face for good luck before he and Crockett ran off. They found their car and headed back toward Hollywood. That was crazy.

Lawrence Tierney slept it off. When he awoke later that day, the incident may even have slipped his mind. He did make the papers on June 21, but the story had nothing to do with West Channel Road. Back in Brooklyn, Jack Lait Jr., the columnist who'd jumped the gun when he called Larry, Roddy, and Eddie the first instance of "three brothers being film stars at the same time," wrote in the *Daily Eagle* that, in light of the good reviews Eddie was receiving for his work in *The Hoodlum*, "it looks as though that's what's going to happen. . . . [Critics] all agreed he shows excellent promise as an actor, and there seems to be no reason why he can't continue on in his brothers' footsteps and achieve early stardom."

The other shoe dropped on June 27, when Robert C. Nye, the Los Angeles deputy city attorney, announced that Lawrence Tierney was being charged with battery and disturbing the peace. Nye said the misdemeanor complaint was issued at the request of John M. Naylor, a twenty-eight-year-old University of California graduate and Dianetics auditor who resided at 117 West Channel Road with his mother, Frances. Naylor told detectives that on June 21, he heard noises outside his home at five thirty in the morning. When he went outside to investigate, he claimed he was beaten, knocked unconscious, and had his jaw broken by two men. He could not identify one of his attackers. The other, he recognized from a photograph: Lawrence Tierney.

Nye asked Bill Shiffrin to arrange for the actor's surrender.

When Lawrence Tierney turned up in Los Angeles Municipal Court in the downtown Hall of Justice on Friday, July 6, he denied he had beaten up John Naylor. It must have been two other guys. He pleaded innocent to the charges and asked for a jury trial. The trial was scheduled for July 27.

Professionally, this couldn't have come at a worse time for Tierney. Not only were executives at Paramount very happy with his work and performance in *The Greatest Show on Earth*, but he'd found a champion in director-producer Cecil B. DeMille. At DeMille's recommendation, the Paramount executives were ready to offer Tierney a contract.

Tierney later told the Murphys: "My agent said, 'Just behave yourself now. Within a month they're gonna sign you to a seven-year contract with a big salary and the first picture you're gonna do is opposite Yvonne DeCarlo in a big Technicolor film called *Hurricane Smith,* all about a pilot.'"

Sheilah Graham reported on July 9 that the studio also had plans for Tierney to star in *The Story of Mrs. Murphy.* "Mrs. Murphy" was a whisky bottle. Tierney would play the alcoholic who named it.

While Shiffrin tried to keep a lid on the Naylor case and salvage the Paramount contract, Tierney was on his way to Santa Fe, New Mexico, to star in a stage production of Tennessee Williams's *A Streetcar Named Desire.* Tierney had been cast as Stanley Kowalski, the role that made Marlon Brando a star on Broadway (and would lead to his first Oscar nomination for the film version, released in September 1951). Austrian-born actress Maria Palmer was the tragic heroine, Blanche DuBois. The play's director was named, somewhat ironically in this case, Jack Daniels.

Streetcar opened on July 25, 1951. After Lawrence Tierney walked offstage from that first performance, all hell broke loose—and not in a good way.

16

5:30 A.M.

The reaction to Lawrence Tierney's debut as Stanley Kowalski at the theater El Teatro in Santa Fe, New Mexico, was very positive. El Teatro, the ambitious troupe billed as "The Southwest's Only Professional Summer Theatre," had another hit with *A Streetcar Named Desire*. The show was scheduled to run through Saturday, July 28, then move on to Los Alamos and Albuquerque.

The 250-seat playhouse was packed the following night, the audience anticipating the 8:30 curtain, when producer Ann Lee walked onstage. The thirty-year-old blonde was a successful Broadway actress who'd built the theater three years earlier and managed to attract top talent from New York and Hollywood, including Kirk Douglas, who'd starred in *Detective Story* to prepare for his role in the film. Lee had bad news: The evening's performance was canceled, due to the illness of Lawrence Tierney. The actor had told Lee he'd been "sick all day," perhaps with acute appendicitis. The cancellation was a disappointment on many levels. This was the first time in the El Teatro troupe's four seasons that the show did not go on.

After the audience filed out and everyone went home, Alfred Paschall, the actor who played Kowalski's poker buddy Mitch Mitchell, stopped in at a downtown bar—and was stunned to see Lawrence Tierney, whisky glass in hand. The leading man was bombed. He'd been drinking there since the afternoon.

When word got back to Ann Lee that evening, the producer wasted no time. She phoned Arthur Franz, a veteran Broadway and movie actor who'd portrayed Kowalski in touring companies in the United States and Australia. Franz, currently onscreen in *Bud Abbott and Lou Costello Meet the Invisible Man*, agreed to fly out to Santa Fe and take over the role. Lee fired Tierney on Friday morning. "I learned he was drinking at a Santa Fe bar Thursday night after I had been told he was too ill to go on the stage," she told a reporter. "That finished me with him."

Tierney, meanwhile, had another date on Friday morning. He was supposed to be at the Hall of Justice in downtown Los Angeles. His trial in the beating of John Naylor was opening in municipal court.

Tierney didn't make it. His attorney, Jack W. Hardy, stood alone before Judge Joseph L. Call and requested a continuance on the grounds that Tierney was in New Mexico for a two-week stage engagement. Hardy told the judge that the city attorney's office had assured him one would be granted.

"If you wanted a continuance, you should have requested it before the date of trial," the judge said. "Furthermore, it is the court, not the city attorney's office, that grants continuances!" He ordered Tierney's $500 bail forfeited and issued a bench warrant for his arrest. Bail was increased to $1,500.

Arthur Franz flew into Albuquerque from Hollywood later that day and arrived in Santa Fe in time for the evening performance. Lawrence Tierney was expected to arrive back in Los Angeles on Saturday.

Then came another dark hour, just before the dawn. Nick Salliras, manager of the Mayflower Café, a popular downtown restaurant, cocktail lounge, and bar, phoned the Santa Fe Police Department at 5:30 a.m. A man was drunk and very disorderly. He was tearing up menus and had kicked down a screen door.

By the time police arrived, Lawrence Tierney was gone. A warrant for his arrest, charging him with being drunk and disorderly in the café, was issued, and a search for the suspect was launched.

Tierney managed to make a getaway. Upon arrival in Los Angeles, he didn't mention the Mayflower incident, and insisted he'd missed the *Streetcar* curtain Thursday night because he "didn't have the vitality to go on." "I was sober when I arrived at the theater, but I had been violently ill and couldn't go on," he said.

Tierney and his attorney arrived at Judge Call's courtroom on Thursday, August 2, to have the earlier arrest warrant lifted. They showed up too late. Judge Call had left for the day. Presiding Judge Byron Walters sent Tierney to see a third judge. Judge Joseph Marchetti recalled the bench warrant and exonerated the bond on Tierney's promise to be in Judge Call's court for trial the following morning.

When Tierney's trial opened for a second time that Friday, Jack Hardy was in the courtroom. His client was not. Hardy told the judge he had no idea where Tierney might be. He withdrew from the case and Judge Call issued another bench warrant. Tierney's bond was raised to $2,500.

Lawrence Tierney and his father arrived in court that afternoon, four hours late.

"Sorry I was late," Tierney told the judge, "but my car battery went dead and I got a traffic ticket on my way down here."

"You've been treating this as a joke, but these matters are no joke," Judge Call said. "This case should go to trial on schedule—not at the whim of the defendant. You're not going to be tried when you feel good and ready; you're going to be tried on the date set by the court."

Tierney's father, the ex–police chief, stepped in with a hat-in-hand plea. "There are a lot of extenuating circumstances, Your Honor," he said. "My son had trouble starting his car this morning, and when he finally picked me up in Hollywood, we got a ticket for going through a stop sign."

Judge Call listened, then ran down a list of thirteen of Tierney's arrests and five forfeitures of bail. "In my opinion, this conduct is willful and deliberate and without justification," he said. "I declare the defendant in contempt."

He sentenced Tierney to five days in jail and rescheduled his trial to begin on August 13. After serving his time, if Tierney wanted to remain free until the trial, he'd have to post another $2,500 bond.

The judge turned to the bailiff. "Take him into custody."

A jury of eight women and four men was seated on August 13 for Lawrence Tierney's trial in the court of municipal judge Ben S. Beery (no relation to the acting Beerys, according to the *Los Angeles Times*, but a surname particularly fitting in Tierney's case). In opening arguments, Tierney's new attorney, Joseph Ryan, indicated that his client would plead self-defense.

The first witness called by the prosecution was the alleged victim's mother. Frances Naylor testified that she was awakened at about 5 a.m. on June 21 by two intruders outside her house. She identified one of them as Tierney. She said she watched her son, John, run out of the house to the sidewalk. Tierney, she said, was standing on a terrace. Mrs. Naylor testified she saw Tierney kick at John's head.

John Naylor testified that when he came out of the house that morning, Tierney was standing on a ledge three feet above him and kicked him so hard that his jaw was broken in three places. "I saw one of his feet coming toward me and the next thing I remember is reeling and wondering if my teeth were knocked out," he testified.

Naylor said he retreated into his house, got a twelve-inch butcher knife from the kitchen, and went back outside. That, he said, was when "everything got fuzzy."

The defense called four witnesses. First up were the Ulvand sisters. Nancy and Elizabeth both testified that they were not awakened by the racket under their window.

The most important witness followed. Defendant Lawrence Tierney took the stand and unspooled his story of what happened that morning before dawn. He testified that he showed up at the Naylor house on the evening of June 20 to visit a girlfriend who was rooming there. The girlfriend and her sister had "callers," so he and his friend Robert Crockett went across the street and spent the rest of the night and early morning playing shuffleboard. At around 5:30 a.m. on June 21, he and Crockett were cutting through the yard of 117 West Channel Road when Mrs. Naylor sicced the collie on them. Tierney, who had been accused of hitting Hella Crossley's dog in a parking lot altercation in 1946, said he regretted kicking the Naylors' dog when it attacked him.

Tierney testified that he was about to apologize when John Naylor rushed toward him from the house. When Crockett shouted a warning that Naylor had a knife, Tierney hit Naylor in self-defense, to save his own life. He denied kicking the Scientology auditor.

"I hit him with my hand," Tierney said. "I hit him twice. When somebody has a knife, I'm going to hit as hard as I can."

Crockett, who was identified as a contractor from Tucson, Arizona, backed Tierney's story. He said that Naylor was wielding a butcher knife the first time he ran out of the house. He testified that he shouted a warning to Tierney, who turned and punched Naylor with his fist. Crockett said Tierney never kicked the man.

On the third day of trial, Naylor filed a civil suit in superior court against Tierney for assault and battery. The complaint claimed that Tierney's "unprovoked" attack led Naylor to undergo an operation, have his jaws wired shut for thirty days, be forced onto a liquid diet, be unable to work for five weeks—and possibly need additional medical care. Naylor demanded $30,587.50 in damages.

Tierney's case went to the jury that day. The jury deliberated for four hours before returning with a verdict that evening. Tierney was found not guilty of disturbing the peace—but guilty of battery. The probation hearing and sentencing would take place on August 30. Tierney remained free on $2,500 bail.

"I am not guilty."

Lawrence Tierney stood defiant before Judge Ben Beery on August 30 as he faced sentencing on the battery charge. His attorney had already made a plea for probation or a new trial. "Because it was Larry Tierney and because he is in pictures," Ryan told the court, "his escapades have been blown to undo proportions."

"His trouble is alcohol," the judge replied. "Every time he has been in trouble, there has been alcohol involved."

Judge Beery said he believed the jury acted on the facts of the case and didn't know about Tierney's film career or past arrests.

"That's a matter of opinion," Tierney shot back. There was silence in the courtroom.

"Look, I realize that society must do something with a dope like me. I am not a criminal, not a thief and my actions have harmed only myself. Before, I pleaded guilty because I was guilty," he said, alluding to his lengthy police record, "but this time it will be very difficult to accept, very difficult to go to jail, because I am innocent.

"I know that I may sound just like another guy who doesn't want to go to jail, but I'm going to the Court of Appeals and farther if necessary."

The judge listened. He sentenced Tierney to 180 days in jail, but in light of the spirited plea, lopped the sentence in half. Tierney would serve ninety days. The judge granted him a one-day stay, to allow time for his lawyer to file an appeal.

Tierney remained free on bail. No matter the outcome, he could forget about any contract with Paramount—and any future movies, at all.

That was Thursday. On Friday, producer Jack Broder signed Tierney to star in *The Bushwhackers,* a Western set in post–Civil War Independence, Missouri. Broder, who was Tierney's pal, said Tierney's fate would determine the production schedule. If he received a postponement and avoided jail, filming would start immediately. Should Tierney be sent away, *The Bushwhackers* would wait.

That announcement was almost as stunning as the latest verdict and sentence. Dorothy Manners, filling in for the vacationing Louella Parsons, wrote that "this is the first time in Hollywood history that an actor with a jail term hanging over his head has been given a picture."

Tierney's latest legal troubles coincided with an outbreak of misbehavior and controversy among Hollywood stars. Cesar Romero, Bruce Cabot, and Shirley Temple's ex-husband John Agar had all been arrested for drunk driving in August. In September, Robert Walker died at thirty-two at his home on Sunset

Boulevard after his psychiatrist injected him with a sedative; Jean Wallace's ex-husband Franchot Tone was beaten into a coma by actor Tom Neal, the ex-boxer boyfriend of his on-and-off fiancée Barbara Payton; Rita Hayworth filed for divorce from Aly Khan; the House Un-American Activities Committee began sending out subpoenas for new hearings on Hollywood communists; and Errol Flynn was in arrears with taxes and reportedly "down to his last yacht."

All these scandals played out while the Council of Motion Picture Organizations was weeks away from launching "Movietown, U.S.A.," a massive publicity campaign celebrating the fiftieth anniversary of motion pictures (and attempting to counter the competition from television). Full-page ads had been taken out in newspapers, and a hundred movie stars were about to be dispatched to premieres and events in cities across the country, to tout the wholesomeness of Hollywood, its product—and stars.

Columnist Harold Heffernan suggested that the Hollywood missionaries might abandon the idea of "trying to sell Hollywood as a town of high morals and ideals" when facing local Kiwanians and Rotarians, and instead focus on the quality of the product. "They can say an honest mouthful on that one," he wrote, "for, to paraphrase the old line: 'Maybe not Hollywood, but motion pictures are better than ever.'"

Awaiting the appeal of his three-month jail sentence, it appeared that Lawrence Tierney was doing his best to get "better." He wrapped his role on *The Bushwhackers* in mid-September, and Jack Broder said he was pleased with Tierney's work as a henchman to an evil, arthritic rancher. (Broder was even happier that he had a high-profile actress in a film that was already in the can and ready for release: *Bride of the Gorilla*, starring Barbara Payton, the soft corner of Hollywood's most scandalous love triangle, who became the bride of Franchot Tone on September 28, two weeks after the groom was pummeled by his love rival.)

When Erskine Johnson reported that Edward Tierney, the aspiring writer, was penning a fan magazine piece entitled, "My Brother's a Screwball," there was a punchline: "Surprise—it's about Scott, not Lawrence."

Few people knew that Lawrence Tierney had been greatly affected by the death of Robert Walker, who'd returned to the screen earlier that summer in Alfred Hitchcock's *Strangers on a Train* after a long stay at the Menninger Clinic. Tierney had experienced a serious alcoholic relapse, and in the fall of 1951 was undergoing intense psychiatric treatment in an effort to kick the booze for good. He was at home, under a doctor's care and guarded by a nurse. His recovery seemed to be on track until October 8, 1951.

17

Barefoot

St. Monica Roman Catholic Church in Santa Monica, California, a grand limestone structure built a half mile from the ocean in 1925, was the inspiration for the 1944 film *Going My Way*, which won seven Academy Awards, including Best Picture, Actor (Bing Crosby), and Supporting Actor (Barry Fitzgerald). Best Director and Original Screenplay statuettes went to Leo McCarey, a St. Monica's parishioner who based Fitzgerald's old Irish priest Father Fitzgibbon on the church's former pastor.

At approximately six a.m., shortly after sunrise on October 8, 1951, Santa Monica police were called to St. Monica's to investigate reports of a man, described as a "shabby, barefoot loiterer"—a "bum"—prowling outside. Officers Dan Cooke and Roy Livingston rolled up and immediately spotted a white male, approximately thirty years old, unshaven, wearing a plaid sport shirt and soiled old trousers. He was barefoot.

As they approached, the man bolted and ran into the church through a back door. The policemen followed and encountered Lawrence Tierney inside. He was babbling incoherently, seemingly panicked—in their words, "mentally imbalanced"—as he ran through the church's nave, up the center aisle past worshippers who were there for early morning mass, and toward the altar. Tierney stopped short at the communion rail, genuflected, made the sign of the cross, and then rushed into the sanctuary, where he fell to his knees before the altar, praying furiously. Officers Cook and Livingston watched cautiously as Tierney prayed, hands folded, eyes clenched shut. Realizing that he was speaking "gibberish," they spoke softly to him, in an effort to coax him out.

"No!" he suddenly yelled. "You can't arrest me!" He leapt to his feet, in a fighting stance. "You can't take me! *I have sanctuary!*"

Tierney was invoking an old tradition that allows churches to harbor criminals, and a belief that police are not allowed to arrest anyone who claims sanctuary inside a church. In fact, there was no law preventing police from arresting a suspect in any house of worship. The two cops weren't so certain. One of them found a parish priest and asked for his opinion. The priest told him it was perfectly fine to arrest the man because he was causing a disturbance.

The lawmen moved in, a bit more forcefully this time. Tierney erupted, violently—swinging, punching, kicking, and clawing. He vaulted over the communion rail, hopped over the pews, and ducked into a side room. The two officers kept him penned in there until they managed to overpower and restrain him with a makeshift straitjacket made of leather straps. As they led him away, Tierney continued to prattle what the cops said were wild, convoluted stories about alcoholism and people who were out to kill him.

"*They want to murder me the way they murdered Robert Walker!*" he cried.

In the squad car on the ride to the Santa Monica Police Station, Tierney gave his age as thirty-two and his address as 333 North Doheny Drive. The police at the station made an emergency "hurry up" call to Edward Tierney. When Edward arrived at the station, his older brother punched him in the face. The police again placed Tierney in restraints before walking him to an ambulance to take him to a nearby psychiatric hospital, the Los Angeles Neurological Institute.

The press was waiting outside for the celebrity perp walk. Cameras clicked. Flashbulbs popped. The resulting photograph that appeared in the *Los Angeles Times* and on front pages across the country was a head-to-toe shot of Lawrence Tierney, hands in front of him, wrists bound by leather straps, led by the arm by a doctor, flanked by an ambulance attendant, and followed by cops. His shirt is tucked neatly. He is still without shoes or socks. He stands tall and looks straight into the camera lens with an intense glare. No image of Dillinger was so menacing, cold, or defiant as was Lawrence Tierney in that photograph.

Few photos were so heartrending.

After the ambulance drove away, Edward faced the press, in tears. "Lawrence is a sick boy," he said. "He has been under treatment by doctors and psychiatrists at his home. He needs treatment."

When the reporters brought up Tierney's past arrests, police told them that in this instance, he was not drunk. No charges would be filed against him.

The headlines the following day befitted such a sensational page one story.

MAD ACTOR TAKES REFUGE IN CHURCH

HOLLYWOOD ACTOR IS FOUND BABBLING INCOHERENTLY BEFORE

CHURCH ALTAR

LAWRENCE TIERNEY

TIERNEY GOES HAYWIRE IN HOLLYWOOD CHURCH
ACTOR TIERNEY GOES BERSERK AGAIN; CAPTURED BAREFOOT IN
CHURCH
LAWRENCE TIERNEY IS TAKEN IN STRAIT JACKET TO HOSPITAL
TIERNEY, ACTOR OF DILLINGER ROLE, IN PSYCHO WARD
MOVIE TOUGH GUY IN NUTTY WARD; ESCAPED NURSE

Doctors at the Neurological Institute said Tierney was "accepting hospitalization," and attendants confirmed "he is not presenting any trouble." Over the next few days, there were reports that Tierney's Alcoholics Anonymous buddies had rallied to help him.

Columnists had their own takes and morsels of information. "Iffy The Dopester" at the *Detroit Free Press* joked that "Lawrence Tierney, movie tough guy, has been placed in a psychopathic ward because he went to church in his bare feet. It seems he left his shoes, however, at the last bar he visited." Harrison Carroll alleged that several days before he sought sanctuary in church, Tierney "had turned fanatically religious. Spent hours praying and quoting verses from the Bible."

All of Hollywood was waiting for Jimmie Fidler to weigh in with another "I told you so." He didn't disappoint. On October 23, Fidler remarked upon "what appears to be a serious mental breakdown."

"It's been apparent that his story would end in tragedy unless he were recognized for what he was—a mentally sick man—and treated accordingly. . . . Bad as it is, it could have been a lot worse. . . . It's almost miraculous, in view of Tierney's savage belligerence when under the influence of alcohol, that the final tragedy finds him the only victim."

"*The final tragedy.*" With those words, Jimmie Fidler was closing the book on Lawrence Tierney. After all of Fidler's lectures and warnings, the final chapter ended with Lawrence Tierney as the sole victim, bound in a straitjacket in a rubber room in a psycho ward, not to be seen in public or heard from, for a long, long time.

Hours later, Tierney showed up in a bar.

The bartender at the joint at West Eighth Street and South Ardmore Avenue had no choice but to grab the phone and call the cops. It was shortly after midnight on October 24. A big Irish-looking mutt had come storming in and announced to the drinkers at the bar, "I'll whip anyone in the place!" Then he began swinging, shoving, arguing, and threatening damage. Officers J. B.

Evans and D. B. Weld from the Wilshire division pulled up in their black-and-white and pulled out the billy clubs before walking in. They found the battler right away. He was the one with the crazy look in his eyes—the one who was barefoot. He told the cops he'd been drinking for three days straight. They quoted him in their report: "I can hold my liquor. I've been drinking double shots for three days without any sleep at all and I can still carry on a conversation."

The conversation was simple enough. "What's your name?"

"Lawrence Tierney."

"Address?"

No, he wasn't giving it.

"Occupation?"

Tierney replied: "Bum."

The two officers placed Tierney in the back of their chariot, and delivered him to the Wilshire police station, where he was booked on drunk and disorderly charges, and then transported to the Lincoln Heights jail. Despite his recent hospitalization and well-publicized cry for help in the sanctuary of the *Going My Way* church, there was little sympathy for the barefoot, disheveled man. The papers said it was his thirteenth arrest in seven years. The actual number was twenty, at least.

Tierney was escorted into municipal court before Judge Harry R. Sims later that day. He pleaded "not guilty" and requested a jury trial. The judge scheduled the trial for November 23 and set bail at twenty dollars.

With Tierney back in the papers for the same wrong reasons, each of the Hollywood gossips jumped in to tear off a piece of the red meat. Danton Walker claimed he'd heard Tierney's legal and medical bills were being paid by his brother, Scott Brady. Broadway columnist Hy Gardner placed Brady's tab at "around $10,000 to keep the screen Dillinger out of the pokey."

Sheilah Graham had a scoop that could have been a simple deduction made from the police report when she claimed that Tierney's breakdown was not the result of psychosis or alcoholism. It was "lack of sleep. He wouldn't allow his doctors to give him sedatives—scared off by what happened to Robert Walker." If that was so, wasn't there a place Tierney could go to cool off? Hedda Hopper posed the question. "If drunkenness is a sickness, there are sanitariums to take care of him, and for nuisances, society has other places even more restrictive."

Should the jury convict him in this latest case, more restrictive surroundings would most likely be in Tierney's future. When he returned to court on November 23, Tierney changed his plea to "guilty." In passing sentence, municipal judge Roger Pfaff offered Tierney a deal.

"If I place you on summary probation," the judge asked, "will you give this court your word of honor that you will quit drinking? Just lay off the stuff entirely—not even a short beer?"

"Your honor," replied the actor, "I'll give you my word of honor on that. I give you my word of honor I won't drink again. And I've never given my word of honor before."

Six weeks after Tierney's breakdown at St. Monica's, four weeks after his relapse, the judge took Tierney at his word. He sentenced the actor to 180 days in jail—but suspended all but three days of the sentence under strict conditions. There would be a three-year probation period, during which Tierney must not drink intoxicants—not even that short beer; he must not enter any bars ("to keep you out of trouble, and to save you money," the judge clarified); and he must attend regular meetings of Alcoholics Anonymous.

"People can always make mistakes," the judge said. "But they can turn over a new leaf, too."

"The judge was very fair," Tierney commented to reporters as he was taken away to serve seventy-two hours behind bars, "and I intend to stick by my word to him."

The next day, in his jail cell, Tierney told a reporter he was finished with drinking "for good."

Harold Heffernan wrote that even Tierney must have been surprised by the judge's "chummy lecture" and suspended sentence. "Once again, tempestuous Tierney walked out a free man and once again, Hollywood is holding its breath, awaiting developments."

As Christmas approached, Harrison Carroll's aide Armand Archerd penned the annual celebrity wish list column. The letter to Mr. S. Claus listed what his "little friends in Glamorville" would "like to find in their stockings." Lawrence Tierney? "One more chance."

Most everyone in Glamorville seemed to agree that Tierney's best chance was with Alcoholics Anonymous, which Sheilah Graham reported he had again joined. "Hope he sticks with it this time."

On December 28, Jimmie Fidler, who'd written Tierney's career epitaph two months earlier, returned to Tierney one last time in 1951—to correct his "final tragedy" eulogy. Tierney's career was not dead, after all. "I'm reasonably sure that no other actor in Hollywood history has had as much bad publicity as he has had," Fidler wrote. "If bad publicity can ruin a career, his should have been wrecked beyond repair long, long, ago."

Fidler shared with his readers the reason for his rant. The Hollywood trade papers had reported that a new, independent company called Kendall-Kirkwood Productions was planning to produce a movie called *The Roughneck*. The actor signed to play the title role was none other than Lawrence Tierney, "the confirmed (until now at least) alcoholic who only two or three months ago, went on such a rampage that he had to be committed to an institution for psychiatric treatment."

The producer behind the headline was Jack Kendall, who did not appear to have any other pictures under his belt, but did seem to possess a good sense of the international publicity his announcement would generate.

"I don't feel like I'm taking a chance," Kendall told a United Press reporter. "Tierney's convinced me of his sincerity to make good. I don't feel he has any worse problems than anybody who's down on his luck and doesn't know how to get back. He just needs a chance to show what he can do. He's a very good actor. That's why I choose him."

Kendall said Tierney was simply a victim of typecasting. "We signed him to play a peace officer in one movie and a truck driver in another," Kendall claimed. "They're all nice guys. After he gets a couple of good roles under his belt, people will forget that Dillinger legend and the heckling will stop.

"Before I signed Larry, I invited him to my home. When he's away from Hollywood and the Sunset Strip, he loses his tension and becomes a different, relaxed person. He's intelligent and has a sense of humor. He's a member of Alcoholics Anonymous. When I offered him a drink, he stuck to orange juice. . . . When I offered him the role, he didn't believe it at first. He joked that it must be a jail picture, since he had experience for that.

"Many producers wanted to hire him, but I think they were afraid to," Kendall said. "I don't think he'll be any problem."

Once again, Hollywood was holding its breath, awaiting developments.

18

Socialite Socked

The world premiere of Cecil B. DeMille's Big Top epic, *The Greatest Show on Earth,* took place on January 10, 1952, at Radio City Music Hall. Bosley Crowther at the *New York Times* called the film "a piece of entertainment that will delight movie audiences for years. . . . Glittering in marvelous Technicolor—truly marvelous color, we repeat—this huge motion picture of the big-top is the dandiest ever put upon the screen." The picture received four out of four stars in the *Daily News.* Kate Cameron wrote, "*The Greatest Show on Earth* is just that."

Betty Hutton, Cornel Wilde, and television actor Charlton Heston starred. James Stewart, Dorothy Lamour, and Gloria Grahame played supporting roles—and Lawrence Tierney had a part as a racketeer who runs crooked games on the midway. Tierney was billed ninth, between Lyle Bettger and real-life clown Emmett Kelly, but his showy and pivotal role put him in A-list company and had him on screen in the best theaters.

Days after the Radio City triumph, Dorothy Kilgallen reported that Tierney still had a desire to check in at the Menninger Clinic—but couldn't afford the treatment. If he was determined to confront his problems, there was another potential rehabilitation route. The week after the *Greatest Show* premiere, he was off on a promotional tour for *The Bushwhackers.* First stop was Chicago, and the movie's premiere at McVicker's Theater on Madison Street. Tierney was traveling with a group that included costar Dorothy Malone—the on-again, off-again girlfriend of his brother Scott Brady. Sheilah Graham reported that Brady denied sending Dorothy Malone an ultimatum to marry him. "I'm not ready to marry," he said, but Graham knew better. "He'll marry Dotty if she will only give him the nod."

The *Chicago Tribune's* critic wasn't impressed by *The Bushwhackers.* Mae Tinee called it "a third-rate western . . . acted by as hammy a group of amateurs as ever cluttered the screen. Most of these sorry souls are eventually killed off during the gunplay—but not nearly fast enough to suit my taste."

The tour continued through February, and Tierney received high marks for his interviews on television, and his good behavior, which was attributed in part to the presence of Malone. There were no reports of dalliances with his brother's love. Al Salerno of Tierney's hometown *Brooklyn Daily Eagle* called the actor "a model of the virtues." Kilgallen disclosed that Tierney had another gal, anyway: singer Joan Whitney, "who once had King Farouk on her string of admirers."

Roger Kendall made news on March 12, 1952, when he announced, in Erskine Johnson's column, another future Kendall–Kirkwood production. *Prisoner of War* would star the radioactive Tom Neal and Barbara Payton. Neal and Payton were again an item—with her estranged husband Franchot Tone the odd man out and seeking a divorce. The couple had been as good as blacklisted since Neal's brutal assault on Tone, but that didn't stop Kendall from casting Neal (whose career had peaked with the 1945 film noir *Detour*) as an American soldier and Payton as an army nurse. Kendall claimed that movie exhibitors were "crying" for a Neal–Payton picture. "The public," he proclaimed, "is the first to forgive stars who have made human mistakes. Tom's a good actor and Barbara's box office."

Cameras never rolled on the picture.

Kendall–Kirkwood never came through with the promised Tierney movies, either. In any case, Tierney wouldn't be available in the near future. He was in jail.

That news was revealed the day after Kendall's latest announcement. Tierney's attorney, Bentley Harris, showed up in Los Angeles Municipal Court to file an appeal in the John Naylor battery case. Harris said he'd located witnesses who'd back Tierney's claim that he acted in self-defense. Meanwhile, Harris's client had slipped into court six days earlier and was sentenced to serve the ninety days. Before the press could get wind, Tierney had been processed back into the Wayside Drunk Farm.

Tierney celebrated his thirty-third birthday on the prison farm. He was released on May 12, after serving sixty-four days. Judge Beery modified Tierney's sentence to time served, after Harris told the judge his client had "an important" role coming up at Eagle-Lion Studios. The attorney also pointed out that Tierney had been a model prisoner and was again a "devout" member of Alcoholics Anonymous. Judge Beery replied that Tierney was entitled to sentence modification because of his good behavior, regardless of any movie contract. Tierney would remain on probation for three years—no drinking, no bars, all AA—terms set by municipal judge Roger A. Pfaff after the last drunk conviction.

Franchot Tone got a divorce from Barbara Payton on May 19, 1952. Payton went off with Tom Neal, for a while. Tone would go off with Lawrence Tierney.

(Neither Payton nor Neal was talented enough to transcend the scandal. She slid into alcoholism, drug abuse, and street prostitution, and died of heart and liver failure on the floor of her parents' bathroom on May 8, 1967. She was thirty-nine. Neal quit Hollywood and became a landscaper in Palm Springs. He was fifty-eight when he died of natural causes on August 7, 1972, eight months after he was released from prison, where he'd served six years for shooting his third wife to death.)

Tierney's "important role" at Eagle-Lion did not materialize. Tierney would not be returning to a Hollywood studio lot, but setting off on the straw-hat circuit in the play *The Petrified Forest*.

Robert Sherwood's two-act drama is a tale of existential desperation set in the Black Mesa Bar-B-Q, a gas station and lunchroom at a highway crossroads in the Arizona desert. Among the crowd is a waitress who dreams of becoming a painter in Paris, a destitute British writer whom she sees as her ticket out, and a desperate gangster (very much like John Dillinger) who shows up and holds everyone hostage. The play was published in 1935, opened on Broadway at the Broadhurst Theatre on January 7 of that year, and ran for 197 performances. Leslie Howard played the writer Alan Squier. Peggy Conklin was waitress Gaby, and Humphrey Bogart took the stage as badman Duke Mantee. Bogart won the role in part because of his physical resemblance to Dillinger, who'd been gunned down the previous July and on whom the character was based. Bogart and Howard reprised their roles, with Bette Davis as Gaby, in the 1936 film version. It was Bogart's ticket to the Warner Bros. gangster gang—and movie stardom.

Forty-seven-year-old Franchot Tone, as Squier, was the marquee name in this summer stock version. Gaby was embodied by Betsy von Furstenberg, a twenty-year-old Broadway and television actress whose name columnists mocked as, among others, "Betsy Von Liverwurst" and "Betsy Von Thingamajig." Betsy, three years and nine months younger than Barbara Payton, was Tone's latest fiancée. The tour would be something of a pre-honeymoon getaway. Tone planned to act, win kudos, and spend nights with his young love, far from the eyes and spies of the gossip press. There was a hitch in Tone's plans when Betsy pushed hard to cast Lawrence Tierney as Duke Mantee. Tone relented and offered Tierney the role on the condition that he stay far away from alcohol during the run. For the most part, Tierney did. He did not stay away from Betsy.

The tour opened on June 9 at the Cameo Summer Theatre in Miami Beach. Herb Rau of the *Miami News* was on the aisle, and on the streets of Miami the next morning with a review of a "choppy presentation" that, "despite its flaws—and there were many . . . still provided a measure of entertainment for what was termed a 'good house.'"

The showbiz columnist-turned-theater critic found that Tone's "tongue-in-cheek treatment seemed to conflict with what is obviously the role of a dreamer." Betsy von Furstenberg "played the desert girl with little authority or impact." And Lawrence Tierney? "More down-to-earth, and fitting the role to the first letter of his last name, Lawrence Tierney played gunman Duke Mantee to the hilt. Bogart couldn't have done better."

"Fitting the role to the first letter of his last name." Word of Tierney's strong performance reached Hollywood. Jimmie Fidler, who'd had his fill of Lawrence Tierney by this point, pulled out a one-liner to run that morning: "Amazing how Lawrence Tierney's career continues to prosper when you consider how many bottle necks it's encountered!"

From Miami Beach, it was fourteen hundred miles north and across the border for six shows in Ontario, Canada, at the Niagara Falls Summer Theatre, operated by Tone's aunt, Maude Franchot. By the middle of the run, Fidler toned down the sarcasm, commenting, "Most Hollywoodites seem to be of the opinion that the teaming of Franchot Tone and Lawrence Tierney in a stage presentation of *The Petrified Forest* is perfect typecasting."

Greater plaudits were ahead at the Triple Cities Playhouse theater, 220 miles southeast in Binghamton, New York. Tierney, Tone, and von Furstenberg checked into the Colonial Motel on the Vestal Highway on the afternoon of Sunday, June 22, then headed straight to the Masonic Temple on Main Street to rehearse. The rehearsal, with a cast consisting of Broadway actors and locals from the Playhouse, went into the early morning.

The Binghamton *Press and Sun Bulletin* reported that Tierney was on the straw-hat tour in preparation for his first appearance on Broadway. Its review of Monday night's opening performance made it clear he was ready: "Mr. Tierney, for one, is probably the most convincing killer we have ever seen on the stage. Terse, tough and able to snap attention to himself with one word, he is shudder-provoking." Years later, Von Furstenberg told Rick McKay that when Tierney was onstage, "no one even saw her or Franchot." Von Furstenberg considered Tierney "a natural, with a God-given brilliant stage presence," who "knew all of Shakespeare" and "taught her everything about acting" while they were on the road.

It was evident that the stage—and distance from Hollywood—brought out the artist in Lawrence Tierney. He'd shined brighter than Tracy and Gable in *The Last Mile*, stepped into Brando's role in *A Streetcar Named Desire*, and now had not only outdone Bogart in *The Petrified Forest* but was also the subject of newspaper stories that didn't involve violence or insobriety. According to *Press and Sun Bulletin* columnist Tom Cawley, when Tierney asked local radio host Vicky Levene if he could borrow a book from her library, she pointed him to "the blood-and-thunder thrillers." Tierney passed them up for a volume of poetry by W. H. Auden.

For many in Hollywood, these months of dedication proved that Tierney could be a good boy, after all. People were ready to believe in him.

Not Jimmie Fidler. On Saturday, the day of Tierney's final two performances in Binghamton, Fidler erupted over another columnist's quote that "a fine actor has to leave Hollywood to be recognized by Hollywood—as witness Lawrence Tierney's road success in *The Petrified Forest.*"

"That one REALLY left me gasping," Fidler raged, professing to be shocked that "any Hollywood producer has been courageous enough to trust him with a job of any kind in view of his record."

Fidler may have known more than he let on. Offstage, Tierney was not the model citizen the local papers portrayed, and he'd broken his vow to "stay dry" through the run of *The Petrified Forest*. The truth came out three years later, when Vince Bird of the *Scrantonian* revealed that during the Binghamton stand, "Mr. Tierney . . . consumed more than a fifth between matinee and evening show each afternoon and probably trebled the dosage from final curtain until the 1 a.m. curfew each night."

Bird recalled that Tierney had paid attention to a "local chick" at the closing night's party, sending "Von-watzername . . . into a paroxysm that was better than her emoting in the show."

Betsy von Furstenberg confirmed the gossip when she spoke to McKay. "Betsy said he was great, didn't drink, and stole the show," McKay wrote. "Until the last of the run anyway, when there was an 'incident.' She did not want to go into details, but it ended with a chair being thrown through a window in an upstate New York motel room and the police coming."

Jimmie Fidler was certain there was more trouble to come. The only question was when . . . and where.

The stars of *The Petrified Forest* returned to New York City—and the Broadway columnists were rubbing their hands together in anticipation. Kilgallen and Wilson caught on in mid-July to Tierney's fling with von Furstenberg, after the couple were sighted at the weekly jam session at Lou Terrasi's jazz club on West Forty-Seventh Street. Dorothy Manners surmised that their dates indicated that von Furstenberg's affair with Tone "can't be too serious." It was serious enough, but his encounter with Tom Neal still fresh in his memory, Tone had wisely stepped back—if not out of the picture.

Despite the three-year probation and drinking ban back in Los Angeles, Tierney returned to his old stomping grounds, and was seen in the drinkeries that lined the sidewalks under the Third Avenue elevated railway. On Friday night, August 8, he was back at P. J. Clarke's. He had just walked in and found a place at the bar when a stranger pushed through the crowd toward him.

Tierney wasn't in the mood to deal with strangers, fans, or another drunk proving to his pals that Dillinger wasn't so tough, after all. He just wanted to drink some gin, in peace. It was a quarter to nine when he entered Clarke's and walked toward the bar, only to have this swell leave his table, and greet him like he was the manager or something.

"Lawrence Tierney!" he announced. "Just wanted to welcome you—"

Tierney glanced at the intrusion. "Get away from me, ya crumb," he growled, and brushed him off with an arm.

The "crumb" was Seward Heaton, a thirty-five-year-old Philadelphia "socialite," now living across town on West Fifty-Fifth Street. Heaton was an annoying and well-known member of the "awfully social set." In 1946, he'd been beaten up by Veronica Lake's husband Andre de Toth at the Stork Club. Heaton shrugged off Tierney's brush-off and returned to his party, which included his date, a tall, blonde television actress named Joyce Quinlan. Everyone laughed and got back to their drinks. Tierney took a seat at the bar.

Seward Heaton got up again and attempted once more to say "hello." Tierney ignored him, mumbled for the fella to be on his way. The third time—it may have been the fourth—Tierney had had enough.

Seward Heaton only wanted to say "hello"—Tierney turned, swung, and punched him right between the eyes. Heaton was launched back. His forehead was torn in a half-inch gash and blood trickled down his face. Before he had a chance to react—if this socialite would even choose to fight back—some good men of café society got between the two men in sharp suits. Somebody called the cops. Someone else called the papers.

When the police arrived, Seward Heaton didn't want to press charges. He and Joyce Quinlan made their way to a car at the curb. She stopped to pose in the flashbulb lights for photos that would appear in the *Daily News* and other papers in the morning: she, smiling as if she were at a premiere; Heaton with his cut head, looking sheepish behind her. The *News* got a shot of Tierney, walking away from the cameras, a cop leading him, not to jail but out of the line of fire.

That was the night the tables turned again. The next day, it wasn't Lawrence Tierney the stage actor making headlines, it was Lawrence Tierney, "who has been arrested thirteen times in the last eight years on charges ranging from drunkenness to assault," in another bar fight. "TIERNEY BRAWLS AGAIN," the *Daily News* trumpeted. "SOCKS SOCIALITE IN BAR." "BARROOM CHAMP DEFENDS TITLE." "LAWRENCE TIERNEY FLATTENS SOCIALITE." The headlines were variations on a theme: Tierney, the victor in another one-punch bout, just like in the old days.

This wasn't Hollywood. Columnists in Manhattan were not in the business of defending the movie industry. Their job was to collect and spill dirt with a quip, and they thrived on action. When metro reporters were assigned a story about a Hollywood tough guy, those East Coast city boys would lace it with mockery. How else would a cynical New Yorker react to the bad boy behavior of a grown-up Hollywood movie star? Lawrence Tierney made for good copy. Nothing personal.

In the days after the incident on Third Avenue, the spies were on the lookout. Wilson was tipped that Tierney was seen with actress Sandra Scott at The Embers, the piano jazz club and restaurant on East Fifty-Fourth Street. A few weeks later, Kilgallen reported on a second meeting between Tierney and Seward Heaton. This time, the two men shook hands "and made up."

Tierney's name remained in the papers almost every day over the next couple of months, but only in the movie ads. He wasn't getting calls or offers from Hollywood. The *Los Angeles Times* reported interest in Tierney starring in one of two pictures focused on American Indians: *Custer's Last Stand* and *Chief Sitting Bull*. The project was being pushed by Hy Signer, a Canadian executive with the Hansen Packing Company of Butte, Montana (best known for its Vitamont canned dog food), along with Canadian investors who wanted to shoot exteriors in Calgary.

When Tierney returned to the columns in November, it wasn't because of his next project.

Danton Walker, November 12: "Lawrence Tierney around town making the same tiresome publicity (two 'incidents' already reported)."

Dorothy Kilgallen, November 17: "Lawrence Tierney slugged a newspaperman, for no apparent reason, outside a Third Avenue saloon the other morning." [The newspaperman was later revealed to be Ed Wilcox of the *Mirror*.]

Leonard Lyons, November 17: "Lawrence Tierney's latest scrap in N. Y. was with James Reardon, the ex-detective involved in the Harry Gross bookie case." [Reardon was a former NYPD detective, convicted of perjury in a graft scandal in which dozens of policemen were convicted and more than two hundred fired or reassigned.]

Walter Winchell, November 30: "Lawrence Tierney's latest target, George Frazier (at Clarke's)." [Frazier was a jazz critic, journalist, and magazine writer whose favorite word was "duende."]

One item that escaped notice was Tierney's ongoing affair with Betsy von Furstenberg. While gossips including Kilgallen and Fidler reported that Franchot Tone was on schedule to take Betsy as his latest bride over the Christmas holidays, in reality von Furstenberg was still besotted with Tierney, who was helping her prepare for her next role on Broadway.

She was signed to play the lead in *Josephine,* a comedy based on short stories by F. Scott Fitzgerald. The show was scheduled to open in February, but by December, during rehearsals, the affair had fallen victim to Tierney's drinking and temper. Von Furstenberg told Rick McKay that the last time she saw Tierney, "he was on a binge and trying to break into her apartment and the police were involved then, too." When *Josephine* opened its out-of-town tryouts in Wilmington, Delaware, on January 8, 1953, Franchot Tone flew in from the West Coast to be in the audience. The play, which costarred Orson Bean and Leslie Nielsen, moved on to Washington, DC, Chicago, and Philadelphia, but closed before reaching New York. By March, von Furstenberg was onstage in

St. Petersburg, Florida, in another production: the "gay, sophisticated comedy," *The Second Man*. Her costar was "former flame" Franchot Tone. In part because of von Furstenberg's feelings for Tierney, she and Tone never married.

Back in New York, three-year probation be damned, Lawrence Tierney was on another binge. Erskine Johnson quoted a letter he'd written to a pal back in Hollywood that summed up his plight. "It's funny having kids stop you on the streets for autographs when you're wondering what the hell you're going to do next."

19

Making Faces

I've never been asked to Morocco's Round Table
To me the Cub Room is strictly a fable,
I don't read Variety—don't even know Abel
And I never get tips straight from Vanderbilt's stable . . .
And to show the drabness of my life's jeerney,
I've never been slugged by Lawrence Tierney.

LEE MORTIMER, NEW YORK CONFIDENTIAL, AUGUST 11, 1953

Lieutenant Edgar Hicks of the Santa Monica Police Department was driving toward an intersection in the Ocean Park section of the city on the evening of Tuesday, February 10, 1953, when he eased on the brakes. A taxicab was stopped in the middle of the street and blocking traffic. Lieutenant Hicks watched as a large man stumbled from the back of the cab and approached the car directly behind him. The man stood in front of the vehicle, blocking its path, and began waving a bottle and . . . *making funny faces.*

Lieutenant Hicks stepped into the street and could see there were three women in the car. Their reactions to the man leaning toward their windshield ranged from amusement to fear. As the policeman got closer, the man staggered away, toward two men seated on a bus stop bench. He slid in between them and loudly, sloppily, urged them to help finish off the bottle. It was a bottle of gin. It was half filled.

Lieutenant Hicks took custody of the bottle. After questioning the man, he took custody of him too, placing him under arrest for drunkenness and disorderly conduct.

The man was Lawrence Tierney.

When he was booked at the police station, Tierney was asked his age. He replied, "I'm 140 years old."

Asked his address, Tierney answered, "I'm just a little pigeon who has no home."

He was walked to the drunk tank.

George Tolch, the taxi driver, followed Hicks's car back to the station. Tierney still owed him the seven-dollar fare.

Tierney's appearance in Judge Thurlow T. Taft's courtroom Wednesday morning attracted extra attention because he shared the docket with Shirley Temple's ex-husband, the actor John Agar. Agar had been transported from county jail, where he'd been locked up since February 1 on drunk driving charges that violated his three-year drunk driving probation. Agar and Tierney were portrayed in the press as a sad doubles act. Jack Kofoed in Miami Beach tagged them as "two of the most tragic figures in Hollywood," who'd taken a worse beating by John Barleycorn "than Chuck Davey took from Kid Gavilan." It was forgotten that only weeks earlier, Edith Gwynn had the exclusive news that "Scott Brady's incorrigible brother" (Tierney was now second-billed in the family) was about to make another comeback in an Eagle-Lion picture called *Brass Check*.

Taft set Tierney's bail at $100 and ordered him to return to court at 9:30 a.m. Friday. When Tierney was a no-show, the judge ordered his bail forfeited, reset bail at $500, and issued a warrant for his arrest. The search began at 710 North Doheny Drive on the edge of Beverly Hills, which Tierney had given as his address.

Tierney didn't surface for seven days. When he did, it was in New York City.

The first sighting was Friday night at the Blue Angel nightclub at 152 East Fifty-Fifth Street, where comedian Robert Clary had recently joined the New Faces Revue. Dorothy Kilgallen reported that the "Hollywood bad boy" stomped in on February 20 and turned the air blue, cursing out the waiters and "really asking for a bashed nose" because "two of them are good enough with their dukes to spar with Rocky Graziano." Lucky for Tierney, "a couple of cooler heads rushed him out of the place just in time."

A week or so later, Earl Wilson reported that Tierney had given "a press agent a shiner." Kilgallen identified the victim as Chic Farmer and the location as P. J. Clarke's. After the one-puncher, Tierney apologized, "confessing it was just 'drunk stuff.'"

The following night, Tierney was seen at the bar in the Trader Tom Steakhouse on West Forty-Eighth Street. Kilgallen commented that "he appeared to have repented," because he wasn't drinking, but playing chess.

While Lawrence Tierney rampaged through the niteries of Manhattan, younger brother Ed made headlines back in Los Angeles. He was being sued for divorce.

Who even knew he was married? The twenty-four-year-old, who'd been doing some television acting, had gotten hitched in Palm Springs on January 25, 1952. His bride was Hannelore Axman, a red-haired, German-born actress best known for the 1949 film noir, *The Red Menace*. In the divorce filed by Hollywood attorney J. George Bragin, she gave her age as twenty-six. That was her Hollywood age. She was actually pushing thirty-two. Hannelore was charging cruelty and claimed that she and Edward Tierney had been living apart since August 1.

The twenty-fifth Academy Awards ceremony took place on March 19, 1953. The Oscars show was the first to be televised and, with audiences in the RKO Pantages Theatre on Hollywood Boulevard and the NBC International Theatre on Columbus Circle, the first to take place in Hollywood and New York City simultaneously.

The Academy Award for Best Motion Picture went to *The Greatest Show on Earth*, over a slate of nominees that included *High Noon* and *The Quiet Man*.

Lawrence Tierney followed up the prestigious honor for the film he'd helped lift by getting into a scrape outside a nightclub in Greenwich Village. Jimmie Fidler had the exclusive, thousands of miles away in Hollywood. He reported that Tierney had taken a swing at another publicity man, but that "fortunately for Tierney there were few people around," and he avoided arrest and more headlines in the New York tabloids.

Earl Wilson got even and got a laugh the following day, with his one-liner: "Lawrence Tierney punched a cocktail party wit who called him 'a star of gin-erama.'"

Hannelore Axman got her divorce from Edward Tierney on April 21. The actress testified that her husband's frequent, unexplained absences led to a separation after six months. She claimed that she'd been unable to sleep and became so nervous that she couldn't work in movies or television, "because my husband would stay away from home" as often as three nights a week.

The next morning, one paper headlined the story, "Tierney Divorced by Reich-Born Actress."

❧

He may have been a star of the Oscar-winning Best Picture, but in the spring and summer of 1953, Lawrence Tierney was just another New Yorker. He moved into an apartment at 40-28 102nd Street in Corona, deep in the borough of Queens, but only blocks from the elevated train that would transport him into Manhattan. That was where, in the bars and nightclubs, he did his acting, always counted on for "being colorful," as Kilgallen reported on June 10 when Tierney "took a stranger's girl away from him, slugged the fellow, and left in a cab with the girl before police arrived."

While Tierney carried on, the gossips in Hollywood continued to spit up the lines fed by press agents and publicists. Tierney "hasn't touched a drop of liquor in three months," Louella Parsons decreed three days after his return to the columns for slugging that poor sap and making off with his date. Parsons had the scoop that Tierney would start rehearsals in July for his Broadway debut in a show called *Black Candle*. "Larry says he will be conspicuously missing from the nightspots while he learns his script and keeps out of the way of temptation." According to Kilgallen, the producer decided to take a chance on Tierney after witnessing him help a downtrodden vagrant.

Earl Wilson followed along with the new angle that the actor was "retired as a barroom brawler." He had Tierney "sipping orange juice and playing chess with a girl at the Shelburne Café." When Louella Parsons was handed a sighting, the girl was identified as former showgirl and Broadway comedy actress June Kirby; June and Tierney were holding hands and drinking milk. In Kilgallen's sighting of the couple at Club Zanzibar, Tierney appeared to be "sober, amiable and unmenacing . . . so maybe the reform wave is on." Even so, June was "brave."

Tierney's most controversial scenes during the early summer were tied to the weather, which was particularly hot and sticky. Actor Gordon MacRae was the first to perform the shocking act in public, at Bruno's Pen & Pencil steakhouse on East Forty-Fifth Street. Tierney followed suit days later, when he walked into Little Bohemia, singer Vera Niva's restaurant on East Sixty-Sixth Street, sporting a yachting cap—and wearing Bermuda shorts. Tierney's and MacRae's solution to beating the heat—venturing into public establishments "with their knees hanging out"—made news, stirred debate, and helped lead to a loosening of the men's dress code at a time when suits and ties were de rigueur, at the office by day, and in restaurants and bars in evenings.

This was a summer of change for Lawrence Tierney. Even Winchell, in a column dedicated to the "passing parade" of celebrities in the city, noted Tierney's "winning smile when he isn't ruffled by bores."

Tierney continued his unruffled run until the twenty-fifth day of July, when he appeared on Broadway. Tierney's debut was not opening night for *Black Candle*. This was a two-man show, early in the morning, on the sidewalk at the corner of Fifty-Second Street.

Even at 3 a.m. on a Saturday, Lawrence Tierney managed to attract a crowd. As many as two hundred people stopped to watch this performance, a few doors east of Gallagher's Steakhouse, a few blocks west of the row of jazz clubs known as Swing Street. Tierney and another man were squared off, about to take swings at each other.

Tierney pulled off his jacket, tossed it to the sidewalk, put up his dukes, and challenged his opponent to take his best shot. The other man, younger, even more muscular, jutted his chin forward, spat back insults, and shrugged off his own coat. Swearing, daring, shouting, and circling under the streetlights, the two men looked ready to box.

No one threw a punch.

Patrolman James McDermott arrived and told the pair to break it up and move along. Tierney and his foe continued to curse each other, loudly, daring the other to initiate the battle. McDermott's reinforcements moved in and the two reluctant boxers were arrested for, as the Associated Press reported, "making ferocious pugilistic gestures at each other." Neither man had been hit or even attempted to strike a blow. Neither would say what they were arguing about.

At the police precinct, Tierney's opponent was identified as twenty-four-year-old Michael Santobello of Queens, also known as Mike Sands, a former welterweight boxer and nephew of Miami Beach fight impresario Chris Dundee. Officer McDermott wrote up the pair for being "boisterous, using abusive language and causing a crowd to collect," and Tierney and Sands were charged with disorderly conduct.

The two of them appeared in court later that day. As the court clerk read the complaint they faced, Tierney interrupted him and began to protest the charges and arrests.

Bang! Magistrate Louis J. Pagnucco slammed down the gavel and cut him off. "Look, Tierney," he said, "I know you're an actor, but you don't have to act in this court."

The judge set bail at $100 for each no-punch pugilist and set a hearing for the following Friday. Tierney made bail and headed home to Queens.

On Monday evening, he was back in Manhattan, making the rounds of bars. It was past midnight, early Tuesday morning in the Tiger Lily Lounge on East Forty-First Street, that the trouble started all over again.

The Tiger Lily Cocktail Lounge was a piano bar just down the block from the Third Avenue El and the strip of taverns in its shadow. After Monday night, July 27, 1953, blended into the wee small hours of Tuesday morning, Benjamin Martini was on the job, at the piano, tickling the ivories, warbling the standards, and taking requests. Tierney was drinking at the bar when he was moved to join in. He walked up and asked the piano man if he knew the song, "I Wonder Where My Old Girl Is Tonight."

Martini nodded in the affirmative. Tierney took the heavy microphone and Martini began to play. Tierney, no Sinatra, even after a few drinks, began to vocalize.

He warbled the first verse, and made it to the line, "'and I wonder where my old girl is tonight,'" when a voice boomed from the bar and through the small club.

"*I bet your mother's wondering, too!*"

Tierney stopped, and after a few more notes, Martini stopped playing. Tierney squinted toward the bar, or wherever the voice had come from.

"Hey pal, I'm no professional singer," he said defensively.

There was no response from the heckler.

"And he . . ." Tierney, looked sneeringly at his accompanist, and announced, "is no piano player!"

Tierney gave Martini a look. Martini picked up the song.

Tierney made it through another eight bars—"'And I wonder'"—and stopped. He raised the microphone in his hand and bopped Benjamin Martini over the head with it. Martini's hands went from the keyboard to his skull. Tierney stormed out of the place.

Benjamin Martini went to Roosevelt Hospital to be treated for lacerations on his scalp. He also stopped at the police precinct to file a complaint—an action that made the papers later in the day.

For Tierney, they were more bad headlines in a bad week to be in them. On Friday, July 31, he was back in Mid-Manhattan Court, side by side with Mike Sands, the former pro boxer he didn't hit, and who didn't hit him, on the corner of Broadway and Fifty-Second Street. Magistrate Charles Solomon couldn't hide his disgust at this waste of the people's time.

"All the world is *not* a stage," Solomon lectured. "This is the sort of stuff that is grist for the Moscow propaganda mill." He addressed Tierney. "What is the sense of this thing? What is the trouble? Do you want to ruin a career?"

As he had in the bail hearing, Tierney told the judge he never should have been charged in the first place. "I don't feel I was in the wrong in this instance," Tierney replied.

"Don't you feel you owe something to the movie industry that has made you a star?"

"I don't believe I owe the industry anything," Tierney said. "I've earned ten million dollars for RKO."

The judge could only shake his head. He fined both men twenty-five dollars and sentenced them to thirty days in jail—but suspended the sentences.

Tierney's attorneys paid his fine. When that was done, two detectives moved in and took Tierney into custody, to be charged with felonious assault on Benjamin Martini. In his felony court appearance the following Tuesday, Tierney claimed the "attack" on the pianist was an accident. The charge was reduced to simple assault, and trial was set for special sessions court. A panel of three judges would decide his fate.

After a parade of arrests in Los Angeles, the relocated Tierney was now "compiling a similarly black reputation in New York," with two recent incidents that "might easily have resulted in someone being killed or permanently injured." That, of course, was the opinion of an observer on the West Coast who was prompted by the recent riot of Tierney headlines to weigh in one more, most likely futile, time. Jimmie Fidler tried a new tack: focusing on Scott Brady and Tierney's family. Fidler announced on August 11 that he no longer felt sorry for Tierney's relatives because of the embarrassment the eldest son had caused them. "Now I am convinced that they, too, are open to criticism for their failure to commit Larry to an institution where he would receive badly needed treatment." Fidler argued that no matter how bitterly Tierney would react to the intervention, it would be preferable to him serving a long jail sentence—or killing someone. "With that knowledge, there should be no further delay on the part of Brady or other members of Tierney's family in signing the necessary commitment papers."

Hiding out in a mental institution might not have been the worst option in light of the potentially deadly fix Tierney had gotten himself into between court appearances. The day after the Martini ruling, Earl Wilson reported that Tierney was "slated for a slugging" after getting into a fight with the brother of a mobster. Shrugged Wilson: "The boys will handle it." Lee Mortimer had the skinny on August 12 on how it would be handled: "Three goons have been hired at $250 each to rearrange Lawrence Tierney's profile." The price, he mused, was "cheaper than a good nose-job."

Two days later, Mortimer reported that a woman in a Third Avenue tavern beat the goons to the job: she smashed two chairs over Tierney's head. "Did she get the dough? Meanwhile the bandaged Tierney has been barred from Clarke's, Glennon's and practically every other saloon in town and this is notice that he is now barred from this column."

Tierney was in special sessions court on Monday. A three-judge panel—James Breslin, James Mulcahy, and Myles A. Paige—would decide the "simple assault" charge. The alleged victim, Benjamin Martini, was first to testify. Revealing his age as forty-two and his legal name as Benjamin Azzara, the pianist said he was at the keyboard in the Tiger Lily Cocktail Lounge on July 28 when the defendant requested and began to sing "I Wonder Where My Old Girl Is Tonight." Martini told about the heckler, Tierney's response, and how the defendant ultimately brought down the heavy metal microphone onto the piano player's cranium.

Tierney testified that the microphone had been knocked over accidentally. A waiter and two bartenders supported his version.

The three judges deliberated for ten minutes before returning with a split decision. Justice Paige registered a "guilty" vote. The two Irishmen, Breslin and Mulcahy, voted to acquit.

Tierney walked free, but not into the sunshine. The following morning, he awoke to Earl Wilson's claim that he'd "staged" the street corner brawl, "thinking it'd be good publicity for an actor buddy." A week later, Wilson reported that "Lawrence Tierney lost another street corner decision."

While September was surprisingly noneventful—Wilson reported Tierney had gotten the bum's rush from the Beekman Tower Hotel, not for fighting but for wearing Bermuda shorts—October was more cruel. On October 9, a Winchell tipster placed Tierney back at the Tiger Lily, "doing the posies-in-the-hand bit for Barbara Kelly," who owned the joint. Tierney was begging to get back in her good graces, but he had more serious amends to make. Kilgallen reported the same day that Benjamin Martini was suing him for $50,000.

The most unfortunate, and truly sad news for Tierney arrived in a double dose from Hollywood that weekend. Edith Gwynn filed the first report on Saturday. Younger brother Edward Tierney, the kid brother who Larry had eased into Hollywood (and the criminal justice system), was putting his literary aspirations aside and sticking to acting. There was a catch: Edward Michael Tierney was also distancing himself from his brother. He would now be billed as "Ed Tracy."

An even more surprising blow to the Tierney family brand was provided by the former Gerard Kenneth Tierney. The stolid middle brother had years earlier taken the stage and screen name Scott Brady—a name change that columnist Howard Heffernan said was "mandatory" because "no brother could hope to travel anywhere on Lawrence's sorry reputation." Scott Brady had earned a reputation as the clean-living antithesis of the boozing, brawling Lawrence Tierney.

On Saturday, October 10, Scott Brady attended a party in Beverly Hills. He left the party sometime after midnight, got in his car, and drove off down Sunset Boulevard, heading home.

Los Angeles police lieutenant Sam Posner spotted the car driving erratically, and witnessed the driver steering with one hand—and drinking from a highball glass in the other! When the cop pulled the car to the curb, Brady tossed the glass over his shoulder into the backseat. Brady submitted to a "drunkometer test" at the police station and failed. He was booked under his given name, Gerard K. Tierney.

Facing misdemeanor drunk driving charges in Los Angeles Municipal Court, Brady admitted that he'd been at a party and left with "one for the road." He was fined $250 and swore he was on the wagon, "for life."

Scott Brady went to work at Republic Pictures on *Johnny Guitar* on October 19. The Western was directed by Nicholas Ray and also starred Joan Crawford, Sterling Hayden, and Mercedes McCambridge. In November, Brady and screenwriter Mel Dinelli were Crawford's dual escorts at the annual Hollywood Press Photographers' Costume Ball at the Mocambo. Sheilah Graham sidled up to Brady and asked if there was any news about his brother, Lawrence Tierney.

"He's just about to sign for a movie in New York," Scott replied.

There was indeed a movie. The only catch was that Tierney didn't sign and was not part of the cast in November when director Elia Kazan began filming *On the Waterfront*, a tale of corruption among longshoremen, in Hoboken, New Jersey. The film starred Marlon Brando as former prizefighter Terry

Malloy. Tierney had been offered the role of Terry's brother Charley, the one who "shoulda looked out for . . . shoulda taken care of" Terry, "just a little bit." Tierney was not happy with the salary offer and demanded more money—too much money. The role, and eventual Academy Award nomination, went to Rod Steiger.

20

Year of the Wag

In his annual "Hollywood letter to Santa Claus" the week before Christmas 1953, Armand Archer once again included Lawrence Tierney's potential Christmas wish: "Another chance." Two years earlier, Archerd had Tierney asking Santa for "one more chance."

Tierney's final column appearance of the year took place the day before New Year's Eve, when Earl Wilson warned New Yorkers that Tierney was out and about, "wearing his new shiner." To the journos who found him a handy space filler, Tierney was almost a ghost, materializing in a Manhattan bar or Hollywood nightspot to throw back a drink, throw a punch, and disappear until the next tavern eruption or court appearance. Across America, though, Tierney remained a robust, if B-list, presence. His appeal had now spread beyond the movie houses and drive-ins that in early 1954 continued to run his old films. He was now directly inside American homes, through television, as syndicators sold local stations non–prime-time packages of original shows and mostly low-budget pictures. *The Hoodlum* was showing up on television schedules at all hours of the day and all days of the week. Within weeks, *Kill or Be Killed* would make the move to the home screen.

Tierney remained on the East Coast in January. He was seen in Greenwich Village, playing bocce, the bowling game popular among New York City's Italian immigrants, outside the Jumble Shop restaurant in MacDougal Alley. That same day, back in Los Angeles, a judge approved an out-of-court settlement in the $30,587 damage suit filed by John Naylor over the Santa Monica jaw-breaking incident in the summer of 1951. Tierney would have to pay Naylor $5,000—but only $2,500 if he paid in cash within nine months.

Tierney was, by all appearances, back on his "milk wagon" routine while keeping up appearances on the boulevards. Kilgallen squealed on a scene at the jiggly Club Samoa on Fifty-Second Street, where stripper Sherry Britton put Tierney in his place, "right out loud . . . scared him so he took off." Kilgallen also had him sitting all alone, at the counter of a Broadway drugstore—"sipping away at an ice cream soda, and no chaser!"

When Tierney's name did hit the papers, leaping from the gossip columns to the crime sheets, it was in the most sordid of circumstances. His name was in the lead paragraph of every story in every newspaper—and not only was he completely innocent of the crime, he had nothing to do with it.

Blame Arthur Godfrey. The scandal that began to unfold on the sidewalk on the Sunset Strip might never have come to pass at all, had the entertainer and broadcaster not fired Julius La Rosa from his morning television and radio program on CBS. The Old Redhead did the firing live on the radio the previous October, claiming the twenty-three-year-old singer lacked "humility" by hiring a personal agent and manager without informing him. Godfrey's stunt backfired. He became the butt of jokes, while La Rosa became a front-page celeb. His single, *Eh, Cumpari,* shot to no. 1 a few weeks later and $185,000 in bookings fell into his lap.

The earnest, dark-haired kid from Brooklyn was pulling in $10,000 a week when he made his "West Coast debut" at Ciro's. On opening night, Friday, February 26, 1954, traffic was jammed and the sidewalk was crawling with damp, screaming bobby soxers, the teenage girls who'd swoon at the sound or sight of whichever crooner happened to be making the charts that week.

Inside the nightclub, Jimmy Durante, Terry Moore, and Barry Sullivan jammed ringside tables among a crowd that brought La Rosa back for six encores. Outside, the underage girls milled, hoping for a glimpse, or more. Some even carried scissors on the off chance they'd get close enough to snip off a lock of La Rosa's hair.

The bobby soxers were still out and about in mid-March, about two weeks into La Rosa's engagement. Two of the girls, both aged fourteen, assumed that their patience had paid off when they were approached on the sidewalk by a man who said he was La Rosa's manager. He invited them to a party, which he promised would be attended by the star.

The girls arrived at the party. While Julius La Rosa did not attend, Betty Lou Shanker was there to greet them. Mrs. Shanker resided at 8351 West Sunset Boulevard, just a couple blocks east of Ciro's, which was very convenient for the business she was in and for the opportunities she offered the two fourteen-year-old girls.

Betty Lou was a pimp.

Over the course of the next week, Betty Lou Shanker arranged for the girls to meet and have sex with men. The girls' mothers became suspicious about their absences and behavior and contacted the police.

Sgt. W. O. Reynolds of the juvenile division and Dep. Walter Howell of the vice squad got on the case. This wasn't exactly a Black Dahlia mystery. Within days, they'd arrested twenty-eight-year-old Betty Lou Shanker and charged her with suspicion of procuring for prostitution and contributing to the delinquency of a minor. The two girls were charged with suspicion of prostitution. They were held at juvenile hall, where they began to talk. The fourteen-year-olds said that in the past couple of weeks, Mrs. Shanker had introduced them to and arranged for them to have sex with nine or ten men. One of the girls gave details about an encounter that took place on March 23, in an apartment at 710 North Doheny Drive—about a mile and half from Ciro's, south of the Strip. The girls said the man who lived there gave them liquor and had sex with one of them.

Reynolds and Howell surveilled the suspect and moved in to make the arrest on Friday, April 2. They dragged him into the West Hollywood sheriff's station and booked him on a charge of statutory rape.

Edward Tierney denied the charge. He was held without bail, pending arraignment.

Lawrence Tierney's kid brother Ed was in the soup, big-time, but when the news broke on Saturday, his screen monicker "Ed Tracy" was not mentioned in any of the stories containing words like "attack," "rape," and "morals charge" in the headline. One name that did appear in headlines was Lawrence Tierney's. Most every lead paragraph reported the arrest of the "brother of actor Lawrence Tierney . . . brother of the trouble-beset actor, Lawrence . . . twenty-five-year-old brother of actor Lawrence Tierney . . . brother of Lawrence Tierney, movie bad man."

Though featured so prominently, Tierney was not asked for comment.

Betty Lou Shanker was arraigned in juvenile court on Thursday, April 8, and charged with two counts of contributing to the delinquency of a minor for introducing the two fourteen-year-old girls to Edward Tierney. When Ed Tierney was arraigned in the same courtroom later that day, he caught something of a break. A grand jury did not return an indictment for rape. The complaint issued by Deputy District Attorney Joseph W. Chandler charged him with four counts of contributing to the delinquency of two fourteen-year-old girls. Ed Tierney was freed on $1,000 bail. His preliminary hearing before Superior Judge William B. Neeley was set for April 20.

After the arraignment, Ed told reporters that he'd met the girls—"casually." He denied having done anything wrong. "This is all a misunderstanding," he said.

Many newspaper reports mentioned that it was a year to the month since Ed's wife, actress Hannelore Axman, divorced him because he'd stayed away from home as often as three nights a week. Hannelore had since returned to Germany.

Ed Tierney celebrated his twenty-sixth birthday on May 13. It must have been a low-key celebration. A week later, he was in superior court, where he pleaded guilty to one count of contributing to the delinquency of a minor. He admitted that on March 23, 1954, the girls were inside his apartment and that he'd given liquor to one of them. Judge William B. Neeley sentenced him to ninety days in county jail, and three years of probation. During the probation period, the judge said, Tierney must not associate with any minor girls, except in a professional capacity (and not the profession the fourteen-year-olds had been lured into). Neeley also fined him $100.

A week after Eddie trudged off to serve his time, Sheilah Graham reported that Scott Brady was headed to Europe with Raymond Burr to shoot *Mannequins für Rio,* a German–American drama cowritten by the blacklisted—and uncredited—screenwriters Dalton Trumbo and Michael Wilson. Filmed in Hamburg, Munich, and Rome, the "white slavery" picture would be released in the States as *They Were So Young,* and include Hannelore Axman in a small role. Graham didn't mention younger brother Ed's predicament, but did observe that she hadn't heard anything at all in recent days about older brother Lawrence, "who could've had a fine movie career—with just an added ounce of will power."

Lawrence Tierney was, in fact, in the midst of what would be his most concentrated and longest-lasting burst of willpower, faith, determination, and artistic endeavor. Over the course of the next fourteen months, he would act in three movies—his last motion picture work for the decade—continue to flex his chops onstage, and begin a new career, not as lucrative as in films, but potentially steady, as a television actor. He'd also keep off the booze, at least to the extent that he would be declared "on the wagon," and remain off the police blotter—until he stumbled, and was exiled, figuratively and literally.

Tierney was a regular in the New York City gossip columns in spring 1954, reported by Earl Wilson to be "on the wag," seen strolling down Broadway in his Bermuda shorts, and spotted on restaurant dates: with television actress Diane Herbert at La Lune d'Argent, a little French joint on Second Avenue and Fifty-Second Street; at Monsignore on East Sixtieth Street, with singer and oil heiress Angela Lamb (daughter of Oklahoma oil millionaire Tony Lamb); and at Joe Marsh's Spindletop steakhouse on West Forty-Ninth Street, table-hopping to spend time with Christine Jorgensen, formerly George Jorgensen, the twenty-seven-year-old ex-GI who in 1952 became a celebrity after undergoing sexual reassignment surgery.

By mid-June 1954, however unreliable the math (considering his "shiner" item in late December), Earl Wilson declared that Tierney had "been on the wagon eight months." That kind of publicity led to work. Tierney was cast as a convict in *The Steel Cage*, director Walter Doniger's sequel to *Duffy of San Quentin*, his film noir that was released in March. He also showed up in *Singing in the Dark*, an independent drama produced by comedian Joey Adams and starring cantor and Yiddish theater actor Moyshe Oysher. In his first English-speaking role, Oysher played a former inmate of a Nazi concentration camp who arrives in America with total amnesia due to the horror he'd witnessed. Directed by *Dillinger's* Max Nosseck, it was one of the first American movies to focus on the Holocaust.

Television came calling next. Reports spread that the man with "Dillinger" as a middle name in so many newspaper accounts would star as a detective in a new series. *The Concrete Jungle* would be the first project from a company led by and named for actor Ray Gordon, who'd recently played a priest on an episode of *The Loretta Young Show.* Tierney would play an instructor in a New York City detective school. Each episode would dramatize another case in flashback. Gordon planned to film the first half-hour episode in New York in July, ready to sell in the fall.

The project did not come to fruition, but another police drama did. Executives at the CBS network offered Tierney a role on the police anthology series *The Man Behind the Badge*. This time, he was cast more to type, as homicidal mobster Al Baker, a role that one reviewer called a "virtual carbon copy" of John Dillinger. *The Case of The Last Escape*, based on an actual breakout attempt at Oregon State Penitentiary, aired on July 11. The cast also included Harold Stone and Jason Robards.

Tierney hit the straw-hat circuit in July. He was reported to be on tour in *Rope*, the 1929 play based on the Leopold and Loeb murder case, and as a detective in a version of the 1947 Broadway play *Laura* at the Summer Theatre in Litchfield, Connecticut.

Tierney was back in the spotlight on August 4, when he was mobbed by fans outside the Rivoli Theatre in Times Square at the star-studded premiere of Alfred Hitchcock's *Rear Window*. Ed Sullivan checked his calendar mid-month and decided that Tierney had been on the wagon for *six* months when he was seen "consuming a quart of ice cream at one sitting." Sheilah Graham upped the stakes a couple of weeks later, estimating that Tierney had gone "*ten* months without one drop of the liquid that is supposed to cheer." Or was it nine? On September 17, Winchell countered with Tierney "on the Wagon since New Year's" (that would be eight months and sixteen days), and groaning, "But nobody'll print that!"

There was little doubt that things were looking up. In September, Fred Finklehoffe, who'd tried to cast Tierney in his World War II stage play, *Mike McCauley*, in 1950, now wanted him to star in a Broadway version of Nelson Algren's novel *The Man with the Golden Arm*. Finklehoffe told *Variety* he was seeking Orson Welles to direct, and had sent Welles a script after tracking him down in Spain. Finklehoffe said that Tierney, whom the trade described as the "film actor who has gotten himself straightened out after his recent personal difficulties," was "a natural" for the role as the ill-fated Chicago card dealer. (The play never opened; a movie version, directed by Otto Preminger and starring Frank Sinatra, went into production in 1955.)

Tierney stayed busy into the fall. He was seen on the town with a pair of hyphenates: model and fashion photographer Lenore Lester, and singer and actress Libby Dean. At boxer Bob Olin's On-The-Park Restaurant in the Mayflower Hotel, he was spotted with Arly Roberts, a former screen actress and production coordinator of *The Fifth Season*, a comedy currently on Broadway at the Cort Theatre. In November, he filmed a low-budget quickie titled *Girl Murdered*. The role may have fit *too* well: an off-duty cop who gets so plastered at a bar that when an actress is murdered across the street, he can't remember if he killed her. The film was shot in six days. John Carradine costarred, and a pneumatic blonde named Jayne Mansfield was featured in her first acting role. Mansfield allegedly was paid $150 for her work, and when she wrapped, returned to her seventy-five-cents-an-hour job selling popcorn at the Stanley-Warner movie theater on Wilshire Boulevard in Hollywood.

The film was produced by actor Burt Kaiser and directed by chubby character actor Bruno VeSota. Both men had roles in the picture, which remained on the shelf, unreleased for months, until events suddenly made it bankable.

෨

Tierney portrayed a crusading, heroic newspaper reporter in *The Case of the County Dictator*, an episode of *The Big Story* that aired on NBC on November 5. It was another feather in his cap, more proof that he'd show up and bring home the goods. John Lester wrote in his syndicated Radio and Television column on December 17 that Tierney had "behaved himself for such a long stretch another network is beginning to believe he means it this time and plans to take advantage of his many dramatic talents."

The Steel Cage premiered on the last day of 1954. The three vignettes in the sequel to *Duffy of San Quentin* focused on different aspects of prison life: comedy, the desire for freedom, and the need for spiritual solace. Tierney, as a convict involved in a doomed escape try, demonstrated the desire for freedom.

The turning of the calendar page to a new year meant that it could be said officially, no matter the columnists' timetables, that Lawrence Tierney had been on the wagon for an entire year. He was on big screen and small, and had recently begun rehearsals for his long-awaited debut on Broadway. He was on a winning streak. How long could it last?

21

Pink Elephants

It was Lawrence Tierney's social life that made news in the first month of 1955. His latest date and very newsworthy companion was Gloria Vanderbilt, the twenty-nine-year-old heiress, socialite, artist, and actress (and great-great-granddaughter of the Commodore). Twenty years earlier, Gloria had been at the center of the Depression era's "trial of the century." She was the "poor little rich girl" caught in a custody battle between her widowed mother, also named Gloria, and her aunt, Gertrude Whitney. Gertrude had sought guardianship of little Gloria, charging that her sister-in-law was an unfit libertine. After hearing allegations of maternal neglect, drinking, pornography, and lesbianism, the judge ultimately awarded custody to Gertrude; mother could visit on weekends.

While she was dating Lawrence Tierney, Gloria was still married to, but estranged from her second husband, the seventy-two-year-old orchestra conductor (and *Fantasia* star) Leopold Stokowski. She'd married the maestro in Mexico in 1945 and would get her Mexican divorce in October 1955. She was also on a break from an affair with Frank Sinatra, who was separated from wife Ava Gardner and had won an Academy Award in March 1954 for his role in *From Here to Eternity*.

Tierney and Vanderbilt met in rehearsals for a Broadway revival of William Saroyan's 1939 Pulitzer Prize–winning drama, *The Time of Your Life*. The play starred Tierney's straw-hat colleague Franchot Tone and was directed by acting guru Sanford Meisner. Tierney was cast, and would finally act on Broadway, because Jean Dalrymple was the latest producer to decide that he deserved another chance.

Vanderbilt had a small part in the play, but her notoriety led her to stand out among the large cast. She recalled her first meeting with the "mad, bad, and dangerous-to-know Lawrence Tierney" in her 2004 "romance memoir," *It Seemed Important at the Time*. "Eyes like steel found me, made me sense that I could be the stream to feed the roots," she wrote, "for his love seemed like a tree, needing a strange alchemy from my eye." Tierney, it can be translated, was needy, and Vanderbilt was willing to write off stories of his past exploits as "only gossip from those jealous of his gorgeous good looks and sensitive talent."

Vanderbilt and Tierney spent time in coffeehouses, where they philosophized and the sensitive actor scribbled poetry on paper napkins—"obscure bits and pieces, passed wordlessly across the table like furtive notes in school, strange and brilliant but making no sense," wrote Vanderbilt. "But what is 'sense' coming from a poet, inarticulate and shut off from everyone save the few such as *moi* who had the sensitivity to understand him? . . . All he needed was me to ease his dark-blue pain."

Tierney won the girl but lost the role when he showed up at a rehearsal and director Meisner believed that he was drunk. In Vanderbilt's eyes, the firing made Tierney "more fascinating than ever."

The Tierney–Vanderbilt combo was first picked up and played cute by Dorothy Kilgallen on January 13, 1955, six days before the play opened for a two-week, Tony-qualifying run at the City Center. Kilgallen reported that the twosome were table-sharing at the Louise Jr. restaurant on East Fifty-Third Street, he "now a model of deportment who has been on the wagon for exactly a year." After dinner, the couple took in a track meet.

After the premiere, Vanderbilt realized that Tierney and the relationship were becoming "more and more out of hand—complicated." On Saturday night, January 29, Tierney showed up at the stage door after the eleventh performance, "not dark blue but a disturbing shade of wicky-wacky dark red." Translated: he was upset and possibly drunk. The uproar continued the next day, when Vanderbilt and Tone were scheduled to perform a scene from the play on *The Colgate Comedy Hour,* the variety series that aired live on the NBC television network. Shortly before her entrance, there was a phone call from Tierney. He sounded "ill, in dire need—rattled, off-balance." The call rattled Vanderbilt, who blew her lines, blew the scene, and as a result lost a starring role in "a Jack Webb movie." She realized then that she couldn't be Tierney's "Florence Nightingale." In a twist, she began an affair with Franchot Tone.

In reality, Vanderbilt the romantic did not let go of Tierney so easily. There were more sightings of the couple: he keeping her waiting for forty-five minutes at McCarry's Steak House on Second Avenue at Forty-Fifth Street; he teaching her to use chopsticks at Carl Henderson's new East of Suez restaurant on East Fifty-Eighth; they, a combo at the Tuscany Room at East Thirty-Ninth Street . . . through the end of March, when Kilgallen had Tierney dividing his time between Vanderbilt and Lenore Lester, that "pretty photographer."

〜

On March 30, Lawrence Tierney saw a pink elephant.

"Seeing pink elephants" is a term long used to describe the hallucinations caused by alcoholic hallucinosis or delirium tremens (the DTs, the most serious form of alcohol withdrawal). The term, mentioned by Bim, the drunk ward nurse in the 1945 film *The Lost Weekend,* originated in the nineteenth century, when it replaced the euphemism "seeing snakes." It appeared in the entertainment and news pages in April 1955, when Earl Wilson reported that noted alcohol abuser Lawrence Tierney was observed observing a pink elephant at Madison Square Garden.

The occasion was the opening of the eighty-fifth season of the Ringling Bros. & Barnum and Bailey Circus, highlighted by a star-studded "Dream Circus," produced by the showman Mike Todd to benefit the New York Arthritis and Rheumatism Foundation.

Milton Berle was ringmaster for the celebrity portion, announcing the entrance of the "Celestial Calendar Cavalcade," a parade of colorful floats, animals, and celebrities in glittering costumes. Leading the parade was Marilyn Monroe, barely dressed at all in a black-and-white leotard and black fishnet stockings, riding an elephant that had been spray-painted pink. When she came into view in the arena, the band stopped playing and there was an audible gasp from the crowd of eighteen thousand. Then, after a moment's silence in which one could hear a mouse squeak, the Garden erupted in spontaneous cheers and applause. From atop her pink elephant, Marilyn blew kisses toward the rafters.

That was why, at an event that attracted stars including Marlene Dietrich, James Cagney, Red Buttons, Sammy Davis Jr., Martha Raye, Sonje Henie, Arnold Stang, and Dave Garroway (and his *Today* show sidekick, chimp J. Fred Muggs), Hollywood has-been Lawrence Tierney made the news that week. The wily Earl Wilson, in a comment that was repeated and reprinted, noted that Tierney was unfazed by the sight of the pink elephant. "Having quit drinking he no longer sees elephants that shade."

It was a backhanded compliment to Tierney's supposed sobriety.

Tierney got something else out of that night. Dorothy Kilgallen reported on April 14 that "Lawrence Tierney's newest fancy is a young lass with the Circus." The circus girl was one of many. Two weeks later, someone tipped Hy Gardner that Tierney was at Peter's Backyard restaurant on West Tenth Street in the

Village with actress Tina Louise. A few weeks later, Gardner had him back with Gloria Vanderbilt—"holding claws" at The Lobster on West Forty-Fifth Street.

While Larry kept his name in the papers and trouble at arm's length, his brothers were keeping the Tierney brand, if not name, alive in Hollywood and internationally. It was announced in May that Scott Brady would be seen in Cinemascope and Technicolor alongside Jane Russell and Jeanne Crane in the United Artists musical picture *Gentlemen Marry Brunettes* (an attempt to repeat the success of *Gentlemen Prefer Blondes,* a giant hit in 1953). Kid brother Ed Tierney, as Ed Tracy, had put his jail sentence behind him and costarred in a movie that premiered on May 18. In his last picture before being sent away, the US Army veteran portrayed a navy pilot in the Korean War drama *Men of the Fighting Lady.* In his latest film, Ed was an army captain and POW in a World War II comedy. The big difference was that the picture was *Heldentum nach Ladenschluß* (Heroism after Closing Time), produced, filmed, and screened in West Germany. Ed, who spoke the language (and had a German ex-wife) had pulled up stakes and left America to live in Germany and work as a German actor. He'd eventually sign a contract with the Munich-based N. I. International, be tutored to perfect his German, and make many films in Germany and in France—most often playing American army officers.

"The Germans," he told an interviewer years later, "are a very energetic people. You go on location, for instance, and the maids come in and roust you out of bed at the crack of dawn with a crisp 'Achtung!'—in my case adding, 'Let's go!'"

He'd remain in Europe for the next six years. When he wasn't working as an actor, he sold Volkswagens.

Lawrence Tierney would soon leave New York City for a short period, as he again set out on the straw-hat theater circuit. There was a full house at the Lakewood Theater in Lakewood Park, Pennsylvania, about 130 miles west of Times Square, on June 27, opening night for *Detective Story.* For six days and eight performances, Tierney starred as Detective James McLeod, the role he'd lost six years earlier when he turned up drunk at a reading for the Chicago production. The rest of the cast—two dozen actors in all—consisted of locals and professionals from New York, including Woodrow Parfrey and Steve Gravers, both at the start of long and busy careers as television and movie character actors.

Marian Shaefer took in the premiere for the *Pottsville Republican.* "The utter silence before the curtain goes up and the enthusiastic applause as it goes down after the third act is always a sure sign of a good opening and continued success for any play. The premiere of *Detective Story* . . . was thus received," she wrote. Tierney "did a fine job in an unaccustomed role" as "the detective who has no warmth in his heart, who knows only that right is right and wrong is wrong."

Shaefer noted that Tierney also played a detective in *Hangover,* a movie he'd recently completed but that was not yet released. *Hangover* was the latest title for *Girl Murdered,* which the producers were having a hard time selling. There would be a couple more title changes by the time the picture hit theaters in a big way.

Two evenings after the Fourth, Tierney was atop the New Jersey Palisades cliffs, across the Hudson River from Manhattan, among a diverse collection of wits, intellectuals, and artists that included "silken speech" radio announcer Norman Brokenshire, columnist and media personality Frank Farrell, music producer and conductor LeRoy Holmes, actress Clair Luce, and "Take My Wife, Please" comedian Henny Youngman. The gathering was not a salon or roundtable summit. They were onstage at Palisades Amusement Park, tasked with selecting a Miss New York 1955, to compete later that month in the Miss USA pageant. The judges chose Patricia Ann O'Kane, a blonde, nineteen-year-old secretary from Valley Stream, Long Island. The papers informed readers that the new Miss New York was five feet, eight inches tall, one hundred and thirty-eight pounds, and measured 36–24–36. (The Miss USA title would go to Miss Vermont.)

On July 23, Tierney boarded a Long Island Rail Road train at Penn Station for the forty-mile ride to the hamlet of Bay Shore, where he would step onto a ferry to Fire Island, a thirty-mile-long barrier spit paralleling Long Island's south shore. Much of Fire Island had been set aside for state parks and wilderness areas, but several villages and hamlets maintained a seasonal population. The ferry and private boats offered the only access, and the sign at the dock warned that there were no public bathhouses and no picnicking allowed on the beaches. There was a hotel or two, a few restaurants and bars, and most visitors stayed in cottages. No automobiles were allowed on the island. Foot transportation was primarily on boardwalks. The preferred means of carrying groceries or luggage was to pull them on Red Flyer toy wagons. For most of the year, Fire Island offered a peaceful, pastoral setting.

Summers were another story. Since the 1920s, the island had attracted literary and artistic types, the show business crowd, and homosexuals, who found an isolated offshore paradise where they could express themselves freely.

"Get mixed up with the fugitives from Broadway, the television studios, Tin Pan Alley, Hollywood and the Greenwich Village bars," Kilgallen warned, "and you are suddenly in the middle of something strongly resembling an alumni reunion at a loony bin."

It was a loony bin that Lawrence Tierney could not wait to bounce around in that summer. After more than a year—close to *two years*—of keeping his boozing on the q.t., he'd be able to sit in a bar and knock back a shot or two. Or three, even.

During that fourth weekend of July, Tierney made enough of a scene to put him back in the columns. Kilgallen had the scoop. If Jimmie Fidler had been infuriated each time one of Tierney's run-ins made news, Kilgallen took pleasure exposing "Fire Island's most exciting moment of the weekend." It was a fight in a pub between Tierney and former football star John "Shipwreck" Kelly, ex-husband of debutante and heiress Brenda Frazier (another "poor little rich girl" who'd been the object of a multimillion-dollar custody battle). Shipwreck was trying to impress a woman at the bar when she began flirting with Tierney. Tierney responded in kind. Punches flew. Other patrons broke it up.

Tierney left the pub only slightly ruffled. The to-do was hardly a bar brawl, but significant because it was noticed, and reported. Tierney's eighteen-month so-called sobriety streak was officially over. But his streak on Fire Island had only begun.

22

Banished

The village of Ocean Beach on New York's Fire Island was bedeviled in the summer of 1936 by a gentleman purse snatcher who would engage with gullible married women, ply them with alcohol, and then rob them. The suave crook had been working the scam for three summers, and lawmen in Suffolk County were at their wit's end, trying to catch him in the act.

Then Mary Polywoda spoke up. A tiny brunette stenographer and secretary for District Attorney L. Barron Hill, Mary suggested that she be given a chance at snaring the criminal—using herself as the honey trap. Her boss and the other men in the room were frustrated enough to hear her plan and agree to put it into action. With fifty dollars in marked bills to stash in her purse, Mary arrived in Ocean Beach and strolled the boardwalk in the warm evening breeze. William J. Gardiner, an investigator for the district attorney, and Police Chief C. W. Morris lurked nearby.

At about 9 p.m., a refined, slim, dark-haired young man walked by, smiled at Mary, and raised his hat in greeting. Mary responded with a coquettish smile. The man took the bait, stopped, and asked if they hadn't met the previous summer. "He flirted with me," Mary later told reporters, "and I flirted back. I just had a hunch that he was the man I was after."

Mary agreed to accompany the man to a tavern. They were seated. The two lawmen took seats nearby. Mary told the man she was married but had quarreled with her husband. The gentleman was sympathetic. She ordered a scotch and soda. He ordered rye. She paid for one of the rounds, opening her purse wide enough for him to get a good look at the cash it held. Mary knocked back another drink, and another, before pretending to suddenly feel ill. That was when the man grabbed her purse and made a move for the door. Gardiner and Morris made a move for the cad. Mary Polywoda had gotten her man.

The suspect was identified as twenty-three-year-old Clement Levy, also known as Bert Lyons. He said he was a radio singer from Manhattan.

Levy was taken to jail and, on August 18, into police court in Ocean Beach. Judge Raymond J. Knoeppel declared him guilty and sentenced Levy to six months in the Riverhead, Long Island, jail and fined him fifty dollars. The judge offered to suspend the jail term and fine, however, on one condition: that Clement Levy never return to Fire Island. The young man agreed. He boarded the ferry and never set foot on Fire Island again.

For her ingenuity and bravery, Mary Polywoda was reassigned as the Suffolk County district attorney's first female investigator. By accepting the deal, Clement Levy became the first person in modern times reported to be banished, officially, eternally, from Fire Island.

Lawrence Tierney would be the second.

In July 1955, Shipwreck Kelly knew how to handle the news that he and Lawrence Tierney had been involved in a bar fight on Fire Island. He denied it. Shipwreck, who pursued a respectable career in investment banking and real estate when not in the columns, declared not only that he never had a spat with the actor, but that he hadn't even been on Fire Island. Kilgallen printed Shipwreck's correction, but suggested he make his way to Ocean Beach and track down the double who was using his name.

Shipwreck shrugged off the incident. Tierney remained on Fire Island and kept drinking until he punched his way into history.

It was the evening of Sunday, August 7, 1955. The temperature had been above ninety every day for the first week of the month, so the thunderstorms that afternoon were something of a relief. Tierney was cooling down in a popular Ocean Beach tavern. His drinking companion, Patsy Mottalo, was about forty years old. He was from Patchogue, Long Island, a town just across the Great South Bay on the south shore. The two of them were getting along fine, downing their shots, discussing life, until, for whatever reason, Tierney punched Patsy Mottalo in the nose. Patsy responded in kind. This time, police were called in and Lawrence Tierney was arrested.

Tierney was called into court in Ocean Beach on the morning of Friday, August 12, charged with disorderly conduct. Magistrate John J. Dwyer reviewed the case, took Tierney's past record and recent behavior into consideration, and fined him fifty dollars. Tierney might have shrugged off the fine, but there was more. Dwyer looked Tierney in the eye and told him to take the 5:40 p.m. boat back to Long Island—and never return. Ever. Clement Levy had at least been given a choice in 1936. Lawrence Tierney was not. He'd been arrested on Catalina Island off the California coast; he'd been a terror on Manhattan

Island and been banned from many bars, but this was the first time he was banished completely.

Tierney accepted the sentence. Before he boarded the ferry and left the vacation spot for the last time, he returned to the bar and had a few friendly drinks with Patsy Mottalo.

Patsy waved goodbye and watched the ferry sail off on Great South Bay. "He's a nice guy, I guess," Patsy said.

Leonard Lyons observed that Lawrence Tierney had "survived almost the full season at Fire Island" before returning to the city, where the headlines darkened prospects even more. Broadway folks who'd sashayed barefoot on Fire Island had seen and heard too much of Tierney's behavior to risk giving him a chance on stage. The only date on Tierney's schedule in September was an appearance at a benefit for Red Cross flood relief at the West End Casino in Long Branch, New Jersey.

Later that month, Tierney spent some time in Hollywood, where brother Scott Brady announced that he'd purchased the rights to the original story "The Long Night," which he hoped to turn into a film starring all three brothers: Brady, Tracy, and Tierney.

The dream project was never realized.

Will Success Spoil Rock Hunter?, a comedy written and directed by George Axelrod, opened at Broadway's Belasco Theatre on Thursday, October 13, 1955. Axelrod had written *The Seven Year Itch,* a 1952 hit that ran for 1,141 performances and led to Billy Wilder's film that featured the iconic image of Marilyn Monroe standing over a subway grate, her white pleated dress billowing up over her hips as she catches the breeze from an Uptown 6 train roaring by below. *Hunter* was a Faustian Hollywood satire about a magazine writer who sells his soul to the Devil to become a successful screenwriter and have Hollywood's platinum blonde sex queen—a lampoon of Monroe in Wilder's movie—fall for him. Orson Bean played the writer. Jayne Mansfield was the sex goddess, Rita Marlowe.

The play received decent reviews. Brooks Atkinson at the *Times* said the actors, including Martin Gabel and Walter Matthau, were "all right," but that Mansfield played her part "with commendable abandon." John Chapman at the *Daily News* was especially taken by the twenty-two-year-old actress, who was "ash-blonde, bosomy and behind-y" and "splendid as a sexy but typically dumb broad."

After months of pushing her 40–21–35½ attributes in Hollywood, it took a Broadway show to make Jayne Mansfield a star. Her success rubbed off on Lawrence Tierney. That six-day cheapie he'd shot with John Carradine a year earlier—the one titled *Girl Murdered,* then *Hangover,* and now, as the columns indicated, *Panic*—would make it to the big screen, after all, after one last title change to capitalize on the girl who shot her scenes when she wasn't shoveling popcorn on Wilshire Boulevard.

The first annual Audience Awards, supposedly based on a poll of millions of moviegoers, were handed out at the Beverly Hilton on December 6. *Mister Roberts* was voted Best Picture, Jennifer Jones won top honors for *Love Is a Many Splendored Thing,* and to no one's surprise, James Dean took Best Actor for *East of Eden.* Dean had been killed in a car crash two months earlier.

Sheilah Graham buttonholed Scott Brady at the event. He was with his longtime, if intermittent, love Dorothy Malone and had just wrapped *The Vanishing American,* a Western based on a Zane Grey novel, at Republic. Brady told the gossip that brother Ed was now a "big star" in Germany, while Lawrence was "touring a play back east."

Lawrence Tierney was indeed back east, but for the most part taking in the sights and playing in restaurants and pubs. He had another chance at Broadway in the play *The Hot Corner,* but despite a terrific, mic-drop audition in which he walked in, played a scene without a script, and walked out, director Sam Levene, who'd encountered Tierney in the past, said he couldn't take a chance on hiring him. (The baseball comedy, no *Damn Yankees,* opened on January 25, 1956, at the John Golden Theatre and closed three nights later.) Tierney remained a fixture in the columns because some women, including Philadelphia socialite Barbara Gainsborough and singer Gayle Andrews, were brave enough to take a chance and be seen with him, but the only films he had in the can were no-budget independents, television work was scarce, and he was definitely in Hollywood's rearview mirror. On December 30, he even rated a "Where Are They Now" entry in the *Boston Globe*: "Q—What has happened to Lawrence Tierney?—H.K., Lawrence. A—Tierney has been devoting his time to the stage and is not at present assigned to a film."

Tierney lost Gloria Vanderbilt for good in January 1956. She went off on a Caribbean vacation with television director Sidney Lumet, and the affair heated up from there. The couple would marry in August, in the West Seventy-Second Street apartment of Sidney Kingsley, the *Detective Story* playwright.

Burt Boyar of the *Philadelphia Inquirer* reported on February 2 that Tierney "took an eight-count at that Third Avenue saloon. An unknown, meek little feller picked up the floor and clobbered him with it." Tierney skipped the premiere of Joey Adams's Holocaust picture, *Singing in the Dark*, at the Cameo Theater in Miami Beach on February 9. (The *Miami News* said the independent picture had a "promising" premise but was "spotty in quality.") After a lunchtime rumble at the end of the month, he added the Old Knick on Second Avenue at Fifty-Fourth Street to the list of taverns where he was no longer welcome.

In April, producer Burt Kaiser added "discoverer of Jayne Mansfield" to his business card and found a taker for his movie in which she appeared with Tierney and John Carradine. Distributor ARC would have the picture in theaters in June, while Mansfield was still onstage on Broadway. The picture's new title was *Female Jungle*, and the girl who had a minor role would be the selling point.

That, at least, appeared to be a stroke of good fortune for Lawrence Tierney. Then he had to go and pop a cop.

23

Diminishing Returns

New York City police officer Joseph Incorvaia was on foot patrol in a posh neighborhood on Manhattan's Upper East Side, working the twelve-to-eight shift on a cold Monday morning. It was forty minutes into April 9, 1956, and the temperature a few degrees above freezing, when he saw trouble waiting to happen not more than a block and a half from Gracie Mansion, the official residence of Mayor Robert F. Wagner Jr. Near the corner of York Avenue and Eighty-Eighth Street, a fellow was in danger of being run over.

The man was staggering, attempting to make his way across Eighty-Eighth Street against the light, and traffic. Officer Incorvaia was eager to help the man to the other side, maybe into a yellow cab, before he was clipped by one. As the cop got closer, he ran through a quick visual checklist: white, thirty-five to forty, well dressed, not a skel, but worse for wear and, by all appearances, drunk. His suit was rumpled. He wasn't wearing a tie. Bright red lipstick was smeared across his face. *Bright red lipstick?*

The man stepped into traffic. Incorvaia reached out to take his elbow— suddenly, the man spun around, gave him a shove, and then—*whap!*—walloped him, knocking him to the pavement. *What the—?* The officer was up in a second. The billy club was out. He subdued the suspect and called for a radio car.

The disorderly drunk was transported to the Twenty-Eighth Precinct house on 104th Street. As soon as the cops walked him through the door, the tip went out that Dillinger was in custody, and *Daily News* photographer Ed Peters was there in no time flat. Officer Incorvaia, who'd nabbed the most high-profile suspect of his career, led Tierney, docile and uncuffed, toward the booking desk—a "walk" for the photographer. With his left hand, Incorvaia gripped Tierney's upper right arm. It could have been a photo of a Dillinger arrest, except instead of a tommy gun, Incorvaia had the nightstick in his right hand. Detective Nilo Mingrone entered the frame to take over, and as

171

he did, Tierney threw a right uppercut. Mingrone leaned away, grabbed hold of Tierney's left wrist—and Ed Peters's Speed Graphic bulb flashed with a *whoosh* and lit the scene, catching the trio in mid-scuffle. From right to left, it was Mingrone in trench coat, stepping back, avoiding the punch; Tierney, hair sweaty and messy, shirt untucked and spilling across the front of his pants, focused on the detective, looking simultaneously fearsome and confused; and beat cop Joe Incorvaia, who can't quite keep the smile off his face.

Lawrence Tierney was booked on a charge of disorderly conduct and led to a cell to sleep it off.

Later that morning, Tierney was in Manhattan Arrest Court with the arresting officer alongside. Tierney admitted that he'd had one too many the previous evening and apologized to the patrolman. Magistrate Walter Bayer looked to the officer for a reaction. Incorvaia had sympathy for the sad sack. "I locked him up more for his own safety than because of his condition," he told the judge.

Tierney pleaded guilty to disorderly conduct. The judge suspended the sentence, and Tierney went on his way. The story made the papers that day. Ed Peters's photo was on page five of the *Daily News* on Tuesday: bottom of the page, under a follow-up on the acid-throwing attack that blinded *Daily Mirror* columnist and organized labor critic Victor Reisel as he walked out of Lindy's restaurant on April 5. The Associated Press picked up the Tierney photo and it was published in papers across the country. This minor incident, a flailing swing at a street cop while stumbling drunk in upper Manhattan, had, through this action photo, become the last straw. Tierney knew it was over for him careerwise, and for the next several years, it was.

A few days after the latest embarrassment, Robert Sylvester at the *Daily News* used a gagster's one-liner. "Lawrence Tierney didn't reform after all," he jotted in his Dream Street column. "He was just in training." Burt Boyar was back with another Third Avenue scoop, and gag, the following week. Tierney had lost to a saloon's "'power behind the thrown.' The bouncer."

Female Jungle was released in June, containing a line from Tierney's character that could have launched a thousand gags: "I won't deny it. I drank. But I'm cured now." The movie was billed as "a gripping murder mystery" and opened on a double bill with *The Oklahoma Woman*, a Western directed by Roger Corman and starring Richard Denning and Peggie Castle (and featuring character actor Dick Miller in his second film role). The ads, touting a pairing of "two all new shockers! Broadway's Boldest and The West's Wildest!," said it all. The press release focused on Jayne Mansfield, still on Broadway, as the "blowtorch blonde girlfriend of the maniacal killer. . . . *Female Jungle,* a thrill-packed Burt Kaiser production brings to the screen Broadway's current rage, a voluptuous blonde bombshell dubbed by Time Magazine as 'sex on the rocks.' Her name is Jayne Mansfield. Her measurements are 40 inches, 21 inches, 35 inches; good indications that she will become the object of America's biggest wolf whistle in the coming year."

Kilgallen, joyful killjoy that she was, got reaction from Mansfield, who'd signed with 20th Century Fox to film *The Girl Can't Help It,* directed by Frank Tashlin, in September, after her Broadway run ended. Now a forgotten cheapie had gotten the jump on her big Hollywood coming-out, so she was understandably "all upset. . . . She doesn't think the picture does justice to her current abilities as an actress."

None of it meant much to Lawrence Tierney's acting career. In fact, he was thinking of walking away and entering a monastery in California. Danton Walker attributed the story to Tierney's "friends," and even he wasn't sure if they were on the level. Two days later, Walker took a left turn and reported that Tierney was not only staying in New York, but had taken a job on Wall Street, working for a former Stork Club page boy who'd opened a stockbroker's office.

Jack Eigen, Chicago's late night radio talk show host, found the hook in his *Tribune* column. Movie musical singer Tony Martin wanted to play a dramatic role. "It's the old story: a comedian wants to be a tragedian; a tragedian wants to be a comedian . . . and Lawrence Tierney doesn't know what he wants to be."

In September, Lee Mortimer tattled in his New York Confidential column that Scott Brady was "in a tail-spin over a N. Y. cutie." Actress Barbara Burgess once dated Scott's older brother, Lawrence Tierney, he reported, "and what became of him and who cares?"

Lawrence Tierney had a new picture opening in theaters around the country, maybe not the best theaters, but he was on the big screen. *The Bushwhackers, Born to Kill,* and *Bodyguard* were only a few of his movies in regular rotation on television. But not a dozen years after he became a star overnight, what had become of him? And who did care?

Hy Gardner cared enough to find out, and had the exclusive on September 5, 1956, the day after Mortimer's dismissive dig. Tierney was located in Brooklyn. He was working, not on a movie or television series, but on a construction site, "cracking rocks instead of chins."

"Yeah, I'm working as an iron man on construction jobs in New York City," Tierney confirmed. "If you think I'm going to tell you exactly where, you're crazy! Do you think I want crowds of people gaping at me? I've been at it for some weeks—I want to get in condition and lose a little weight for a movie role in the fall, a lead role. I play a man who comes out of prison and tries to reform himself."

Tierney may have been trying to save face. There would be no movie work in the fall, in the winter, or the year to follow. While Tierney was building with iron that September 1956, his father was hosting a thirty-second-birthday lunch for son Gerard—Scott Brady—in Hollywood, and gifted him with an original oil painting of Emmett Kelly, the clown billed directly below Lawrence Tierney in *The Greatest Show on Earth*. Danton Walker followed up with an item about young Eddie. "Ed Tracy" had six pictures under his belt in Germany, and a fat new contract.

Tierney had another shot at a stage comeback in October, with the Equity Library Theatre, a nonprofit group that provided a showcase for actors, directors, and technicians. The job didn't pay, and there was no admission fee, merely a request for donations, for the show at the Lenox Hill Playhouse on East Seventieth Street. Tierney was to star in another production of *The Last Mile*—until he got into a fight with the director and stomped out of rehearsals. The show went on without him on October 31.

From his perch in Cyprus Hills, Brooklyn, at the *Kings County Chronicle*, Harry Schreiner saw it like this in his Like I See It! column: There would always be acting work available for Lawrence Tierney. "The only reason you haven't seen him of late is that he just doesn't seem to want to work." Paul Pepe, who wrote the Broadway Showcase for the *Weekly Star* in Greenpoint, Brooklyn, observed in the last week of 1956 that Tierney still "manages to make a complete fool of himself on the streets of New York." What was news in Tierney's home borough no longer made news across the Brooklyn Bridge. Tierney was off the radar far into the new year, and when he did make the news—and the *News*—even his arrests lacked the color and flair of his past escapades.

The weather was mild, skies partly cloudy in midtown Manhattan at 1 p.m. on Saturday, March 30, 1957, when, amid the usual weekend cacophony, there was the sound of a crash. In the middle of Seventh Avenue and Fifty-Seventh Street, where Carnegie Hall loomed at the southeast corner, Lawrence Tierney had slammed his car into a vehicle driven by Robert Folks of Valley Stream, Long Island. After the initial shock, Tierney stepped into the street and approached the other driver, who remained in his car. Tierney didn't ask for insurance details. He spat on the man and began punching him. Police arrived, and as the *Daily News* reported, Lawrence Tierney, thirty-eight, "who used to play tough-guy roles in the movies and never got over it" was arrested for drunken driving, driving without a license, and simple assault (the term "road rage" had yet to be coined). Tierney said he was unemployed and lived in a rented room at 1789 Davidson Avenue in the Bronx. He spent the night in jail. The following day he was in weekend court, where magistrate Hyman Bushel set a hearing for April 22 in vehicle accident court. When Tierney was a no-show that Monday morning, Hyman Bushel, the latest in his history of fed-up judges, issued three warrants for his arrest.

"I called this case three times," Bushel said. "At his first appearance, I felt sorry for him, he looked so shabby. Now he is taking advantage of this court, so I will issue a warrant on each charge."

Tierney showed up the next day, very apologetic. He explained that he'd been out looking for work, not as an actor but, having received a union work permit as a construction worker the previous week, as a wire lather (using wire and metals to build structural frameworks for plaster and other materials). Tierney said he'd assumed his lawyer had gotten an adjournment. The magistrate set bail at $500 and adjourned the case until Friday.

Tierney's attorney cleared up those charges. On May 20, Earl Wilson reported that Tierney had once again joined Alcoholics Anonymous—possibly a condition of a plea deal.

A week later, Tierney led two police cars on a wild chase through the borough of Queens. When cops caught him at the intersection of Queens and Woodhaven Boulevards, they wrote out summonses for running two red lights and reckless driving. When Tierney showed up on time in Queens Traffic Court in Kew Gardens the following Tuesday, his attorney got that case pushed far into the future, for trial on October 17.

Tierney didn't give a reason for the joyride, but he could have been rushing home for dinner. Though it had never been publicized, Tierney was living, and continued to live on-and-off for the next decade and a half, in Bayside, Queens, and later on Long Island, with Vito Frisina and his family: wife, Marie, and children, AnnMarie, fourteen at the time, and eleven-year-old Kenneth.

"My father was a very close friend of Larry. In fact, they were almost inseparable," AnnMarie Frisina Guertin says. "If you ask me how they met, I have no idea, because my father was a very quiet man, very well-respected. He wasn't a drinker and he didn't allow drinking."

AnnMarie may have a hint of how the pair became acquainted. Vito Frisina was a businessman who his daughter admits "wasn't exactly legitimate."

He was a bookie and loan shark who in the 1940s served time in Sing Sing for armed robbery. When Frisina went on his rounds, collecting money from businessmen along Queens Boulevard and Hempstead Turnpike, Tierney often came along, as muscle. "Larry was almost like a bodyguard," AnnMarie says. "My father was not a violent man, but if he'd say, 'Hey, you gotta pay or else,' if they'd see Larry, they knew they'd get the crap knocked out of 'em."

In exchange, Vito gave Tierney a place to sleep and eat when he was on the East Coast. "Larry used to bring in some really hot women into the house in Bayside," AnnMarie says. "My father would allow it, but he wasn't encouraging it. That was our Uncle Larry. Everybody loved him. Everybody. My neighbors were starstruck.

"He had these habits," AnnMarie recalls. "He would growl when he ate. And he used to say, 'AnnMarie, please massage my head.' He used to have a lot of pain in his head. That was probably from a lot of drinking, and the beatings he had taken."

Tierney's relationship with the Frisinas paid off on Sunday, July 28, when police in Manhattan responded to an early morning report of a fight between two men at the corner of Broadway and 100th Street. They arrived to find Lawrence Tierney on the pavement and a younger man standing over him. The officers quickly determined that there had not been a fight after all, but that Tierney had been struck by a motorcycle while walking across Broadway. No charges were filed against the motorcyclist, Francis J. Mulligan, a twenty-one-year-old army private stationed at Fort Bragg, North Carolina. Tierney was taken to Knickerbocker Hospital in Harlem, where doctors checked out his bruised back and sent him home, which he listed as 35-37 206th Street in Bayside, Queens.

The address he gave was Vito Frisina's house, and is key to what actually took place. "My father went to pick up Larry in the city, because he had gotten drunk, and wanted to take him home," AnnMarie says. "Larry was in the backseat and my father had stopped for a red light, and Larry saw something happen while they were stopped. He jumped out of the backseat and got hit by a motorcycle."

The initial reports of a fight were correct. "Larry beat up the guy on the motorcycle," AnnMarie says. "But my father had a tremendous way of calming people down, especially Larry. So he may have given the guy some money. That was my father. He always took care of business."

What could have been a serious charge that led to jail instead became a newspaper chuckle about the tough guy "knocked flat on the seat of his britches." It would have been a fitting finale for a former movie star transitioning into the construction and goon trades. Turns out, it was merely a prelude.

"Lawrence Tierney, who is still playing 'Dillinger,' smashed his face in a fall from a motorcycle, was barred from plush Armando's and got the stand-up from Georgette McDonald, and all this in one day!" Lee Mortimer's item a week later was familiar, but one-third of it would take on great importance. Georgette McDonald was a model whom society columnist Cholly Knickerbocker described as "gorgeous . . . the girl who makes Jayne Mansfield look like a boy." Georgette would rocket Tierney back into the headlines, and onto the police blotter and courtroom dockets in a spectacular, dramatic incident. It would be a low-budget, B-movie noir version of the infamous "Wrong Door Raid" of November 7, 1954, when Frank Sinatra and Joe DiMaggio busted into an apartment, expecting to find the Yankee Clipper's ex-wife Marilyn Monroe in bed with her lover, only to find a secretary in bed alone, because they had the wrong address. This would be bigger than the Battle of Decker's Lawn.

Talk about a comeback!

24

The Burglar

A Hollywood producer visited New York recently with the specific purpose of investigating the possibility of a movie based on the rough-and-tumble career of actor Lawrence Tierney. The film executive spent one night following the free-swinging Tierney around his 8th Ave. bar beat, and booked himself on the next plane to Los Angeles. His confidential report on the project: "Impossible for movies."

DOROTHY KILGALLEN ON BROADWAY, AUGUST 31, 1957

Eileen Keenan was a career woman in New York City. She worked in advertising and had an apartment just a couple of blocks from Madison Avenue, at 166 East Fifty-Sixth Street between Third and Lex. Eileen was twenty-seven, tall, tanned, blonde, beautiful, and on the afternoon of Friday, August 23, 1957, fast asleep. Her roommate had recently moved out, and for now, Eileen had the place to herself. She was alone in the apartment, taking a nap at around 3:30 p.m., when her doorbell rang. It rang again, and again, as she sat up, clearing her head. She was up and halfway to the door when the ringing stopped and the pounding began—*BAM! BAM! BAM!*—and shouts, gravel-voiced and angry, along the lines of "I know you're in there! Open the door!"

Eileen froze in terror. "*Open the damn door!*" She looked to the phone by the couch, then to the window. "Georgette!" *BAM! BAM! BAM!* Eileen responded. "She doesn't live here any—" *CRASH!* There was a sudden explosion of wood and hinges, as the door was kicked open—*CRASH!*—and slammed against the wall, revealing a glowering hulk in the doorway, his eyes cold and darting in all directions.

Eileen let out a piercing scream. In her words, she became "hysterical" as the man pushed past her, searching for Georgette, opening closet doors, looking under the bed. Eileen Keenan continued to scream as she ran to a window above Fifty-Sixth Street. She leaned out onto the fire escape and called for help.

The intruder took one last look around and made a getaway. When he hit the sidewalk and beat feet toward the Third Avenue bars, Eileen was leaning out above him, still shrieking for the police.

When Eileen stopped screaming and used the telephone to call the police, she had no problem identifying the man who kicked down her door. It was Georgette McDonald's boyfriend, or ex-boyfriend, she didn't know for sure because Georgette had moved out. Eileen knew it was that guy who used to be an actor.

Lawrence Tierney got word that weekend that the cops were looking for him. On Sunday morning he made himself presentable, strolled to the Seventeenth Precinct house on East Fifty-First Street, and turned himself in. Just a misunderstanding, he told the desk sergeant—before he was charged with burglary. *Burglary?* Tierney told the cops that was ridiculous. He wasn't stealing anything. As he was being booked, another *Daily News* photographer was there to immortalize the proceedings. Tierney didn't take any swings this time. His white shirt was tucked in. He held his jacket over his left shoulder with two fingers. He looked toward the ceiling, then straight into the lens, dispassionately, as if he were on line for Dodgers tickets.

Tierney repeated to felony court magistrate Thomas Fitzpatrick that he was victim of a misunderstanding. Burglary? He'd been dating this gal named Georgette McDonald for a few months now, and he'd gone to the apartment to see her, unaware that she no longer lived there. Kicking down the door? The only reason he did that was because he thought Miss Keenan was telling him the door was stuck and that she needed help opening it.

The judge looked to Eileen Keenan, who was in the courtroom and very annoyed about the entire situation. She, too, was surprised that Tierney was charged with burglary. "He didn't take anything," she told the magistrate. "I just want him to stay away from me." Fitzpatrick set bail at $500 so Tierney could find himself a lawyer. He set a hearing for Thursday.

Lawrence Tierney returned home, which he told police was now at 142 West Ninety-Second Street on the Upper West Side, a short walk from Central Park. The story hit big in the papers the next day. Hollywood and the rest of the country had been consumed with the *Confidential* magazine trial, in which publisher Robert Harrison, ten other people, and five companies were charged with conspiracy to publish criminal libel and obscene material, because of the salacious stories they'd published about Hollywood stars in the scandal mag. The trial was star-studded and sordid, but Tierney's latest scrape was colorful enough to elbow in on page five of the *Daily News,* with photos. The story even received decent placement in the *Los Angeles Times,* as the wire stories were picked up by just about every paper in the country. Readers hungry for Hollywood dirt in their local dailies got a lagniappe of Lawrence Tierney, as the headlines blared.

SCREEN DILLINGER ARRESTED AGAIN, NOW FOR BURGLARY

LAWRENCE TIERNEY ARRESTED AS BURGLAR

LAWRENCE TIERNEY AGAIN IN THE SOUP

BLONDE'S MAD, ACTOR'S IN DUTCH—AGAIN

TIERNEY HELD IN BAIL AS BLONDE YELLS COP

So what if the wise guys at the *Daily News* referred to him as an "ex-actor"? Papers everywhere were trotting out Tierney's greatest hits. The press settled on "at least nineteen" or "nearly twenty" as the number of times Tierney had been arrested "since he played gunman John Dillinger on the screen" (the actual number was twenty-nine, at least), and as past headlines were exhumed, it was obvious that much of his story had passed into Hollywood myth (e.g., United Press embellished the legend of the Battle of Decker's Lawn in 1946, claiming, inaccurately, that Tierney had been arrested after "tangling" with Diana Barrymore at a party at Errol Flynn's house).

Felony court magistrate Louis S. Wallach reviewed the facts on August 29 and reduced the burglary charge to unlawful entry. "It seems unfortunate that a man of your talents has these things happen because of drinking," he lectured the defendant. "There's no reason why you can't stop this nonsense." Wallach then dismissed the case altogether. "Behave yourself," he said.

Before he left the courtroom, Tierney apologized to Eileen Keenan. In the hallway, a *Daily News* photographer convinced Tierney and the young woman to pose for a re-creation of that apology. The photo showed Eileen Keenan, the statuesque blonde with dark (most likely cherry red) lipstick, in a high-neck white dress with cinched waist. Her bare shoulders have a Coppertone tan. She holds out her right hand limply as Tierney, wearing a buttoned suit coat and tie, holds her fingers and appears to be repeating the apology. His attorney Harold Frankel stands between them, behind the handshake, looking up at the young woman, smiling with satisfaction. It's the look on Eileen Keenan's face that makes the photo a classic. Chin down, lips parted, frowning, she looks up at Tierney with an expression of fear and loathing so evident that Tierney's image could be replaced with that of Gargantua. The photo caption described her expression as "a bit wary."

Tierney's obsession with Georgette McDonald didn't end with the disposition of the court case. He continued a very turbulent, passionate relationship not experienced since his public clashes with Will Rogers's daughter Mary in 1949. Turned on by jealousy and violence, Tierney and Georgette played a dangerous game. She kept seeking out new suitors, whom Tierney kept seeking out to attack.

According to Cholly Knickerbocker on October 5, Tierney had the "quaint habit of slugging her male friends, telephoning threats or invading their apartments in search of what he insists is 'my girl.'" The columnist claimed there were too many instances to give a complete listing, but singled out "bon vivant Bunty Lawrence, boulevardier Paul Schwartz and Bill Wakeman, the carton king. . . . Less fortunate still was Philadelphia's George Cummings, whose apartment door and jaw were smashed."

Tierney's brother Scott Brady was keeping busy in Hollywood. He'd wrapped the Western *The Restless Breed,* opposite Anne Bancroft, and was getting work on television series like *Studio 57* and *Zane Grey Theatre.* He was living, apart from the family, at 8929 Hollywood Hills Road, a secluded, three-bedroom hideaway deep in Laurel Canyon, north of Sunset Boulevard. In August 1957, his friend Desmond Slattery was staying with him at the hacienda. Slattery was forty-three, a colorful, self-promoting "man about town" and bit actor. In 1951, he'd produced a television pilot in which he starred as Robin Hood. The pilot didn't sell, and his most notable role since was as a contestant on the Groucho Marx comedy quiz show, *You Bet Your Life.* Slattery also earned money as a publicist, and had gotten some publicity himself in March, when he came up with the gimmick of selling crickets as household pets.

On the evening of Thursday, August 15, the two friends were at the house, entertaining a pair of young women, one a pretty blonde, the other described as an intriguing Eurasian. As the evening progressed, there was music; there were libations. Everyone was relaxed and having a fine time, until Slattery followed the blonde into the kitchen and watched as she stood at the window, "moving shutters around, as if signaling." Signaling? He passed word to Brady, who stepped over to another window and peered outside. Wouldn't you know it? "Hey, somebody's out there!"

Before he could investigate, there was a pounding on the door, then the door was open and four cops busted in. Sgt. John O'Grady of the Los Angeles Police Department's narcotics squad identified himself. O'Grady's men searched the house and rounded up the quartet in the living room. Flashlights were shined in eyes. The women checked out, he said. The men's eyes did not dilate in the bright light—a sure sign, O'Grady said, of marijuana use. So was the evidence one of the cops said he found outside in the bushes. It appeared to be exactly what the narcs were looking for: a portion of a marijuana cigarette.

O'Grady told the women they could leave. He told the men not to leave town. The cigarette would be sent to the lab for analysis.

The next afternoon, Brady and Slattery were in a restaurant on Melrose Avenue, trying to make sense of what had gone on the night before, when Sergeant O'Grady showed up with more police officers and arrested them in public. The cops took Brady and Slattery to central narcotics division for questioning before the men were charged with marijuana possession, booked— Tierney under his legal name, Gerard Kenneth Tierney—and released, each on $2,500 bail.

When the arrests were announced that day, Sergeant O'Grady strutted before the press. He said he and his men had acted on a tip that Brady had "invited two girls up to blast some tea and get high." O'Grady said his officers had found a marijuana cigarette that Slattery had flicked outside into the weeds when Brady warned him of the raid, and a marijuana cigarette butt on the premises. "The girls," he said, "had nothing to do with a narcotics charge. They were brought there by Scott Brady from some place in Hollywood."

O'Grady had been involved in the arrest of Robert Mitchum in the 1948 "reefer resort" raid in Laurel Canyon. At the time, Mitchum expressed regret. Brady and Slattery did not. As soon as they posted bail, they faced the press. Two respectable men in suits and ties, one a movie and TV hero, the other familiar to reporters, sat at a table in front of a wall of lockers and encouraged the photographers to shoot away. These were not jazz-grooving hepcats or a couple of rebel hopheads. They were two angry men. "This was a frame-up," Brady announced, slamming his fist on the table. He said he didn't want to say anything more, not until he'd hired an attorney. Slattery had no such qualms. The women, he said, were "plants."

Brady muttered to his housemate that he really shouldn't be "talking too much," but Slattery wasn't through. "All I can say is a woman is the cause of it all," he said. "You can't shake down every woman who comes into your place. We didn't know them from Eve."

He told the newsmen about finding the blonde in the kitchen, "moving shutters around as if signaling." The police, he said, arrived moments later.

"They came in," Brady added, "like the Russian Army."

The two men walked into municipal court for arraignment on Monday morning, loaded for bear and represented by the 1957 equivalent of a legal Dream Team: attorneys Robert A. Eaton, son-in-law of California's Governor Goodwin J. "Goodie" Knight, and Jake Erlich, a legendary celebrity lawyer from San Francisco whose motto was "Never Plead Guilty." Brady and Slattery were arraigned before Judge Louis W. Kaufman, who'd presided over one of Lawrence Tierney's arraignments eleven years earlier. A preliminary hearing was set for November 19. Brady and Slattery were each permitted to remain free on $2,000 bail.

After the hearing, the defense attorneys said they'd already begun investigating the "bizarre and unusual conduct" of police in the case. In the weeks to follow, they got down to business, filing motions, winning continuances, outsmarting the prosecutors, and making demands that would expose the way showboat John O'Grady and the LAPD Narcotics Division selected their targets and made their arrests.

The defendants and their lawyers returned to Judge Kaufman's courtroom on December 9. The judge entered, the gavel came down, and the proceedings began with a statement from Manley Bowler, chief deputy district attorney, concerning the continued prosecution of Gerard Tierney, aka Scott Brady, and Desmond Slattery. A police officer involved in the case had advised the DA that disclosing the identity of the two women who were at Brady's house at the time of the arrest, as the defense had demanded, would unmask one of the narcotic squad's "most reliable informants." The officer said he could not do that "in good conscience." The district attorney's office also admitted that there was not sufficient evidence to prove guilt beyond a reasonable doubt. Bowler recommended that the charges against Brady and Slattery be dropped. Municipal judge Kaufman dismissed the case. Scott Brady and Desmond Slattery walked free.

25

Get Your Kicks

*Why does a 39-year-old guy like Lawrence Tierney keep getting
in fights? Why doesn't he act his age, like Jack Benny?*

ROBERT SYLVESTER, *NY DAILY NEWS*, OCTOBER 18, 1958

One of the last gossip items to feature Lawrence Tierney in 1957 was published
the day after Christmas. Cholly Knickerbocker wrote that Tierney had "hung
one on Bill Wakeman's whiskers in a Third Avenue bar and then walked off with
the prize—Georgette McDonald." Translated: Tierney had punched Wakeman
in the face, he was still allowed in some of the *Lost Weekend* saloons, and he
continued to wreak havoc over the woman who Cholly had observed made
"Jayne Mansfield look like a boy."

So what could the New Year bring? In early 1958, more of Tierney's film
oeuvre was running on television daily. *Step by Step, Born to Kill, Kill or Be
Killed, Dillinger, The Devil Thumbs a Ride*—he could even be seen in the
pre-*Dillinger* Leon Errol comedy, *Mama Loves Papa*. Yet, surely, one would
think that by this time, Tierney was lost to show business.

One would think.

On January 9, Leonard Lyons reported that Tierney had joined the teaching staff of a drama school in Brooklyn. Cholly reported two weeks later that
he'd played a real-life scene with Georgette at her place of work, and the scene
was so dramatic that she was fired. Kilgallen alleged on February 10 that Tierney was on the verge of an "aisle-waltz"—not with Georgette, but the "wealthy
divorcee" Helen Kellogg. Cholly volleyed in March, announcing that a group
of Broadway investors was serious about setting up the oft-arrested former
movie star in a real-life detective agency. By then, Earl Wilson already had

the only scoop that mattered: Lawrence Tierney was about to make another comeback, as star of a Hallmark television series called *Civil Air Patrol.*

Tierney was in north Florida in April to film the television pilot (also referenced as *Wings for Hire*) in and around the Silver Springs Airpark Field outside the city of Ocala. To prepare for the leading role as a pilot who ran a private charter service, the unpredictable alcoholic, convicted drunk, and reckless driver took flying lessons. His costar was Sammy Petrillo, a twenty-three-year-old nightclub comedian and Jerry Lewis impersonator.

"In the pilot I was ferrying in a bunch of rattlesnakes and I got bitten and had to crash-land," Petrillo told Todd Rutt in *Psychotronic Video.* "Then Larry comes and saves me."

The producers assigned Petrillo another task besides flying and providing comic relief. "They told me I had to keep Larry busy, running track and playing cards with him so he doesn't drink. I said okay. So I'm a little skinny kid. I'd be exhausted running track with him, before we'd shoot, after we'd shoot. Then we started playing cards, but he wanted to bet money. It cost me eight hundred bucks to keep the guy sober."

The television pilot did not get picked up.

More of Tierney's old movies were added to the television rotation in May, including *The Bushwhackers, Badman's Territory, San Quentin, Bodyguard,* and *The Hoodlum.* Moviegoers could still ogle Jayne Mansfield in *Female Jungle* in theaters and drive-ins.

By June, Hazel Kellogg was history, at least in the columns, as Kilgallen relayed the sighting of a "tamer" Tierney with "schoolteacher" Esther Landrau at Downey's, an Eighth Avenue steakhouse that attracted a Broadway and showbiz clientele.

Lawrence Tierney was being seen in all the right places, at least until 7:30 on the evening of Wednesday, July 23, when he stepped out of the Hotel Astor into Times Square, and NYPD Lieutenant William Nevins stepped up and restrained him with handcuffs.

Tierney protested, nonviolently this time, but went along to the Nineteenth Precinct house on East Sixty-Seventh Street. The cops had been looking for him since May, intending to charge him with felonious assault. The last time he'd been booked in Manhattan, it was on the complaint of an advertising woman. This time, it was an advertising man, thirty-two-year-old Gary Jennings. Tierney had allegedly been drinking in Jennings's apartment at 39 East

Sixty-Fifth Street, when he struck Jennings and fractured his jaw. This time, Tierney allegedly used a fist, not a foot.

Tierney was charged and held overnight until his arraignment. He wore a gray suit, tight blue sweater, and brown shoes when he appeared before Magistrate Reuben Levy in felony court. The judge set bail at $500. Tierney posted the bail and headed home, which he told police was the address in the Bronx.

Tierney had work ahead. He'd been cast in an episode of *Naked City*, a television police drama that starred John McIntire and James Franciscus as a pair of detectives investigating cases around New York. The series was shooting at Gold Medal Studios (the former, historic Biograph Studios) in the Bronx and on location in nearby neighborhoods and Manhattan. The series would premiere on September 30, 1958, on ABC.

The surprise arrest didn't affect that job, nor did it have much of an impact on Tierney's swath through the city. He continued to drink and rumble. On August 6, Tierney was involved, according to Lee Mortimer in his New York Confidential column, in a not-so-confidential brawl at an apartment house on West Fifty-Eighth Street. He did not stray far from that neighborhood for his next blockbuster appearance.

It was Monday, October 13, the day after 750,000 people lined the streets of Manhattan for the annual Columbus Day Parade. Police in Midtown received the first alert around noon that Lawrence Tierney was on a bender. He'd shown up at the door of a woman he'd been seeing, and when she wouldn't let him in, he got angry. On this occasion, he didn't kick in the door. He smashed a window of her building. Tierney was gone by the time police arrived, but they remained on the lookout. Tierney hit some saloons, and got into a couple of fights as the afternoon progressed. Around 5 p.m., somebody hit the panic button at the Gorham Hotel on West Fifty-Fifth Street between Sixth and Seventh Avenues. Tierney was there, raising hell. By the time the squad car pulled up, he was already in the wind.

Sometime along the way, Tierney hooked up with Arthur Kennedy—not Arthur Kennedy the actor, but a construction pal—a thirty-two-year-old fellow lather from Lynbrook, Long Island. Tierney and Kennedy stopped in at several taverns and dives near the Gorham Hotel, and managed to be involved in several scraps, looking more bruised, their clothing more disheveled, and their eyes more bleary, at each successive stop.

Shortly before midnight, the pair came crashing into the Midtown Café at 1362 Sixth Avenue at the corner of Fifty-Fifth Street, not a block from the

Gorham. The two of them were loud, disruptive, battle-scarred, and so obviously drunk that barmaid Esther Zinman took one look and knew they'd had enough. When she refused to serve them, Tierney and Kennedy complained loudly and harassed the few customers who remained. Tierney cursed and challenged any and all to a fight.

The hubbub brought owner Louis Pfaff to the bar. Pfaff was no stranger to aggressive drunks. He told the two Irishmen to scram, and when they refused, made the call to the local police precinct.

Officers Louis Romano and Samuel Saipan pulled up on Sixth Avenue, walked into the Midtown Café at 12:05 a.m. on October 14, and encountered a couple of loud louts and a very angry bar owner. Louis Pfaff demanded the men be arrested for disorderly conduct. They'd not only caused a disturbance, he said, but Tierney had used "boisterous language" in front of his barmaid. The cops could believe it, because, they later reported, Tierney continued to be "loud, boisterous and filthy-mouthed" in their presence. Both Tierney and Kennedy looked as though they'd been in a half dozen fights and were ready for a couple more. "Let's go," Romano ordered. Tierney refused at first. Romano led the two men out to the sidewalk. Saipan followed.

It was once they were in the early morning air, according to Officer Romano, that he placed the pair under arrest. Tierney began to resist. "I'm going to punch you two all around!" Tierney declared, and suddenly turned and swung. He popped Romano in the face, kicked at Saipan's legs, and then thumped Romano in the chest before delivering the coup de grâce, stepping back and kicking the cop square in the groin. With the hard toe of the leather shoe banging directly into his testicles, Romano folded like a deck chair and dropped to the sidewalk. Saipan moved in, right into the fist end of Tierney's roundhouse. He, too, hit the concrete. Romano rose to his feet and was pulling out his billy club when Tierney kicked him again. Now Kennedy whipped off his coat and began kicking at Saipan. Passersby stopped and watched the two sweaty, crazy construction workers take on two uniformed police officers. The fight didn't last long. Kennedy cocked a fist, but before he could deliver the punch, a whack of Saipan's nightstick quieted him. It wasn't so easy to tame Tierney. An enraged and aching Romano got up for the second time and brought his club down on Tierney's head.

Tierney kept fighting, dead-eyed, animal-like. Romano swung again and again, opening a gash on Tierney's scalp that sprayed blood across the sidewalk. Both cops kept swinging and bashing until Tierney was under control. The suspects were handcuffed, squeezed into the back of the squad car, and sped to the Midtown North precinct house on West Fifty-Fourth Street.

A press photographer was waiting to get the shot of Tierney being dragged in for booking. The shutterbug didn't care about the non-acting Arthur Kennedy, so the arresting officers got in place for the photo of Tierney being walked between the two of them. Saipan has him by the right elbow; Romano clutches his upper left arm. The cops are all business and camera-ready in their heavy uniform coats with shiny gold buttons and hats. Tierney is another picture altogether. His wrists are shackled in front, his shirt torn and open, chest and stomach exposed. His hair is matted, jaw swollen, and face bruised and caked with blood that poured from the wound over his right eye and splashed down his ripped shirt, neck, and bare chest onto his trousers. He is dazed from the booze, brawls, and beating. He is a man who has had his head handed to him.

The cops knew Tierney's appearance didn't reflect well on them. Romano told a reporter that Tierney and Kennedy were already looking "about that bad" when he and his partner arrived at the Midtown Café. Tierney was fighting so wildly and ferociously, Romano said, "we were forced to use the stick on him." When Kennedy got into the act, "he kicked both of us, then drew back a cocked fist . . . but that's as far as he got. We had to bop him."

Tierney and Kennedy were charged with felonious assault. Tierney, who gave his address as the Belvedere Hotel at 319 West Forty-Eighth Street, was also charged with disorderly conduct. After the booking, the cops let Tierney button his shirt and gave him a sports jacket for another news photo. They sat Tierney in a chair and Romano stood over him, pretending to be asking questions. In the photo, Tierney's head wound continues to bleed down his face and onto his shirt. He looks up at the cop hovering close to his left side, seemingly confused and uncomprehending, yet his left leg is crossed, defensively, and his left hand is on that knee, tense, balanced on four fingers, directly in line with the cop's crotch, as if at any moment this wild animal might reach out suddenly to grab and tear out his bruised testicles.

The photo session ended without incident. Tierney and both cops were taken to St. Clare's Hospital on West Fifty-First Street in Hell's Kitchen. Romano was treated for his aching groin, and Saipan complained of ankle injuries from all the kicks. Their prisoner would not accept treatment. A hospital spokesman said that Tierney was cursing so profusely and lashing out so violently, that the staff was unable to handle or treat him. He was returned to a cell, according to the *Daily News,* "shrieking, cursing and challenging one and all to fight."

Later that day, when Tierney and Kennedy were arraigned before Magistrate Francis X. O'Brien, Tierney was still belligerent. His plaid shirt stiff with blood, he said he intended to plead innocent and demanded an attorney.

O'Brien ordered him held on $4,000 bail—$3,500 on the felonious assault charge, and another $500 for disorderly conduct. He set Kennedy's bail at $500. When Kennedy announced that he wanted to plead guilty on the spot, the judge suggested that he find himself a lawyer and save his plea for the hearing on Monday, October 20.

According to the *Daily News,* Lawrence Tierney had the last word. As he was led out of the courtroom to jail, he turned to Officer Romano and snarled, "I'm a cop hater from the word go. You only made me more of a cop hater."

Of course, every newspaper editor worth his salt ran at least one photo of the bloodied Lawrence Tierney. Many headlines mentioned the "one-time bad man movie actor" or "ex-movie tough guy" who was arrested on one of his "periodic rampages." The New York *Journal-American* beat them all by publishing a close-up photo of bloody Tierney under the headline: "FACE OF A 'COP HATER.'"

Before Tierney and Kennedy returned to court, Tierney's lawyers had gotten the charges reduced to simple assault. If there was any justice in the case of the Midtown Café brawl, it was reported by Earl Wilson. Tierney, who'd broken the jaws of Dianetics auditor John Naylor and ad man Gary Jennings, was eventually treated for his wounds from his battle with police.

Among his injuries was a fractured jaw.

Meanwhile, he was back on television.

26

Skidville Avenue

The fire in an apartment house on Ocean Front Walk, overlooking Santa Monica Bay, was reported to Fire Station 63 in Venice, California, on the afternoon of Thursday, February 5, 1959. When firemen arrived at number 2109, smoke was pouring and flames were licking from a window of one of the units. The eighty-three-year-old neighbor who'd escaped the smoke when he was pulled through a window told them a woman was still inside.

The firefighters worked their way into the tiny apartment. On the floor of the bedroom, they found the body of a woman. She was identified as Gruili A. Cross, forty-five years old; she'd lived there alone. Everything in the room, including Mrs. Cross, had been burned. The rest of the small abode was also destroyed—with the exception of one extraordinary item. Neighbors later brushed the ashes from a scrapbook that contained pages of newspaper clippings, magazine articles, photos, and memorabilia revealing Gruili A. Cross's life story and true identity.

The woman who died in obscurity in a cheap apartment in a rundown seaside neighborhood was born in Copenhagen and was once very famous. Gruili A. Cross used to be Gwili Andre, one of the top fashion models of the 1930s. Gwili (pronounced Jee-lee) had been photographed for the covers of *Vogue* and *Harper's Bazaar* and was in great demand in the United States and Europe when David O. Selznick signed her to RKO Radio Pictures. She was cast in the film *Roar of the Dragon*, alongside Richard Dix and Zasu Pitts in 1932, and the studio went all out to promote their "tall, blonde Norse princess out of Hans Anderson's fairy tales . . . with the mystery of Garbo and . . . the fascination of Dietrich."

Gwili had the looks. She had the allure. She did not have the talent and simply didn't click on the big screen. RKO dropped her the following year. She continued to model as her screen career slid to a halt by 1942, a year before

Lawrence Tierney arrived on the RKO lot. Gwili's life unraveled when her second marriage ended in 1948. She turned to the bottle, lost custody of her son, and lived out her years in that apartment in Venice, alone and forgotten. Her neighbors and friends had no idea about her past life and fame.

When she died, Gwili was fifty-two, not forty-five as reported. Forty-five was her Hollywood age.

Lawrence Tierney had the alcoholism and RKO links to Gwili Andre, but on the surface, little else. The week after Gwili Andre's body was found, he was on television in a fresh role as a murderous elevator operator in "One To Get Lost," an episode of *Naked City*. So it could have been perceived as a cheap shot on February 16 when Joseph L. Haas included Tierney in a syndicated story about Gwili Andre titled "Some Movie Greats Have Found Skidville Ave. Steep, Fast Road." Tierney was used as an example of a star who lost his footing at "the top of the tinsel world of filmdom" and learned "it can be greased skids all the way to rock bottom. . . . Can Tierney beat Skidville Ave., a steep, fast road with a few u-turns? Only time will tell."

In the short term, the outlook may have been bright. Tierney, looking to lose the "bad man" image, turned down a television series focused on America's leading mobsters since the 1800s. He reached a milestone in March, turning forty. Dorothy Kilgallen reported that month that he'd switched his membership in Alcoholics Anonymous from the East Coast to a West Coast branch, as he returned to Hollywood to attempt a movie comeback. On May 3, it was reported that Tierney was headed back to New York to appear in an episode of *The Lawless Years*, a new NBC crime drama set in the Roaring Twenties. Unfortunately, that very day, he was arrested in Hollywood.

Nine thirty on a Sunday morning: Officer L. F. Jones was driving his patrol car through the heart of Hollywood, when, just south of Hollywood Boulevard, he came upon a ruckus in the middle of Cahuenga Boulevard. One man was against three, shouting, harassing, and haranguing them. The apparent antagonist was Lawrence Tierney. Officer Jones could see he was "plain drunk."

Once he sorted out the stories, Jones was satisfied that Tierney was the instigator, having verbally abused the trio as they were on their way to church. He sent the three worshippers on their way. He placed Tierney in the back of his car and drove him to the Hollywood jail.

"He was pretty well loaded, but no force had to be used to bring him in," a cop at the jail told a reporter. "He was too belligerent in jail to process right away, so we left him in the drunk tank."

When he sobered up enough, Tierney was booked for drunkenness. He posted twenty dollars bail and was released later in the day. He was ordered to appear in municipal court on Monday.

That morning, the *Los Angeles Times* reported that "the one-time screen badman" had "notched up another episode in his career." UPI reported that the "movie and real-life tough guy who once played outlaw John Dillinger" had been "arrested at least fifteen times on drunk charges on both East and West Coasts." (The actual count was higher. This was at least Tierney's thirty-second arrest on various charges.) That same morning, Tierney failed to show up in court. Judge Howard Schmidt ordered his twenty-dollar bail forfeited.

Scott Brady, meanwhile, had relocated temporarily to New York City. The previous summer, he'd tried his hand at the straw-hat circuit, with his father serving as his publicist. On April 23, 1959, he became the first Tierney to make it to Broadway, when *Destry Rides Again,* a musical loosely based on the 1939 movie, opened at the Imperial Theatre on West Forty-Fifth Street. Brady was third-billed behind stars Andy Griffith and Dolores Gray. Brooks Atkinson grumbled in the *New York Times* that a lot of "talent and labor have been squandered on a conventional western story," but said the audience "seemed to be beside itself with admiration." The critic highlighted Brady's "shrewd acting" as the bad guy.

As summer approached, Lawrence Tierney was gone from New York, but not forgotten, as Earl Wilson wrote in his column on June 11: "A Third Ave. bar sports a sign: 'Lawrence Tierney Fought Here.'" Scott Brady didn't forget his brother, either. In *Destry Rides Again,* he played, in the words of correspondent Whitney Bolton, "a really arrogant, dirty-trick, low-down villain . . . of superbly felonious stature." It didn't escape him, that had circumstances been different, the role would have been perfect for Larry. Talking to Bolton during the publicity rounds for *Destry,* Brady gave credit where he knew it was due.

"Hal Wallis gave me a screen test because my brother took me to lunch and Wallis saw me," he said. "From that test to my first paid job is exactly two years. I think I made more tests than Wasserman ever did in his laboratory."

"Speaking of my brother, I want to mention him. His name is Lawrence Tierney and he has been mentioned in the press as getting into this and that brawl. Be that as it may, I'm beholden to him. Without him, I'd never have stuck it out in Hollywood. He is a hell of a good actor, a hell of a good brother, and I want that on the record."

Scott Brady put it on the record again in Mel Heimer's syndicated column, My New York. "'Without my brother's encouragement to fall back on, I'd never stuck it out,' Scott says. The wistful part about it all is that inch by inch, after that, Brady climbed up the path of security—while mile by mile, swiftly and tragically, Lawrence slid down it to the point where every couple of months the cops seem to be taking him off to the pokey for brawling."

That sounded disturbingly like Skidville Avenue, but even after fifteen years of troublemaking, there was another chance for Lawrence Tierney, so long as he announced that he was back on the wagon.

"For good this time, he tells me," Hollywood columnist Mike Connolly relayed on August 3, leading to his scoop that the actor was collaborating with Ronnie Shedlo, Errol Flynn's nineteen-year-old personal assistant, on a script called *Christmas Story* for General Electric Theater. "Doesn't mean Larry's giving up his acting career. Just means he's between jobs and writing is one way of letting off steam."

It was also announced in August that Scott Brady would be returning to Hollywood and a regular role on television. *Shotgun Slade*, a Western pilot that aired in March on the CBS anthology series, *Schlitz Playhouse of Stars*, was rolling out as a syndicated series in November. Brady would star as a detective who got around on horseback and toted a unique sawed-off shooter (with a shotgun barrel for close work and rifle barrel for distance). Though set in the Wild West, the series, according to IMDb, had more in common with modern detective series like *Peter Gunn* and *77 Sunset Strip* than *Gunsmoke*.

When Brady filmed his series on the Revue Studios (soon to be Universal Studios) backlot over the hill from Hollywood, his older brother would be working, as well. The Cahuenga Boulevard incident apparently cost Tierney a gig on *The Lawless Years*, but Kilgallen reported days after Connolly's item that he'd be handed another "comeback chance" in *Captain of Detectives,* a television series starring Robert Taylor as the leader of a police squad chasing down crimes in an unnamed city. Ultimately retitled *The Detectives,* the series was filmed on the Republic lot on Radford Avenue in Hollywood and would run for three seasons. Tierney was featured in the eleventh episode, which aired on Christmas Day.

So once again, in the summer of 1959, Lawrence Tierney was back. Earl Wilson reported on September 4 that he'd "reformed—he sticks to orange juice and carries a pocket chess set to the local cafes."

Two weeks later, Tierney was arrested, drunk and fighting.

On Friday, September 18, two men were exchanging punches on the sidewalk outside Hollywood High School on the corner of North Highland Avenue and Sunset Boulevard. One was a sturdy, middle-aged man who appeared to have a knowledge of the art of fisticuffs. The other man was somewhat smaller, visibly older, and though trading swings, getting the worst.

The elderly man clambered away, scrambled into the school, and took refuge inside. The other man followed, and the shouting and fighting continued inside the halls of learning. A vice principal and several male teachers collared the aggressor, forced him back outside, and held him until police arrived.

The arresting officer reported that the suspect, Lawrence Tierney, "reeked of whisky." Tierney was booked on a plain drunk charge at the Hollywood station and locked in the drunk tank. He was released the next morning after posting twenty-one dollars bail.

27

In Like Flynn

On October 14, 1959, Errol Flynn died laughing.

That at least was the account initially given to reporters by Dorothy Caldough, Flynn's hostess in Vancouver, British Columbia, where he'd traveled to negotiate the sale of his yacht to Dorothy's husband, and where he breathed his last at the age of fifty. According to Mrs. Caldough, the reckless, roguish former movie idol was at a cocktail party, regaling guests with tales of his adventures, when he complained of back pain, went into a bedroom to rest, and lost consciousness.

The truth was somewhat more complicated, and sadder.

The Errol Flynn who landed at Vancouver International Airport from Los Angeles five days earlier was graying, swollen, paunchy, and bloated. The survivor of two heart attacks, he was afflicted with cirrhosis, back trouble, an intestinal disorder, genital warts, and a touch of malaria. There was vomit on his shirt, the residue of a reaction to the vodka he'd swilled on the flight, and on his arm was Beverly Aadland, a seventeen-year-old blonde he'd been paired with since she was fifteen.

Flynn had traveled to the Canadian province on a heartbreaking mission. His career at its lowest ebb, in debt to the IRS and past wives, and drowning in legal bills from his third divorce, he was forced to sell off his last prized possession—and sometime home since Warner Bros. dropped him in 1952—the sailing yacht, *Zaca*, to stock promoter George Caldough.

The Caldoughs were driving their guests back to the airport when Flynn complained of severe pain in his back and legs. George Caldough made a detour to the home of Dr. Grant Gould (uncle of pianist Glenn Gould), who resided in the "penthouse" apartment of a two-story building at 1310 Burnaby Street. The doctor gave Flynn a shot of Demerol, and feeling better, Flynn did entertain Gould's neighbors with tales of the Bundy Drive days before he retreated to a bedroom for a nap from which he did not awaken.

Although Errol Flynn was one of his heroes and he'd always claimed that his defense of Flynn was the reason he threw the punch that launched the Battle of Decker's Lawn, Lawrence Tierney was not among the Hollywood celebrities sought out by reporters and columnists seeking tributes to the late, great actor.

It would be several weeks before Lawrence Tierney earned headlines on his own. The story was all too familiar. Another binge. Another woman. Another door she refused to open.

Tierney got a surprise when he forced his way into Beatrice Colgan's apartment in West Hollywood in the early hours of Sunday, November 8, 1959. He'd shouted that he was searching for "Mary," with whom he'd spent time on Saturday night. Once he bulled his way through the door, he realized that he'd crashed a small party. Among the guests was Carroll Coates, a thirty-year-old British-born songwriter and film composer. Two of his songs had been recorded by Frank Sinatra and his tune, "The Drive-In Rock," was featured in the recent film, *Blue Denim*. For some reason, Tierney focused on him.

"I didn't recognize him," Coates says. More than sixty years later, at age ninety-one, he recalls Tierney's entrance like it was yesterday. "He was drunk. An intimidating figure. I'm about a hundred and seventy pounds. He was probably well over two hundred. I was standing and talking to some people and he said something like, 'Oh you, you goddamn Limey,' or something like that—and *boom!* Broke my front tooth. It was a shock. I was just standing, talking to somebody, and he muttered something and then hauled off and hit me! I think he thought I was going to steal his girlfriend or something. I didn't fight back because he'd knocked my front tooth out—half of it. So I was looking for the piece."

Others hustled Tierney out of the place. He tore up some drapes along the way.

Tierney was arrested and charged with drunkenness, battery, and disturbing the peace. He gave his address as 8690 Lookout Mountain Avenue in Laurel Canyon, and later in the day, after the sun was up and he'd sobered up, Tierney was arraigned in Beverly Hills Municipal Court. He was released on $288 bail.

In Judge Adolph Alexander's court on November 23, Tierney pleaded innocent to all the charges. He denied punching Carroll Coates, claiming he "only bumped" him. Tierney was ordered to stand trial on January 7.

Coates wasn't called to testify in court, and unlike some others on the receiving end of Tierney's fist, didn't sue. He did need to see a dentist. "I had to have that tooth removed and a false one with a post put in," he says. "I was sort of in a state of shock afterwards. I was scared of him, and after that happened I was worried that when I was going around to parties and things like that, that I would run into him again, or he'd run into me, literally. He scared me."

Twenty-six days before his trial was set to begin, Lawrence Tierney was arrested again. In this case, he was the recipient of a punch to the mouth.

The spiraling trouble of Saturday, December 12, began on Wilshire Boulevard. Tierney, twenty-three-year-old Allan Wem, and another fellow were walking from one bar to another when Tierney and Wem began to argue and engage in physical combat. The fight became lively enough to annoy and alarm holiday shoppers. Someone called the police, but by the time officers arrived, the men were all fought out. All three were sitting on the curb. Tierney, unkempt, unshaven, less than coherent, and very drunk, was dripping blood from a split lip. He was the only one placed under arrest.

Tierney's mouth was bleeding heavily enough that before transporting him to the city jail, the cops made a stop at the Central Receiving Hospital on Sixth Street for sutures. They were inside the building when Tierney suddenly went berserk. He tackled the cops, cursed at the nurses and orderlies, and flailed at the doctors until he was overpowered and strapped by his wrists to an examining table. He was straining at the straps, kicking at the cops, and shouting when one of the uniforms came up with a way to quiet him. He stood over Tierney, and with his left hand pressed Tierney's head into a pillow. A news photographer documented what he did with his other hand. A caption accompanying a wire service photo describes the picture.

"Hush Up: LOS ANGELES, Calif.—Officer Roman Fromm rams a towel into the mouth of Lawrence Tierney to muffle his words as the actor tries desperately to kick Fromm off. The policeman succeeded in shutting Lawrence up."

"I've tried hard. I just can't make it. Even Alcoholics Anonymous couldn't turn the trick with me. It's a great organization, but I didn't have the willpower to stick it out."

On the first day of the 1960s, newspaper readers encountered the words of a candid, chastened Lawrence Tierney. Tierney admitted to syndicated columnist Harold Heffernan that after "a couple of drinks," he would lose control. In Heffernan's words, "If he imbibes one, it always means another—then one more encounter with the police."

"Some fortunate people can solve their problems by normal outlets, such as eating, playing golf, tennis or swimming," Tierney said. "But as for me—well, I don't go much for food and not at all for exercise. My troubles always seem to begin when I have to work late. And there's very little to do in this town then except go to a bar."

The interview with the Hollywood journalist, published two weeks after his Wilshire Boulevard drunk arrest and subsequent towel-eating incident, didn't take place in the visiting room of a prison or sanitarium, but in the commissary on the Twentieth Century–Fox lot in West Los Angeles. Tierney had spent the night in jail for that last publicized arrest, and on the following day, December 13, was sentenced to an additional day behind bars, but the sentence was suspended. Tierney was still looking forward to his trial on January 7 for forcing his way into Beatrice Colgan's apartment and punching Carroll Coates in the face (and, if Heffernan's later stories were accurate, newspapers didn't even bother to report that he'd been cited twice during this period for drunk driving).

Tierney was now seated among the stars, with a lunch of boiled beef in front of him and his father at his side, to promote his latest "comeback," a guest role on the ABC television series *Adventures in Paradise,* which starred Gardner McKay as a Korean War veteran who sails his schooner around the South Pacific. The conversation centered on Tierney's disappointment that he lived alone in a small apartment and had never married. He told Heffernan that if he had a wife and kids to come home to, he might have kept out of bars, and trouble.

"All three of my boys live here in town, but in their own places," the elder Tierney interjected. "We're an independent lot—but come trouble and we're as one. This boy here is a handful, I admit. And to think—if it hadn't been for hooch he might have become one of the biggest stars in Hollywood."

Tierney hadn't touched that boiled beef from the commissary kitchen and after those words, he wasn't about to. He said that he'd "gone on the wagon" every December 31 for the last ten years. "Once he made it through January," Heffernan wrote. "More often the skid came in a matter of hours."

This time, Tierney didn't last a week.

Tierney had an appointment with Judge Alexander in Beverly Hills Municipal Court on January 7, 1960. He entered a not-guilty plea to charges of drunkenness, disturbing the peace, and battery in the Beatrice Colgan incident, and the judge postponed the case until February 4.

A few hours later, Tierney got word that his mother was dead.

According to early reports, Lawrence H. Tierney had called his sons to their ailing mother's bedside in their apartment at 931 North Spaulding Avenue in West Hollywood. All three brothers arrived around the same time as the fire department rescue squad, and were there when she passed. Those reports also added some intrigue by noting that "police found a bottle of sleeping pills nearby." Within hours, it was clear that Ed Tracy, back from Germany, had found his mother dead in the apartment he shared with her (it was never publicized that Marion "Mary" Alice and Lawrence Sr. had split up some years earlier). The youngest son told police that she'd been released from a hospital three weeks earlier and was still recuperating from the heart attack that put her there. Mary Alice Tierney had apparently succumbed to another heart attack at sixty-five, but the presence of the pill bottle led police to mark the death as a "possible suicide."

That night, sheriff's deputies in West Hollywood spotted Lawrence Tierney staggering along a nearby street, "unsteady of gait and loud of voice." After arresting him for drunkenness, the deputies showed some sympathy for their frequent guest, pointing out in their press release that Tierney had been picked up hours after his mother's death, and did not resist. The Associated Press followed suit, reporting that Tierney was taken in while "sorrowing over the death of his mother."

When Tierney failed to show up in court the following day to answer the latest intoxication charge, Judge Alexander was informed of the situation and did not order Tierney's arrest.

The Cunningham and O'Connor Mortuary on Melrose Avenue handled the funeral arrangements. Rosary was recited for Mary Alice Tierney on Sunday evening at St. Ambrose Roman Catholic Church on Fairfax Avenue, a few blocks from where she died. A requiem High Mass was said at 10 a.m. Monday. She was interred in a mausoleum at Holy Cross Cemetery in Culver City.

Most evidence leads to the conclusion that Mary Alice Tierney's death was accidental. "She didn't leave a note," Timothy Tierney says. "She had stress in her life and was dealing with it in maybe not the best way. She drank too much, and she needed sleeping pills to get to sleep every night. She took too many pills and too many drinks at the same time, and that was it."

At the time, the Tierney family wasn't so sure. They knew that her eldest son was a major cause of Mary Alice's distress. "I certainly heard that Larry got blamed by my dad, and maybe other people in the family, for driving her to this point where she did die," Tim adds. "And it wouldn't surprise me if Larry blamed himself as well."

According to "family legend," their mother's death eventually led to a "colossal fistfight between Lawrence Tierney and Scott Brady on a Hollywood street," and an estrangement that lasted until 1983, when another family tragedy prompted a shaky truce.

Through all these tumultuous first days of the 1960s, Lawrence Tierney could be seen at all hours of the day on television, as Dillinger and the bodyguard, in *Born to Kill* and *Female Jungle.* Added to those now golden oldies were two new roles, in episodes of popular television series that happened to run back-to-back on ABC on January 25.

At 9:30 p.m., it was *Adventures in Paradise,* the show he'd promoted in the Fox commissary. Tierney played a bitter ex-army man in the episode "Walk Through the Night," set in the New Guinea jungle, but filmed in the Santa Monica Mountains at the 20th Century-Fox Ranch near Malibu.

The episode was followed by *Man with a Camera,* starring Charles Bronson as a former combat photographer who solved crimes in New York City. In "Hot Ice Cream," Tierney fit the part as a murdering, dope-dealing amusement park ice cream vendor—another tough, tight-lipped, and threatening—if middle-aged—bad man. The climactic scene, in which Tierney engaged in a lively brawl with Bronson, gave viewers an idea of what it might have been like to witness Tierney in action after he had one too many at a nitery.

"Actor Lawrence Tierney rejoined AA, ordered a Shirley Temple cocktail (ginger ale) at Armando's."

Earl Wilson's "sighting" of Tierney at the end of January, in New York City and abstaining at the café society hotspot, showed that the cycle would continue into a third decade, and that the sometime actor still made for good copy. With his deep history of scandal, Tierney would always be afforded column space, if only as a cautionary tale. The day Wilson's item was on newsstands, a separate stack of papers held Harry Schreiner's column debunking the "mistaken attitude that . . . being related to a star is the show biz kiss of death." Among the array of children and siblings who beat the "Hollywood family jinx" was Scott Brady, whose "trouble prone brother, Lawrence Tierney . . . had much too much and not too soon either. After only a few movies and finally stardom as Dillinger, he hit the juice and the skids at the same time."

Harold Heffernan returned on Valentine's Day with a feature on claims that Los Angeles judges were giving preferential treatment to celebrities arrested for drunk driving. The case of John Agar sparked the "fair play" campaign, but Lawrence Tierney, an infrequent driver, was cited "as by far the most frequent offender."

Tierney was even drawn into a scandal involving celebrities he didn't know. William Talman, who played the hapless district attorney Hamilton Burger on the CBS series *Perry Mason,* was arrested on March 13. Sheriff's detectives had raided an apartment on North Curson Avenue in Hollywood expecting to bust up a marijuana party, only to interrupt Talman and seven other naked people entwined in a Benzedrine-fueled sex orgy.

Tierney was not among the nude revelers. According to Danton Walker, he was "making different news in Hollywood, bringing friends into the Alcoholics Anonymous fold at the rate of one a week." But Tierney was featured prominently in the May 22 *New York Daily News* feature, "Can The Good Guys Be Bad Guys Off-Screen?" cited as "Hollywood's most tragic example" of an actor whose original bad guy screen role led to a "personality merger."

"The on-screen Dillinger began a new off-screen career as an adult delinquent (although) he never came close to Dillinger's level of crime. When he was arrested last December as a plain drunk, he hardly made the papers."

With Tierney proselytizing for Alcoholics Anonymous and working hard on television, the dredging of his past could be seen as a little unfair.

Until nine days later.

28

Chinatown

Grand Macnish blended Scotch whisky was created in 1863 by an ornery tea, tobacco, wine, and spirit merchant in Glasgow. Robert McNish set out to create a lighter and smoother version of the harsh usquebaugh of the day and came up with a recipe that became known as the finest Scotch whisky of all. The popularity of Grand Macnish spread throughout the United Kingdom and into North America. The brand was featured in Robert MacKendrick's 1949 film, *Whisky Galore!* Ernest Hemingway gave the blend a boost in 1952 by giving it his highest recommendation. In 1960, a bottle of Grand Macnish had a costarring role with Lawrence Tierney in a scene that could have been taken from a screwball comedy, but was, sadly, a rerun of a playlet acted too many times before.

It was the evening of Monday, May 30. A young woman named Carma Monson called the Beverly Hills Police Department to report a man outside her apartment, attempting to break down the door. She was less frantic than annoyed. Officers arrived to find Lawrence Tierney waiting quietly. He was unsteady, swaying slightly, and cradling something in his arms, as if it were a precious baby. Closer inspection revealed that Tierney was holding a Grand Macnish whisky bottle. The bottle was empty. The officers asked Tierney to identify himself.

He pointed to the label of the bottle. "I'm Mr. McNish," he said.

Had Tierney been carrying a bottle of Macallan or Glenlivet, his response would not have had the same comedic effect. The "sh" sound at the end of "McNish" provided Tierney's rejoinder with the classic slurring speech of the comic drunk. The scene would have been classic comedy, if Tierney hadn't been awaiting trial on charges of battery, disturbing the peace, and drunkenness for forcing his way into another woman's apartment in West Hollywood in November 1959. He was booked, once again, on a plain drunk charge and moved to the jail in Beverly Hills. After five hours behind bars, he was sober enough to be released on twenty-six dollars bail.

When reporters visited Carma Monson in hopes of collecting colorful details, she told them to go away. "I don't want to talk about it," she said.

Tierney was ordered to show up in court on Tuesday. He did not, and so forfeited his twenty-six dollar bail. He'd be in a courtroom soon enough. His trial for the break-in at Beatrice Colgan's apartment was finally set for July 28, but by the time the case reached Judge Adolph Alexander, the charges had been slimmed down to a simple drunk count. Although the defendant had been arrested on at least five occasions since the incident, Judge Alexander dispatched the case quickly. He fined Tierney $200, gave him a sixty-day jail sentence, suspended the sentence, placed him on a year's probation, and ordered him to quit drinking.

Yes, as part of his sentence, Lawrence Tierney was ordered to refrain from drinking alcohol. A review of his past record would indicate that would be easier ordered than followed.

Lawrence Tierney faded into the background in the weeks to follow, but while he remained out of the news and all newspaper sections save the television listings, there were several notable events in his life. He teamed up again with Sammy Petrillo in a low-budget film shot at a resort in the Catskill Mountains. *Unholy Alliance* was never released, and possibly never completed. "Lawrence Tierney and I were hitchhiking from a guy that was gonna kill us," Petrillo told Todd Rutt in 1991. "I don't even remember what it was about."

On September 3, there was an event at the Fifth Avenue Presbyterian Church in Manhattan that could have caused him to stick his head into another running electric fan. Georgette McDonald, the woman for whom he punched many men in the nose and first broke down an apartment door, married John Otis of the Otis Elevator fortune.

Even more momentous was a day that went unreported, and that at the time may have seemed very unremarkable to him. On or about November 12, 1960, Lawrence Tierney spent time with a woman. Two hundred and eighty days later—forty weeks, or nine months and seven days—on August 19, 1961, a child would be born. A girl. His daughter. Tierney would never acknowledge the identity of the mother—and for good reason—but her name would be linked with his in the weeks ahead.

❧

Q. Who played the lead in "Dillinger," Humphrey Bogart or Lawrence Tierney?—L.O., Endicott, N.Y.
A. It was Tierney, in 1945.

Q. I recently saw a movie on the life of John Dillinger. I recognized
Scott Brady as the actor playing the lead, but the narrator never
named him or any of the other actors. This often happens. Don't
you think viewers would like to see the names of the cast of these
old movies?—C.P., York, Pa.
A. We must agree with that. It's often very irritating to recognize an
actor and not be sure of his name. A listing of the cast at the end
would have saved you a little confusion too—that it wasn't Brady, it
was his brother, Lawrence Tierney.

If "viewers" had forgotten that Lawrence Tierney had played John Dillinger
fifteen years earlier, they were reminded once again on December 15, 1960, by
reports that "Actor Lawrence Tierney, 41, who played gangster John Dillinger
in a movie, was arrested early today on a drunken driving charge."

Sheriff's deputies M. H. Chance and J. E. Barrett had clocked Tierney
doing sixty in a thirty-five-mile-per-hour zone on La Cienega Boulevard by the
time they pulled him over near Santa Monica Boulevard in West Hollywood.
He was driving a car owned by Anne Winterburn. Anne was in the passenger
seat. She was twenty-four, a beauty from Pasadena, a graduate of the May-
field Senior School of the Holy Child Jesus (a private, Catholic, all-girls high
school), and this wasn't the first time she'd made news in the passenger seat of
an automobile driving too fast. In Pasadena on July 28, 1953, sixteen-year-old
Anne was in a sedan driven by her friend Carol Murray, also sixteen, when
Carol lost control on a steep hairpin curve. The car rolled thirty feet down
an embankment before crashing, upside-down, in a driveway. The impact
crushed the car's roof down to the dashboard and both girls suffered ankle
fractures, cuts, and other injuries. The accident made national news because
of a wire service photo showing Anne, in her schoolgirl dress, lying under the
overturned auto, a policeman kneeling at her side.

More recently, Anne had been among the line of leggy dancers in the Las
Vegas–style revue, *Showgirls of 1960*, at Bimbo's 365 Club in San Francisco and
had achieved a degree of local fame when she was crowned Miss Shellfish at
Bernstein's Fish Grotto on Powell Street. Now, she remained in the passenger
seat, playing it cool while her date got hot under the collar.

"There was some difference of opinion," Deputy Chance later told reporters. "He was trying to get belligerent, but we didn't give him a chance." Chance and Barrett slapped the handcuffs on Tierney. No punches were thrown.

Tierney gave his address as 7606 1/2 Lexington Avenue in West Hollywood, a half mile from the apartment in which his mother died. The deputies escorted him to jail, charged with drunk driving.

Anne Winterburn said that she lived at 652 North Veteran Avenue, across from the Los Angeles National Cemetery. The cops let her go. She took the car and drove off. This, however, would not be the last time she'd be a part of the Lawrence Tierney story. In 2002, Tierney's nephew Michael Tierney revealed that Anne Winterburn was pregnant at the time, and on August 19, 1961, gave birth to Lawrence Tierney's daughter. Michael knew the family secret because Anne Winterburn was also his mother. Edward Tierney married Anne on May 23, 1964, and raised Elizabeth Tierney as his own daughter.

"I have a three-quarter sister by (Lawrence)," Michael, who was born on January 24, 1965, confirmed to Rick McKay. "It's pretty confusing, but he met my mother first, before my dad, and had a kid by her, but my dad ended up marrying her. She's my sister, but we have the same mother and her father is my uncle. Very *Chinatown*."

It was a familiar sight the following Thursday: Lawrence Tierney and his lawyer in Beverly Hills Municipal Court. Tierney and Judge Henry Draeger had met more than once, many years earlier. The judge took Tierney's latest "not guilty" plea, this time to the drunk driving rap, and ordered him to return for trial on February 9.

Tierney could be seen on network television the night after Christmas, in an episode of the NBC private eye series *Peter Gunn*. Tierney played a thug who locked horns with star Craig Stevens. For those who may have forgotten, the critic for the *Boston Globe* mentioned that Lawrence Tierney "is the older brother of Scott ('Shotgun Slade') Brady and bears a remarkable resemblance to him."

While his trial was delayed further, Tierney did day work at Desilu Studios, playing a detective in a couple of episodes of NBC's *The Barbara Stanwyck Show*. He received some international attention in February when the *Sydney Morning Herald* in Australia ran a story about "a new Hollywood ailment—success sickness. The symptoms? They range from 'an acute anxiety neurosis' to a 'deep-rooted career complex.'" Tierney was declared recovered from his own "Dillinger complex," and was "reformed and . . . on the verge of a comeback."

"I'm done with drinking," he was quoted, "and I'm done with the fear of failure, the fear of not holding on to the top. From now on I take what comes with good grace."

Tierney accepted, with grace, the decision of Judge Charles J. Griffin in Beverly Hills Municipal Court on May 4, in the drunk driving case: a $158 fine, summary probation, and a suspended jail sentence if he stayed out of trouble for twelve months. The judge suspended Tierney's driver's license for thirty days, but said he'd recommend that the Department of Motor Vehicles not revoke the license for good.

Dick Powell hosted the thirteenth Prime Time Emmy Awards on May 16, 1961, at Frank Sennes's sprawling Moulin Rouge theater and nightclub on Sunset Boulevard. A few days earlier, UPI's Hollywood man Vernon Scott showed how real life and television roles had merged for the three lead actor nominees. The office of Raymond Burr, unbeatable trial attorney on *Perry Mason,* was crammed with law books, and Burr often spoke to legal groups. Jackie Cooper, a Navy doctor on *Hennessy,* had an office on the same General Services Studio lot, full of nautical mementos and "medical doodads including a fancy stethoscope." Robert Stack, G-man in *The Untouchables,* was proud of his many shooting trophies.

Scott acknowledged that his theory wasn't new, but one that had been talked about for more than fifteen years: "Remember Lawrence Tierney? After playing John Dillinger he had more troubles with the cops than the original desperado. It's something to think about."

Remember Lawrence Tierney? Lawrence Tierney would make them remember. He may have been considered by producers and casting directors to be just another generic face to fill supporting roles as detectives or thugs, but he was about to crash the A-list, literally, costarring with two of the biggest stars in the world. Alongside them, he would make headlines around the globe. Everyone would remember Lawrence Tierney.

Of course, not in the way one might prefer.

29

Incident at P.J.'s

The Moiseyev Dance Troupe of Moscow launched its second American tour on April 18, 1961, at the Metropolitan Opera House. The troupe of one hundred Bolshoi-trained folk dancers and full orchestra had first arrived in New York City three years earlier for a ten-city North American tour that also opened at the Met. American audiences were thrilled and awestruck by the virtuoso dancing, whirling, spinning, and leaping displays of vitality and abilities that seemed beyond human capacity.

The excitement had spread nationwide by the time the Moiseyevs stepped off the SP Lark at Union Station in Los Angeles on June 20, 1961. That night the troupe performed the first of ten sold-out shows at the downtown Shrine Auditorium. As there had been in cities on both Moiseyev tours, protesters were outside the Shrine, holding placards and waving American flags, objecting to the trade with the Communists, but inside the auditorium, politics was not an issue among the audience of sixty-six hundred, including many members of the "Hollywood film colony."

Of all the Hollywood stars who witnessed the performance that opening night, few were as impressed or mesmerized as Elizabeth Taylor and Eddie Fisher. The Hollywood power couple had married in scandal two years earlier (she had been friends with Fisher's wife, the wholesome actress Debbie Reynolds), but Taylor won sympathy in March when a bout with staphylococcus pneumonia while filming the title role in the 20th Century-Fox film, *Cleopatra*, left her near death and requiring a tracheotomy. She recovered, and in April won the Best Actress Oscar for *BUtterfield 8*. Fisher, a popular singer, was a costar in the film. His nightclub career was thriving.

The week the Moiseyevs were in Los Angeles, the couple played host. They invited the troupe to the Fox lot to watch movies, presided over a dinner at the posh L'Escoffier Restaurant in the Beverly Hilton, and, after the final performance on June 28, treated the visitors to what they hoped to be a typical, all-American, Hollywood party.

The couple bought out P.J.'s, a swinging new nightclub and restaurant (said to be named after P.J. Clarke's, Lawrence Tierney's old Third Avenue drinking and fighting ground) at 8151 Santa Monica Boulevard in West Hollywood, for the event. Festivities began not long after midnight Thursday. More than a hundred Russian dancers and orchestra members and an equal number of Hollywood celebrities mingled in the club's dark, wood-paneled rooms. A jazz trio played in the main room. A piano soloist tinkled in another. A jukebox played during breaks.

Hamburgers, chili, barbecued spare ribs, and steaks were on the menu. The Russians particularly loved the chili. They drank mostly beer and Scotch. The ones who sat in the booths, at tables with checkered tablecloths, were fascinated by P.J.'s gimmick: earphones for customers to listen to their favorite tunes in private. Movie stars were everywhere. There was Mel Ferrer. Joan Collins made an entrance. Tony Curtis and wife, Janet Leigh, swept in. Soon, Leigh was standing by the piano and teaching a swing step to a young male Russian dancer. Laurence Harvey, another *BUtterfield 8* star, showed the Russians how Americans dance to jazz.

Of course, Eddie Fisher was itching to get up onstage in the main room. Backed by the trio, he sang "Around the World in 80 Days." The Russians cheered. "Bravo! *Bis! Bis!*" ("Wonderful! Encore!"). When he followed up with the popular Soviet song, "Moscow Nights," everyone sang along.

Janet Leigh moved to the foyer. She led four of the phenomenal dancing girls through some swing and Latin steps. They led her through some folk dance moves.

Elizabeth Taylor and a group of dancers posed for the news cameras out front.

"We love these people," Fisher told reporters. "We've never met them before their opening night here. And we don't consider this a function. It's just something we wanted to do because they're so darned nice."

Everyone was having a great time.

It was after 3 a.m., and the celebration was winding down, when Lawrence Tierney pushed his way past the off-duty police officer at the door and through the crowd of Russians, deeper into the dark, smoky, boisterous club, closer to the music and the nearest bar. He had one goal: another drink. When he couldn't get one, he wasn't happy. One of the security men had a few words with the party crasher and led him back toward the door. Tierney cooperated, until he was a step from outside, when he suddenly and unexpectedly lashed out with punches.

Other guards moved in and the tussle moved out to the driveway. The fight didn't last long, but was in full view of Taylor, Fisher, and some of the guests. The Russian dancers had gotten a treat. They'd not only been able to experience a Hollywood party, but witnessed a traditional Hollywood party brawl.

Tierney was booked at the West Hollywood sheriff's substation on charges of assault, disturbing the peace, and that old standby, drunkenness. When it was obvious that he was too intoxicated and surly to attend a 9 a.m. court hearing, he was transferred to the county jail. He was stashed in a cell, where he quickly fell asleep. Later in the day, he was released on bail of $393.75 and ordered to return to Beverly Hills Municipal Court the following Wednesday, after the July Fourth holiday, for arraignment.

Elizabeth Taylor and Eddie Fisher's party for the Moiseyev Dance Troupe was a major Hollywood event, star-studded, culturally significant, and even historic. It would lead the US State Department to choose the couple to represent the United States at the Moscow Film Festival in July. But in the days following the event, everything was overshadowed by Lawrence Tierney's cameo appearance.

Every newspaper article in every newspaper across the country focused on the attempt by the forty-two-year-old actor who once played Dillinger on the screen to crash the Red bash. The headlines included "TIERNEY FIGHTS COPS AT PARTY," "LIZ AND EDDIE'S PARTY ENDS WITH CRASHER IN JAIL," and perhaps the most colorful: "NAB TIERNEY FOR RUSHIN' EDDIE-LIZ RUSSIAN PARTY."

If anyone assumed that his actions were meant as a patriotic stand against Communism, Tierney made it clear he had nothing against the Russians. He was objecting to not being served. It was a phenomenon in itself that the star of the story was the town drunk. Well past his prime, fifteen years after his great opportunity at stardom, essentially kicked out of movies and relegated to support spots on television series, Tierney had managed to snatch the glory from A-list, Academy Award–winning, chart-topping, gossip column–headlining actors and performers, as well as the dance troupe that was America's flavor of the month. Poignantly, in this case, it truly was a last hurrah. The glory days of the one-punch fight and sidewalk brawls on the Sunset Strip were in the past. Ciro's had closed in December 1957. The Mocambo shut its doors for good the following July.

P.J.'s was on the vanguard of a new nightclub scene, the era of the discotheque. There would be fights, but the combatants were a generation removed from Lawrence Tierney, a relic from a Hollywood gone by.

Tierney showed up alone in court the day after the Fourth. He said his attorney was out of town, and so was granted a continuance until July 12 before entering a plea. When he returned with a lawyer to Judge Adolph Alexander's courtroom, he pleaded innocent to charges of battery and being drunk on private property. He asked for a jury trial. Trial was set for August 23.

The judge then ordered that Tierney be returned to county jail for sixty days, because the latest arrest violated his probation from his drunk driving arrest in December 1960. The bailiffs cuffed his wrists, and Tierney was led away.

The fallout from Tierney's arrest didn't end there. The publicity over his actions almost cost P.J.'s nightclub its entertainment license. Charles Murano, who operated the joint for the owners, was called before the county public welfare commission. Staff assistant Neal Abrahamson reminded him that P.J.'s license didn't allow for public dancing. The commission, however, took no action.

With Tierney jailed until September 10, his P.J.'s trial was moved back to Monday, September 25. It never took place. On Friday, September 22, Tierney made a surprise appearance in Judge Alexander's courtroom and pleaded guilty to one count of battery. Judge Alexander accepted the plea and suspended the drunk charge. He sentenced Tierney to another year of probation, and once again ordered that he not drink alcohol during those twelve months.

The day that Tierney's trial would have opened, Elizabeth Taylor went back to work on *Cleopatra*, which would become Hollywood's most expensive and troubled production.

By the time he'd shaken off another sixty-day residency in the county jail, the Hollywood landscape shifting beneath him, this experience of sharing headlines with the superstars of the day seemed to be Tierney's last stand. He certainly was no longer the chiseled, frightening character people recognized. He was carrying more weight. He was middle-aged. What could be next for him after falling so far?

Another comeback, of course.

Lawrence Tierney, as practically everyone in Hollywood who knew him would attest, was a very "nice guy" when he wasn't drinking, and there were still people in Hollywood willing to give him another "last chance at a comeback." So, while Elizabeth Taylor was in Rome shooting *Cleopatra* for 20th Century-Fox,

Tierney was filming on the 20th Century-Fox lot in West Los Angeles. He had a small guest role on an episode of *Bus Stop,* the ABC anthology series based on William Inge's Broadway play. Inge, one of the most successful playwrights of the 1950s and winner of a Pulitzer Prize for his play, *Picnic,* was the show's script supervisor. He and Tierney, both struggling alcoholics, had struck up a friendship in New York City during Inge's heyday.

Even more helpful was William H. Wright, who'd produced *The Barbara Stanwyck Show,* including the two episodes that featured Tierney in guest roles. Wright was currently producing *Follow the Sun,* an adventure series about a pair of freelance magazine writers based in Hawaii. The show had premiered on ABC the week that Tierney pleaded guilty in the P.J.'s case. Wright offered Tierney the sizable, featured role of a mobster in an episode that paired him with singer and actress Julie London.

Word of this latest last chance hit hard and fast and spilled across the gossip columns. Harrison Carroll broke the somewhat surprising news on November 9 and phrased it as a question: "Isn't Lawrence Tierney set to play a heavy in a 'Follow the Sun' TV segment?" Dorothy Kilgallen one-upped her competitor four days later, saying that Tierney seemed "to be hitting the comeback trail instead of the bottle. Those who witnessed his first performance in the TV series 'Follow the Sun' report that he was splendid." The following day, Dorothy Manners, filling in for Louella Parsons, wrote that virtue was paying off for Tierney, who'd "kept on the straight and narrow so well lately" that producer-director Stanley Kramer spoke to him "about playing Bobby Darin's father in *Point Blank.*

"Ironically, the part is that of a dypso, an affliction not unknown to Tierney," she typed. "But everyone on the 20th Century-Fox lot where he's now making a TV show reports that Larry has been a model of deportment and very cooperative."

The story was next handed off to Harold Heffernan, who ran with it on November 19. In a rerun of late 1959, when Tierney was making another "comeback" on *Adventures in Paradise,* Tierney was sitting across from Heffernan in the Fox commissary, and again, Tierney's father was at his side. Lawrence Sr. was now his bodyguard, guarding the actor against himself, driving him to the studio in the morning, staying with him throughout the day, and driving him home at night, helping avoid all temptation. The familiar feature story was summed up in its headline and subtitle: "LAWRENCE TIERNEY'S STRUGGLE TO STRAIGHTEN HIMSELF OUT: ACTOR'S CAREER ALMOST RUINED BY BOOZE, HE'S NOW ON WAGON FOR GOOD."

"Big, rugged, quiet-voiced and sincere" Larry Tierney, who "all but ruined a brilliant career with a jaded kind of release calling for booze," was now nursing a soda water and twist of lime, and announcing in a semi-whisper, "I don't drink anymore, and even the magazines I buy don't have liquor ads in them. . . . I haven't had a drop of booze for three months. I work out every day and I'm in pretty good shape. I feel better than for a long time."

It was another mea culpa in which the actor admitted what everyone already knew: that he'd been a resident of "drunk tanks" in at least a half dozen city jails. "The last time they booked me in Hollywood," Tierney said, "the desk sergeant cracked: 'Larry, if this doesn't stop, we'll have to get you a cell with a revolving door.'"

Tierney insisted he did all his drinking in his off-hours, was never drunk on set or late for a call or meeting, and never played his most famous role in private life.

"I've got no respect for a no-good bum like Dillinger or anyone who thinks he can do it with a gun," Tierney was quoted. "Remember, my father was a cop. My brothers and I came up with a lot of respect for the Badge Boys. Some of my father's friends were shot down by guys like Dillinger. I'm not trying to prove I'm a tough guy. I have no chip on my shoulder. I just can't handle liquor."

He credited William Wright for giving him a break that even he called a "last chance at a comeback."

"Wright wanted a guy to play a tough dame-beating type who learns the error of his ways in the end," he said. "He asked me if I wanted the role and said he was sure I could do it. All we did was shake hands on the deal. No agent, no contract. Well, we've just finished it. Julie London was great in her dramatic scenes. And the fellows on the set told me it is one of the best episodes yet. There was something happened to me during the filming I'll never forget. After I did a dramatic soliloquy-type scene the whole crew applauded. I got all choked up."

Heffernan asked Tierney about his previous scene—the one at P.J.'s when he crashed Eddie Fisher and Liz Taylor's party for the Russians. "Remember it? You might as well ask me if I remember what I was doing the night Lincoln was shot. It's a complete blackout. Everyone's got problems. Mine comes in bottles. A. A. couldn't help me, and it's a wonderful outfit. Lately, I've been doing something else to beat the problem—and I've been doing it on my knees."

"Night Song," Tierney's well-received episode of *Follow the Sun,* was broadcast a week later. Percy Shain, the *Boston Globe*'s television writer, wasn't very impressed with the show, but wrote that Tierney, in "something of a comeback

... showed no evidence of rustiness in his depiction of a roughhouse promoter who tries to muscle Julie out of a singing career and then dies in a final shooting duel with an ex-associate."

Once again, by maintaining his sobriety, staying out of trouble for only a few months, and reminding producers that he could hit his marks and deliver, Lawrence Tierney had regained the respect of Hollywood. Television and film offers were again coming his way.

So how would Tierney follow up this triumph that aired on the evening of Sunday, November 26, 1961?

By getting himself arrested again, four days later.

30

Fights

A guy walks into a bar. He spots one of his friends, shouts, "Where's my ten bucks?!" and then slugs him!

That's how the sluggee, John A. Fox, described the chronology as he nursed his aching jaw and told the cops what happened on the evening of Friday, November 30, 1961. He was having a quiet drink at a bowling alley bar when Larry Tierney came storming in.

The fifty-three-year-old accountant said he knew Tierney. They were acquaintances, if not close friends, and by the way, Fox added, he didn't owe Tierney any money! Popped in the kisser over a sawbuck? Fox signed a complaint, and Lawrence Tierney racked up another arrest, this time for battery.

At some point during the next two weeks, Tierney made amends with his latest victim. Fox told Los Angeles deputy city attorney John M. Concannon that he'd changed his mind. He didn't want to prosecute his sometime friend, after all, and he wasn't going to testify against him in court. Concannon had no choice but to drop the case.

After all the positive publicity and good faith Tierney had earned since his embarrassing arrest at the Eddie Fisher–Liz Taylor party, the incident was a disappointment to his supporters, and a potential reason for him to return to jail for violating probation. Lucky for Tierney, the cops didn't arrive on the scene to witness his condition or haul him in.

When the charges were dropped on December 14, Tierney had seventeen days to get through the year and move on to 1962 without another arrest on his record.

He made it through twelve days.

Early on December 26, after Christmas Day turned into Boxing Day, Tierney got into a bare-knuckle boxing match on the corner of Sunset Boulevard and Highland Avenue. It was the same location where his fight with an elderly man in September 1959 carried on into the halls of Hollywood High School and led to another drunk charge.

Tierney's sparring partner got in his licks and went on his way on this morning, leaving the actor bloodied, with cuts on his knuckles and left knee. The officers who responded to the call took Tierney to Hollywood Receiving Hospital to get patched up on the way to the station and the drunk tank. He was freed later that day on twenty-one dollars bail.

This holiday season arrest did not go unnoticed. In early January 1962, the North American Newspaper Alliance syndicated a news item reporting that "two famous imbibers . . . had run afoul of the law within a few hours of each other." The two drunk arrests were actually separated by eight days, but it was true that John Agar, known forever as Shirley Temple's ex-husband, had been busted on December 18 at Jones Restaurant on Ventura Boulevard in Studio City. The story estimated it was Agar's eleventh arrest. Citing Tierney's Boxing Day bust, the article noted that "police have almost lost count" of his arrests, and that "only a few weeks ago Tierney finished another 'comeback' role, declaring at the time that he'd finally found himself, that his craving for liquor had been stilled."

Storms of Biblical proportions battered and deluged Southern California in February 1962. For six solid days, rain pounded onto land and hillsides that had been baked to dust by a decade of drought. There were flash floods and mudslides, bridges were washed out, and homes destroyed. There were at least twenty deaths before the first rays of sun peeked through.

Before dawn on February 12, hundreds of pounds of moving mud pressed against a retaining wall in the Hollywood Hills and burst through in a powerful surge that pushed a house off its foundation before exploding in the middle of a road, sending automobiles sliding and careening downhill, crashing into parked vehicles all the way down to Hollywood Boulevard. That main thoroughfare was closed. Hollywood stars including Rhonda Fleming and Richard Boone were forced to evacuate their homes. This disaster in the heart of the entertainment industry was a major news story, and the celebrity selected to represent Hollywood's elite in the photo that the Associated Press transmitted to newspapers around the world was Lawrence Tierney. This time, he wasn't battling a policeman, an actor, or fellow drunk, but the elements, pictured waist-deep in mud, struggling to rescue an overstuffed chair from the grip of the oozing muck that had poured into the apartment house garage where he'd stored his belongings.

The photo could have been a metaphor.

Given recent events and headlines, it came as no surprise that producer Stanley Kramer did not cast Lawrence Tierney in the Bobby Darin film, after all. *Point Blank* had begun shooting in November, and would be released in October 1962 as *Pressure Point*. Darin played an American Nazi sympathizer charged with sedition, and Sidney Poitier was the prison psychiatrist assigned to treat him. The role of the abusive, alcoholic father went to James Anderson, who'd appeared in several episodes of *Perry Mason*.

Stanley Kramer was a man of his word, however. In early 1962, he hired Tierney on another film. *A Child Is Waiting* was an exposé of the institutionalization and cruel treatment of intellectually disabled (identified at the time as "mentally retarded") children. The important, high-quality production starred Burt Lancaster and Judy Garland (Elizabeth Taylor had been considered for the role), with a script by Abby Mann. The director was John Cassavetes, in his third feature. Kramer offered Tierney a four-week guarantee at $1,000 a week. It was his first motion picture work in six years.

Louella Parsons reported the casting on February 19. Tierney promised her that he'd stay busy with the film, but "said nothing will interfere with his attendance at Alcoholics Anonymous meetings on the average of three to five times a week.

"Tierney had a break in *Follow the Sun*. . . . Now he's finding that sobriety pays off," Parsons wrote. "I have always liked Lawrence Tierney, and his mother used to talk to me about him. She had such faith in him. Lawrence is unfortunate that he has been accused often when he hasn't deserved it, and of course, sometimes when he has."

Director Cassavetes also had faith in the actor. "He took Lawrence Tierney and put him in *A Child Is Waiting*, and Larry was a huge drunk. He would tear a phone off the goddamn wall. I mean, he was wild, though he was a great guy and a great actor," Seymour Cassel related in David Spaner's book, *Shoot It! Hollywood Inc. and the Rising of Independent Film*. Cassel made his film debut in (and received an associate producer credit on) Cassavetes's first feature, *Shadows*, and would go on to have a long association with the director. "John said to him, 'If you take one fucking drink, I'll beat the shit out of you. This is the best part you've found in a long time. You get twelve weeks of pay. Don't drink.' And I started laughing and had to turn away because Lawrence Tierney was seven inches bigger than John and heavier. I knew John was kidding, but he was intense. You believed him when he said something."

As it turned out, Judy Garland's alcohol issues caused tension on the set. "Judy was drinking a great deal and it was a big effort to get herself together and get in shape to work," Lancaster later recalled. "I had to kind of nurse her along with it."

Tierney made the best of the opportunity. Sipping a conspicuous coffee, he told UPI's Vernon Scott that he was again on the wagon and that his brawls were "all in the past."

"I felt like a famous boxer," he said. "Every time I went into a bar some guy wanted to take a poke at me so he could tell his friends about it. For a while I thought I had to uphold my reputation as a tough guy. So I fought 'em. But I finally realized I had nothing to gain, even if I won the barroom fights.

"I've learned a number of important things in the past few years. One of them is that cops don't like to get slugged." He waited for the laugh, or at least a knowing smile from his interviewer. "I'd also like to make it clear that if there is anyone in this world who doesn't want to get mixed up in a fistfight, it's me.

"I've done some TV work. 20th Century-Fox helped me out on a couple of shows—*Bus Stop* and *Follow the Sun*. But I never had any complaints about my acting. Drinking and the notoriety that went with my idiotic escapades held me back despite the fact that—contrary to rumor—I never held up a picture or failed to appear because of alcohol.

"I'm not a tough guy in this new picture," he said. "Now maybe people will treat me like any other actor. Lord, I hope so."

The interview was syndicated under various headlines. The *Press & Sun-Bulletin* of Binghamton, New York, came up with the most original: "ONLY CLINK IN HIS FUTURE IS OF COINS, SAYS TIERNEY." In March, Kilgallen picked up on that last quote—"Now maybe people will treat me like any other actor. Lord, I hope so"—and remarked, "So do a lot of people. Lawrence has a lot of rooters."

In early 1962, Scott Brady's syndicated series, *Shotgun Slade*, the Western detective show with the jazzy modern score, was in reruns, having been canceled after two seasons and seventy-eight episodes. Brady was working on the road, in a traveling stage production of Gore Vidal's satirical political melodrama, *The Best Man*. Good guy Brady played unscrupulous presidential candidate Senator Joe Cantwell. "There's nothing in the world like this for really learning your craft," he told an interviewer in Atlanta. "For one thing, it requires a lot of self-discipline. You've got to be on time for the job every night. In television, if you're late getting on the set, it's no great worry since they can shoot around a particular actor."

Brady said he hoped to star in another television series, next time a "modern adventure." He expressed mixed feelings about *Shotgun Slade,* and the "sort of nonsense . . . doing the same thing day after day in seventy-eight shows.

"It was very lucrative nonsense," he clarified, "and it's the kind of thing you don't mind having children watch. I prefer to do light comedies. My first movie role was the part of a boxer, but I really got my start in the play, *Heaven Can Wait,* which was a pretty good comedy."

Whenever he did an interview, Brady was asked about Larry, "best known for his portrayal of John Dillinger." Brady said big brother was "doing fine in TV now." He made no mention of the animosity between them. Kid brother Ed was nearby, not only as Brady's manager on the road, but "partner" in a construction business. Scott financed the B and T Construction Company (for "Brady and Tierney"—Ed had reverted to the family surname), building houses in Woodland Hills and on Wonderland Avenue in Laurel Canyon, around the corner from Brady's home on Hollywood Hills Road.

Lawrence Tierney completed his role in *A Child Is Waiting* commendably. With the added attention from the second airing of his *Follow the Sun* episode on May 13, the first five months of 1962 represented another remarkable turnaround for an actor struggling mightily with the bottle. At forty-three, Lawrence Tierney may at last have been winning the struggle.

Then came another early morning in Santa Monica: Friday, June 1, 1962, after midnight at an all-night restaurant. When Lawrence Tierney barged in—he had a habit of barging in—there were more than a couple of dozen customers in the place, and most were soon aware that the big man was having a disagreement with night manager Daniel Hashaway. The disagreement got loud. Tierney's language turned blue. Cook Tommie Wagner stepped away from the grill to see what the trouble was, and by now Tierney was cursing out anyone in sight. The manager called the Santa Monica police.

Hashaway was upset that Tierney had used profane and abusive language in front of his customers—thirty-five of them, he said. The cook backed him up on that, but the cops only needed to take a look at Tierney to get the picture. They clanked on the cuffs.

Later that day, Tierney was in Santa Monica Municipal Court before Judge Hector Baida. The charges were familiar: disturbing the peace and drunkenness.

Tierney's response was familiar: he pleaded innocent and demanded a jury trial. Judge Baida set a court date for June 25. Bail, erroneously reported by UPI as $5,250, was $52.50.

On the last day of June, Tierney wandered into the Hollywood police station to check in on a pal who was detained there. The desk sergeant told Tierney to take a seat and picked up the phone. Additional policemen arrived in the lobby, and before Tierney could react or realize what was happening, he was again under arrest. There was a stack of outstanding warrants in his name in Van Nuys, a neighborhood in the San Fernando Valley about eleven miles northwest of the Hollywood station. Tierney was in Van Nuys Municipal Court on Monday, charged with drunkenness, malicious mischief, and disturbing the peace. He returned to the Van Nuys courthouse on Wednesday, July 18, pleaded innocent to the charges, and asked for a jury trial. Judge Charles Hughes set the trial for September 11.

Despite the distractions, Tierney completed a role on *The Lloyd Bridges Show*, an innovative, post–*Sea Hunt* anthology series on CBS, in which Bridges introduced a story about a news event before being transformed into the main character in a reenactment. Tierney was cast in "A Pair of Boots," a Civil War story directed by John Cassavetes, and featuring Seymour Cassel and Bridges's son Beau.

The bad luck streak resumed soon enough, on Friday, July 20, when Tierney got into a fight with an actor in a restaurant on LaBrea Avenue in Hollywood. Dimitrios Georgopoulos was forty-two, a year younger than Tierney, and due to a previous injury, sporting a neck brace. Tierney splashed a cup of hot coffee in his face, followed by a whisky chaser, and then attempted to pull off his medical collar. When he failed at that, Tierney went for the payphone and tore it out of the wall.

Then he was gone.

Georgopoulos, soaked, stained, and stunned, adjusted his collar and filed a battery complaint.

Hours later, in the early hours of Saturday, a pair of police officers in Hollywood observed Tierney in the middle of the street, narrowly avoiding being run over by a car that swerved at the last second. When the cops approached, Tierney waved them off.

"Leave me alone!" he ordered. "I'm just walking off a fight."

The cops did not leave him alone. They accompanied him to the Hollywood station, where Georgopoulos's complaint was waiting. Charges of battery and disturbing the peace were added to public drunkenness.

Tierney's continuing tear led to professional and personal damage. In the wake of the LaBrea restaurant incident, he lost a role on *The Dick Powell Show*, an anthology series on NBC. The part went to Gerald Mohr, a character actor best known for the early 1950s crime series *Foreign Intrigue*. *Los Angeles Times* TV writer Cecil Smith would commend Mohr for a "remarkable performance because he'd gotten the role only the day before, replacing Lawrence Tierney." Smith's description of the part indicated that it could have been written for Tierney: "a drunken boor who knocks Carolyn (Jones) around."

Tierney was arrested on another drunk charge and was treated at Hollywood Receiving Hospital on September 28, after a bar fight spilled out onto the corner of Cahuenga Boulevard and Selma Avenue. His opponent used a beer bottle as a weapon, cutting Tierney's head and hands. The Hollywood *Citizen-News*, referring to Tierney as an "erstwhile actor," reported that the assailant was still at large, "described as being five feet, four inches in height. Tierney is a good six feet and weighs nearly 190 pounds."

Edward Tierney, who'd turned to artist management and construction since his return from Germany, was suddenly in demand as a television actor. In October 1962, the youngest Tierney brother, now thirty-four, had filmed three television episodes that would soon air on ABC. Two were on the series *Combat!*, a one-hour World War II drama series following American infantrymen fighting their way through Europe; one on *The Gallant Men*, a one-hour World War II drama series following American infantrymen fighting their way through Italy.

In all of the episodes, the tall, robust, Irish Brooklynite portrayed a German Nazi. His years working in German television and movies, when he was almost always typecast as an American army officer, led to the demand. He was fluent in German and had picked up many German characteristics.

"Playing American officers in German war pictures was a bit ticklish for me," he told Allen Rich of the San Fernando *Valley Times*. "I read each script very carefully. I didn't want to portray an American officer in any manner that might reflect discredit on our country. And I can truthfully say that I never did."

Edward had left "Ed Tracy" behind. He was now billed as Ed Tierney. His main focus, however, was not Ed Tierney the actor but Ed Tierney, builder, and his new enterprise with brother Scott Brady. B and T Construction was currently working on a twelve-unit apartment building on Colfax Avenue near North Hollywood.

"Kids will stand around watching, you know, like they do on construction jobs," Ed Tierney said. "Suddenly one will point to Scott and whisper to the others. Then they'll mosey over and say, 'Hey, mister, ain't you Shotgun Slade?' At such times Scott obligingly drops his hammer or shovel and makes with the autographs."

If big brother Larry was signing autographs, it was in the hallway of municipal court, where, on Tuesday, October 20, he and his attorney awaited a hearing on the LaBrea battery case. As soon as municipal judge Bernard S. Selber called the hearing to order, the assistant district attorney informed him that the complaining witness, Dimitrios C. Georgopoulos, could not be located. The judge dropped the charge. Case dismissed; Lawrence Tierney had one less rap to worry about.

On Saturday, October 20, police were called to an apartment on Sunset Boulevard. They arrested the suspect, Lawrence Tierney, on suspicion of being drunk.

31

"Highly confused and largely incoherent"

"Larry really went off the deep end in the early 60s," his nephew Michael Tierney told Gary Sweeney. "I had heard some stories that Larry would just come up to the house that Scott had up in the hills and climb over the fence with a girlfriend at three in the morning and start swimming in the pool. And he'd be drunk and then my dad would come out, because my dad would be staying with Scott, and he'd say, 'Get the hell outta here,' and it would start into a fight. 'I got you started in this business! You wouldn't even have this house if it wasn't for me!' How many times can you say 'thank you' without, 'You gonna just keep rubbing it in my face for the rest of my life?' So Larry had this a little bit of jealousy or animosity towards his younger brother."

A Child Is Waiting premiered on January 9, 1963, in drive-ins around Atlanta, Georgia. "Somebody goofed" when it came to "one of the most poignant movies of this year," Marjory Rutherford observed in the *Atlanta Constitution*. "Drive-ins are wonderful places to see movies but not this particular one, which needs a sedate and more thoughtful setting." The picture opened in theaters two days later. The reviews were respectful, given the difficult subject matter.

That same day, January 11, Tierney was in Los Angeles Municipal Court to plead guilty to two misdemeanor drunk charges. He returned to court a month later for sentencing, and municipal judge A. J. Bernhardt listened as Tierney explained that he was attempting to rehabilitate himself with the help of the motion picture chapter of Alcoholics Anonymous. A probation department report indicated that he'd been attending AA meetings regularly. After reviewing Tierney's past record (and public statements as recently as 1960 that "even Alcoholics Anonymous couldn't turn the trick with me"), Judge Bernhardt had

222

the opportunity to take the action that columnist Jimmie Fidler had argued and wished for, long ago in 1949: "to sentence Lawrence Tierney to a stay of indeterminate length in a sanitorium and to scientific treatment designed to rehabilitate him as a useful member of society."

Judge Bernhardt sentenced Tierney to probation. The headline in the *Pensacola News*: "'DILLINGER' GETS BREAK."

Scott Brady's latest picture, *Operation Bikini*, opened on March 27, 1963. The World War II submarine drama was a low-budget production from American International Pictures, which included in the cast many actors from its beach party movies, including Tab Hunter, Frankie Avalon, and Eva Six. At thirty-eight, Brady continued to get television and film work, and having beaten charges from the 1957 "narco raid," had maintained his reputation as the "good" Tierney brother. So it may have seemed an April Fools' joke when, on April 1, Brady was named in a horse racing scandal.

The New York State Harness Racing Commission, which regulates the races in which trotting horses pull drivers on two-wheeled carts, had launched an investigation into "alleged undercover ownership of horses by bookmakers." In Brady's case, a trotter named First Flyer had been put up for sale at Yonkers Racetrack in April 1962. Brady, a former Yonkers resident who held a New York state harness license, was announced as the buyer, allowing the horse to keep racing.

In December, a routine gambling raid on the home of a convicted bookmaker named Michael Yannicelli turned up Brady's ownership certificate, and evidence that Yannicelli, not Brady, had purchased the horse for $4,700 in cash, and was paying all horse-related bills and expenses. Brady was exposed as the front for the bookie. The commission found no evidence of race fixing, but Brady was one of eight men banned from harness tracks, for life. (Timothy Tierney says his father had played beard only as a favor to Yannicelli, a friend "from the old neighborhood.")

Lawrence Tierney continued to get second chances. Amid his legal troubles, he filmed "Death of a Cop," an episode of *The Alfred Hitchcock Hour* (written by Leigh Brackett, female screenwriter of Howard Hawks's *The Big Sleep*) on the Revue Studios lot. It was a small but featured role as the boss of a gang of hoodlums. The episode was scheduled to air on CBS on May 24.

Tierney's next arrest took place twelve days before the episode aired. This time, Tierney faced the most serious charge of his criminal career: assault with a deadly weapon. The only thing that separated Tierney from the criminal John Dillinger was the choice of deadly weapon.

That made people laugh.

Saturday night had turned to Sunday morning on the streets of Hollywood on May 12, 1963, when Lawrence Tierney, stumbling out of another gin mill, was arrested again for public drunkenness. The cops were very used to hosting their frequent guest and deposited him in the drunk tank at the Hollywood station. A few hours later, when Tierney appeared to be sobered up, they sent him on his way. It wasn't a long walk to the room he kept on Las Palmas Avenue, north of the Musso & Frank Grill, but Tierney didn't head straight home. He stopped in at a few more of his favorite haunts along the way, and got his blood alcohol concentration back to its most argumentative level.

By late Sunday evening, standing at the corner of Hollywood Boulevard and Cherokee Avenue, he was about two blocks from sleeping it off. The neon Musso & Frank sign was a directional marker across the boulevard to his left, but Tierney was attracted to a beacon on the northeast corner, across Cherokee and half a block east of the famed restaurant. The neon signage over the bright red façade advertised "Sontag, Original Cut Rate Drug Stores" and "Fountain-Grill." Sontag was one of the largest drugstore chains in the country, and this Hollywood Boulevard flagship featured a wide array of pharmacy and sundry items, from prescriptions to pipes, as well as a sixteen-seat lunch counter.

Tierney was pretty well hammered as he made his way inside, slid onto a stool at the counter, and leaned in to order a coffee. Pete Dzelebdzic was working the counter. Pete was fifty-five. He'd seen all kinds on the night shift and more than a few drunks slurping coffee in hopes of sobering up before heading home. This fella was no different, though maybe he looked familiar. The fella ordered a coffee. Dzelebdzic took his order and poured the cup of java. As he turned away, the fella shouted something. The coffee was too cold or too hot or didn't taste right. Dzelebdzic turned back, shrugged, and as he reached over to remove and replace the offending cup, the fella took a swing at him. *What in the—?* Instinctively, Dzelebdzic responded by slapping Lawrence Tierney in the face. Maybe that would sober him up. Tierney's eyes got wide. He jumped back off the stool and threw a spoon at the counterman. He cursed and screamed, grabbed a saucer, and hurled it toward Dzelebdzic's head. Then the coffee cup. A glass. Dzelebdzic didn't have much room to find cover behind the counter, but did his best to dodge the flying crockery. Tierney began "throwing everything in sight," including those heavy glass sugar bowls that were spaced along the counter. You could knock a guy out with one of those. Dzelebdzic took a hit to the head, but fired back with whatever he could grab. Tierney began to beat a retreat. He was bolting for the door when Dzelebdzic took aim, wound up, and like Don Drysdale, fired a metal cream dispenser down the middle. The can bounced off the back of Tierney's head.

And then he was gone. The bloodied counterman called the police and said he wanted to file an assault charge. He had to go to the hospital to get stitches in his head, where the sugar bowl had bopped him. The cops, who'd had possession of Tierney earlier in the day, knew where to find him: fast asleep in his room on Las Palmas. The cops roused him and took him to the receiving hospital to have his own head stitched before they delivered him to the Hollywood station for booking. This time the charge was suspicion of assault with a deadly weapon. If prosecuted as a misdemeanor, it could mean a year in the county jail; as a felony, serious prison time. The deadly weapon in question?

The sugar bowl.

Lawrence Tierney remained in jail until Wednesday. The district attorney reviewed the case and decided there wasn't enough evidence to issue the felony charge. The charges were reduced to battery and disturbing the peace. Tierney was let go after posting $262 bond.

After all these years, a drunken Lawrence Tierney fight still warranted headlines—especially one featuring assault with a deadly sugar bowl. Jack Kofoed in the *Miami Herald* had more than once in the past decade referred to Tierney as a tragic figure, tag-teamed by King Bourbon and John Barleycorn. Eleven years after Tierney was so impressive in a straw-hat theater production in Miami Beach, he was on Kofoed's radar again. "Tierney is one of the real tragedies of the movie colony. He's a good actor, but what producer wants to sign a bottle belter? I met Larry here years ago when he was a guest star in *The Petrified Forest*. He was on the wagon then, and swore he'd stay there forever. He fell off a week later. It's too bad. He's really a nice guy."

The nice guy didn't let half a week pass before falling off again, in a major way, into a potential charge that was even more serious than the felony rap he'd escaped so narrowly. The complainant was Sylvia Toboas, who described herself as a twenty-nine-year-old housewife. She told police that on the evening of Wednesday, May 22, she was leaving a restaurant on Sunset Boulevard when Lawrence Tierney grabbed her and forced her into her car. He took the wheel and proceeded to drive her for seven hours through Hollywood and Beverly Hills. Mrs. Toboas said she managed to escape when Tierney pulled over at a hotel and got out of the car "to see someone."

When the police arrested Tierney, they said he was "highly confused and largely incoherent." He was sent off to jail and Mrs. Toboas was ushered into the Hollywood police station, where she filed a kidnapping complaint. In California, a kidnapping conviction could put a person away in prison for eight years. While detectives checked out her story, they found that Sylvia Toboas was a scofflaw with two outstanding parking tickets. The police arrested her and put her in a cell, in lieu of twenty dollars bond.

The district attorney must have had similar issues with Mrs. Toboas's story. When the case came to court a week later, it was decided that despite her claims, there was insufficient evidence of a kidnapping. Tierney would face less serious and more familiar charges: battery and disturbing the peace. The charges would be folded into identical ones filed in the lunch counter sugar bowl attack. Trial was set for Friday, June 14.

Tierney was, somewhat predictably, a no-show for his latest moment in Los Angeles Municipal Court. Judge Mario L. Clinco issued a bench warrant for his arrest, and as police searched for Tierney on Saturday, the *Miami Herald* took home the prize for headline originality, or at least, nostalgia: "LAWMEN HUNT 'JOHN DILLINGER.'"

Peter Dzelebdzic, the soda jerk who was Tierney's alleged battery victim—target not only of a punch, but a thrown sugar bowl that led to lumps—sued Tierney on June 19 for $65,000. Tierney did not respond to the suit. He'd skipped town.

Twenty years after he'd first arrived on the RKO lot in Hollywood, Tierney had escaped to his hometown. Earl Wilson sounded the warning on July 23—"Actor Lawrence Tierney's around town with Latin ¼ showgirl Darlene Larsen"—but aside from that sighting, Tierney managed to lay low for weeks, even months.

It was during this period that he befriended a kindred spirit, the Irish poet, novelist, and playwright Brendan Behan. Considered to be one of the greatest writers in Irish history, Behan was also one of its most bawdy, singing-and-dancing public scene makers, and hopeless, unhinged alcoholics. He'd arrived in New York City in September 1960 for the Broadway premiere of his play *The Hostage,* and over the next few years carried on a loud, drunken, public sweep through Manhattan stages and taverns. Tierney would later have many discussions with his friend C. Courtney Joyner about his friendship with

Behan, their elbow-bending binges, and times they spent reciting stanzas of poetry and acting out classic scenes.

"It just made sense," says Joyner. "They were both Irish. They were both drunks."

By the autumn of 1963, Behan was back in Dublin, where he'd literally drink himself to death four months later, at age forty-one, and Lawrence Tierney was back in the headlines.

At four o'clock in the morning on October 17, Tierney was a passenger in a car piloted by a drinking buddy, cruising up Broadway on Manhattan's Upper West Side. John Joetze, who was forty-nine, was approaching Eighty-Fifth Street when patrolmen Peter Wenz and Eugene Ione spotted him driving in an "erratic manner."

The cops hit the cherry top, pulled over the car, and determined that Joetze was very clearly intoxicated. One cop observed that he was "bombed." They were placing the driver under arrest when the passenger started acting up. According to the cops, Tierney got out of the car and began yelling "in a loud and boisterous manner." He became aggressive and began pushing and shoving the officers. That constituted interfering with police in the performance of their duties, and that meant Tierney was headed to the Twenty-Sixth Precinct on West Sixty-Eighth Street along with his pal.

The pair were arraigned in criminal court before Judge Maurice K. Dowling. Joetze gave his address as 39-20 Greenpoint Avenue in Long Island City, Queens. Tierney said that was his address, as well. They were both released and told to return for a hearing on October 31.

Hollywood awoke to scandalous news on the morning of Friday, November 22, 1963, and Jack I. Schwarz was at the center. Schwarz was a producer who'd made dozens of B-movies in the 1940s and '50s, including *The Hoodlum,* which starred Lawrence Tierney and introduced kid brother Ed in his first credited screen role. On Thursday, Schwarz had been in municipal court, facing the same trouble and charge that sent Eddie to jail for ninety days in 1954. Police had shined a light into his car after a Hollywood party and caught him snuggling with a fifteen-year-old girl. Schwarz was sixty-six. He was convicted of contributing to the delinquency of a minor and sentenced to 180 days in county jail.

Schwarz wished for some event to push that story out of the papers. His wish was granted at 10:36 a.m. when the ABC radio network reported that shots had been fired at President John F. Kennedy's motorcade in Dallas. At 11:25, the report was broadcast that JFK was dead.

As transistor radios and television sets blared the news of the assassination, Hollywood ground to a halt. Production stopped on the pilot episode of *Bewitched.* It was lights out for Audrey Hepburn filming *My Fair Lady* with George Cukor on the Warner lot in Burbank; James Garner, shooting a comedy scene for *The Americanization of Emily* on the MGM lot; Jack Lemmon on *Good Neighbor Sam* at Columbia; Debbie Reynolds and *The Unsinkable Molly Brown* at Universal.

Reporter Armand Archerd, who was now "Army Archerd" with a column in *Variety,* was at the entrance to Desilu Studios in Culver City, where he noticed a clown from *The Greatest Show on Earth,* the new ABC television series based on the only film featuring Lawrence Tierney to win the Academy Award for Best Picture. The clown, Archerd wrote, "sadly waited at the gate," with "the mournful makeup grotesquely accurate for the day."

Frank Sinatra and Sammy Davis Jr. were in a cemetery in Burbank filming a scene for the Rat Pack movie, *Robin and the 7 Hoods.* Both had campaigned for Kennedy, both were later snubbed by him—Sinatra because of his mobster associates and alleged affair with JFK's sister, Pat Kennedy Lawford; Sammy due to his interracial marriage to Swedish actress May Britt. Sinatra and Davis expressed shock and offered customary tributes. According to Bob Thomas, another actor on the picture, Jack La Rue, collapsed when he heard the news. He was rushed to St. John's Hospital in Santa Monica with a suspected heart attack. La Rue would be remembered as the attempted peacemaker who wound up in the hospital in 1946, after Lawrence Tierney punched him in the nose during the Battle of Decker's Lawn.

Lawrence Tierney was not among the Hollywood notables asked for comment on the death of the president. He was back in the swing of New York City, once again a regular at the Third Avenue saloons and gin mills on Eighth Avenue. Winchell columnized in early November about "the steady boozers at '21,' Toots, P.J.'s etc., who call themselves 'The Lawrence Tierney Garden Club.'" When Tierney's cop-shoving case finally made it to court on December 27, he pleaded guilty to disorderly conduct. Judge Benjamin Gassman gave him a brief lecture, reminding him that "a man in your position should know better." The jurist gave Tierney the choice of paying a twenty-five-dollar fine or serving time in lockup. "Five days in jail or pay the fine," he said. Tierney paid the fine.

The *New York Daily News* headline made the story more sensational than it was: "TIERNEY FINED AS A PUSHER."

32

World's Fair

I did see him once again years later on Broadway as I came out of a theatre. He was almost unrecognizable slumped against a parked car in no condition to catch my eye. My impulse was to go to him. But I didn't. I walked on by. I knew there was nothing I could do to save him.

GLORIA VANDERBILT, *IT SEEMED IMPORTANT AT THE TIME*

Lawrence H. Tierney was at his son Scott Brady's home on Hollywood Hills Road when he suffered a heart attack on Thursday, February 13, 1964. "I remember my dad saying, 'He died literally in my arms,'" Timothy Tierney says. "'I was holding him, and he collapsed. I picked him up, and he died in my arms.'" The senior Tierney was seventy-two.

As they had after the death of Tierney's estranged wife, Mary Alice, four years earlier, the men at the Cunningham and O'Connor Mortuary handled the arrangements. A Rosary was said for Lawrence H. Tierney in the funeral home chapel on Melrose Avenue at 8 p.m. on Friday. There was a requiem High Mass at St. Ambrose Church on Saturday morning. His body was slid into the crypt near Mary Alice in the mausoleum at Holy Cross Cemetery in Culver City.

The continued confusion over fraternal relationships among Hollywood actors was displayed in the *New York Daily News* on Monday, when Ed Sullivan wrote in his Little Old New York column that "Lawrence Tierney and Scott Brady lost their dads." Sullivan was probably still trying to differentiate among the Beatles, who'd made their second live appearance on his CBS variety show the night before.

Lawrence Tierney was in New York City that day. He wasn't singing "I Want to Hold Your Hand." He had his hands full. They were around a man's neck, choking the life out of him. It led to his first arrest of 1964, and happened in time to make the *Daily News* on Tuesday.

This incident occurred at 2:45 in the afternoon. Tierney was a passenger in a yellow cab driven by forty-one-year-old Jack Brass of Forest Hills, Queens. The cabbie was transporting Tierney along East Thirtieth Street toward the East River Drive. Traffic was heavy, the typical stop-and-start, sudden braking, horn-honking trip though Murray Hill in Manhattan. A hack in front of them stopped in the middle of the street so a fare could disembark. He didn't leave enough room to pass. Brass hit the horn. He gave a yell. The other cabbie yelled back.

They sat in traffic for a few moments. Tierney, suddenly, frustrated, leaned toward the driver and ordered, "Lemme out here!"

Jack Brass hit the flag on the meter. "A buck forty-five," he said, referring to the fare.

"I ain't paying you a cent," Tierney replied. "You're a lousy driver!"

Brass hit the lock button on the passenger door and Tierney slammed forward over the seat and grabbed the driver by the throat. Brass struggled and tried to fight back, clawing at Tierney's meaty paws as if he were being garroted in a gangster movie. He kicked. The taxi horn blared.

Outside, cars stacked up behind them, tangling up traffic to Second Avenue, leading to a din of car horns and shouts, and attracting the attention of police. A beat cop worked his way toward Jack Brass's cab. Tierney continued to strangle. Brass was blue. For a moment, he blacked out.

A policeman was there. "What the hell is going on here?"

Tierney loosened his grip. Jack Brass stumbled from the car, coughing. "He tried to kill me! He wouldn't pay the fare. He strangled me! And he owes me a dollar and forty-five cents!"

Tierney stepped onto the street.

"Why don't you pay him the dollar forty-five?" the officer asked him.

This time, Tierney responded with a wisecrack, not a punch. "What the hell are you?" he replied, "A collection agency?"

"Okay. You're under arrest."

Tierney's next stop was the Thirteenth Precinct station house on East Twenty-Second Street. Brass followed, to press charges. Asked for his address, Tierney said he didn't have one. He was booked for felonious assault and locked up overnight. By then, he'd given cops his address: 748 Lenore Lane in Elmont, Long Island, the new home of Vito Frisina and his family.

"Larry would come and go," AnnMarie Frisina Guertin says. "When he was on a binge, he'd disappear, and then he'd get in touch with my father. My father would get him, and make sure he was okay, and bring him home and get him clean."

Tierney was cleaned up and in Manhattan Criminal Court on Tuesday. Judge Ambrose J. Haddock set a March 16 hearing on the assault charge. Tierney was held on $1,500 bail. The hearing was postponed to Thursday, March 26, when the judge reduced the charge to the less serious third-degree assault, which was prosecuted as a misdemeanor.

The trial on Monday, April 20, and subsequent sentencing, was something of a public reckoning for Tierney. This was the first time in months that reporters got a chance to get a good look at him, up close. At forty-five, Tierney was not only older than the chiseled, dangerous bad man whose televised films gave style tips to a new generation of would-be tough guys. After a year away from the cameras, Tierney barely resembled the middle-aged actor seen in guest roles on current television dramas.

"The lean and dynamic Hollywood problem child had," Jack Kofoed scribbled in the *Miami Herald*, "become beefy and florid."

"You'd have hardly recognized him as the icy-eyed villain from 'Dillinger,' 'San Quentin,' 'The Hoodlum,' or 'Born to Kill,'" according to the *Daily News*. "Larry has put on a lot of weight since his lean-faced killer days; his neck bulged over his collar and he was badly in need of a haircut."

A three-judge panel, consisting of John M. Murtagh, chief judge, and Judges Benjamin Gassman and Evelyn Richman, heard Jack Brass testify about the cab ride, Tierney's refusal to pay the fare, and the attack that rendered him unconscious.

Tierney took the stand and denied all. Brass "was endangering my physical welfare" by driving recklessly and arguing in the street with another cab driver, he testified. He wasn't choking the man, but merely trying to reach past him to turn off the taxi's ignition. That's what Tierney had claimed from the start.

The judges listened and returned a verdict of "guilty." Tierney was allowed to remain free on $1,500 bail pending sentencing.

The reporters from the *Daily News* always got a kick out of Lawrence Tierney's misadventures, and their coverage always contained a bit of fun at the expense of the Brooklynite who went Hollywood, hit it big in a gangster picture, and spent the next two decades playing the hard-drinking tough guy in real life. So on Wednesday, April 29, Michael Mok pounced when he spotted Tierney in the hallway outside the courtroom. The defendant was sitting on a bench awaiting sentencing, all by himself, forlorn in a rumpled sports jacket, gray trousers, and shirt with button-down collar and tie.

Mok sat on the bench next to him and began to extricate Tierney's tale of woe. "The whole beef could have been settled for $1.45," Tierney told him. "That's what the cabbie wanted but I wasn't going to pay him because I didn't like the way he was driving. So this cop comes along and says, 'Why don't you pay him the $1.45?' and I said, 'What the hell are you, a collection agency?' and the first thing you know I was under arrest.

"I just reached over the cabbie's shoulder to turn off the ignition and he said I was trying to strangle him. But all that's academic because they found me guilty, anyway."

Mok almost bought the story, but like readers of his paper, he knew Tierney's "bad rep as a cop fighter that stretches from here to L. A. and back again." So Mok squeezed in a few softball questions, almost giggling in anticipation of Tierney's response—like asking if he'd ever been arrested before.

"Once or twice that I can remember." Tierney grinned when he said that. "Out on the Coast I got my pants ripped off on a car door and grabbed some corrugated tin off a roof to make sort of a skirt. Then I went into the bar and ordered a drink and was pinched for not wearing a necktie or something."

"Didn't I read about you kicking somebody in the face and breaking his jaw in three places?"

Tierney "rubbed a hard hand across his beefy face" before replying. "I don't remember. I honestly don't remember."

The interview was cut short when a court attendant told Tierney his sentencing was coming up. In court, Tierney stood with his hands behind him, "at a kind of parade rest," as Mok described it, as he and his lawyer faced three judges.

"My client has a drinking problem," the lawyer said. "And if you will approve some sort of probation, I will see to it he gets help."

Disbelief was reflected in the face of Judge Murtagh. "You're asking for probation?" he said. "Do you know that your client has been in court twenty times on similar charges?"

"Tierney just stood there and took it, twisting his fingers behind his back," Mok observed. "He didn't look like Dillinger at all—just like a guy who has lost too many battles to the bottle."

Tierney's attorney claimed that his client hadn't had a drink in weeks and was attempting to cure himself. Murtagh may have heard that line before.

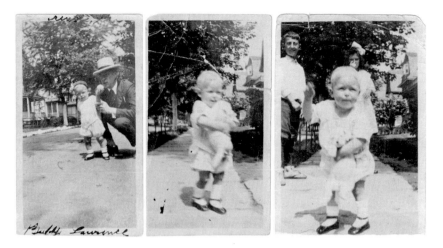

"Baby Lawrence," circa 1920, already a tough guy. (courtesy Timothy Tierney)

Grandfather Tim Crowley, who taught seven-year-old Larry to fight by smacking him across the living room. (courtesy Timothy Tierney)

Baby Gerard Kenneth Tierney, known as "Roddy," the future Scott Brady. (courtesy Timothy Tierney)

Baby Edward Michael Tierney, the youngest brother, who'd sometimes be billed as Ed Tracy. (courtesy Timothy Tierney)

(*left*) Young lifeguards Roddy and Larry Tierney. (courtesy Timothy Tierney)

(*below*) Lawrence H. Tierney, chief of the NY Aqueduct Police (left), with colleagues and his son, young Edward Tierney (center). (courtesy Timothy Tierney)

(*left*) Larry, mother, Marion "Mary" Alice, and Roddy, who'd recently enlisted in the US Navy, circa 1943. (courtesy Timothy Tierney)

(*below*) Navy man Gerard "Roddy" Tierney with his parents and older brother Larry. (courtesy Timothy Tierney)

Young Edward Tierney, with a great future behind him. (courtesy Timothy Tierney)

Mary Alice Tierney and her three sons. (courtesy Timothy Tierney)

Mother, Mary Alice Tierney: Some family members believed that Lawrence contributed to her untimely death. (courtesy Timothy Tierney)

An early 8×10: "Best wishes, sincerely, Larry Tierney." (courtesy Timothy Tierney)

(*left*) Portrait of a movie star. (courtesy Timothy Tierney)

(*below*) Lawrence Tierney's first screen credit: *Youth Runs Wild* (1944). He played a bad guy.

Lawrence Tierney and Bonita Granville in Youth Runs Wild at the Paradise today through Thursday.

Dillinger had its world premiere at the Strand Theatre in downtown Cincinnati, Ohio, on April 6, 1945.

After *Dillinger* opened at the Victoria Theatre in New York City's Times Square, Lawrence Tierney became an overnight sensation.

The face of Public Enemy No. 1: Lawrence Tierney as John Dillinger.

Dillinger behind bars: Life would soon imitate art.

Dillinger walks toward death. Anne Jeffreys as The Lady in Red and Lawrence Tierney filming Dillinger's final scene. (courtesy Timothy Tierney)

Lawrence Tierney, Hollywood's new tough guy. (courtesy The Del Valle Archives)

At the wheel in Hollywood. (courtesy The Del Valle Archives)

Taking notes: Younger brother Roddy watches big brother Larry in action. (courtesy Timothy Tierney)

(*left*) Lawrence Tierney appeared onstage in Baltimore in February 1947—and was lucky to make it out of the city alive.

(*below*) Tierney hated the cold-blooded killer he portrayed in *The Devil Thumbs A Ride*—"I thought of myself as a nice guy who wouldn't do rotten things." (courtesy The Del Valle Archives)

May 1, 1947: Outside court with eighteen-year-old brother Ed, after their arrest for a street brawl. (Los Angeles Times Photographic Archive, Library Special Collections, Charles E. Young Research Library, UCLA)

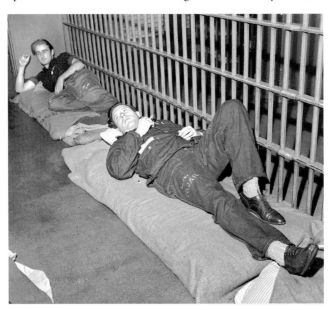

Sentenced for his fight with Ed, Lawrence Tierney is forced to sleep on the floor in a corridor of the crowded Los Angeles County Jail. (Los Angeles Times Photographic Archive, Library Special Collections, Charles E. Young Research Library, UCLA)

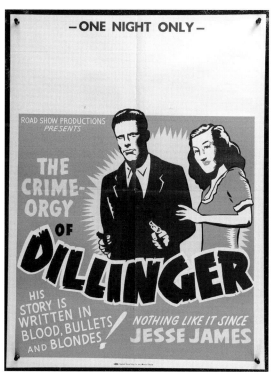

(*above*) Lawrence Tierney at his baddest in *Born to Kill* (1947), with *Dillinger* costar and good friend Elisha Cook Jr.

(*left*) The roadshow goes on: *Dillinger,* "one night only." (Author's collection/PopGallery33)

Scott Brady watches as kid brother Ed Tierney gives acting a shot at his alma mater, the Bliss-Hayden School of Acting. (courtesy Timothy Tierney)

Lawrence Tierney got younger brother Edward a costarring role in *The Hoodlum* in 1951.

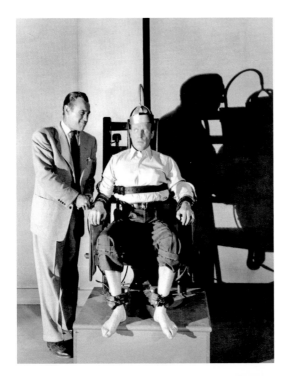

Publicity still for *The Hoodlum*. (courtesy The Del Valle Archives)

Lawrence Tierney is led barefoot to a psychiatric hospital after a breakdown in a church on October 8, 1951. (USC Digital Library. Los Angeles Examiner Photographs Collection)

Two weeks and two days after the church incident, Tierney was arrested, barefoot in a bar, offering to "whip anyone in the place." (Los Angeles Times Photographic Archive, Library Special Collections, Charles E. Young Research Library, UCLA)

Tierney didn't mind signing a photo showing him as a bad guy in *The Bushwhackers* (1951). (courtesy The Del Valle Archives)

Tierney with Charlton Heston in *The Greatest Show on Earth*, winner of the Oscar for Best Picture at the twenty-fifth Academy Awards on March 19, 1953.

So Sorry, Says Sober Tierney

(NEWS foto by Ed Peters)
Patrolman Joseph Incorvaia tries to hold Tierney as the movie tough guy aims a right at Detective Nilo Mingrone, at E. 104th St. station house after Incorvaia had picked up Tierney.

NYPD patrolman Joseph Incorvaia attempts to suppress a grin as a drunken Tierney aims a right at Det. Nilo Mingrone, after the tough guy's arrest for disorderly conduct on April 9, 1956. (Ed Peters/*New York Daily News*)

(*above*) August 27, 1957: A disgusted Eileen Keenan is forced to shake hands with Tierney, who's very sorry for kicking down the door of her apartment. The actor's attorney, Harold Frankel, is pleased that charges were dropped. (Phil Greitzer/*New York Daily News*)

(*left*) October 14, 1958: Lawrence Tierney is hauled into the NYPD's Midtown North precinct house after picking a fight with two New York City cops armed with nightsticks. (Ken Korotkin/*New York Daily News*)

October 14, 1958: Patrolmen Samuel Saipan and Louis Romano, looking no worse for the wear and tear, escort their opponent to St. Clare's Hospital, where Tierney's fight will continue. (Ken Korotkin/*New York Daily News*)

Scott Brady and his parents visit Vito Frisina's house—Larry's home away from home. (courtesy AnnMarie Jackie Guertin)

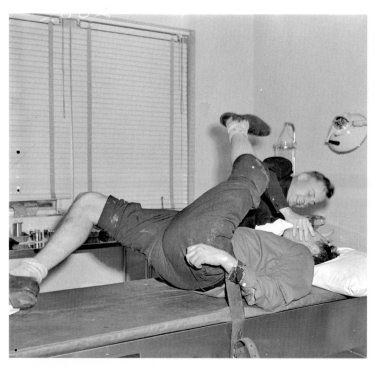

(*above*) December 12, 1959: LAPD officer Roman Fromm quiets a boisterous Tierney at Central Receiving Hospital—strapping him down and cramming a towel into his mouth. (Los Angeles Times Photographic Archive, Library Special Collections, Charles E. Young Research Library, UCLA)

(*left*) Tierney is escorted into a police van on October 17, 1963: Arrested for shoving an NYPD cop—the *NY Daily News* headline described him as a "pusher." (Bob Costello/*New York Daily News*)

(*above*) Like father, like son: Lawrence Hugh Tierney, aka "Lawrence Tierney Sr." (courtesy Timothy Tierney)

(*left*) "From Stardom to Hansom": Lawrence Tierney makes national news in October 1974 when it's revealed he's working as a Central Park horse and buggy driver. (Associated Press)

The comeback is under way: Tierney attracts notice in a pivotal scene with Liza Minnelli and Dudley Moore in the 1981 movie *Arthur*. Moore played the drunk.

He's ba-a-a-ck! Lawrence Tierney had his first starring role in years in director John Russo's 1982 exploitation horror film, *Midnight*.

Tierney and Phyllis Diller were squabbling would-be exorcists in a 1985 episode of the syndicated horror anthology series *Tales from the Dark Side*.

"I just deep-sixed two heads." Tierney stood heads above the rest of the cast as Ryan O'Neal's father in Norman Mailer's 1987 film noir, *Tough Guys Don't Dance*.

In May 1987, Tierney had the last words in the last scene of the last episode of the groundbreaking NBC police drama *Hill Street Blues*.

Tierney crashed for weeks at the home of his friend, film historian David Del Valle. (courtesy The Del Valle Archives)

Tierney's memorable turn as Alton Benes in "The Jacket" episode of NBC's *Seinfeld* (1991) could have led to a recurring role—if not for a scene with a knife.

Quentin Tarantino (right) seemed amused by Tierney in the "Uncle Bob's Pancake House" scene of *Reservoir Dogs*. Then they came to blows.

As Joe Cabot in *Reservoir Dogs*: "My way or the highway!"

(*above*) "Don't kiss me, kid." Lawrence Tierney with friend and fan Todd Mecklem, or as Tierney called him, "Prince Valiant," in Hollywood, 1992. (courtesy Todd Mecklem)

(*left*) Tierney erupted when he was handed copies of this photo to sign at the 1993 Weekend of Horror convention. He preferred "tough guy" pictures. (courtesy Todd Mecklem)

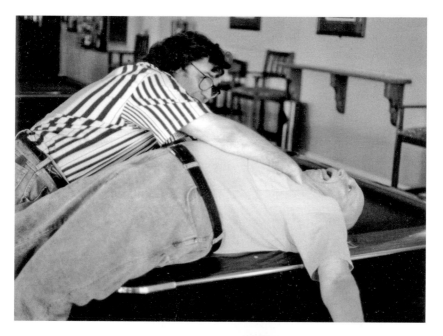

(*above*) Tierney's friend, the author, screenwriter, and film historian C. Courtney Joyner, was often mistaken for his son. Here, at the Hollywood Athletic Club in 1992, he could be mistaken for one of Tierney's bar brawl opponents. (courtesy Todd Mecklem)

(*left*) Clowning around in Santa Monica, circa 1994. (courtesy Will Thimes)

Tierney and his nephew, "Saint" Michael Tierney. (courtesy Timothy Tierney)

As the Regent of Palamar in *Star Trek: Deep Space Nine* (1996).

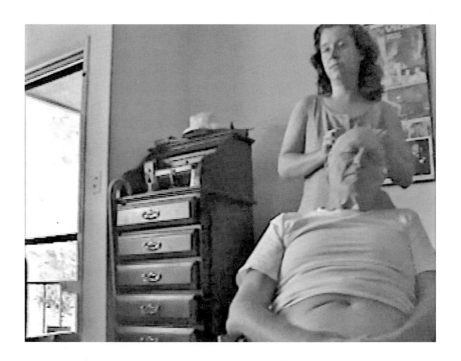

(*above*) Tierney
receives his often-
requested head rub,
while exposing his
knife wound, in *Gimme
Some Larry*.

(*left*) "Cheers." Signing
autographs till the end.
(Author's collection/
PopGallery33)

Lawrence Tierney immortalized as a *Reservoir Dogs* Joe Cabot action figure. (Author's collection/PopGallery33)

Lawrence Tierney (March 15, 1919–February 26, 2002) (The Del Valle Archives)

He had a brief, whispered consultation with the other two jurists, Benjamin Gassman and Bernard J. O'Connell, before delivering the verdict: "One year in the penitentiary—suspended on the condition that you try to help yourself and stay out of trouble. You'll have to check in with this court once a month."

"Thank you, your honor," said Tierney, and walked out of the courtroom.

Stay out of trouble? Jack Kofoed found it hard to believe that a judge familiar with Tierney's past had added that stipulation. "He has never been able to stay out of trouble, and there seems little reason to expect him to do that now. I hope he does. Sober, Tierney is a nice guy, and even the judge doesn't want to see him in the hoosegow."

On May 6, a week after the hearing, Sheilah Graham gave an indication of how serious Lawrence Tierney was about staying out of trouble: "Lawrence Tierney was at it again in New York, in a rage in the lobby of an apartment house, smashing up things. But no one wanted to press charges. What a curse that firewater can be."

If in the past Tierney found himself the target of barroom jokers out to prove that Dillinger wasn't so tough, by the early 1960s, deep into another decade of alcohol abuse, he was more often the aggressor, thirsty for a fight as much as a whisky. "Oh, man, I tell ya, he was a real shit-stirrer," Ray Boylan reminisces. Boylan, a writer and radio host, tended bar at O'Brien's Corner, across Fiftieth Street from Madison Square Garden, in those years. Tierney was a regular at O'Brien's and other saloons on Eighth Avenue. "It was clear that he thought he was Dillinger. I saw it happen a half-dozen times. He would walk in, and if somebody's standing there, he would elbow 'em in the lower back to get 'em out of the way. Or through a snide comment, he'd engage them in an altercation.

"But I found a couple of things interesting: One is that he always punched down," Boylan says. "He would never call out some stud at the bar. He would pick out the weakest person and he would focus on them. And the guy would either walk out with his friends or the guy would be too much for Tierney to handle and Tierney would leave. But there were times when he went toe-to-toe with people. And when he would get his hip pockets bounced off the floor of the bar, they'd take him into the back room, fix him up in the office, and there was always some cop to take him home."

Boylan says he went toe-to-toe with Tierney at Mickey Walker's Toy Bulldog bar, a block south of O'Brien's. "I was talking to a friend of mine, a guy named Mike Reilly. We were talking, I said something, and Reilly laughed. And Reilly laughing pissed off Tierney, apparently. Like 'What the fuck are you laughing at?' Tierney walked over and stuck his finger in Boylan's face. 'I asked, "What's your problem?"' 'You're my fuckin' problem!'"

Boylan says he grabbed Tierney by the wrist, pulled him close, and hit him in the jaw. One punch. "He went down like a throw rug."

While Hollywood wasn't calling, Tierney found a way to make a few dollars off his movieland fame and notoriety through a back door in his own backyard. The 1964 World's Fair had opened in April in Flushing Meadows, Queens. An international exhibition and showcase of mid-twentieth-century technology and innovation, the fair featured pavilions and attractions from eighty nations and close to fifty corporations. At the hub was the Unisphere, a twelve-story, stainless steel model of the earth.

Popular exhibits included General Motors' Futurama; the Vatican Pavilion, where Michelangelo's Pietà sculpture was on display; and two attractions that would later be transported to Disneyland: Walt Disney's *Great Moments with Mr. Lincoln* "audio-animatronic" robot stage show in the State of Illinois Pavilion; and *It's A Small World*. There were also queues for the Hollywood USA pavilion, which celebrated the movie and television industries. Its façade was a scaled-down replica of Grauman's Chinese Theatre, complete with stars' hand- and footprints out front. Inside, a museum showed off costumes, jewelry, props, and other relics. Music from film scores played. There was a display of famous movie monsters, replicas of the throne rooms from *Cleopatra* and *The King and I*, a street from *West Side Story*, and actual gunfights on the set of the CBS television series *Gunsmoke*.

A section of the museum was dedicated to the career of Cecil B. DeMille, who'd died in 1959. A highlight was the small model train used in the spectacular crash scene in *The Greatest Show on Earth*. Lawrence Tierney's part in the picture, along with his tough guy roles, made him a natural presence in the pavilion's central mall, where actual movie, television, and recording stars had been paid to meet the public, sign autographs, and pose for photographs. Tierney was able to keep his face out there and bring in spending cash as movie fans from all over the world got to meet the former Dillinger, if not quite a Madame Tussaud's replica.

The fantasy didn't extend beyond the 650 acres of the World Fair grounds. On August 4, 1964, police in Manhattan were called to a disturbance at a hotel at 253 West Seventy-Third Street, just west of Broadway. The Riverside Plaza was an ornate, formerly posh hotel that had fallen into decline and was a decade away from being turned into a residential drug treatment center.

Tierney, who was calling the place home for the time being, had engaged in a loud argument with one of the telephone switchboard operators. When he threw a pile of mail in the woman's face, the hotel manager stepped in. Jacob Fisher was sixty-six. Tierney punched him.

Police arrived and left with Tierney, who was charged with drunk and disorderly conduct. When he was led into criminal court later in the day, the *Daily News* described him as "subdued and bleary-eyed." A hearing was set for the following Tuesday, August 11. Tierney was ordered held on $500 bail. The *News* estimated this was his thirteenth arrest in New York City "for boozing and brawling."

Two and a half weeks later, *Coney Island Times* columnist Bobby Maurice wrote: "Boozer and brawler Lawrence Tierney still in jail here."

Lawrence Tierney had run from Hollywood to New York City. When he got out of jail, it was time, once again, to run even farther.

33

Exile

In 1965, twenty years after *Dillinger* made him a star, Lawrence Tierney was, at age forty-six, a relic. A former actor. A menace to society. A washed-up drunk. Jimmie Fidler had long ago washed his hands of him and other gossip writers were no longer using his public displays for filler items at the end of their columns. Some of his arrests didn't make the news at all. No one cared what woman he was sharing dinner with or whom he punched. Tierney was out of the country, out of sight, and out of mind of the casting directors looking for a heavyset, middle-aged tough guy to fill supporting roles on television dramas.

For those who remembered, veteran Broadway scribe Louis Sobol, filling in for an ailing Dorothy Kilgallen, provided an update in mid-April. "Lawrence Tierney, who is usually in and out of trouble of some sort, hasn't been in newsprint for some time. Now I hear he has been in Italy playing the lead role in a picture titled 'The Tower Game.'"

Tierney was indeed in Italy, acting in a *giallo*—an Italian horror-thriller—directed by Angelo Dorigo under the name "Roy Morrison" and filmed in expressionistic black and white. He did not have the lead role, and the title was not *The Tower Game*, but *Assassino senza volto* (*Killer Without A Face*). Castello Balsorano in the Abruzzo region of southern Italy stood in for Nottingham Castle in England, where a woman is chased onto the ramparts by someone with a gun and falls to her death. More murders follow. Everyone is supposed to be British, but all the actors speak Italian—with the exception of the creepy, mute, and very suspicious handyman, played by Tierney. (According to UK film blogger Mark David Welsh, the plot did include a "tower game," and although it was "insufficiently explained . . . would seem to be a party game that involves choosing who you would throw off a building if there were three of you and only space for two.")

It was a film that would not make it across the Atlantic to American audiences any time soon. Nor would Tierney, as he picked up voiceover work, dubbing films into English, in France and Spain, scraping his way and getting into trouble away from the prying eyes of the American press. At a time when sideburns had gotten longer and dresses shorter, and the counterculture, sexual revolution, and anti-war movement were stirring, Lawrence Tierney was yesterday's news.

As if to delineate the new era to which the Tierney torch was passed, a fresh Dillinger was introduced in movie houses and drive-ins everywhere in April 1965. Twenty years to the month after the release of Tierney's *Dillinger* came *Young Dillinger*—"young," even though Nick Adams, portraying John Dillinger in this latest incarnation, was seven years older than Tierney when he played the role in 1945. With a jazzy score by Shorty Rogers and little attention to period wardrobe, the film had less to do with the gangster of the Great Depression than with Charlie Starkweather, the nineteen-year-old garbage collector who took along his fourteen-year-old girlfriend, Caril Ann Fugate, as he murdered eleven people in Nebraska and Wyoming in 1957. A precursor in style, attitude, and violent content to *Bonnie and Clyde* and other films of the American New Wave, this Dillinger was heavily influenced by *Rebel Without a Cause,* Nicholas Ray's 1955 film about teenage angst and rebellion. Nick Adams had a supporting role in *Rebel,* the picture that made his friend (and rumored lover) James Dean a legend.

Young Dillinger was described in the *Boston Globe* as "a grade-D imitation of a grade-B Chicago gangster movie," but *Los Angeles Times* critic Kevin Thomas dubbed it "a B picture with Grade A virtues.

"While not erasing memories of the 20-year-old Lawrence Tierney 'Dillinger,' kept fresh by frequent showings on TV, it succeeds in its own distinctive way." Thomas wrote that Adams's interpretation of the gangster was "valid, but Lawrence Tierney's classic tight-lipped steely-eyed portrayal remains easier to accept as an accurate depiction of a vintage gangster."

For Lawrence Tierney, the "old Dillinger," there would be more arrests, more drunken brawls, more undeniably shocking headlines, but the time between incidents would lengthen. Just as Hollywood was releasing fewer motion pictures each year, and movie stars were more selective in the pictures in which they appeared, so would Tierney show up only occasionally with a blockbuster headline.

Dorothy Kilgallen finished typing up her Broadway column and sent it via messenger from her five-story townhouse at 45 East Sixty-Eighth Street to the *Journal-American* offices at 2:30 a.m. on November 8, 1965. Shortly after noon that day, her body was found by her maid and personal hairdresser, sitting up in bed in a third-floor bedroom. The columnist and television game show panelist was fifty-two.

Dr. James Luke, an assistant medical examiner, reported on November 15 that Kilgallen had died of "acute ethanol (alcohol) and barbiturate intoxication." He did not rule whether the death was a suicide or accident. In the decades to follow, conspiracy theorists would allege that Dorothy Kilgallen was murdered because she planned to expose the truth about the assassination of President John F. Kennedy.

The original gossip queen, Louella Parsons, retired from her column that same month. Her longtime archrival Hedda Hopper reported that after fighting various maladies, including pneumonia, shingles of the optic nerve, fractures of the hip and shoulder, two heart attacks, and tuberculosis, Parsons was packing it in at eighty-four, and handing off the column to her longtime aide-de-camp, Dorothy Manners.

If Hedda Hopper took any satisfaction in outliving her competitor, it was short-lived. Hopper died of "double pneumonia with heart complications" at Cedars of Lebanon Hospital on February 1, 1966. She was seventy-five. Parsons hung in until December 9, 1972, when she died in a nursing home in Santa Monica, at ninety-one.

And where was Lawrence Tierney?

Tierney's whereabouts from the time he decamped to Europe in early 1965 to when he washed up back in New York City two years later have been enveloped in mystery and, thanks in no small part to Tierney himself, more than a bit of myth. According to one of the most circulated and disturbing stories, Tierney was in Italy when he headed out on a date in a car borrowed from bodybuilder-actor Steve Reeves. Tierney supposedly crashed the vehicle, killing his female passenger, fled the scene, and was arrested in Portugal, where he was convicted of manslaughter and sentenced to four years in prison. A version of the incident, included in Tierney's biography on an "official" Lawrence

Tierney website, places the tragedy in 1957, while Reeves was filming *Hercules*, and sticks Tierney in a Spanish prison for two years.

"Larry did discuss it with me once or twice," Tierney's close friend C. Courtney Joyner says. "He borrowed a car from Steve Reeves and he picked up a young lady. A pro. And he wrecked the car, and she was killed. That's how he ended up in jail in Portugal. He was in jail for, I think it was four years. And he told me he used to give the Portuguese prison guards shit all the time. When he got out of prison, the army escorted him out of the country, and then he found his way to Spain. And that's when he hooked up with Phil Yordan and was in *Custer of the West.*"

Actor and theater director Stephan Morrow, also close to Tierney in his later years, has a point when he admits, "With Larry, I never knew what was real or invented. . . . I was curious about what he did in World War Two. He said, 'I drove a tank through Europe.'"

Tierney may have managed to walk away from a fatal car accident somewhere along the way, but there is at least one major problem with the manslaughter tale, aside from the fact that Tierney's involvement in such a spectacular tragedy, followed by a trial and imprisonment in a foreign country, would surely have made news back in the States. A review of Tierney's activities confirms there was never a two-year, let alone four-year, gap in his documented work, arrests, court appearances, or whereabouts between 1957 and 1967.

(Steve Reeves died in 2000. "So many times, he would tell me a story involving a celebrity he knew and would retell an amazing historical memory about them," says Christopher LeClaire, author of *Worlds to Conquer,* Reeves's authorized biography. "Unfortunately, Steve never mentioned to me about knowing Mr. Tierney (or) the story involving him borrowing Reeves's car.")

That's not to say that Tierney didn't spend time in jail in Portugal and Spain. John Slaughter, in a recollection on another Tierney fansite, said he was acquainted with the actor in Madrid in 1966. Slaughter recalled that Tierney had been "kicked out of France for torching a dry Christmas tree at a hotel, kicked out of Italy for flooding his bathroom. In Madrid they would just throw him in jail a few days when drunk."

Another American expatriate said he met Tierney that same year at the celebrated Cerveceria Alemana tavern in Madrid and shared a room with him at a pension "for a couple of days" after Tierney had been jailed for fighting. "He showed off his chipped tooth and complained about Spanish dentists."

Alcohol-induced exploits may have been Tierney's most reportable activities in Europe, but his months on the Continent were also filled with higher pursuits. As he did in many off-hours in New York, Tierney spent time reading literature and poetry. Here, he could study in the places where they were written. He taught himself to speak passable Italian, Spanish, and French—which helped in his work dubbing films. He would also make notable acquaintances. In his later years, Tierney would tell Joyner and nephew Timothy Tierney that in Paris, he befriended the author of *The Respectful Prostitute,* a writer who happened to be one of the leading philosophers of the twentieth century.

"Larry's life was so outrageous that you just don't know if everything he ever said was true. But I tend to believe it was," Timothy Tierney says. "He said he knew Jean-Paul Sartre. He said, 'He was my friend.' I doubt that means they were best buddies, more like they saw each other at the café a few times and would say 'Hello,' but he demonstrated a familiarity with the philosophy of Sartre, in regards to being a free agent. He would talk about every man being a free agent."

In the existentialist Sartre, Tierney may have found another kindred spirit, one who validated his choices as he stumbled forward in life.

Back in the States, someone noticed Tierney's absence. Vic Wilmot wrote in the *Arizona Republic* on August 3, 1966, that he was "wondering almost aloud about whatever became of former movie bad guy Lawrence Tierney. He's now an on-and-off good, good guy doing film work in England."

Wilmot was about a thousand miles off. Tierney had remained in Spain that summer, where he'd picked up money doing voice work, and was currently filming his most high-profile project in years. Philip Yordan, who long ago had written the screenplay for *Dillinger* and lobbied for Tierney in the starring role, had cast Tierney in an international coproduction of an American Western titled *Custer's Last Stand.* The movie told the story of US Army commander George Armstrong Custer, who after the Civil War was sent west to fight the Indian Wars and was killed, along with his entire command, in 1876 by a coalition of Sioux and Cheyenne tribes at the Battle of Little Big Horn. The picture was being filmed in Super Technirama 70, the marketing name for a widescreen format that could be printed in 70 mm and screened in Cinerama theaters. Japanese filmmaker Akira Kurosawa was set to direct, but pulled out, and after British director Lindsay Anderson turned down the film, the job went to German film noir veteran Robert Siodmak.

British actor Robert Shaw was Custer. Shaw's wife, Mary Ure, had the role of Custer's wife. Tierney was cast as Custer's superior, General Philip Sheridan. He got to wear a mustache.

Exile

Word that Tierney was in a legitimate picture overseas got back to Earl Wilson in September. "One-time movie bad guy Lawrence Tierney, who lost the battle to booze, is making a screen comeback—as a good guy." Jack O'Brian, who inherited Dorothy Kilgallen's On Broadway column at the *New York Journal-American* and Hearst syndication, reported a few days later that "Lawrence Tierney's nicely on the wagon again and film-acting in 'Custer's Last Stand.'"

The New York columnists were accurate—to a point. According to those American friends Tierney had made in Madrid that year, his boozing and brawling had made him a "legend" among expatriates—and the Guardia Civil (Spain's national police force).

Jack O'Brian delivered the next Lawrence Tierney update, on January 26, 1967: "Poor LAWRENCE TIERNEY's in hot water again, in Paris this time—a brawl in a store over a sweater." The incident was less than a brawl, but more of a crime. Lawrence Tierney had been arrested for shoplifting.

It took some time for word to travel across the Atlantic. Tierney had been taken into custody on January 6 for allegedly trying to steal a sweater from a department store in Paris. Tierney was prosecuted, and the case went to trial on February 28.

A female store detective testified that she watched as Tierney picked up a sweater, examined it, tore off the label and price tag, rolled it up, and stuffed it under his suit jacket. He was walking out of the store when she and security men stopped him. Tierney admitted picking up the sweater, but said he had no intention of walking out of the store without paying for it. He claimed he only wanted to take the sweater outside into the daylight, to get a better idea of the color.

Tierney was found guilty. The penalty was a suspended one-month prison sentence, and a fine of 400 francs, then the equivalent of eighty US dollars.

This was Lawrence Tierney's first publicized arrest for a crime that was not related to boozing and/or brawling (for the most part, his antics in Europe escaped attention), but it was no surprise to AnnMarie Frisina Guertin. She recalls several similar instances, most prominently the day she drove "Uncle Larry" to buy clothing at the Green Acres Mall in Valley Stream, Long Island, ten minutes from home on Lenore Lane. "He goes into a store and he's got on this big coat. He would take the clothes into the fitting room, and he would try on the clothes, and then he'd come out empty-handed—he looked a little heavier, to be honest—and say, 'Okay, I didn't see anything. Let's go home.' And as I'm driving him home, he would be stripping off all of these clothes that he'd stolen from the store!"

Many friends from later in Tierney's life recall instances of his pilferage, from silverware to ketchup packets. "Whether or not Tierney could afford to purchase things is not the point," wrote a friend who became administrator of a Tierney fansite. "Shoplifting for Tierney was a joy unto itself. Every item stolen was a mini-heist that had Tierney feeling a little like a gangster again."

Tierney was still feeling like a gangster when he returned to New York City that year. He told Joyner that he ran into director Gordon Douglas, who was scouting locations for the Frank Sinatra picture, *The Detective.* "Douglas had directed Larry back at RKO in *San Quentin,* and they had a little reunion. He told him, 'Larry, I know about the problems and what's been going on, but there's a real good part in this picture for you. You can get back on your feet, get your insurance back.' Larry thought that was a great idea, and Gordon Douglas went off with his guys to look for locations. Douglas was staying at the Sherry-Netherland hotel and he and Larry were going to meet there to talk about the part and old times. Rather than have the meeting, Larry got his buddies together. They busted into Gordon Douglas' room and wiped him out.

"That was Larry's thinking then. That was his mindset. Larry said he was sure Douglas knew that he was responsible, and never turned him in. Larry felt terrible about it. He apparently wrote Gordon Douglas a letter years later, apologizing. In the movie, Ralph Meeker played the part that Douglas wanted to give Larry."

The Custer movie, retitled *Custer of the West,* opened in the United Kingdom on November 9, 1967, and word reached Hollywood that Tierney's performance was excellent. As was often the case throughout his lurching trajectory of the past twenty years, the good word led Tierney to become something of a commodity. Tierney told Sheilah Graham, and she told her readers, that he wanted a part in *The Boston Strangler,* 20th Century-Fox's film about Albert DeSalvo, who confessed to murdering thirteen women between 1962 and 1964. The picture was to be directed by Richard Fleischer, who directed Tierney in *Bodyguard* almost twenty years earlier. Tony Curtis was signed to play DeSalvo, and cameras were scheduled to roll on January 15, 1968, according to Leonard Lyons, "in the very house where the strangler, DeSalvo, lived."

If the *Strangler* producers were interested, Graham knew where Lawrence Tierney could be found: at Fifty-Eighth Street and Madison Avenue, on a construction site.

34

Fatso

Q. Are Scott Brady and Laurence Harvey brothers?—N.C., Elmira.
A. No. You have your acting Lawrences mixed up. Brady's
brother is former actor Lawrence Tierney.

TV TIME ANSWER MAN, DOVER, OHIO, *DAILY REPORTER*, JULY 19, 1968

Sheilah Graham, entering her twenty-third year of publishing Lawrence Tierney items and exclusives, revealed on December 14, 1967, that the one-time movie star could be found working with a construction gang in midtown Manhattan. Leonard Lyons, entering year twenty of occasional Tierney items, followed up two days later with the details. The "Dillinger" actor was laboring for seven dollars an hour, building the General Motors tower, a fifty-story office high-rise that was taking up the full city block bounded by Fifth and Madison Avenues between Fifty-Eighth and Fifty-Ninth Streets.

Tierney was not cast in *The Boston Strangler* movie, but while he hammered away into the first month of 1968, *Custer of the West* began its first run in Cinerama theaters in American cities. Reviews were mixed for a picture that, despite some contemporary flourishes, was definitely not part of the American New Wave that was launched in 1967 with films including *The Graduate, Bonnie and Clyde,* and *In Cold Blood.* "If you can imagine the script of an average TV western padded to last half the night and then being shot in Cinerama," the *Kansas City Times'* Dennis Stack wrote in a representative review, "you have the idea of *Custer of the West.*" The reception was even more hostile that summer, after the movie left the Cinerama theaters and was released in a standard format. Renamed *A Good Day for Fighting* in some cities on the East Coast, the new version had twenty minutes lopped off the 140-minute running time, and none of the rip-roaring Cinerama-type effects—"That's to move the camera at great speed down an incline," Stack explained, "thus giving us the effect of a wild ride. First it's done with a wagon, then with logs in a river and, finally, with a train."

Add to that an inferior, washed-out print distributed to theaters, and the critics were howling. When *Custer* limped into Manhattan in time for the Fourth of July, *New York Times* critic Renata Adler complained that "the print is abysmal" and contained "so much strange cutting and botching . . . that it is nearly impossible to follow the story."

For all the negative reception, the quick dump to the drive-in circuit, and a script that gave him lines like "I didn't recognize you without your horse," Lawrence Tierney's reputation was enhanced by *Custer of the West*. Kevin Thomas at the *Los Angeles Times* credited him for supplying "what vitality there is" in the film, and the *Boston Globe*'s Marjory Adams wrote that "Lawrence Tierney practically steals some scenes right from under the nose of star Shaw."

By the end of May, Walter Winchell was reporting that Tierney, "who climbed and fell from the Hollywood heights," was "signaturing his first film deal in years."

In the days and weeks after the April 4, 1968, assassination of Rev. Dr. Martin Luther King Jr., rioting and looting broke out in cities across the nation. Walter Winchell tapped out a related item in early May, in a column that was a mix of politics and news with a dash of show business. He painted a "Street Scene at 3 a.m. at 45th Street and 6th Avenue" in which "three young Negroes allegedly flung a heavy wire wastebasket thru a gem store glass door and began looting. . . . The cops nailed them as they fled." When one suspect whined, "I'm only fifteen!," a "Negro passerby interrupted, 'You stupid little punk!' A handsome white giant in the crowd shook his head in agreement . . . Lawrence Tierney, who made stardom in 'Dillinger.'"

Besides revealing inadvertently that Lawrence Tierney, of no fixed address, was wandering midtown Manhattan streets at 3 a.m., Winchell was juxtaposing Tierney's image as a classic movie gangster with his disapproval of contemporary antiestablishment protest. In those turbulent times, Tierney was represented as a figure on the far side of the generation gap, the "old Dillinger" from the old movies on television, as opposed to the nihilistic young Dillinger, played by Nick Adams, who, rebel to the end, had in February been found dead on the floor of his bedroom in Coldwater Canyon, victim of a drug overdose.

(Shortly after this period of unrest, Tierney put his voice-acting skills to use on *Silhouettes in Courage*, an ambitious audio documentary project that traced the history of Black Americans, from 500 BC, through slavery, to the Civil Rights movement and present day. Spread over eight long-playing records, the series featured a cast that included Ossie Davis, Brock Peters, Cicely Tyson, and the voices of Martin Luther King, James Meredith, and Malcolm X. It was produced by composer Charles "Big" Jones, who featured underexposed Black artists through his Silhouettes in Courage record label.)

Perhaps it was a combination of Winchell and *Custer* that turned Tierney into a momentary Hollywood authority. In June, Sheilah Graham sought his take on *Bonnie and Clyde,* which had premiered in August 1967 and was still in second-run and drive-in theaters. Arthur Penn's film, starring Warren Beatty and Faye Dunaway as the Depression-era outlaws, was controversial for its violence, comedy, and pop culture glamorization of the title characters.

"It's a shame the way everyone is lionizing them," Tierney said. "Bonnie and Clyde were a disgrace to organized crime. They were far too ruthless but didn't really have a criminal streak. They were just interested in indiscriminate killing—and shouldn't be made into folk heroes."

On July 2, Larry King, the Miami radio and television host and *Miami Herald* columnist, included Tierney in It's My Two Cents, his column accumulation of non sequiturs: "He hasn't been around in years, but Lawrence Tierney was always one of my favorite actors." It took a reader to remind the future interviewing legend that in the summer of 1968, Lawrence Tierney was everywhere—in several television commercials.

Most notable and controversial was an ad for the Armstrong wide-track, "really built" tire dubbed "Fatso" ("underneath his thick rubber hide, and above his nylon cords, he's got two belts of fiber glass that help keep the tread firm and tough"). "He plays 'Fatso' in that tire commercial where the little old lady goes into a gas station and asked to see 'Fatso,'" King scrawled on July 11. King reminded readers that he'd recently written that Tierney was "a favorite of mine. . . . His portrayal of John Dillinger showed a great understanding of violence and the criminal mind," before relaying a reader's postcard message that Tierney had "gained an unusual amount of weight."

The *Boston Globe* estimated that Tierney had packed on a hundred pounds since last encountered. Jack O'Brian wrote that "Lawrence Tierney in the TV tire commercial has blimped to Orson Welles size," though he set the avoirdupois record somewhat straighter on August 17, with an actual Tierney sighting in a new New York City restaurant called The Mood. As if easing Tierney back into the nightlife items, O'Brian took a cue from the golden olden days of Parsons and Hopper, and described the fifty-year-old man as "a good boy again." According to O'Brian, Tierney "said his career is acting well with two movie roles and two TV dramas; before which he'll melt off 30 lbs."

With all this new fortune—the role in *Custer,* the renewed respect, residuals from national television commercials, and a contract ready to be signed—the Lawrence Tierney whom the gossips and Hollywood producers knew so well had no choice—no choice but to get in trouble again.

Friday, August 9, 1968, a day the mercury tickled ninety, was a sticky seventy-nine degrees at 11 p.m. in Greenwich Village in lower Manhattan. In Washington Square Park, the neighborhood's hub, musicians strummed acoustic guitars and dope dealers sold marijuana and pills under the grand arch, modeled after the Arc de Triomphe, at the northern gateway over Fifth Avenue. People cooled off along the perimeter of the large fountain in the park's center. Some walked in the shallow waters. Music played. Free speech was expressed. In the southwest corner along MacDougal Street, chess hustlers played the suckers at stationary concrete tables.

Three blocks south on MacDougal, past the espresso cafes, falafel joints, bars, and headshops, among the hippies, hipsters, students, and tourists, was the Bleecker Street intersection. A film crew from NBC News was on the sidewalk and in the street shooting a documentary. The portable lighting rigs that illuminated the scene had attracted a small crowd, curious to see if a movie or television show was being filmed. The cameraman was focused on patrolman John Heitmann, who'd stopped a group of motorcyclists on the corner.

The traffic stop was proceeding smoothly when it was interrupted by a sudden commotion on the sidewalk: a crash, and a searchlight sweep across the buildings and faces as the lights toppled; another clattering, and the lights were out. Someone had knocked the lighting rig into the street, deliberately. That someone was the guy from the Fatso tire commercials. Lawrence Tierney had stomped out of one of the nearby bars, impulsively brought down the bright lights that caught his attention, and was now ready to take on people. That signaled the end of the film shoot. Officer Heitmann sent the bikers on their way and turned his attention to the interrupter.

Cameraman Robert Sarro demanded that Tierney be arrested, so the gear was packed up, Heitmann affixed handcuffs on Tierney, and everyone headed west to the Sixth Precinct house on Charles Street, where Sarro could press charges.

At the station, Heitmann plopped the manacled suspect onto a chair and brought Sarro to the desk to discuss the best way to handle the incident.

They could settle things now. Tierney could make good for the damages and everyone could be spared the expense and time of an arrest, booking, and court appearances.

Sarro was very angry, but a reasonable man. He understood what Heitmann was suggesting. Everything could be handled—

Suddenly, big Lawrence Tierney, bigger than ever, bolted from the chair where he'd been stowed and charged the cameraman. In one motion, he thrust out his chest, tilted his big head back, and slammed it forward with force into Sarro's brow. The headbutt opened a cut over the filmographer's left eye, from which blood began to flow.

Everyone in the vicinity pounced on Tierney and wrestled him under control. That changed things, Heitmann realized. Tierney was now facing a pair of charges: criminal mischief—for the attack on the lights—and assault, for making thirty-nine-year-old Robert Sarro see lights. He was booked and spent the night in jail.

The *Daily News* had the story to itself the next morning. Under the headline, "JOUST WITH TV-ERS JAILS TUFFY TIERNEY," Vincent Lee, as was the wont with *Daily News* reporters, had some fun with Tuffy, "who switched from movie tough guy to winning notoriety from here to Hollywood and back as a brawling, sometimes drunken rounder and cop-fighter."

As Tierney awaited arraignment in weekend court, Lee quipped: "What everyone wondered was why Tierney picked a television crew as his latest target since his most visible sign of solvency is his job as a spieler on TV commercials."

In February 1969, former middleweight boxer Jake LaMotta showed up in Spokane, Washington, for an Amateur Athletics Union awards luncheon. He wasn't scheduled to speak, but was happy to unload on Harry Missildine, who wrote the humorous, insightful Twice Over Lightly column for the *Spokane Review-Journal's* sports section. LaMotta revealed that he'd finished writing an autobiographical book that would be published in 1970. The title was *The Raging Bull.* He said he hoped it would be made into a movie.

Speaking of movies, LaMotta let it be known he was doing some film acting of his own. "Recently did a movie in Italy," he said. "The tentative title is *The Spy.* It's got Burgess Meredith, Lawrence Tierney and Connie Towers in it. I play a bartender."

While Tierney kept a low profile in Italy through the early months of 1969, another big break in the States seemed to be in the offing in April. The opportunity was dangled by bestselling crime novelist and pulp fiction writer

Mickey Spillane. The former comic book writer had sold millions of books, seen many of his titles turned into B-movies, and even acted onscreen, portraying his signature character, private eye Mike Hammer. Spillane was born in Brooklyn a year and six days before Lawrence Tierney, and although he was brought up in Elizabeth, New Jersey, shared many of Tierney's tough guy qualities.

Hy Gardner broke the news in his *Daily News* question-and-answer column, Glad You Asked That! "Q. What ever happened to that drunk and belligerent actor who played the role of John Dillinger in a movie, then thought that's who he was, even fighting cops?—D.B., Oakland.

"A. Lawrence Tierney finally sobered up and wised up. He got a job moving furniture to build himself up physically. Mickey Spillane just signed him to play the heavy in 'The Delta Factor,' observing: 'Anyone who overcomes his alcoholic cancer deserves a break—and I'm giving one to Larry.'"

Spillane had big plans, and not only for Lawrence Tierney. On May 8, 1969, he and producer Robert Fellows (who'd cowritten and produced *The Girl Hunters,* the 1963 picture based on Spillane's book and starring Spillane as Hammer) announced the creation of Spillane-Fellows Productions, Inc., an independent movie and television production company to be based in Nashville, Tennessee. The moviemakers planned to construct a movie studio and turn Nashville into the "Hollywood of the South."

Their first picture, *The Delta Factor,* a spy thriller based on Spillane's bestseller from 1967, was to begin filming in June, directed by Tay Garnett, a Hollywood veteran who began his career writing silent films and had directed the 1946 film noir, *The Postman Always Rings Twice.* The two lead roles were up in the air, but Joan Blondell was confirmed for a cameo, and Spillane's wife, Sherri, a former nightclub singer who posed nude for his book covers, was cast as a murder victim. Lawrence Tierney would play "the archvillain."

As soon as that picture wrapped, Spillane-Fellows intended to roll on another. J. B. Williams, who was financing the company, told the *Tennessean,* "We plan to stay in continuous production."

Events did not unfold as planned. Four days after the big announcement, Robert Fellows died at Hollywood Presbyterian Hospital after suffering a heart attack. When cameras rolled in June, seventy-four-year-old Tay Garnett was directing from a wheelchair. Christopher George and Yvette Mimieux had the lead roles. Lawrence Tierney was not in the cast in what would be the one and only offering from Spillane-Fellows Productions, Inc.

According to Jack O'Brian, Tierney, the "good actor whose life is a sad script," was "ailing in Rome." Tierney remained off the Hollywood radar the remainder of the year. He was not in town as fear spread in August after five people were massacred at Roman Polanski's rented home in Benedict Canyon, followed the next night by the bloody murders of Leno and Rosemary LaBianca in their house across town in Los Feliz.

Lawrence Tierney was fifty. He was overweight. While he could get work in commercials and overseas, the "alcoholic cancer" of which Mickey Spillane spoke had done its worst. The surprising twist—and there always seemed to be a surprising twist in the stumbling journey of Lawrence Tierney—is that some of his most memorable film and television work lay ahead. So did his most sensational off-camera escapades. In the 1970s, Lawrence Tierney would grab major headlines. There would be blood. There would be embarrassment. There would be death.

Then, there would be a comeback unlike any other.

35

Stabbed

At the dawn of the new decade, Lawrence Tierney entered a new era in his career and a new stage in his life. The old movies—*Dillinger, Step by Step, The Devil Thumbs a Ride, San Quentin, Bodyguard, Kill or Be Killed*—were still shown constantly on television stations throughout the country. Tierney himself was more elusive. There were sightings, and stories, as there had been in the late 1950s, that he was living, on and off, on the streets. "There was a long time when he was drinking and living in abandoned buildings and hoboing around the streets of New York," Michael Tierney told Rick McKay. "He tried everything, I guess. On the low end, anyway."

Cameo appearances, snapshots, vignettes, and the occasional shocker of a headline kept his name and image alive in the news, while he wrestled with his alcoholism and carried out a slow, inconsistent stagger on a path back to the screen.

The 1970s could have begun with a new lease on Tierney's career. At fifty years old, with a reputation for standing on the elder side of the generation gap, he was a perfect fit for the role of Joe Curran, the loudmouth, homophobic, and ultimately homicidal factory worker in John G. Avildsen's film, *Joe*. Avildsen told John A. Gallagher in his 1989 book, *Film Directors on Directing*, that the producers at Cannon Films were insistent that his own choice for the lead, thirty-four-year-old Peter Boyle, was "too young, nobody would believe that he had been in World War II." Avildsen said he relented and went on to cast an "older actor who was also very good."

The producers reconsidered two days before principal photography began in January 1970. According to the director, the older actor "took a leak in the escalator at Bloomingdale's and slugged a saleslady, so I said, 'Why don't we go with Boyle?'"

Joe became a star-making role for Peter Boyle. Only later was it revealed that the "older actor" was Lawrence Tierney.

Lloyd Kaufman, a production assistant on the picture—and future director and cofounder of the Troma Entertainment production company—had a slightly different recollection when he spoke to *Screen Anarchy* in 2014. "Lawrence Tierney!" he recalled on the website. "We were taking him in to get a fitting at Alexander's department store, and he pissed on my . . . I felt this thing on my blue jeans, like that's a weird feeling. He was urinating on me. He was drunk! They got rid of him!"

The alleged urination incident may not have been the only reason Tierney was axed from the picture. Shortly before filming was to commence, he reportedly was arrested for assaulting a bartender who refused to serve him another drink.

The climactic scene of *The Last Days of Dillinger* was filmed outside the historic Biograph Theater in Chicago on July 22, 1971, the thirty-seventh anniversary of the actual killing of Public Enemy No. 1 by FBI agents on that very spot. The television special was the premiere episode of *Appointment with Destiny*, a series of one-hour dramas recreating historic events at the sites where the events took place. David Wolper produced for CBS. Rod Serling would narrate.

William Wendt, a twenty-eight-year-old veteran of Broadway, regional theater, and television guest roles, played Dillinger. Wendt told his hometown paper in Winona, Minnesota, that he'd secured the role only three days before he had to be on set in Chicago.

"Thank goodness I'd taken a course in speed reading and in a day-and-a-half I read four books about Dillinger's life and studied every available newsreel clip taken of him during that era," he said. "By the time production started . . . I think maybe I knew more about the man than he did himself.

"Above all," he insisted, "we were concerned with creating an absolutely authentic setting for the story and duplicating the events as they happened." The 1945 *Dillinger*, starring Lawrence Tierney, he said, "was full of inaccuracies."

Around this time, Lawrence Tierney was close to the action, while at the same time far from it, in midtown Manhattan. Jack O'Brian wrote on August 23 that Tierney was obviously "happier as a construction hard hat than acting, but he stays on the Broadway scene—still working on a new W. 57th Street skyscraper." A week later, Earl Wilson reported that Tierney had walked into the Metropole Café at Seventh Avenue and Forty-Eighth Street in Times Square, "in hard hat and uniform." The former jazz club was now a drinkers' joint with the added attraction of go-go dancers behind the bar. Tierney told the spy he was "doing construction work on W. 57th St. and couldn't be happier."

How much happier? Weeks later, O'Brian claimed that Tierney had "blown up . . . to a far happier 235 pounds." The columnist had taken to referring to Tierney as the "erstwhile off-and-onscreen baddie," but the hard hat did manage to pick up some film acting work that summer. He had a small role as a hospital security guard in *Such Good Friends,* a film starring Dyan Cannon as a New York housewife who discovers her comatose husband had been unfaithful. Otto Preminger produced and directed a script written by Elaine May (under the name "Esther Dale"). For an "erstwhile" actor, Tierney did well in a brief scene with Cannon. He did not appear to be an obese "Fatso," but solid and sturdy, his hair thinning but dark brown—perhaps aided by a splash of Grecian Formula. The credited role wouldn't draw attention from audiences or critics, but it generated a lot of talk—and complaints—on the set. According to O'Brian, Tierney "upset a few people, including several pinched gals."

Dillinger lived and died again in 1972. Production began in October on yet another film about the Public Enemy, this one taking its title from Tierney's 1945 classic. The new *Dillinger,* from the exploitation behemoth American International Pictures, was the directorial debut of John Milius, a macho screenwriter known for embellishing American male folk heroes in films like *Jeremiah Johnson, The Life & Times of Judge Roy Bean,* and *Evel Knievel.* The cast included John Dillinger look-alike Warren Oates in the lead role, and two 1972 Academy Award winners from *The Last Picture Show,* Ben Johnson as G-man Melvin Purvis, and Cloris Leachman as the Lady in Red. The Biograph Theater finale was filmed in Oklahoma City.

On January 18, 1973, construction worker, sometime bartender, and part-time actor Lawrence Tierney was drinking away the afternoon at the Three Roses Bar, a gin mill on Ninth Avenue in Hell's Kitchen, the working-class Irish and Puerto Rican neighborhood west of Midtown Manhattan. A decade before gentrification would creep in, the rough-and-tumble area was controlled by the Westies, an Irish mob of racketeers and killers that did dirty work for the Gambino crime family. Due to his heritage and reputation, Tierney fit right in. He had a bed at 368 West Forty-Eighth Street, around the corner from the bar, where he was a regular. The Roses was dark, usually quiet except for the television, and patronized by working stiffs, drunks, and mooks concentrating on their drinks. Although Tierney could be an imposing figure even while seated at a barstool, at fifty-three he was no longer the target of some drunk down the rail who wanted to prove that Dillinger ain't so tough, after all.

There was always the risk, however, as he downed shot after shot, that the combination of alcohol and his own hair-trigger aggression or annoyance would lead to some kind of flare-up. On this Thursday afternoon, Tierney got into it with a Puerto Rican guy. Robert Rosado wasn't a youngblood looking for trouble. He was fifty-seven, and lived around the corner from Ninth Avenue, in a rattrap at 436 West Forty-Second Street. The dispute got loud, and the bartender told them to take it outside.

Tierney and Rosado took it outside and began scuffling on the corner of Ninth Avenue. People got out of the way and others watched from a safe distance as the big Irishman and the Latino went at it. The fight carried on for two blocks down Ninth Avenue, with Tierney, in a rage, chasing Rosado, Rosado punching back, retreating. Tierney, bigger and brawnier, seemed to have the upper hand—until Rosado pulled a knife from his pocket and pointed it at him. What was this? *West Side Story*? Before Tierney could adjust to the presence of a weapon, Rosado charged forward and plunged the blade into Tierney's belly. It felt like a punch, followed by a strange intestinal pressure. With his adrenaline flowing and all the booze coursing through his system, Tierney didn't realize at first that he'd been stabbed. Then there was the warmth, the blood spreading across his untucked shirt. Then there was the pain.

Police showed up and hurried Tierney to St. Clare's Hospital on West Fifty-First Street. Rosado was arrested and charged with felonious assault and weapons possession.

Even with a Hollywood star well past his sell-by date, the story was irresistible, and on Friday few newspapers resisted the headline that an actor, or "former actor," had been stabbed in a brawl. The "movie tough guy . . . who gained fame in a 1945 portrayal of John Dillinger" . . . "who won acting fame three decades ago when he played the title role in a film biography of gangster John Dillinger" . . . was "quiet and resting comfortably" in St. Clare's, where he was listed in fair condition, recovering from surgery for a stab wound in the abdomen.

More than a month later, Tierney was still on the mend. Jack O'Brian, who referred to the stabbing incident as Tierney's "latest cruel-life role," wrote in March that he could bide the time while recovering, "watching himself on a hot new Cranapple Juice TV commercial."

"Sometimes my wife gets edgy if I'm not working, and if I turn down a job, she hits the ceiling. To tell you the truth, I can't afford to turn down many parts, not with these kids to send to college. I don't want my boys to be actors.

They meet too many kinky broads. But for me, I'm perfectly happy with the career choice I made."

While Lawrence Tierney recuperated in New York City, his estranged brother Scott Brady was living a very different life than the one he'd enjoyed for close to two decades in his bachelor pad on Hollywood Hills Road. The actor who'd been one of Hollywood's "most eligible" had done what he'd vowed in 1948. He'd found "a gal like Grandma." On Christmas Day 1967, at the age of forty-three, Brady had married a "non-pro": American Airlines ticket agent and part-time model, Mary Lizabeth "Lisa" Tirony. The couple, who'd met nine years earlier at a Notre Dame football party (Brady had a reputation as a diehard Fighting Irish fan), had two children—Timothy, born in 1968, and Terence, two years later—before moving to Northridge, a neighborhood deep in the San Fernando Valley, far from the Hollywood crowd.

Scott Brady continued to work, though no longer as a rugged leading man. His most epic professional decision was made in 1968, when he turned down the lead role in *Justice for All,* a potential ABC television series that after a number of revisions and cast changes would eventually be rolled out on CBS as *All in the Family.* He wasn't so proud of his most recent movies, which included *Satan's Sadists, Five Bloody Graves,* and *Hell's Bloody Devils,* all directed by exploitation master Al Adamson, but Brady was also popping up in guest roles on top prime-time television series, including *Adam-12, McMillan & Wife, Mannix,* and *Ironside.*

Newspaper readers across the country caught up with Brady in June 1973, while he promoted his latest picture, *Wicked, Wicked,* a tongue-in-cheek horror thriller filmed in "Duo-vision" (a fancy name for split screen). Far enough removed from his heyday that he was interviewed for Nancy Anderson's syndicated Yesterday's Stars Today feature, Brady referred to himself, at forty-eight, as "an ex-star."

Anderson described Brady as "the big Irishman who came to Hollywood from World War II to become a movie and television star" and talked "straight from the shoulder but with humor." Brady cracked a few jokes while dishing on famous female costars ("Working with Joan Crawford isn't tough, but as an alternative you could join the Marine Corps") and repeating his origin story ("My first picture wasn't released, it escaped").

In a serious reflection of his character, Brady acknowledged the relative who gave him the opportunity for success.

"When I got out of the Navy, I just drifted into this business because of my brother," he said. "I went to drama school, but I learned a lot—more I guess—hanging around the sets. I had access because of Lawrence."

John Milius's *Dillinger* premiered in Dallas on June 19, 1973. Despite the quality of its cast and vision of the writer-director (Milius would write and direct *Big Wednesday,* and write the screenplay for *Apocalypse Now*), *Dillinger* was an American International exploitation flick, offering not much more than bloody, pulpy fun. Columnist Elston Brooks of the local *Fort Worth Star-Telegram* accused the filmmaker of "blatantly borrowing every trick in the bag pioneered by *Bonnie and Clyde,*" but admitted that the film was "not at all bad, no matter how familiar."

When *Dillinger* opened in New York on August 1, *Times* critic A. H. Weiler wrote that the picture was "fascinating for its speed, action and firepower, but as character studies . . . shoots blanks most of the time. . . . The Dillinger portrayed by Warren Oates is tough and homespun, if little else."

Lawrence Tierney's legacy remained intact, although not everyone recognized it. Entertainment columnist George Anderson of the Pittsburgh *Post-Gazette,* announcing the local opening of Milius's *Dillinger* in July, added, "Does anybody remember an actor named Lawrence Tierney, who played the title role in a quickie film called 'Dillinger' in 1945? He was the brother of Scott Brady."

Surprisingly, during this troubled period, Tierney kept a hand in the acting game. In the summer of 1973, he was booked on the dinner theater circuit. The concept of taking popular plays and musicals to cities and towns far from Broadway and serving them up along with a restaurant-quality meal and, most hoped, alcohol service, was developed in the 1950s, but hit its stride and became part of pop culture in the 1970s. Many current television personalities and aging former movie and theater stars made good money treading the boards in these hybrid establishments. Tierney's knife injury may have been the reason he canceled out of a role at Houston's Windmill Dinner Theatre, in a production of *Gaslight* that costarred *Gilligan's Island* actress Dawn Wells.

Word came from Philadelphia in February 1974 that Lawrence Tierney was returning to the stage, after all, to appear in a Drama Guild production of *Death of A Salesman.* Arthur Miller's Pulitzer Prize– and Tony-winning drama would open on the last day of the month and run through March 17 at the historic Walnut Street Theatre. The director was the brilliant actor and notorious drunk George C. Scott. Jack O'Brian reported on February 20 that Tierney was telling fellow boozers at Pete's Tavern on East Eighteenth Street that he would be starring as traveling salesman Willy Loman. In truth, that leading role had gone to Martin Balsam. Tierney was cast in the small but crucial role of Willy's dead brother Ben, who appears in Willy's memories and troubled imagination.

No one was shocked when there was trouble with a drinker shortly before the premiere—only it wasn't Tierney who drained the bottles, ran off, and disappeared before opening night. It was the director. Scott got into an argument with the playwright and stormed out of town the weekend before the first preview. Miller himself took charge in those final days, and the show went on, as planned. The *Philadelphia Inquirer*'s Howard A. Coffin wrote that Balsam delivered "a powerful, understated and deeply moving performance," and singled out Lawrence Tierney for a "smaller part . . . well played."

Tierney's out-of-town redemption didn't get much attention back in New York City, nor did an item that Charles McHarry ran with on May 22 in his On The Town column in the *Daily News*. It wasn't until later in the year, when someone got photographic evidence, that McHarry's overlooked scoop spread around the world. Forget Philadelphia. Lawrence Tierney had finally returned to Broadway, but not in a way he or anyone else might have expected.

36

"From Stardom to Hansom"

Central Park's newest horse-drawn carriage hackie? That would seem
to be Lawrence Tierney. The former film star was spotted tying up his
rig in front of the Stage Deli for a brief stopover the other night.

CHARLES MCHARRY, ON THE TOWN

The story that the notorious actor had hitched his horse to a parking meter
outside the pastrami sandwich and matzoh ball soup dispensary on Seventh
Avenue between Fifty-Third and Fifty-Fourth Streets ran in the *Daily News*
on May 22, 1974. The gossip item did not get national attention, nor was it
picked up or expanded upon by competing columnists. Three months later,
Larry Fields's nugget in the *Philadelphia Daily News* that "Tierney, who used
to act a lot badder off than on screen, is now driving a hansom cab in Fun
City"—was also met with the sound of crickets.

Earl Wilson's report on August 12 that Tierney had "opened a drama
workshop in Manhattan," and Jack O'Brian's September sighting of Tierney
"kissing a girl's hand in front of Carnegie Hall 'tother aft" spread throughout
the country by power of syndication. Neither was more sensational nor historic than news that the former Hollywood tough guy was at the reins of a
horse-drawn carriage like some character out of a Dickens novel. What would
it take for someone to notice?

It would take a photograph. "DIFFERENT WORLD: Lawrence Tierney, a
onetime actor who no longer is making movies, holds the horse that is his
workmate in New York. Tierney drives a hansom cab in Manhattan, and had
just driven a party to a theater when the picture was taken."

The Associated Press photo was picked up on October 9, 1974, and by
October 10 had been carried by newspapers in every city in the country. It was

a simple portrait of Lawrence Tierney and his horse, standing in the street. The horse's head fills most of the right side of the frame. On the left is Tierney, in slacks, turtleneck, and heavy, knee-length coat with a thick fur collar. His right foot is on the curb; his left hand holds the horse by the bridle. Tierney is obviously balding and what remains of his once-brown hair is cropped close. He's an older, rounder man than even the one in the Preminger film. A full-frame view of the picture, which was cropped tight in most newspapers, reveals that Tierney was in the Theater District, on West Forty-Fifth Street, between Seventh and Eighth Avenues, across the street from the Booth Theatre, where Ray Dotrice was starring in a revival of his one-man show, *Brief Lives*.

The *Los Angeles Times* ran the photo alongside a publicity still from *Born to Kill* that depicted Tierney grasping the wrist of a resisting Claire Trevor. The actress occupies the same space in the frame as the carriage horse in the more recent picture. The caption read "From Stardom to Hansom."

The news from New York was of such importance to readers on the West Coast that the *Los Angeles Times* ran the photos again the following day, adding that "after series of reversals in professional and private life, he took up the reins." When the *Daily News,* a day late on the story, ran the photo on page four, the copy guys had their usual fun, with the headline, "AWRIGHT YOU, WANNA CAB?" Misidentifying the location as Central Park (fourteen blocks north), the *News* wrote that the "legendary movie tough guy has exchanged that career for that of a horse-and-carriage cabbie. . . . At least he still has the whip hand."

Of course, the *News* and the others insinuated the exact opposite of Tierney having "the whip hand"—power or control in a situation. The subtext to each photo cutline was that a man who had everything one could ask for— *stardom*—had been banished from the sacred circle to become an ordinary working lug. Tierney's was an ultimate cautionary tale, a fate worse than being found dead of an overdose on a bathroom floor. "*New role . . . different role . . . hansom role . . . switch . . . Lawrence Tierney . . . who portrayed gangster John Dillinger in the movies . . . no longer in movies . . . may not be seen much on the silver screen, but he is still in the public's view . . . on Broadway . . . with his rig on a Manhattan street . . . just driven a party to the theater.*" The cutlines bled together. Even after a steady, decades-long fall from grace, this tumble, as one paper captioned, "From Ham to Hansom," was the saddest yet. But something was left out in the descriptions of the photograph, something evident from even a cursory look: it's a rare photo in which Tierney is smiling for the camera. He's not grimacing, thrusting a hand to block the lens, or ready to attack. He's beaming. Perhaps for the first time, he's happy to pose for a news photographer. He looks to be more relaxed than he's been in years.

Eleven years later, as a guest on Skip E. Lowe's public access talk show, Tierney looked back fondly. "I was the handsomest cab driver," he said. "I used to say, 'Take a ride in my carriage and see my horse with the handsome behind.'

"I liked doing that a lot because, well, I like children. The adults would sit in the back and once in a while you get a young kid and let them sit up on the seat right between your legs and let him hold the reins and think he's driving. Watch his expression, that was fun. I like young kids, you know. Yeah, it was fun to have the kid think he was driving and a thrill for him. Vicarious thrill for me."

Jack O'Brian had to hand it to Lawrence Tierney. In the first month of 1975, he noted that "spunky Larry" was "still trying," driving a Central Park hansom cab, "even if his film career is abeyant.

"Saddest part, he was one of the strongest, Gable-ambianced young actors on the way up," O'Brian recalled. "No one in showbiz is mad at Tierney for blowing his chances; it would be like being mad at someone for having pneumonia."

With those sentiments, the columnist was one of the few to acknowledge that alcoholism is a medical condition and Tierney's rage a symptom of far deeper issues. O'Brian's words were also a few weeks behind the headlines. Far from abeyant, Tierney's film career had been resuscitated. On New Year's Day 1975, Charles McHarry's column in the *Daily News* had featured another sighting of Lawrence Tierney at the Stage Deli. This time, the "former actor" was telling people he was returning to the big screen, "this time as a TV newscaster in a thinly veiled story of the Patty Hearst kidnapping." This time, people noticed. Earl Wilson picked up the item and ran with it on January 3.

The film was titled *Abduction*, a down-and-dirty "torn from the headlines" sexploitation flick with obvious similarities to the kidnapping in February 1974 of newspaper heiress Patty Hearst by a revolutionary group called the Symbionese Liberation Army. At the time Tierney's participation was announced, Patty Hearst was still missing and had gone from victim to criminal fugitive in the eyes of the law, declaring herself a member of the SLA and shown on surveillance video holding an M1 carbine during a bank holdup.

Oddly enough, *Abduction* was actually based on *Black Abductor*, a pornographic novel by Harrison James that was published a year before the Hearst kidnapping. Now the movie was to be shot in a hurry, in thirty-five days, and rush-released to capitalize on the current events. (Producer Kent E. Carroll denied a *Variety* report that *Abduction* had been conceived as a hardcore porno flick, but admitted to Bob Thomas that some explicit sex scenes had been filmed "because of the reality that the director required.")

Within weeks, Tierney was generating more heat. Bill Gyorfy, another exploitation filmmaker, told the *Greenville News* of Greenville, South Carolina, that Tierney would play "the bad guy" in *Colorado Gold,* an "old fashioned Western" he planned to shoot locally in mid-June. Gyorfy said he'd hired director George Sherman, who'd been working since the Mack Sennett days and had directed dozens of Westerns (as well as the 1952 Errol Flynn pirate movie, *Against All Flags*). The movie would feature old-time cowboy movie stars including Lash Larue, Sunset Carson, Monte Hale, and Red Barry.

Gyorfy also planned to shoot a Western comedy, tentatively titled *True Grits,* simultaneously. Citing his experience helming *Beach Bums on Wheels,* Gyorfy said he'd direct that one himself. (Gyorfy would gain some underground fame as director of the never-completed film *Gas Is Best,* starring Sammy Petrillo as a superhero battling anti-Semitism and powered by flatulence.)

April 6, 1975, was the thirtieth anniversary of the premiere of *Dillinger* in Cincinnati. April 25, 1975, was the thirtieth anniversary of *Dillinger*'s opening in New York City. Mid-June 1975 came and went. Cameras never rolled on *Colorado Gold.*

On June 20, 1975, the day the movie *Jaws* opened in theaters across America, Lawrence Tierney was fifty-six years old, losing the battle of his bulge, surrendered in the war to maintain a hairline, and settling into late middle age. He was an occasional actor, hansom cab driver, a working stiff, and a drunk, just one of seven and a half million stories in the Naked City.

His latest story was about to unfold in a fourth-floor apartment in a five-story walkup building at 132 West Fifty-Eighth Street.

Her name was Bonnie Jones. The papers would say she was a secretary. She was twenty-four years old. She was a redhead, and as Tierney told it, a feisty, fiery one at that. She liked to argue, sometimes crazy argue, especially when they were drinking. *Was she crazy?* Was he? The thing was, she was a kid. He really cared for her. He really did. So how did this happen on the evening of June 20, 1975?

As Tierney told it, they were in her living room, just the two of them, both drinking scotch. He was on the couch. She was waltzing around the small apartment, wearing nothing but a nightgown.

Young Bonnie put down her drink.

"I think I'm going to jump out the window," she said.

37

"I think I'm going to jump"

New York City Police received the first 911 call shortly after 8:30 p.m. on June 20, 1975. A woman had jumped or fallen from a fourth-story window at 132 West Fifty-Eighth Street. Officers from the Midtown North station at 306 West Fifty-Fourth Street arrived at the scene and were told the body had landed on the roof of a one-story extension at the back of the apartment building. Sgt. Patrick Maney and officers John Kelly and Bruce Berman made their way to the second-story setback and found Bonnie Jones in her nightgown, splayed unnaturally. Her head was smashed and blood poured from her matted red hair—but she was alive. The sergeant did what he could to try to stanch the bleeding. The cops maneuvered Bonnie onto a stretcher and got her down to the ground and out to the street, where an ambulance from Roosevelt Hospital was waiting.

The ambulance attendants took over. They slid the stretcher and Bonnie Jones into the back of the emergency vehicle, slammed the doors shut, and hit the siren and the gas.

The ambulance lurched forward, then stopped. The engine had stalled. The driver tried again. The engine was flooded. The emergency vehicle wasn't going anywhere.

The cops moved quickly. They hustled an emergency service station wagon, got Bonnie Jones inside, and raced through the midtown traffic the few blocks to the hospital at Fifty-Ninth and Ninth.

Doctors were waiting at the emergency room entrance.

Meanwhile, in the apartment on the fourth floor, fifty-six-year-old Lawrence Tierney was sobbing as he went over his story one more time for the detectives.

"We were sitting in her living room enjoying ourselves, and suddenly she said, 'I'm going to jump.'"

The cops wanted to get that right. "She said, 'I'm going to jump out the window.'"

"Yeah." Tears rolled down Tierney's face. "She said, 'I think I'm gonna jump out the window.' Then she put her drink of scotch down, walked to the window, and went out."

The detectives looked at each other, looked toward the window, and back to Tierney.

"I couldn't believe it," he stammered. "I thought she was joking. For God's sake, if I knew she was serious, I could have grabbed her." Tierney wept some more. "I really loved the kid."

Bonnie Jones was wheeled directly into an operating room. The impact after falling about thirty-five feet, at more than forty-seven feet per second in less than two seconds, left her with a fractured skull and multiple internal injuries. The doctors made an urgent effort to save her life, but less than two hours later, it was clear there was no hope. They called the time of death at 10:30 p.m.

"We did all we could, but it was impossible," one of the physicians told reporters.

"She was too far gone," a hospital spokesman added.

Sgt. Maney was also on hand. "It was a terrible sight," he told a reporter from the *Daily News.* "I tried to stop the bleeding, but it was impossible."

Meanwhile, the official police statement on Bonnie Jones, "an attractive, red-haired secretary," was that she "jumped or fell to her death."

The cops took Tierney to the Midtown North stationhouse to question him some more. He was truly shaken. He stuck to his story. "She said, 'I think I'm going to jump out the window.'"

Bonnie Jones's death was ruled a suicide. There was no evidence that her drinking companion had thrown her from the window or somehow convinced her to take the leap. Lawrence Tierney was in the clear, free to go back to his hansom cab and wait for tourists outside the Plaza Hotel.

None of the reporters covering the story mentioned that the scenario was reminiscent of the 1951 film *The Hoodlum,* in which Tierney's character, the sociopathic criminal Vincent Lubeck, seduces his younger brother's girlfriend, impregnates her, and drives her to suicide—by throwing herself off a building.

According to David Del Valle, Tierney was more akin to his character in *Female Jungle*: the detective who fears he killed an actress during an alcoholic blackout. "He told me that he couldn't remember," Del Valle says. "We were on the subject of blackouts. If he was blacking out, he couldn't remember, so how could he possibly tell us what happened? Occasionally, Larry would change the story around and say it was an accident. But his one comment stays steady through the whole thing: it wouldn't have happened at all if they hadn't been drinking."

There was one other scenario floated in the weeks following the initial headlines, one that circulated through the industry back in Hollywood: that Tierney had witnessed Bonnie being tossed out the window by a pimp, kept shtum with the cops, and then carried out justice on his own. After many conversations with Tierney that ventured to the edges of the subject, his close friend C. Courtney Joyner subscribes to a version of that theory.

"He told me that Bonnie was a student, but that she was a heroin addict," Joyner recounts. "He was very devoted to her, and he hated the guy who got her hooked on heroin. But Larry would never be completely clear on the specific details of her death. He was usually so articulate about details when he'd talk about his past. I didn't sit Larry down and give him the third degree about all this, but he told me, 'I got the justice.' From the bits and pieces that Larry said, I believe there was a fight with this man in the apartment—whether he was a pimp or a drug dealer—and they were fighting, two big guys, and I think she got knocked out the window. Purely a terrible accident. All he would tell me about what happened was, he got the justice against the dealer or pimp that he blamed for Bonnie's death. Always those exact same words: 'I got the justice.' I never for one second believed it was intentional or that Larry would throw this woman out a window. Never in a million years."

38

Bad

As far as the press was concerned, the death of Bonnie Jones was a fitting final capstone on its coverage of Lawrence Tierney's booze and brawling binge that had been launched thirty years earlier, six weeks after the release of *Dillinger.* The *New York Daily News* explained to readers that Tierney had "gained minor fame for playing tough-guy roles in the movies." In its brief mention, the *New York Times* referred to him as "the former actor." In the new, post-Watergate, *People* magazine era, nothing short of actual murder or perhaps a runaway horse down the middle of Broadway would make Lawrence Tierney newsworthy.

To tabloid editors, he was old news. To Hollywood producers, he was at least three Dillingers removed. Those who'd followed his exploits of the past thirty years, however, knew that at this low point in his life, there was only one thing in store for Lawrence Tierney: another comeback.

Abduction, the "Patty Hearst movie," arrived in theaters on October 24, 1975. The picture opened with a disclaimer making clear it was not based on the Patty Hearst kidnapping, even though the movie's kidnapped rich girl turned revolutionary, played by Judith-Marie Bergan, was named Patricia. The explicit sex scenes were trimmed enough that the film carried an R rating, but Joseph Zito's directorial debut did not win accolades. A reviewer for UPI wrote off the film as a "numbing bore"; the cast dismissed as "unprofessional"—with the exceptions of Dorothy Malone (brother Scott Brady's lost love) and Leif Erikson as Patricia's parents, and Lawrence Tierney, who ended up playing an FBI agent.

"Whatever prompted them to participate in this nasty, ill-intentioned little movie?" the reviewer asked of the named actors. In Tierney's case, the answer would be the paycheck. It was a fortuitous choice. Director Zito would cast Tierney twice more. The role also got him a mention in Earl Wilson's column: "Lawrence Tierney, whose big role was Dillinger, plays an FBI man in 'Abduction.'"

Eighteen weeks after the tragedy, it was as if Bonnie Jones never happened. Just like old times, Lawrence Tierney was back, in boldface.

Tierney's comeback was gradual, in small roles that would lead to attention because of each film's "coolness" quotient, cult status, quality, success, or historical significance.

In June 1976, few people were "cooler" or more significant than the most celebrated pop artist of the century. Tierney was cast in *Andy Warhol's Bad*, the latest offering from the Warhol Factory in Union Square. The film was a "bad taste" shock comedy starring Carroll Baker as a housewife who runs an electrolysis hair removal parlor in her home, while making extra money dispatching women to do "hit jobs." The role had been offered to, among others, Shelley Winters, who turned it down. Following the relative success of *Andy Warhol's Frankenstein* and *Andy Warhol's Dracula*, *Bad* was being sold as Warhol's move to mainstream cinema, and with a budget that topped $1.3 million, 35 millimeter cameras, an eight-week shooting schedule on location in Queens, and an actual script, the picture was as close to conventional as the Warhol group had yet ventured. Jed Johnson, Warhol's twenty-seven-year-old boyfriend, was directing—for the first time.

Tierney played an ex-cop named O'Reilly, a role that could have been tailor-made: an old man who gets drunk in a bar every night, is beaten up by two of the hitwomen while his dog is stabbed (but survives), and gets into a trashcan-hurling street brawl with Warhol "superstar" Brigid Berlin. According to many involved in the production, director Johnson was among the most incompetent. Tierney found the entire experience to be "terrible" and the production "unprofessional."

"Oh, don't mention it," he said when the Murphys brought it up. "That was a terrible film, a terrible film."

It must have been an interesting summer for Tierney. In June, he also worked with a group of NYU Film School graduates, pornography veterans (who knew how to work with small budgets), and *Abduction* cinematographer João Fernandes on *The Kirlian Witness*. Written and directed by Jonathan Sarno and set in Soho in lower Manhattan, *Kirlian* was described by Vincent Canby in the *New York Times* as "a film that sort of dabbles in parapsychology, being about a plant that fingers (leafs?) a murder suspect." Steve Johnson, founder of the zine and film journal *Delirious*, appreciated the movie as "a Brian DePalma film without De Palma." The production could only afford Tierney's services for a single day, so his role as a police detective was little more than a cameo that added a "name" to the cast. *The Kirlian Witness* would not be released for several years, but would develop a cult following.

Most all of Tierney's film work in 1976 was under the radar. He made the news twice that year, but not for his acting. In January, Earl Wilson resurrected him for a "Show Biz Quiz": "Who are the actor-brothers of actors Lawrence Tierney, Peter Graves and Steve Forrest?" Ten months later, he was a question in Marilyn and Hy Gardner's gossip column, Glad You Asked That. "Q: Where can actor Lawrence ('Dillinger') Tierney be found these days?—Mrs. J. Curry, Indianapolis. A: Between infrequent bit parts in television, he can be found standing with his horse and hansom in front of New York's Plaza Hotel, waiting to be hailed for a romantic lark around Central Park."

Tierney had one of his—and cinema's—most unusual acting assignments around the end of 1978: a repair job to help sell an old horror flick to television.

Naked Evil was a 1966 British film about street gangs, a hostel full of Black Jamaican students, and a caretaker who unleashes voodoo terror in an English town (despite the title, without nudity). After *Naked Evil*'s release in the UK, its producers couldn't find distribution in the United States because it was filmed in black and white. Their solution was to tint various scenes in red, green, blue, and amber, and claim the process was a gimmick called "Evil Color."

In the mid-1970s, exploitation and B-movie producer Sam Sherman and his Independent-International Pictures Corporation picked up the film for US release in triple bills at drive-ins. A few years later, Sherman licensed *Naked Evil* for a package of horror films to sell to television. He tackled the Evil Color issue by coming up with a framing device. He wrote a script in an evening and gave his assistant Steve Jacobson $5,000 to shoot the scenes in one day. He hired two movie veterans, Tierney and B-movie cowboy star Robert Allen, and young actors Catharine Burgess and Addison Greene. The shoot took place at a hospital on Roosevelt Island.

Tierney portrayed a psychiatrist, interviewing a man who supposedly witnessed the events in *Naked Evil* (though he was not in the original picture). The events of the movie were edited to appear as flashbacks. Tierney's Dr. Fuller had a "special laser device" that gave colors to certain memories. That would explain the weird tinting.

"I hypnotize him and I tell him whenever there's blue tint, he's gonna remember certain things and red tint, he's gonna remember scenes of violence," Tierney said in 1990.

Tierney remembered "good old Sam Sherman" as "a nice guy, a very clever guy." Sherman remembered Tierney as "miscast." He told horror movie expert Bryan Senn, "He always acts like he's John Dillinger and *we* make him a doctor!"

With fifteen minutes of new color footage, Sherman changed the movie's title from *Naked Evil* to *Exorcism at Midnight*. When *Exorcism at Midnight* made it to American television, Tierney was listed as the star.

In 1979, *Abduction* director Joseph Zito hired Tierney for *Bloodrage,* a film about a young man who accidentally kills a prostitute in his small town, then flees to New York City, where he kills more. Zito directed under the name "Joseph Bigwood." Tierney played a detective named Malone. He was noticeably heavier, his hair silver and a bit too long.

Bloodrage, also known as *Never Pick Up a Stranger,* screened for distributors at Cannes on May 20, 1980, and had a limited release in Europe. In June, syndicated gossip Liz Smith (former ghostwriter for the Cholly Knickbocker column) had news that "Lawrence Tierney, Hollywood's bad boy of the '50s, will be making a movie comeback in a new shocker, 'Never Pick Up a Stranger.' . . . It's Tierney's first film in years." *Bloodrage* didn't arrive in the United States until 1983, on home video.

A reunion with another director that summer proved to be more of a boost for Tierney's rekindled career. John Cassavetes, who'd directed Tierney in *A Child Is Waiting* in 1962, had in the ensuing years become an Academy Award–nominated actor, and as a director, a revered pioneer in independent filmmaking. In June 1979, he was directing a studio picture for Columbia with the working title *One Summer Night*. Cassavetes's wife, Gena Rowlands, played a tough woman protecting a six-year-old boy from Mob hitmen. Tierney was cast as a bartender, another role he'd played in real life in recent years.

For Tierney, the small part in a Cassavetes studio production was a personal triumph. For a few weeks at least, it was just like old times. He was even becoming something of a regular in the gossip columns again. In late November, Liz Smith gave big space to a supposed Tierney autobiography. "The actor who proceeded to brawl his way through the front pages of the '50s after he won fame playing Dillinger," she wrote, "will punch out his life story in all its black-and-blue detail. And he says he'll do it by himself." And "on an electric typewriter," Jack O'Brian later added in his column, "certainly correct for his planned shocking memoirs."

Four days before Christmas, *Daily News* columnist Pat O'Haire reported a Tierney sighting at a restaurant on West Fifty-Second Street. She reminded readers that Tierney was the actor who "achieved a certain fame some years back as Dillinger, then took a beating because of his drinking." Dining at Joe's Pier 52, Tierney "didn't have any alcohol at all" and, as in the old days, insisted "he's been off the sauce for a few years." O'Haire not only got the scoop that Tierney wrapped a role in the Cassavetes film, but got an ironic quote to go along with it: "And I play a bartender!"

Pat O'Haire added the button: "Times have changed, haven't they?"

In 1980, still getting by in New York City, Tierney was again cast in two films on opposite ends of the Hollywood spectrum.

In March, he was in Pittsburgh to not only act but to star—yes *star*—in *John Russo's Midnight.* Russo had status in the horror community as cowriter of George Romero's *Night of the Living Dead.* His low-budget exploitation film distributed by Sam Sherman's Independent-International was truly a comeback role for Tierney, and the first solid introduction of his second incarnation, the one described by author Barry Gifford: "in his sixties now, fat, and completely bald. His gigantic, gleaming skull is absolutely square."

Tierney had top billing over a cast of unknowns as Bert Johnson, a cop who makes his entrance staggering drunk, and then proceeds to maul, molest, and attempt to rape his teenage stepdaughter. She escapes, destination California, but winds up in the backwoods with a family of Satanists who keep their dead mother in a bedroom and are intent on using the girl as a human sacrifice. It was a meaty role for the beefy actor, and in the end, Tierney's character even finds redemption by rescuing his stepdaughter and dying heroically.

Then there was *Arthur.* Cameras rolled in New York City on June 2 for the romantic comedy starring Dudley Moore as a happily drunk billionaire who falls for Linda, a working-class girl from Queens played by Liza Minnelli. Tierney was not a drunk in this film, but Man in Coffee Shop. Dudley Moore's Arthur was the drunk at the coffee shop counter, attempting to propose to Minnelli's waitress. Tierney, seated next to Moore, interrupted with requests for the roll he'd ordered. It was one scene, but memorable—and got laughs. Sharing the screen with the two stars, not to mention his participation among this A-list cast, only added to his renewed appeal.

The Cassavetes film, renamed *Gloria* after Rowlands's character, premiered at the Venice Film Festival on September 5, 1980, where it shared the highest prize, the *Leone d'Oro,* with Louis Malle's *Atlantic City* (which starred Burt

Lancaster, the lead in *A Child Is Waiting*). *Gloria* opened in theaters in October and led to Oscar and Golden Globe nominations for Gena Rowlands.

That same month, Tierney was in Cape May, the seaside town in southern New Jersey, for another Joseph Zito picture. *The Prowler* was a slasher film in which a killer in World War II army fatigues stalks and targets a group of college kids. Farley Granger, perhaps best known as Robert Walker's costar in Alfred Hitchcock's *Strangers on a Train,* was the other Hollywood legend among a cast of young unknowns.

The Prowler turned out to be another feather in Tierney's cap. After its release on June 26, 1981, the movie was hailed as one of the best of the "slasher" genre, and while its focus was on the young, often-topless victims, Tierney and Granger were the selling points in the newspaper ads.

Arthur opened wide on July 17, 1981. It was a critical and financial success, the fourth-highest grossing film of the year. At the Fifty-Fourth Academy Awards ceremony at the Dorothy Chandler Pavilion in Los Angeles on March 29, 1982, *Arthur* was nominated in four categories, and took home Oscars for Original Song ("Arthur's Theme") and Supporting Actor (John Gielgud). The fact that Tierney was part of this cast only moved him closer to Hollywood. (Not so lucky was director and screenwriter Steve Gordon, who was nominated for Best Original Screenplay but lost out to *Chariots of Fire* and, eight months later, suffered a fatal heart attack at forty-four. *Arthur* was the first and only film he directed.)

Hard-living, hell-raising former *Saturday Night Live* star John Belushi had died of a drug overdose at the Chateau Marmont on March 5, 1982, two weeks before the Oscars. Belushi's untimely demise crossed him off the call sheet for *Nothing Lasts Forever,* a science fiction comedy directed by Tom Schiller, an original *SNL* writer known for the short films he directed for the program. The six-week shoot in New York City began on April 21. Zach Galligan and Lauren Tom starred. Featured actors included Sam Jaffe, Mort Sahl, Imogene Coca, Eddie Fisher, and former *SNL* stars Bill Murray and Dan Aykroyd.

Lawrence Tierney was cast in a role that paid him tribute and was close to his heart. He's the driver of a horse-drawn carriage, seen pulling up in front of Carnegie Hall (site of his 1957 road rage arrest, and where he was "caught kissing" in 1974).

Nothing Lasts Forever is another of Tierney's late films that went on to gain cultural prominence. The first movie produced by *SNL* creator Lorne Michaels may be the ultimate cult film. Before its scheduled opening in 1984, it was shelved by MGM/UA, and as of 2022, has never had an official theatrical, home video, or streaming release.

Tierney laid low for much of 1982. He would reveal in 1987 that he'd experienced a minor stroke that year. The medical emergency did not seem to cause permanent damage, but was serious enough to accomplish what Alcoholics Anonymous could not: convince him to cut down on his drinking for the next few years.

The stroke would lend empathy to his next performance.

Liz Smith reported the surprising news in September 1983: James Cagney was signed to star in his first television movie. Cagney was the original movie gangster, whose performance in *The Public Enemy* in 1931 made him one of the biggest stars in Hollywood. Unlike Lawrence Tierney, he fought against typecasting after playing Public Enemy No. 1, and moved on to a long, varied career. Cagney retired from acting in 1961, but returned to the screen twenty years later, after suffering a stroke. He said he took the cameo role in *Ragtime,* directed by Milos Forman, for the sake of his health. "The doctor said, 'Keep the man busy.'"

Now, at eighty-four, Cagney was starring in *Terrible Joe Moran* as a wealthy, old ex-boxer, confined to a wheelchair and showing the effects of too many punches. The two-hour CBS movie interspersed fight scenes from his 1932 boxing picture, *Winner Take All,* and boasted a heavyweight cast of supporting players, including Art Carney, Ellen Barkin, Peter Gallagher—and Lawrence Tierney.

"I played an old prizefighter, an Italian, Pico Marendello," Tierney told the Murphys. "There was a scene in this big mansion house that he had. He was in a wheelchair. Cagney . . . was having strokes at the time and they had these different characters come out. It was like a testimonial to him. . . . I come out and they started asking me questions. 'Yeah, I fought him twice. Both times he knocked me out. He was a good guy. One time he hit me in the chin and I lost my mouthpiece. You know, he stepped back. He even helped me pick it up, put it back in. What a good guy. And then later on he set me up good, when I had to retire. I get into too many fights. He bought me a fruit stand. I'm doing pretty good. Joe Moran was a good guy.' I played him like a tough old guy."

The shoot was not without complications. Cagney was perhaps *too* well-suited for the role. After another stroke and other medical setbacks, he required a wheelchair in real life, and his speech was seriously impaired.

Director Joseph Sargent worked around the obstacles, seldom shooting Cagney in close-up, and showing other characters listening when he spoke. Most, if not all, of his dialogue was dubbed by impressionist Frank Gorshin.

The high-profile television event, which would be Cagney's last movie, was filmed in New York City. Although it kept Tierney in view of casting agents and producers, the movie did not lead him back to Hollywood. Something else would lead to his return to the West Coast at the end of 1983: a death in the family.

39

All in the Family

After filming his guest roles on the *Combat!* television series in 1965, Edward Tierney put acting behind him and dedicated himself to his construction business. Among the houses he'd built in Laurel Canyon, within walking distance of Scott Brady's bachelor pad on Hollywood Hills Road, was a two-bedroom townhouse at 8763 Wonderland Avenue, which in 1981 would be the scene of the "Wonderland Murders," one of the bloodiest and most gruesome crimes in Los Angeles history, and an inspiration for Paul Thomas Anderson's 1997 film, *Boogie Nights.* Other B and T dwellings and apartment buildings were less notorious, but also stood the test of time.

Ed and Anne Winterburn raised three children, Elizabeth (Anne's daughter with Lawrence Tierney), Michael, and Stephen, who was born on July 9, 1966. The marriage was not a happy one. California state records show the couple divorced in July 1967, and again in May 1969. By the end of the decade, the family had moved from Los Angeles to Orange County, where Ed would become interested in, and then obsessed with, the game of chess.

By that point, many things had gone wrong in Ed Tierney's life. Along with two failed marriages (he would remarry Anne in 1978, but the couple would split again), his plans to become a great writer and respected actor never came to be, and his construction business was tied up in lawsuits with another business partner.

Chess was different. With chess, he would become an unqualified success, highly ranked by the US Chess Federation, and highly regarded and well-liked within the chess community.

Ed Tierney's passion was kindled around the time that "chess fever" spread across America. In July 1972, Chicago-born Bobby Fischer faced world champion Boris Spassky of the USSR in the World Chess Championships in the Laugardalshöll sporting arena in Reykjavík, Iceland. The "Match of the Century" was hyped as a Cold War battle between the United States and the Soviet

Union, and when Fischer took the title from Spassky in August after twenty-one games, he was hailed as an American hero. The enthusiasm inspired many Americans to take up the game. Edward Tierney was inspired to teach chess to his sons, seven-year-old Michael and Stephen, six. He became active in the San Clemente Chess Club, participated in tournaments in Orange County, and was mentioned often in the *Los Angeles Times* chess column as a competitor and organizer. The *Times* noted in 1978 that Ed Tierney was a prime mover in building a chess team at Marco Foster Junior High School in San Juan Capistrano. The student team was soon competing for national titles, and the players were treated like star athletes. According to the *Times,* chess became "the hottest thing on campus."

"Ed organized dozens of tournaments, scholastic and adult, and ran them with a warm, caring touch," his friend Kevin Burnett wrote in *Rank & File,* a Southern California chess magazine. "The tables groaned with trophies and medals on display all during the tournament to inspire the kids. Ed didn't just hand out the hardware; he presented it, with ruffles and flourishes, and a personal introduction for each winner."

Taught and coached by their father, Michael and Stephen Tierney became chess champions. In May 1979, when their Capistrano Valley High School team competed in the national championships in Philadelphia, chess led to their first meeting with their Uncle Larry.

"I knew about him from a young age. . . . Larry was the one that used to be an actor who played Dillinger way back when," Michael told Gary Sweeney. "But I never had a chance to meet him. Larry did once in a while call and send us letters . . . and he was on this tennis kick and he thought tennis was a great sport for young adults or teenagers, so he would send us money for tennis rackets, and we started taking tennis lessons in our early teens. And I still hadn't met him.

"Finally, I was in Philadelphia, and Larry came into Philadelphia. My dad arranged it and I got to meet him for the first time. It was pretty funny and pretty awesome. He was a really funny guy. There was definitely some drama between him and my father because they had a lot of bad blood going from way back, but my dad made an attempt to get along with him and introduce him to his boys.

"The funny thing is, Larry showed up to the hotel room. . . . He walks in and greets me and my brother kind of solemnly. And he has this big old suitcase filled with the most outrageous ties I've ever seen, like clown-looking ties. And he really thought these were ties that we would wear. And we just kind of held our breath and tried not to laugh, but it was very comical. We ended up giving these ties as gag gifts for years."

The meeting with their Uncle Larry would quickly lead to chaos and, back in California, a major revelation for their ten-year-old cousin Timmy.

"I remember my dad on the phone getting very upset, and slamming the phone down, and saying to my mom, 'I told him not to do it, and now look what's going on! This is terrible!'" Timothy Tierney recalls. "I remember saying, 'What happened, Dad? What happened?' And he said, 'Your Uncle Larry, he's kidnapped your cousins, Mike and Steve! Ed's really upset. I told him not to do it, and look what happened!'

"And my first words were, 'My *who*? My Uncle *Who*? You have another brother?' And he said, in the most offhanded way, 'Yes. But don't worry about it. He's never coming here. You will never meet him.' Like, '*I'm keeping the monster away from you.*'

"I was just shocked that there was this other guy I'd never heard about, who was apparently so terrible that he had to be kept away from the home forever. And that when my Uncle Ed ignored my dad's advice, he's suffering the consequences. Now, as it turns out, his kids weren't really kidnapped. Larry brought the kids back at the end of the day. He had taken them sightseeing. It was kind of a miscommunication, though Uncle Larry was awfully cavalier with someone else's kids."

In the decade following the interview in which he referred to himself as "an ex-star," Scott Brady kept his distance from the Hollywood social scene but remained available for television and movie work.

"He was at that point what I would call a journeyman actor," son Timothy says. "People knew by his reputation and his many credits that he could do a good job at certain kinds of roles. And he treated it entirely as, 'This is the job that I get up and go to, and I come home at the end of the day to go back to being a regular guy.' He could have been an accountant for all we knew, except for the fact that he didn't go to work regularly like an accountant might."

Brady was sought for a wide variety of roles as he settled into his fifties. He booked many one-off parts in network television series, including *Banacek, Gunsmoke, Get Christy Love!, Hawaii Five-O, Laverne & Shirley, Baretta, The Rockford Files, Supertrain, Taxi, Charlie's Angels, Cagney & Lacey, Simon & Simon,* and *Welcome Back, Kotter.* He was a semi-regular on the NBC series *Police Story,* and in 1976, long after he turned down the lead in the pilot that led to Norman Lear's groundbreaking CBS sitcom, *All in the Family,* won a recurring role in season seven as Archie Bunker's pal, Joe Foley. Be it a comedy, Western, or police drama, whether as cop, coach, or cowboy, he could be counted on to walk in, walk on, and get the job done.

Scott Brady hit two late-career film peaks in his final decade. In 1978, he worked alongside Jack Lemmon, Jane Fonda, and Michael Douglas in *The China Syndrome,* James Bridges's thriller about a safety cover-up and near disaster at a nuclear plant. Five years later, he had a showy role as the semi-corrupt Sheriff Frank, who's done in by mischievous little monsters in the horror comedy *Gremlins.* By then, Brady had begun to struggle, healthwise. A smoker since his days in the navy, he'd been stricken with emphysema. After he collapsed at the Northridge Public Library in 1981, he was diagnosed with pulmonary fibrosis, a disease that causes the lungs to become scarred and hardened, making it progressively harder to breathe. Though he often relied on an oxygen tank, Brady carried on working like the old school pro he was. *Gremlins* director Joe Dante recalled shooting a scene on the Warner Brothers lot in Burbank, when Brady collapsed while ascending a flight of stairs. The crew feared he'd suffered a heart attack.

He'd simply run out of breath.

By the early 1980s, Ed Tierney had added much weight to his six-foot, two-inch frame and developed diabetes and other ailments. He had some difficulties getting around, but his condition didn't slow down his work on behalf of Orange County chess enthusiasts. His most noteworthy success was helping launch a West Coast version of the US Amateur Chess Team and managing to bring the national high school championship games to the West Coast for the first time. The historic event took place at Buena Park High School from December 27 to 29, 1983. Ed Tierney did not attend. The previous week, on December 18, he had died of diabetic shock. He was fifty-five.

An unexpected mourner at the services for Edward Tierney was his eldest brother. Lawrence Tierney showed up at Scott Brady's home in Northridge the evening before the funeral. It was the brothers' first meeting since they fought it out in the street after the death of their mother. "My mom said, 'Your father and Larry have a lot of issues from their past, and they haven't seen each other in all these years,'" Timothy Tierney recalls. "'But your father has made the decision to tell Larry that everything that's happened is all under the bridge, and I forgive you for everything.'"

Lawrence Tierney arrived with Ed Tierney's sons. It was the first time cousin Tim laid eyes on his Uncle Larry. "It could have been a scene from a Larry Tierney movie," he remembers. "He comes into the house, and he's this big, big guy. He moved slowly, he spoke slowly, and he just radiated hostility, anger, menace. He was like a very tightly coiled spring. He looked like he was gonna start breaking things."

In fact, Tierney did break things, snatching a paper toy from the hands of another guest who was trying to make conversation. "My dad's friend, a set artist who we called 'Eddie the Artist,' who was childlike in many ways, had this shiny origami fidget toy, and he's talking to Larry, but because we're all very nervous, he was doing a lot of fidgeting on that thing, probably not even realizing it. Larry took notice and said, 'Gimme that!' And he grabbed it out of Eddie's hands, ripped it into several pieces, and threw it down on the carpet of our living room. So within minutes of coming into the house, Larry is already intimidating people and destroying things.

"My dad was well into his pulmonary fibrosis at this point, and he was on an oxygen tank, and could only move around with a cane or a wheelchair and spent most of his time on the couch. He was not very ambulatory, frankly. But Larry was still in his house, and he was going to not be anything less than the man of the house. I remember watching from a safe distance, Larry coming up to my dad, who was on the couch. It was very tense. I remember them talking, in quiet words that I couldn't hear. But my mom could hear, and Mom was like a tigress. When she got mad, she could really blow the roof off the house. And all of a sudden, my mom is screaming at Larry, saying, 'You're the same son of a bitch you were twenty-five years ago! *You get the fuck out of this house, right now!*'

"Larry wasn't in our home for even twenty minutes before he got kicked out."

"I remember my dad being very angry at Ed's funeral," says Timothy Tierney. "And on the drive out to the gravesite, everybody's in cars, but Larry happened to be in a pickup truck. Larry was standing in the back of the open pickup truck, facing forward, with his hands over the cab of the vehicle, hanging on to the top of the cab for support. And I remember my dad swearing, saying, 'Goddamn it! Look at him, being such a fucking asshole! He's probably drunk, and he's making an ass of himself at Ed's funeral!' He was expressing what I think was clearly a frustration he'd expressed a thousand times before. 'Here's Larry, doing it again.'"

Edward Michael Tierney was buried among other veterans in the Riverside National Cemetery, as "PVT U. S. ARMY, WORLD WAR II." Hollywood and the mainstream news media did not take notice of his passing, but Ed Tierney's community did. "Ed Tierney was a bear of a man," his friend, chess pro Jerry Hanken, eulogized in *Rank & File,* "a big friendly lovable Irishman who could charm the dew off the Blarney Stone. Ed could tell you that you were full of it in such a nice way that you didn't realize what he had said until the next day. And even then you couldn't get mad at him. Lord knows I tried to get mad at him enough times, but when I would see him, all that anger would be washed over by the warmth of his essentially loving nature. And it was loving. Ed loved people, he loved his kids, and he loved chess."

"I know [Scott Brady] thought his brother was crazy and that he couldn't deal with him, and so he'd rather just not think about him. That's probably why he never mentioned him to his son," Michael Tierney told Gary Sweeney. "But when they did meet up again, right after my father died, they tried to talk to each other a few times. But they'd just get real emotional. Scott was having health problems . . . so he had to get Larry away from him because it was just too upsetting."

The two surviving brothers went their separate ways after Edward's funeral. Scott Brady, with his oxygen canister, headed home to Northridge and his crossword puzzles and televised football games. His lung ailment had made it increasingly difficult for him to work. Perhaps coincidentally—Scott Brady might say "ironically"—after Edward was put in the ground at the National Cemetery, Lawrence Tierney began to spend more time in Hollywood.

Despite his behavior, he was welcome in the Brady house. "Which is surprising, but that's how they handled it," Timothy Tierney says. "It was okay for Larry to come by from time to time.

"I remember his return to Hollywood was a role in this commercial series for Anacin headache pills. He came over and he said, 'I'm breaking back into Hollywood.' We were all happy for him, and my dad, too. It was like a victory for the family. That's the kind of compartmentalization that people can do. This guy is a maniac, and we don't want him around, but still, he's one of us, and having success, and we're happy for him."

In his new guise—craggy, bald, with a voice that was a cigarettes-and-alcohol growl—Tierney had already worked with Cagney and Cassavetes, in Oscar-winning films and hip cult movies. Now he began to land some of the roles that might have gone to the dependable Scott Brady when he could walk unaided.

He began to pick up acting work on the West Coast in 1984, with an episode of *Fame*, set in New York City but filmed on the MGM lot in Culver City. He returned to New York later that year to film another prestige role, as a police lieutenant in John Huston's black comedy crime film, *Prizzi's Honor*. "It was a pleasure. I wanted to work with him for a long time," Tierney told Skip E. Lowe shortly after filming. "I'd always admired him. I think he's one of our best American directors—in fact, best directors in the world." The star of the film was Jack Nicholson. "I knew him when he had nuthin'," Tierney said. "Now he knows me when I got nuthin'!"

While shooting *Prizzi's Honor* in Brooklyn, Tierney lived with a girlfriend on Hicks Street, and connected for the first time with relatives Danny and Eddie Leahy, who were living in Flatbush. ("My grandmother and his mother were cousins," Eddie explains.) At sixty-five, Tierney had more than thirty years on the Leahy brothers, but fit right in with them and their friends, regaling the gang with stories of old Hollywood as only he could tell them.

"He said after he did *Dillinger,* he was in a club and Huntz Hall from the Bowery Boys was there," Danny remembers. "He says to me Huntz Hall smacked him in the face! He goes, 'Danny I grabbed him, I cocked my hand, I was gonna punch him right in the fuckin' face—and I held back.' And I'm saying to myself, that ain't Lawrence Tierney! He goes, 'Danny, I felt sorry for the guy. He was drunk and he wanted to fight me. And then I walk outside the club, he's sittin' on the curb. I called him a cab. A couple of months later, I'm in a place and they introduce me to this woman. I take her home and I'm bangin' the shit out of her—it was Huntz Hall's wife!" Danny is laughing. "I'm goin' by what he told me. I don't know if it's true. But it made me laugh!"

(David Del Valle heard many similar stories from Tierney. "I think he equated his sexual prowess with drunken behavior," he says. "'Yeah, I went out with this broad and we had some drinks, and I fucked the shit out of her' ... 'That Huntz Hall, I got back at that Huntz Hall. I went over and fucked his wife!' The macho thing was wrapped up in it.")

"We all got a kick out of him. He was a great storyteller," recalls the Leahys' cousin Donald McManamon. "One night it was him and I in Buckley's, an Irish bar-restaurant on Nostrand Avenue. We were having a few beers at the bar. He might have been drinking Scotch and beer. After that, I get in the car, and Larry's sitting in the front. I'm at the red light on the corner of Nostrand Avenue and there was a police car right next to us. Larry rolls down his window and he waves to get the cops' attention. There were two cops in the car. The driver rolls down his window and Larry goes, 'Hey, just wanna let you know, you got a flat in the back there!' And they're like, 'Oh! Whoa! Thanks a lot, sir, thank you!' So now the light turns green. 'Larry,' I said, 'he had a flat in the back?' He goes, 'Nah! *F those coppers!*' And he let out a big laugh! And now I'm looking in the rearview mirror, and I'm, 'Oh, shit.' And I can see the cop that was the driver looking at his rear tire, then looking up at my car as I'm driving away—looking back at the tire, looking up at my car, like 'What the hell's goin' on? Why would that guy say that?' Larry said, 'F those coppers!' He called them 'coppers!' I'll never forget! I haven't heard that term for a cop since the movies!"

Eddie Leahy drove "cousin Larry" to the *Prizzi's Honor* filming location on Union Street. Months later, when things went sour with his galpal, Tierney moved in with Danny. "He was no problem. He was good," Danny Leahy recalls, and mentions that Tierney also got along with their father, Daniel J. Leahy, a decorated New York City police officer. "Larry always said he hated cops, but he was nice to my father. And my father got a kick out of him."

Tierney left Brooklyn for North Carolina late in the year for a more substantial and darkly comedic movie role in *Silver Bullet*. Stephen King wrote the screenplay, based on his novella about a werewolf terrorizing a small town. Tierney was Owen Knopfler, a tough bartender who wields a baseball bat with "The Peace Maker" carved on the barrel. He may have been familiar with that type of barkeep's equalizer, keeping one within reach when he worked behind bars, or on the receiving end when he caused trouble on the customer side.

Scott Brady was able to complete one final television role after his work in *Gremlins. Whiz Kids* was a CBS sci-fi adventure series about a group of high school computer experts who were also amateur detectives. In the episode that aired on April 24, 1984, Brady portrayed a developer with plans to bulldoze a park to build a munitions factory. He played the part in a wheelchair, with a nasal cannula leading to an oxygen tank. The television audience might perceive a clever take on the villainous Mr. Potter from *It's a Wonderful Life*. In reality, Brady's pulmonary fibrosis was progressing. By the time *Gremlins* opened in June 1984, his condition had worsened. Brady was admitted to the acute care hospital in the Motion Picture and Television Country House retirement community on Mulholland Drive in Woodland Hills. He died there, of respiratory failure, on April 16, 1985. He was sixty years old.

Scott Brady's death did not go unnoticed. The passing of the "ex-star" made headlines worldwide. Brady was eulogized as a "handsomely rugged . . .

menacingly attractive . . . tough-looking . . . leading man in the 1950s whose career spanned Broadway, movies, and television." His recent appearances in *Gremlins* and *The China Syndrome* were cited, as was the cream of his many movie roles, including *Johnny Guitar, Gentlemen Marry Brunettes, Operation Bikini, Battle Flame, Red Tomahawk, Kansas Raiders, Canon City, He Walked by Night, In This Corner, Yankee Buccaneer, Bronco Buster, Montana Belle, Untamed Frontier, Vanishing American, Mohawk,* and *The Loners.*

The United Press International obituary mentioned his television series *Shotgun Slade,* "where he portrayed an odd mixture of a swinging private eye and Western hero working on horseback for banks, insurance companies and saloon owners," and his support of Notre Dame football.

Many stories also focused on Brady's reputation, before his marriage, as "Hollywood's No. 1 bachelor," reported to give advice like, "The first thing to remember is never date the same girl twice" and "When a dame mentions marriage, turn on the Jack Paar show and cry along with him." Stories that mentioned his 1957 marijuana bust added that he'd claimed a frame-up, and that the charges were dropped for insufficient evidence.

Scott Brady's wake took place on the evening of Friday, April 19, at Pierce Brothers Cunningham and O'Connor Mortuary in Hollywood. The vigil was followed by a funeral mass Saturday morning at St. John Baptist de la Salle Church in Granada Hills, not far from his home in Northridge. As were his parents, he was entombed in the mausoleum in Holy Cross Cemetery in Culver City. The name engraved in gold on the front plaque of his crypt—GERARD K. TIERNEY, AKA 'SCOTT BRADY'—showed that he was, and remained, a Tierney. The quote that followed—"SURE AND YOU CAN HEAR THE ANGELS SING"— was a line from "When Irish Eyes Are Smiling," a nod to his heritage and eternal love of Notre Dame's Fighting Irish football team.

Lawrence Tierney was bunking at Danny Leahy's place when he learned of his brother's death.

"He got the call at my apartment," Danny says. "He said, 'Danny, Scott died.' Larry didn't show emotion. He just said to me, 'I got a call from this guy in Hollywood' and 'I got a call from Jack Nicholson to say, I'm sorry.' He left the next day."

Eddie Leahy, at thirty-one a year younger than his brother, accompanied cousin Larry to the funeral in California. "They said, 'Mind him, make sure he's good,'" he remembers. "I was like six foot three, 230 pounds, I'd played semi-pro football and was a longshoreman."

The pair arrived at the wake, accompanied by Royal Dano. The rangy character actor who gave voice to Disneyland's animatronic Abraham Lincoln had worked with Scott Brady in the 1954 film *Johnny Guitar*—and with Tierney on *The Lloyd Bridges Show*, in the episode directed by John Cassavetes.

Tierney stepped up to the open casket and looked down at his brother, laid out in his best blue suit. Lisa Tierney, Scott's widow, walked over and stood beside him.

"They did a good job," she said with a slight smile. "Doesn't Scott look good?"

Tierney grunted. "He looks like shit," he growled. Then he walked away.

Eddie Leahy was dumbfounded. "I looked at Larry. 'Why did you say that?' He looked at me—and then all of a sudden he got a tap on his shoulder and he turned around and Royal Dano flashed a fucking pint of whisky! I was like, 'Larry, no, no!' He goes, 'I'll be right back, kid,' and they went to the parking lot. I came out five minutes later, and the whisky was gone. I'm like, 'What are you doing? You're supposed to be good!' 'Hey, kid, mind your own business.' He was like the fuckin' Dead End Kid."

As another mourner left the funeral home on Santa Monica Boulevard, he witnessed the sixty-six-year-old Dead End Kid walk to the curb, unzip his fly, and urinate into the street.

"After all that happened, we went to a bar," Eddie Leahy says. "I think we were staying at a hotel on Sunset Boulevard. Tom Waits was at the poolside, playing his guitar and singing. Me and Larry had one room there, and Larry's nephew Michael was there with his guitar, and he started playing the guitar and Larry was pissed. He was like, 'Why you playin' the goddamn guitar for?' And Larry grabbed the guitar from his fuckin' hands and he smashed it against the wall into smithereens!

"I'm looking at the kid, the kid's got tears in his eyes. I said, 'Larry, why the hell did you do that?' 'I didn't wanna hear this shit!' I said, 'Hey listen, if you don't punch me, I won't punch you, because I've taken enough punches from my brother in Brooklyn, and you're a tough guy and all that stuff, but you either fuckin' get the fuck outta here, or I'm gonna fuckin' hit you.'

"And he turned around and he grabbed his suitcase and he left. The next morning, we're going to the funeral, he was sitting at the bus stop with the suitcase in his hand." Eddie laughs at the memory. "I pulled over and we got him in the car, went to the cemetery. I asked him, 'Why did you break your nephew's guitar?' 'I didn't wanna hear that shit.' He was a moody guy. He was a good guy, he was a crude guy, he was a wild guy, but I tell ya, I loved him."

40

Renaissance Man

I play what they cast me in.

LAWRENCE TIERNEY, 1985

After Lawrence Tierney zipped up and made his way home from his brother's funeral, he walked into a refreshed career. At sixty-six, his presence in a film or television episode added a dimension of menace, authority, sly humor—or a mixture of the three. Audiences might not place the face, but producers and writers knew his unique place in Hollywood history and often hired him because of it. Thanks to a video rental market that had expanded greatly in the past half decade, Tierney was also appreciated by a new generation of cinephiles educated on VHS tapes of vintage films they could study, over and over again. One of the most intense "students," a twenty-two-year-old movie obsessive, was hired in 1985 as a clerk at the Video Archives store in Manhattan Beach, California. Quentin Tarantino would spend the next five years there, watching movies, taking notes, and writing scripts.

Tierney was no longer considered a frightening, incorrigible menace to Hollywood society, but an entertaining if unpredictable relic of a more genuine age. He settled into a small apartment in Hollywood and began befriending many movie fans much younger than himself. It was a natural connection. While many of his contemporaries had died or long been domesticated, he continued to frequent the Hollywood dive bars and taverns that were now patronized by young people as well as old drunks.

It was this group of relative youngsters—filmmakers, writers, movie fans, scenesters, and others in his path—that in this late stage of Tierney's career would take the place of the gossips and newspaper columnists of old. They would chronicle and spread word of his exploits and outrages in person, in print, and years later, through social media.

"Larry knew he could get away with murder with people who respected his film career. And he did," Del Valle observes. "People that have lived rough, that literally have stripped themselves of all pretension, become very manipulative, because being on the street you get to read people instantly. You know exactly where you can go with whatever it is you're trying to do. And Larry was that. Larry got away with murder because he was a movie actor."

"He was such an outsized personality, a truly unique person, and he was the first person I met who had a connection to old Hollywood," recalls Todd Mecklem, who was in his mid-twenties when he became friends with Tierney. "And the dichotomy of this big, powerful guy with the sweetness, but then the edge—it was kind of exciting. He took a liking to me, and once he liked you, you were part of the club, you were his pal."

Joyner, the screenwriter and director, was twenty-six when he met Tierney in October 1985. "My friend [movie director] Jeff Burr and I had gone to the Chinese Theatre and seen the movie *Silver Bullet*. Larry was in it, playing a rough and tough bartender who takes on the werewolves," he says. "Later, Jeff and I were down at Boardner's [bar], which was our regular hangout, and had been one of Larry's since the forties. And in he walked! I got introduced to him. When I told him I was a big fan, Larry goes, 'What are you a fan of?' I said, 'Well, I really loved *The Ghost Ship*.' 'Okay, *Ghost Ship*, that was a good one. All right. Where you sittin'?' And the next thing you know, he was sitting with us!"

Tierney invited the young men and their friends—a group that included writers and actors Will Huston and Ron Zwang—to his apartment on North Beachwood Drive. "I had an MG Midget and he wanted a ride home," Huston says. "I said, 'Well, it's a two-seater and I already have somebody in the seat.' And he sits down on the hood of my car and says, 'Let's go.' I said, 'Get off, Larry.' 'No, I ain't getting off. Take me home.' So we drove down Hollywood Boulevard and up to Beachwood, all the way with Larry sitting on the hood of my MG Midget."

"On the way, he wanted to stop at the Mayfair market to pick up a few things," Jeff Burr recalls. "And not knowing Larry, that sounded completely innocent. It's probably two in the morning, after the bars closed, and there are very few people in the market. He just starts walking down the aisles, opening up stuff—and he would say stuff like, 'Smell this cheese, it smells like my brother's feet,' as he'd pick up pieces of bread and ham, making himself a sandwich. He ended up shoplifting a whole bunch of stuff, just stuffing it down his pants! And this was our introduction to him! It was unbelievable—and he had absolutely no guile about it."

"We ended up in his apartment, and he made us sandwiches," Joyner remembers. "And of course, the place looked like a bomb had gone off, which I found out was Larry's norm."

"Stacks and stacks of newspapers from who knows how far back," Huston says. "Looked like he'd lived there for twenty years, and he'd lived there for like three months."

"It just started from there," Joyner says, "and the old, 'Listen kid, gimme your phone number, 'cause I'm gonna be calling you.' And boy, did he ever."

Huston adds: "Like they say in *Devil Thumbs a Ride,* they gave him a ride home and changed their lives forever."

The fortuitous meeting would also lead to a major change in Tierney's life, career, and fortunes. For his young friends, though, it was a red flag. "Looking back on it now, it's not really a laughing matter, because I guarantee you he was bipolar, either non-diagnosed or self-medicated," Burr says. "I think that certainly fueled the manic ups and downs of his career and just a willful screwing up of real possibilities.

"And another thing, and he probably did it that night—he had a big thing about public urination. I mean, there's twenty empty stalls five feet away, he would choose to open a door and urinate outside or on Hollywood Boulevard. This wasn't when he was infirm. This was fifteen years earlier, when he was absolutely able to get around. It was a choice, just a blatant disregard for anything or anybody, authority-wise."

Joyner says Tierney eventually developed a cordial relationship with his daughter, Elizabeth. "Sometimes we'd be sitting in Boardner's and she'd come by. I remember when she came with a pizza and sat around with us for a night. They weren't lovey-dovey. But I never saw them in conflict."

Tierney struck up a much closer kinship with his nephew Michael. Edward Tierney's son had acting ambitions of his own, and in the years to follow would take on the role of his uncle's caretaker, aide, and de facto manager. "He came into my life at the same time that my father died," Michael told Rick McKay. "He was in the process of putting his acting career back together, and I helped him and he helped me. Our relationship sort of developed from that. In some ways, he's like a father figure to me. And in some ways I'm a mother to him!"

(Timothy Tierney didn't get so close. After his mother's death in 1993, he sought out his uncle as the last living link to his family's history. "I wanted to know what it was like, the early Hollywood days and all that," he says. "But he would just not answer a direct question. Ever. He would tell a random story about something or deflect a question and talk about something else. And so I never got anything coherent from him. I really got the impression that he was, in a sense, addled. That he just could not keep a proper chain of thought.")

Tierney had substantial roles in three series that aired during the fall 1985 television season. In NBC's romantic crime drama, *Remington Steele,* he was the father of a professional wrestler; he and Phyllis Diller played it for scares and laughs as would-be exorcists on the syndicated *Tales from the Dark Side*; and Tierney was the first person seen and heard in the premiere episode of the sixth and penultimate season of NBC's police drama, *Hill Street Blues.* The first of his seven appearances as Sergeant Jenkins, Hill Street station's night shift roll call sergeant, would pay off in the series' final episode.

Murphy's Law began filming on location around Los Angeles in November. The action-thriller starred sixty-four-year-old Charles Bronson as Jack Murphy, an LAPD detective falsely accused of murdering his ex-wife. Twenty-five years earlier, Tierney had played a bad guy in an episode of Bronson's television series, *Man with a Camera.* This time, he was a private eye. It wasn't quite a reunion. He and Bronson didn't share any scenes.

Tierney made news as a defender, if not relic, of Old Hollywood on November 14, when he spoke at an annual tribute to the actor Tyrone Power at the Hollywood Memorial Park cemetery. Twenty-seven years to the day earlier, Power had suffered a fatal heart attack in Spain while filming a dueling scene on the set of *Solomon and Sheba.* Three thousand fans had mobbed his funeral in 1958. About fifty people gathered for the tribute at Power's resting place, a white marble tomb that doubled as a bench. Tierney, one of the few present who'd actually met and known Power, threw a knuckleball into the proceedings by attacking recent biographers who'd written about the actor's alleged bisexuality. They were, Tierney growled, "despicable"—as were the writers who claimed that his hero Errol Flynn also enjoyed occasional male-on-male action.

Scott Alexander and Larry Karaszewski were recent graduates of the University of Southern California's School of Cinematic Arts when they sold their first movie script in 1986. That year, the young screenwriters spent afternoons working in Karaszewski's apartment on North Beachwood Drive. Lawrence Tierney lived a few doors down.

"He must've seen me with a script, and it was like, 'Oh, you're in the movie business? I'm in the movie business, I'm an actor,'" Karaszewski recalls. "I immediately looked him up—and looking up Larry in the days before Google was a matter of opening my *Hollywood Babylon* book. It was like every picture I could find of Larry had him with a bloody face. But he was just a big old guy who lived next door. And such an overwhelming personality. He loved the fact that we loved Hollywood."

"I was living in West L.A., so Larry K. and I were taking turns working in each other's houses," Alexander says. "On Beachwood days, Larry Tierney would see me pull up and know that we were both in there. And then treat Larry K's front door like Kramer on *Seinfeld*."

"He was the only person I've ever known that literally was like a sitcom character," says Karaszewski. "You know how they'd walk into the room and they don't have to ring the doorbell or anything?"

Says Alexander: "He would *barge* in!"

Both men remember Tierney as intelligent, well read, and very funny, but also unfiltered, without boundaries—and often frightening.

"He was so entertaining," Alexander says. "We wanted to hear him tell us stories, and he would be charming—but then he'd just turn on you on a dime. If you made a joke and he took it the wrong way, all his muscles would freeze up and he would turn and give you the death glare. And then you're like, 'Oh my God, he's gonna choke me. And kill me.'"

Karaszewski agrees. "There was always a sense of danger with Larry. We were . . . almost like—" He pauses to find the right words. "Battered wives? We were always on edge."

Alexander interrupts. "I just remembered a detail. Larry drove an old, used Volkswagen Bug. And it had a bumper sticker on it that clearly was from the previous owner with a lipstick kiss and the words 'I love your smile.' And the image of big, burly Larry squeezing himself into this fucking little car, and he's such an angry person, and it says, 'I love your smile.'"

"If we ever wrote a movie like the Coen Brothers movie with Javier Bardem as the murderer," Karaszewski adds, "we would have the mass murderer have a car with 'I love your smile' on it."

About a week after *Murphy's Law* arrived in theaters in April 1986 ("sleazy"— *New York Times*), Tierney was called to Roger Corman's studio on Main Street in Venice, California. Jeff Burr was directing *From a Whisper to a Scream*, a low-budget horror anthology starring Vincent Price, and cowritten by Tierney's new friend C. Courtney Joyner. Tierney was needed to play a prison warden witnessing an execution.

"We had wanted different people in cameos," Joyner says, "and we were talking about Forrest J. Ackerman and genre folks that we knew. And somebody fell out, and it just goes to show you, I called up Larry and he gave me the old, 'Sounds like you're in trouble, kid. I'll be right down there.'"

"Looking back on it, it was amazing," Burr says. "It was a very small part, but he couldn't have been easier. He was fine."

Tierney's next role was far more than a cameo, and would be regarded by many critics as the finest work of his second career. *Tough Guys Don't Dance* was written and directed by Norman Mailer, based on his 1984 novel. Film was not the first language for the aging macho, boozing, brawling author, and although he'd written and directed three semi-improvised 16mm "underground films" in the late 1960s, *Tough Guys* was Mailer's first mainstream picture. A mix of mystery, comedy, and film noir, it at least *looked* like a Hollywood production, and featured some serious and unintentionally comedic emoting by major mainstream talent, including Ryan O'Neal, Isabella Rossellini, Wings Hauser, and Frances Fisher.

O'Neal starred as Tim Madden, an ex-con and struggling writer prone to blackouts, who awakens with a hangover, an unexpected tattoo, blood in his Jeep, and the severed head of a blonde behind the rock where he stashes his weed. Tierney was cast as his father, Dougy Madden, a tough old bartender dying of cancer, but strong enough to help his boy by "deep-sixing" a couple of severed heads and a half dozen corpses in the ocean.

Tierney told the Murphys that when he first read for the part, Mailer "liked me so much" that he expected to be cast immediately. When days went by without a decision, Tierney "had a couple of drinks" (revealing that he'd resumed his alcohol consumption), got Mailer on the telephone, and roared, "Fuck the goddamn picture, you don't want me anyway!" Mailer had been leaning toward Tierney all along, so producer Tom Luddy arranged for a second reading. "I did about three lines and Norman said, 'Stop, we're wasting time. He's got the part. He's the only guy to play it.'"

The seven-week shoot commenced on October 27, 1986, in Provincetown, on the tip of Cape Cod in Massachusetts. Tierney said he found Mailer to be "a very charming, nice, kind-hearted guy"—and a fellow alumnus of Boys High School in Brooklyn. "I used to always sing the high school song, 'Morning

Renaissance Man

sun greets many banners, on this western track . . .' Finally, he got fed up. He said, 'I went there, I don't want to hear about it.'"

Tough Guys Don't Dance premiered at the Cannes Film Festival on May 16, 1987. *Variety* panned the picture, but praised Tierney as the "biggest, baddest, nastiest" tough guy of all. Earlier that week, on May 12, Tierney's work on *Hill Street Blues* paid off unexpectedly and memorably with the airing of the series finale. In "It Ain't Over Till It's Over," Tierney's Sergeant Jenkins shares the final scene with Detective Norman Buntz, played by Dennis Franz. Buntz is leaving the fire-damaged Hill Street precinct house for the last time, after being fired for punching out the police chief.

"Hey Norm," Jenkins says, looking around at the repair work under way. "You believe that? With all the fire and everything else, this old place is still sound."

"Yeah," Buntz replies. "Believe that."

Buntz folds a stick of gum into his mouth. A phone rings as he walks away and tosses the wrapper. As Buntz pushes open the door, Jenkins picks up the phone. "Hill Street."

Fade to black. Lawrence Tierney had the last words in one of the most influential shows in television history.

"He actually took me to that movie. 'You need to see my new movie, *Tough Guys Don't Dance*. I'll take you to it.'" Derek Bell was in his late twenties, an army reserve helicopter pilot and flight instructor when he was introduced to Tierney at Boardner's bar. "He walked up to the box office and said, 'Hi, I'm Lawrence Tierney. I'm in this movie. Here's a friend of mine. Can you let him in?' He told me, 'Go on, I'll be back after it's over.' He didn't even watch it with me. I went in there and I watched. He came back and we had lunch later."

Bell, who went on to become a well-known chopper pilot and traffic reporter on Los Angeles television, also recalls the day Tierney showed up unannounced at Santa Monica Airport, where Bell was giving flying lessons. "It just so happened that the student I had was an acting coach, Larry Gilman. He saw Larry Tierney walk in the door and he knew exactly who he was. Larry said, 'Can I get a ride in that airplane?' And I said to Larry Gilman, 'Would you like it if Larry came along with us?' He said, 'Sure.' So it was kind of a little Hollywood moment for him, as well. After we lifted off the runway, we both looked back to see what his reaction was. Larry was sound asleep. He slept the whole flight."

After *Tough Guys Don't Dance* opened across the country in September 1987, it was regarded as a "bomb," raking in less than a fifth of its $5 million budget. Most critics found the film to be risible, if not incomprehensible, but many pointed to Tierney's performance as a bright spot. Michael Wilmington of the *Los Angeles Times* called him "an amusingly gravelly noir icon." Roger Ebert of the *Chicago Sun-Times* wrote that Tierney was "the film's best character."

In the aftermath of *Tough Guys,* solid television work came Tierney's way, including a guest spot on the ABC sitcom *The Slap Maxwell Story* and a pair of roles that paid tribute to his film noir legacy. On *Hunter,* the NBC detective series starring former NFL defensive end Fred Dryer, Tierney was a retired police detective who not only solves the real-life, forty-year-old Black Dahlia murder mystery, but also a second killing by the same perpetrator. He was 1940s gangster Cyrus Redblock (a spin on Sidney Greenstreet from *The Maltese Falcon*) in "The Big Goodbye" (a mash-up of Chandler's *The Big Sleep* and *The Long Goodbye*), the eleventh episode of the syndicated *Star Trek: The Next Generation.* (The inclusion of the retro character in a series set aboard a twenty-fourth-century starship was achieved via a contrivance called a "holodeck" that allowed crew members to enter a virtual reality environment.)

With *Tough Guys* gaining an ironic fanbase and the *Hunter* and *Next Generation* episodes scheduled to air the second week of January 1988, the Hollywood publicity machine began working for Tierney for the first time in decades. His past brawls, binges, and busts were no longer embarrassments, but colorful memories of old Hollywood machismo.

"You think Sean Penn has a talent for getting into trouble, even for landing in jail?" Mitchell Smyth asked in the December 6 *Toronto Star.* "He's a pussycat, a non-starter, compared with Tierney in the 1940s and '50s. . . . In fact, Tierney was arrested more than 20 times, much more often than '30s 'Public Enemy No. 1' Dillinger (three arrests, two jailbreaks)."

In the feature, titled "'Dillinger' has finally wised up," Tierney said, "I haven't had a drink in, oh, five years now. Yeah, I finally wised up. I'd say it was about time. Heck, I threw away about seven careers through drink."

Tierney would later contradict the sobriety statement, but during this period, most of his friends say he was making an effort. "Most of the time that I knew him, he was trying to stay away from alcohol," Bell says, "which is a good thing, because one time I was with him, he was drinking pretty heavily and demons were starting to come out. He was conflicted but he was focused on moving on, focused on working, focused still on being a professional."

Joyner happened to witness one of Tierney's last hurrahs in the late 1980s, when he bailed Tierney out of jail at the Hollywood police station the morning after another drunken bar fight. His shirt stained with blood, Tierney insisted that Joyner follow as he traced his steps in search of the wallet, cash, and keys he'd left behind the night before. The hunt devolved into a tour of dives and speakeasies, with Tierney downing tumblers of scotch at every stop, until he and Joyner arrived at a bar called the Power House, site of the previous night's altercation. "Some guy came up and said something to him. I don't think Larry even knew him—and Larry turned around and just knocked this guy across the room," Joyner says, still amazed that Tierney was slugging at his advanced age. "My God, those hands, those huge hands, with those calcified knuckles. . . . It was like swatting a fly."

Offscreen exploits aside, Tierney kept working. In April 1988, he played the manager of the California Angels baseball team in *The Naked Gun*, the gagfest starring Leslie Nielsen and O. J. Simpson; in August, a prison warden in *The Horror Show*, a slasher flick produced by Sean S. Cunningham of *The Last House on the Left* and *Friday the 13th* fame; in November, Armenian Robber #1 in *Why Me?*, a heist comedy based on a Donald Westlake book; and a few days before Christmas, a slavemaster in the comedy fantasy, *Wizards of the Demon Sword*, banged out by prolific low-budget filmmaker Fred Olen Ray—reportedly hastily, on sets left over from Roger Corman's remake of his own *Masque of the Red Death*.

Amid this run, a notable figure in Tierney's life passed on. Jimmie Fidler, the gossip columnist who'd wasted many column inches attempting to get him help or to change his ways, died on August 9, at eighty-nine. Tierney's own achievements were recognized on September 12, when the Masquers Club, an old Hollywood actors' fraternity, presented him with the "Platinum Violin Case" at the "Gangsters and Their Molls Ball" at the Hollywood Roosevelt Hotel. Tierney was honored for his role as Dillinger, but the *Los Angeles Times* cited his work in *Tough Guys Don't Dance*—now referred to as "last year's instant classic"—and his "immortal line" from the picture: "I just deep-sixed two heads."

Tierney played a hardboiled police chief in *The Runestone*, a horror adventure picture lensed in March and April 1990. He had the title role of an illegal nuclear arms dealer—and his name above the title—in *The Death Merchant*, a direct-to-video feature directed by Jim Winburn, a stuntman who worked on *The Naked Gun*.

In May, Hollywood came to Milwaukee, as David L. Wolper Productions began filming the ABC television movie, *Dillinger*. In this latest telling, the role of the bad guy was given to a television good guy, Mark Harmon, best known as Dr. Robert Caldwell on NBC's medical drama *St. Elsewhere* (but who played against type as serial killer Ted Bundy in a television movie in 1986, the year he was *People* magazine's "Sexiest Man Alive"). The telefilm was unremarkable but for the respect it paid to the original. Lawrence Tierney was cast as the heroic, real-life Sheriff Jess Sarber, who was shot and killed on October 12, 1933, when the Dillinger gang broke their leader out of jail in Lima, Ohio.

Cincinnati, Ohio, was Tierney's next stop. John Sayles, the independent filmmaker and 1983 MacArthur "genius grant" recipient, was filming *City of Hope,* an ambitious story of politics, racism, and corruption. Among three dozen featured characters, Lawrence Tierney had a memorable scene as a *Godfather*-like Irish powerbroker. "Larry loved John Sayles," Joyner says. "And whatever buttons Sayles pushed, I think that is one of the best acting jobs Larry ever did."

(One of Sayles's early efforts was the screenplay for the 1979 Dillinger-themed film *The Lady in Red,* which Quentin Tarantino called "the best script ever written for an exploitation movie." In Tarantino's 2021 novel, *Once Upon a Time in Hollywood,* Tarantino remakes *The Lady in Red* with Michael Madsen as John Dillinger.)

All that and a guest role on the ABC legal drama *Equal Justice* would have made for an impressive year, but there was more ahead. In late 1990, two major opportunities were handed to the seventy-one-year-old actor. Unfortunately, both would add to his growing reputation as an actor who was not only versatile, but dangerous—and possibly crazy.

Scott Alexander and Larry Karaszewski scored a hit in 1990 with the movie *Problem Child.* Signed to write a sequel to their black comedy about a monstrous kid, they created a character for Karaszewski's former neighbor.

"Larry [Tierney] was always doing a routine for us where he'd pretend to be a sexy Latina maid who is vacuuming in the nude," Alexander says of their Beachwood days. "Then the phone rings, and she answers it and pretends to be her boss. It was really silly shtick. He had this hilarious voice he did as the girl. So we wrote a long opening sequence that would star Larry. He'd play a burly, lying moving man who does a con and has to switch to the funny girly voice. Then he gets caught and ends up in a big expensive action scene blowout with the kid. It was a lot of fun, all designed to showcase our pal."

Although he was a shoo-in for the role, Tierney had to audition for the director, producers, and Universal Pictures' head of casting. He arrived at Universal's "black tower" headquarters, and encountered a roomful of actors waiting to read for the same part. They were large, muscular, some twenty years younger than he. Bubba Smith, the six-foot-seven former professional football player, was among them.

"Larry's a fantastic actor, but he was in one of his moods," Alexander recalls. "He set out to fuck with their heads. Scowling at them. Rage in his eyes."

"He was discombobulated, he was a ferocious lion," Karaszewski says.

Faced with Tierney's unsettling behavior, Bubba Smith left without auditioning. "I witnessed that he fled from that elevator bank," says Alexander. "He was so scared."

Karaszewski clarifies: "Probably not scared as much as I think Bubba said, 'Life is too short to maybe get a part in *Problem Child 2*.'"

When it was Tierney's turn to read, "he 'innocently' asked if he could eat one of the bagels in the corner," Alexanders recounts. "Everybody was waiting for him to read, but instead, he methodically toasted a bagel, slathered it with cream cheese, then sat down and slow-w-w-ly ate it. He was just glaring at everybody, chewing slowly, his face smeared with cream cheese. He looked like a rabid dog. He was like a ticking bomb about to explode. It was total silence. People in the room were frozen. Absolute fear. 'Larry don't you, don't you—' I'm talking to myself—'Don't be fucking doing this, don't be doing this. I've seen you scare people, this is not the time or the place.'"

"'We're trying to get you a job,'" Karaszewski says. "'Please don't fuck this up, please don't fuck this up—' Oh, he's fucking this up."

The five-page sequence was cut from the film.

In November 1990, Jerry Seinfeld and Larry David finished polishing the script for the third show of the second season of their NBC sitcom, *Seinfeld*. In "The Jacket," Seinfeld, playing a fictionalized version of himself, and Jason Alexander as best friend George Costanza, are invited to dinner with the father of Jerry's ex-girlfriend, Elaine Benes, played by Julia Louis-Dreyfus. Alton Benes is a war veteran and famous writer who intimidates both men. Barney Martin, who played Liza Minnelli's father in *Arthur* and had been cast as Seinfeld's father on the series, suggested that his friend Lawrence Tierney would make a perfect Alton Benes.

Tierney arrived at CBS Studio Center on Radford Avenue in Studio City on November 28 for the table read, despite the fact that, according to Joyner, "he didn't get" the script. "He kept saying to me, 'Do you think this is funny? I don't find this humorous at all.'"

"He stayed with me when he was doing this episode of *Seinfeld*," Del Valle says. "It's a great episode, and Larry had absolutely no idea what it was about. On the first day of rehearsal, he came back to the house and said, 'You know, that Seinfeld, I don't think he's funny. I've known every comic from Jack Benny, you name it. This guy is not funny. How the fuck did he get a TV show?'"

The episode was taped before a live audience on Soundstage 19 on December 4. By all accounts, the episode was very funny, and Tierney was deadpan hilarious as Elaine's father, adding surprise levity to his trademark menace.

"He was intimidating, which the character was supposed to be," director Tom Cherones said in a *Seinfeld* DVD retrospective.

Added Alexander: "He was brilliant . . . and it was every reason in the world to have that be an ongoing character because . . . there was so much tension between him and every other character."

All agreed that Tierney would have returned as Elaine's father, if not for an incident that took place on the Seinfeld apartment set. Other cast members were onstage when Tierney strolled over to the kitchen area, looked around, pulled a butcher knife from a block on the counter, and slipped it under his jacket. He assumed no one had noticed. Others did notice. They were shocked, but no one expected anyone to call him on it.

"I wasn't about to ask him for it back," Cherones said.

Jerry Seinfeld was not so reticent. He walked up to Tierney and confronted him. "Hey Lawrence," he said, "what do you got there in your jacket? What's with the knife?"

"You see the color drain out of Tierney's face because now he's been caught," Alexander said.

Tierney responded with an attempt at humor. "I thought I might need it to stab you in the heart," he said. He then pulled the knife from his jacket. Raising it over his head, he made stabbing motions toward Seinfeld, while imitating Bernard Herrmann's screeching string sounds from the bloody shower scene in Alfred Hitchcock's *Psycho*.

"He thought it would be funny," said Louis-Dreyfus.

"Jerry didn't back off, so I don't know what was in his mind," Alexander said. "And I remember looking at Tom, looking at Julia, and just going, 'We're in the land of the sick now. We're in really scary territory.' Lawrence Tierney, I think, scared the crap out of all of us."

"But he was a good guy," director Cherones insisted. "He worked hard and did the job for us."

To Louis-Dreyfus, "he was a total nutjob" but "a wonderful actor, because he was so amazing in that show. And it's too bad he was so cuckoo because I'm sure he would've been back otherwise."

Del Valle says he wasn't surprised that Tierney attempted to swipe the knife. "He was a kleptomaniac. He would steal things," he says. "Larry would go into Jerry Seinfeld's office and take all this stuff off his desk and bring it back to my house. And then Jerry's office would call my house, saying, 'Do you know where all of our stuff is? Like paper clips, tape, pens?'"

"He had a tendency to just pick things up," says Joyner, "so running errands with Larry could be a problem. I remember he and I were with a mutual friend at a car wash, and when our buddy went to pay, it was twenty-five dollars more than he'd expected because Larry'd put a pair of sunglasses in his pocket and walked out. If you went into a cafeteria with him, he'd shove glasses and silverware into his pockets! You'd never finish eating because he needed to beat it out the door with all their stuff. He'd say, 'Go ahead kid, just go—move, move . . .' And he'd be rattling out the door with the cashier and waitresses watching.

"The nicest thing that came out of that period was that I was able to bring Larry together with Quentin."

41

Reservoir Dog

Quentin Tarantino assumed that Lawrence Tierney was dead. When he completed his latest script—which he was determined to direct—Tarantino had typed a note at the top of the first page, before directions for the opening scene: "This movie is dedicated to these following sources of inspiration," followed by eight names. The roll call of young Tarantino's cinematic influences reads as follows: Timothy Carey, Roger Corman, Andre DeToth, Chow Yun Fat, John Woo, Jean Luc Godard, Jean Pierre Melville, and, before Lionel White—the crime novelist whose books were the basis for films including Stanley Kubrick's film noir, *The Killing,* and Godard's *Pierrot le fou*—Lawrence Tierney.

By 1991, Tarantino had pushed his way from Video Archives in Manhattan Beach into Hollywood. *My Best Friend's Birthday,* an amateur film he'd cowritten, directed, and starred in while working at the video rental store, had become the basis for a script called *True Romance.* Tarantino would sell *True Romance* to director-producer Tony Scott. He was holding *Reservoir Dogs* for himself.

C. Courtney Joyner was a friend of Tarantino's (both were represented by manager Cathryn Jaymes). He had the opportunity to read the *Reservoir Dogs* script early on and was struck by the Tierney dedication.

"Lawrence Tierney!" Tarantino said. "He was the toughest guy of 'em all. He was a wild man, and he got killed in Mexico. Shot to death in a whorehouse."

"No," Joyner replied. "He lives right behind the Hollywood library, off Fairfax. I see him like every other day."

Joyner hosted a Christmas party. Lawrence Tierney was invited. So was Quentin Tarantino. "Quentin was all excited," Ron Zwang says. "I said, 'Quentin, here's Larry Tierney.'" Zwang puts on an obsequious voice: "'Mr. Tierney, your films . . . they captured a time in cinema which was the epitome of the postwar period, which spoke so much for the generation.'" As Tierney: "'Yeah kid, you're real smart, you're a real smart guy. Tell me, do you know where the can is?' And then he walked off to the bathroom. That was it. That was Quentin's introduction to Larry Tierney."

"One day my phone rang and it was Lawrence Bender." Will Huston is talking about a phone call from Tarantino's producer. "He said, 'I hear you know Lawrence Tierney really well.' 'Yes, I do.' 'Well, we're thinking about hiring him. What do you think?' Having experienced Larry on film sets before, I said, 'Well, you need to have somebody with him, almost like a Larry Tierney handler, because he gets impatient. I actually saw him walk away from sets because he was bored, and he would engage other people—just people on the street—and start hanging out with them. So you need somebody to do that.' And Lawrence pretty much dismissed me and said, 'I think we can handle him.' I'm like, 'Okay. Good luck.'"

Reservoir Dogs was ostensibly a heist movie. Harvey Keitel was the bankable name in the cast, one of a gang of strangers brought together to pull off a diamond robbery that goes very wrong. Michael Madsen, Tim Roth, Steve Buscemi, Edward Bunker, and Tarantino played the other crooks. Chris Penn was Nice Guy Eddie, son of Joe Cabot, the old criminal who assembles the team and assigns each a name from a color chart, so no one can squeal if they're caught. Joe Cabot was played by Lawrence Tierney.

Madsen, a modern-day tough guy actor, portrayed Vic Vega, aka Mr. Blonde, a sadistic psychopath and the most "Tierneyesque" character of the bunch. "I had never even heard of the guy until I was doing *Dogs* with Quentin," Madsen says, looking back more than thirty years. "Quentin says, 'Guess who's playing Joe? Lawrence Tierney!' And I did not know who the fuck Lawrence Tierney was. When I looked him up, and when I finally figured it out that he was John Dillinger, I was kind of embarrassed. And I was kind of starstruck—which I'm not very often by most actors I've met. But gosh, he was really a mountain of a man."

Filming got under way in L.A.'s Highland Park neighborhood on Monday, July 29, 1991. Tarantino should have remembered the adage about meeting one's heroes—or at least recalled that first meeting—because Tierney was a problem from the start. He was forgetful, angry at his director and fellow actors, and wasted valuable time when he flubbed his lines. And just as he didn't understand what was funny about *Seinfeld*, Tierney didn't "get" the references, humor, poetry of the dialogue, or artistry of the expletives in Tarantino's script. He let the director and everyone else know it.

"Tierney was a complete lunatic by that time—he just needed to be sedated," Tarantino told BBC television and radio host Francine Stock at a BAFTA event in 2010. "We had decided to shoot his scenes first, so my first week of directing was talking with this fucking lunatic."

"Quentin said, 'Listen, don't give Lawrence any alcohol. He has a problem with drinking. Whatever you do, don't give him a drink,'" Madsen remembers that first week. "And so obviously, me and Tim were pretty curious to see what would happen if we did. And so we took him over to Musso & Frank's, and we're all sitting at the bar, and he put away a couple of vodka grapefruit juice pretty quick. And he said he's going to go to the bathroom. He got up, and ten, fifteen minutes later, he didn't come back.

"I said, 'Tim, where the fuck did he go?' He goes, 'I don't know.' So I ran over, I looked in the bathroom, we didn't know where he was. And suddenly, we heard a bunch of cars honking out on Hollywood Boulevard. And one of the maître d's and some of the people in the other dining room were all up in the front of the restaurant. We walked up there, and there was Lawrence outside, standing in the middle of Hollywood Boulevard with his pants down around his ankles. And cars were honking at him to get out of the way. Me and Tim walked out there, and we said, 'Lawrence, come here, man.' And he hiked up his pants, and we took him back to the restaurant. And he was just acting like nothing strange had happened at all.

"I made some joke about him being drunk, and he took this wild swing at me—like a big haymaker swing. I ducked out of the way, and he just missed me by about two inches. And I'm really glad that he didn't connect, because I think he probably would have knocked me out. He had a big fist."

"He didn't like my dialogue," Tarantino said in a Tierney tribute included on the *Reservoir Dogs* tenth anniversary DVD. "He had a hard time remembering it and it was, 'Ugh, this fucking shit is too fucking convoluted! This thing is so fucking repetitive! . . . Whaddaya mean? Whaddaya mean? And I don't want to say that joke you gave me. That fucking dirty joke's disgusting!'"

Then there was Tierney's habit of walking away while Tarantino was giving direction. "Right in the middle of your talking! Not like, 'Fuck you.' You know, just *voom*—you're just supposed to be trailing after him. He was personally challenging to every aspect of filmmaking."

Madsen, for his part, remembers Tierney as "a big giant teddy bear that got crabby once in a while." He also recalls Tierney's difficulty filming the scene in which Joe Cabot assigns "colorful" names to the thieves. "Quentin wanted all of us in the room, so we were all sitting in the chairs, the way it looks in the film, and Lawrence was standing in front of us handing out the colors. But for some reason, he couldn't get it right. He didn't know who to look at for which color, and he was looking around in the opposite direction."

Tierney began to argue with Tarantino. Then he turned to Madsen. "I have a tendency to move around," Madsen says. "I'll scratch my nose or I'll cross my legs. Quentin called it being 'mannered.' I was doing my thing, and all of a sudden, Lawrence yells at me! 'Madsen, stop scratching your fuckin' face! And stop movin' around! I can't concentrate with you fuckin' moving around!' I said, 'Oh, my God. Lawrence, I'm sorry, man. I wasn't trying to be disrespectful, buddy. I'm sorry, man.' Quentin had enough, and he said, 'Okay, you guys get out of here.' And Quentin shot that scene of Lawrence in a close-up, or a medium of him handing out the colors to everybody, but nobody else was there except him."

"By the end of the week everybody on set hated Tierney—it wasn't just me," Tarantino insisted. "Tim (Roth) wouldn't even act with him in the same room!"

"Tim gets very dramatic about things," Madsen says. "In Tim's mind, Lawrence was being unprofessional, or being difficult when he should have been really happy to be out of retirement on a Quentin Tarantino film. I think Tim took it personally. I found Lawrence to be charming, and I thought he was funny."

Roth's character in *Dogs* got some revenge with an apt description of Joe Cabot's—and Tierney's—physical appearance: "You remember the Fantastic Four? The Thing. Motherfucker looks just like The Thing!"—"The Thing" being the heavily muscled, rocklike, and monstrous Marvel comics superhero.

It all boiled over on Friday, August 2, the last day of the first week of filming. The production was on location at Pat & Lorraine's Coffee Shop on Eagle Rock Boulevard, northeast of downtown Los Angeles, shooting that opening scene: Uncle Bob's Pancake House. The heist crew is assembled around a table, finishing breakfast.

"I was on the set that morning," Joyner says. "Larry was already on edge. I saw that Quentin was making a mistake with Larry. He kept touching him. I watched Quentin take Larry by the shoulders and try to position him for the camera. And Larry always had that thing: if he didn't invite that physical contact, watch out. Those hands would go up—those big ham hocks with the busted knuckles."

Tierney had expected that Joyner would stay for lunch, but when his friend left before the break, the old man's mood darkened further. Filming resumed in the afternoon. Tarantino has told his version more than once: With twenty minutes before the martini shot, he was speaking to Tierney when the actor began to walk away. This time, Tarantino grabbed his arm. "Lawrence," he barked. "Stay here!"

Tierney pulled away and gave the director a hard shove. "Get your fuckin' hands off me!" he growled.

Accosted by an actor on his set, in front of his crew? A defining moment for any director, let alone a first-timer getting through his first week. "All right, this fucker's gonna touch me on my set? Fuck him."

Tarantino lunged toward the old man. "Fuck you, you fat fuck! You're fucking fired! Take your fat fucking ass off my fucking set!"

Madsen and Keitel moved in to separate the pair and block the punches. Tarantino and Tierney stormed off in opposite directions. There was a moment of stunned silence.

Then, Tarantino said, the crew broke into applause.

Thirty years later, the incident is fresh in Madsen's memory. "We were all sitting at the table, and Quentin wanted Lawrence to look back and forth between Harvey and Steve Buscemi. And Lawrence felt like maybe Quentin was trying to make a fool out of him by making him look from one guy to the other guy, back to the other guy. He was really uncomfortable with it. And so he started to yell at Quentin. Q had had about enough of him at that point. He just said, 'You're fucking fired!'

"And he pointed his finger at Lawrence, and Lawrence jumped up out of his chair! All the rest of us were just sitting there like, 'Oh, my God. Lawrence Tierney is going crazy.' It was like seeing Frankenstein! It was like this monster got up from the table! He and Quentin actually started swinging at each other, and Harvey Keitel, as I remember it, stood right in the middle of them and separated them. And everybody else was up at that point. I said, 'Lawrence, Lawrence! What the hell's the matter with you?' And he goes, 'Gimme twenty bucks.' Every day, at some point in the day, he would ask me for twenty bucks. But it was an odd time for him to say, 'Gimme twenty bucks,' and I wondered if he created the whole thing—if he wanted me to pay him twenty dollars for the entertainment!

"Lawrence walked out of the Pancake House, started walking up the block—not on the sidewalk, but right up the middle of the street. And he was about a hundred yards away, and Lawrence Bender came in the room, and he goes, 'Oh, my God, Quentin, you can't fire Lawrence! He's already been established in the film!' I said, 'What the fuck are we gonna do? We're gonna have to get another actor and reshoot?' Which wasn't possible, because of the budget we had. And so Quentin and Lawrence Bender went out on the street to see him and they were all friends when they came back."

Madsen says he understood Tierney's issues. "Lawrence was an old guy who knew his craft very well. He had been around Hollywood way before any of us, and just wanted to be respected. I think he knew a lot about movies, and I think that he had lost his idealism for acting. And all of a sudden, he's sitting on a set with a bunch of young guys in black suits and black ties, and I think he was a little overwhelmed, but wasn't sure why. He must have looked across the table of people and was like, 'Who are these bunch of fuckin' kids trying to pretend like they were gangsters?' I mean, after all, he played John Dillinger. 'Who the hell do you guys think you are?' And I don't blame him. I get it."

Tarantino said he was certain he'd be fired over the incident. Keitel, who was also a coproducer of the movie, smoothed things over. The shoot carried on. The director had made it through the week.

Lawrence Tierney was only getting warmed up.

By the time Tierney arrived back at his apartment in Hollywood, his anger was still building. He called Joyner, told him he'd been fired, and said he wanted to meet him at Boardner's bar. "I knew what that meant. It would be real trouble," Joyner says. "Larry was really furious. And while we were on the phone, Quentin and Lawrence Bender beeped in. And I'm waiting, and waiting, and waiting, and he gets back on the line with me. They rehired him. Obviously, the reality was that they didn't have the money to recast or reshoot.

"I said, 'So Larry, you're okay now. You don't have to go out and have a night on the town,' or whatever it was he was planning to do. Later, I called Boardner's and the bartender George got on the line, and he told me that Larry had been there, and there had been a fight."

The next morning, Joyner's answering machine began filling with messages. Lawrence Tierney was in jail at the Hollywood police station. It would cost $5,000 to get him out. That meant bail had been set at $50,000.

"Michael Tierney filled in those blanks. Larry had hit the bouncer at Boardner's and broke the glass in the front door. When he left, he was joined by another regular, and they went back to his place, and they kept drinking. And they drank to that real bad tipping point. And that's when Larry called Michael, and Michael came over."

Some time after Michael Tierney arrived, his uncle became irritated, pulled out a .357 Magnum handgun, and fired at him. The bullet missed. Michael scrambled for cover, and Tierney fired another shot through the wall, into the next apartment. Once in the street, at a safe distance, Michael called police to report an "accident." This, according to Timothy Tierney, prevented a SWAT team incident, and possibly saved not only Tarantino's shooting schedule, but Lawrence Tierney's life.

"I called Cathryn Jaymes, and she said, 'For God's sake, do not tell Quentin, and don't tell Lawrence (Bender)!'" says Joyner. "She didn't want to jeopardize the completion bond or the insurance, so it was this big effort from all of us to get Larry out of the jug. His manager, Don Gerler, was prepared. He put up the lease on his condominium as collateral for the bail. Cathryn and I were able to get Larry out of jail with Don Gerler's help, and he was able to get onto the *Reservoir Dogs* set that Monday morning."

"What could I do? Let him sit in jail?" Gerler asked historian McKay. "I like him, and even more importantly, he has that amazing talent. I wouldn't have put up with this shit if he didn't have that talent. He's a Brando, except for the money he gets paid."

"Quentin chided me later about this, because we really did a great job as secret agents," Joyner adds. "He had no idea about any of this until it was over."

(Though charges of attempted murder were floated that weekend, Tierney was allowed to remain under a form of house arrest until he completed the film. The charge was bargained down to "shooting at an occupied dwelling or occupied vehicle," a felony which carried a possible penalty of seven years in prison. With his age as a factor, Tierney was sentenced to time in a halfway house in the San Fernando Valley. Stephan Morrow recalls picking him up there. "I went in and there's all this screaming, and there's Larry, triple the age, if not more, than most of the people in a halfway house, carrying on like he was another twenty-year-old.")

The *Reservoir Dogs* shoot wrapped at the end of August. For all his troubles with the script, Lawrence Tierney must have appreciated the iconic line Tarantino had written for him in the final scene.

JOE. You don't know jack shit. I do! The cocksucker tipped off the
cops and had Mr. Brown and Mr. Blue killed.
MR. PINK. Mr. Blue is dead?
JOE. Dead as Dillinger.

Mr. Blue was played by Edward Bunker, a career criminal turned successful author, screenwriter (*Straight Time, Runaway Train*), and actor whose fifty-seven years were written on his face as clearly as Tierney's seventy-two. When he first arrived on set, Bunker recognized Tierney immediately. They'd met "in the fifties," when Bunker drove into the parking lot of a Hollywood restaurant and encountered Tierney "beating the shit out of his brother." Bunker intervened, and Tierney beat him up, too. When Bunker brought up their history, Tierney said he didn't remember Bunker or the fight.

Chris Penn, who would die of heart disease in 2006, was the cast member who was closest to Tierney. The youngest of the *Reservoir Dogs* stars and younger brother of actor-director Sean Penn, he was twenty-five in the summer of 1991. He met the man who'd play his father a few weeks before rehearsals, at an informal cast barbecue at the Malibu beach house rented by Keitel. Penn later extended a vague future barbecue invite to Tierney. He was surprised when the old man phoned him at 8 a.m. the next day, asking for directions.

Tierney found his way to Penn's parents' house on Point Dume in Malibu and made himself at home. He ate, drank, slept, and after surveying the property, offered his host a gift of lawn furniture. "And there's lawn furniture everywhere," Penn said in the tenth anniversary tribute. "The day progresses. . . . I've definitely told him there's no way I want the lawn furniture."

When it was time to head home, Tierney asked for a ride back to his apartment in Hollywood. He said he had videotapes of his movies to show Penn. As they were leaving the house, the young actor witnessed one of Tierney's unfortunate habits: he scooped a pewter vase from the dining room table and walked out with it.

Penn waited until he'd pulled his truck up to Tierney's apartment building before saying, "And by the way, you know, what's with the vase?"

"I didn't take a vase," Tierney insisted. "I didn't take nothin.'"

Tierney entered the building and returned with the tapes—and "a shopping basket full of lawn furniture." Penn reminded Tierney that he didn't want the furniture. Tierney barked, "Well, what the fuck did you make me bring it down here for?"

"And then he walked away," Penn recalled. "That's Lawrence Tierney in a nutshell."

Madsen adds a punchline to Penn's familiar story: "Way after we finished *Reservoir Dogs,* I was at the Hollywood Athletic Club shooting pool, and somebody said, 'Lawrence Tierney's here.' And I went outside and he was standing there. 'Gimme twenty bucks.' And I go, 'No, Lawrence, I can't. I'm not going to do it anymore. The movie's over.' And he says, 'Well, I got some lawn furniture.' '*What?*' 'You know, lawn furniture. Do you want it?' And I said, 'Do I want it? No, Lawrence, I really don't have a need for it.' And he's like, 'Ah, fuck! All right, you asshole—' or something like that. And he walked away.

"A couple days later, I was at El Coyote and I ran into Chris. And he goes, 'Madsen! Why did you do that?' I said, 'Why did I do what?' He goes, 'You told Lawrence to give me that fucking lawn furniture!' Apparently, Lawrence had driven up to Chris's house in a truck, and he unloaded the rusted lawn furniture on the front lawn. Chris came out and said, 'What the hell are you doing?' And he said, 'Madsen told me to give it to you.'"

Reservoir Dogs was screened at the Sundance Film Festival in Park City, Utah, on January 21, 1992. It was picked up for distribution by Harvey and Bob Weinstein's Miramax Films and given a limited release on October 23. The picture was praised for its energy, black humor, dialogue, structure, and camerawork, criticized for its violence, and hailed as the debut of a major cinematic writing and directing talent. It was not, however, a huge financial success. *Dogs* grossed only about $2.8 million in North America, though it did more than twice that number in the United Kingdom, where it was released as a mainstream movie (and later banned on home video).

The film was the apotheosis of Lawrence Tierney's official comeback. In his enthusiastic review in the *New York Times,* Vincent Canby wrote that Tierney "more or less presides over the movie." Roger Ebert was less thrilled by the picture but admitted that "the movie has one of the best casts you could imagine, led by the legendary old tough guy Lawrence Tierney, who . . . is incapable of uttering a syllable that sounds inauthentic."

Reservoir Dogs represented a new peak in Tierney's later life. With roughly ten years ahead of him, he would carry on with movies, television, and even more scandal, but at seventy-three, all the troubles of the past fifty years had finally paid off. The question was, what now?

42

Natural Born Killer

He's sorta one-part chiseled, good-looking actor meets Tor Johnson. There's something about Larry's face that every crevice, every wrinkle tells a hundred tales. You can look in that face and you can see bar fights and dysfunctional relationships with women, and every hardship that he endured, from alcohol to everything, it's all in that face. I mean, they don't make faces like that anymore.

CHRIS GORE, DIRECTOR, *RED*

Reservoir Dogs gave Lawrence Tierney an unexpected second shot at mainstream pop culture fame, but within the industry also solidified his reputation as a slightly mad and potentially violent old man with anger and memory issues who was difficult to work with.

The director, ensemble cast, and crew of *Reservoir Dogs* were not the only ones to walk away with tales of Tierney. During the *Dogs* shoot, Tierney spent a day filming a small part in *Eddie Presley,* an independent feature written by and starring Duane Whitaker (based on his one-man play) and directed by his friend Jeff Burr.

"Larry always called it 'Eddie *De*Presley,'" Burr says. "We paid him $500 cash and all the craft service he could eat and stuff in his pockets."

Tierney's disruptive and argumentative behavior in what should have been a simple walk-on role took on more import when Tarantino, who also was friends with the filmmakers, took a few hours off from *Reservoir Dogs* to film an *Eddie Presley* cameo. When footage from both movies later wound up at the same film lab at the same time, Whitaker and Tarantino spent time commiserating. "We'd see Lawrence Tierney in *Dogs* in one room and then see Larry in our movie in another room," Whitaker told Scott Voison in the book, *Character Kings 2.* "We mostly just talked about Larry Tierney and what a nightmare he was to work with. We had kind of a common enemy."

"Duane Whitaker has the Tim Roth opinion of Larry," Burr says. "He hated working with him." Burr, who'd hosted Tierney in his West Los Angeles apartment for eight months leading up to the *Reservoir Dogs* shoot—"Imagine the worst roommate you could have. It was really like having this psychotic grandfather in the house"—was more understanding. He even included an affectionate tribute to Tierney when *Eddie Presley* was released on DVD in 2004. "Tierney's Tyranny" contained outtakes from Tierney's scenes, and visual proof of what a pain he could be to a young director on a tight budget. "He likes me so much he threw a peanut butter sandwich at me," Burr says in the mini-documentary. "I was kidding around with him and he was kidding around with me and all of a sudden he snapped and I walked away and I felt a huge blob of peanut butter sandwich whiz by my head and explode on the floor right in front of me. I think we got some good stuff, but I was practicing dentistry, pulling teeth."

But the featurette also showed Tierney joking avuncularly with the young crew members, and charming one young woman, first by speaking in French and then reciting a poem by Yeats: "When You Are Old."

"He had a steel trap mind," says Burr. "He probably had hundreds of poems memorized that he could do at a moment's notice. Before and after, Larry would come to our set and just hang around. Everybody liked him because they got a kick out of him. And this was before *Reservoir Dogs*. He didn't have that cachet, whereas two or three years later, every young filmmaker would want to work with him because they loved that movie."

"Larry was very well-read, very well-educated," Del Valle says of his one-time houseguest, "but he never bragged about it or made you aware of it. The one thing that proved to me he was an intellect was that he could do the crosswords in record time. He'd do those crossword puzzles like an Oxford don. He had a tremendous vocabulary. He was just a very interesting person."

"When he was home, he would read, and he would watch movies," Joyner recalls. "But he would get restless. I mean, that was really the drinker part of him, that he couldn't sit still. And so he'd get on the phone, he'd call me, he'd call whoever, 'Let's go get some ice cream, let's go do something.' He didn't know what to do with himself and he couldn't stand being alone."

"He was always on the phone!" Del Valle adds. "He loved to talk on the phone."

In private, Tierney dealt with the indignities of age. When he bunked with Del Valle, his host remembers that "he kept an empty coffee can by the bed so he could pee without getting far out of bed. He had prostate issues." When out in public, especially among his acolytes, Tierney remained a wild card. "As he got older, his personality got more colorful," Del Valle says.

His younger friends still trade stories of Tierney's hijinks during this period: couch-surfing; compulsive shoplifting; public urination; come-ons to and flirtations with young women on the street, in supermarkets, and movie houses; and pranks, like arriving at Del Valle's party for Cornel Wilde with drag queen Vicki Venom as his date. "Cornel said, 'Wow, Larry sure has gotten some weird tastes in his old age,'" Del Valle recalls.

For all the entertainment he provided, Tierney, with his constant calls for car rides and companionship, could be a burden on young people working to break into Hollywood.

"It was always an adventure to be around Larry, but it was a 24-hour job," Burr says. "He demanded that sort of attention, or he would light himself on fire. One night we were out in a bar, with a friend who was a director, and Larry felt he wasn't getting enough attention so he poured some rum on his chest and lit it on fire, just as an attention-getting act! And all of a sudden, you see him patting it down because he'd really burned himself!"

"He was very amusing," says Ron Zwang. "He loved young women to rub his head. And most of the time they did it. It's a strange request, but he seemed docile at the time. And he'd sometimes come up to you in the middle of a party: 'Okay, take the number 374, divide it by twelve, add number seventeen, and divide that by 362. Whatta ya get?' And I said, '*What?*' 'I told ya!' And he gives me the numbers again. 'Whaddaya get?' 'I don't know, Larry.' 'You know, for a while there you were showing signs of human intelligence!'

"He was a smart guy. But at a certain point, he'd become a pain in the ass. 'Hey kid, I'm having a heart attack. You gotta come over here.' 'Call an ambulance! I'll be right over!' 'I don't like ambulances.' 'Call your doctor.' 'I don't trust doctors. Come over here now—I'm dyin' . . . *agghh . . . I'm dyin'!*' So I drop whatever I'm doing, I rush right over there and he's standing on the sidewalk in front of his place. 'Larry! How are you feeling?' 'Fine. Let's get a drink.' 'I thought you were dying!' 'If I said I wanted to drink with you, you'd tell me to wait till you weren't busy or something.'

"He didn't have many friends because he wore them out. He wore me out," Zwang says with a sigh. "Calling me constantly. 'This is Mr. Blowjob. Can I speak to Ron? He called me earlier.' The phone would just constantly ring and he constantly wanted to do something. Who has time for all this? He wanted constant attention. I could either be his friend or have a career. I couldn't do both. At one point when he was driving me crazy, I said to somebody, 'Why couldn't I have met Don Ameche?'"

Tierney did meet up occasionally with survivors of the "old days," but according to Joyner, "his co-workers and old buddies from those days were few and far between during the time we spent together. [There were] not many of them left." Tierney spent time with directors Burt Kennedy and Hubert Cornfield; actors Timothy Carey, Robert Clarke, and John Finnegan. Jack Nicholson took his calls. Says Joyner: "There were so many folks who floated in and out of Larry's life, and he sure burned a lot of bridges, but the loyal people were loyal, because he was loyal, and he gravitated towards new people all the time."

Tierney was in Joyner's apartment—"As was his wont, Larry had moved in for a while"—when he phoned his old friend Elisha Cook Jr. at his home in the High Sierra region about four hours from Los Angeles. (In contrast to the squirrely characters he played, the slight Cook was a rugged outdoorsman who decades earlier took Tierney on hunting trips.) "I think Larry wanted to see 'Cookie' one last time, probably to make amends for something he did or said back in the forties," Joyner says. "But Cook refused to see him. He was happy to see Larry, but not if he had been drinking. And it upset Larry quite a bit. It hit him hard, as he was making a sincere effort. I have no idea if Larry ever tried to contact Cook again or made the long drive up to Bishop for a visit, which is what he wanted us to do. But I doubt it."

New friends, most all in their mid-twenties, replaced the ones who'd been aged or worn out, and most found the trade-offs to be worthwhile—until they weren't. And while Tierney gave headaches to established directors, he encouraged neophytes he befriended, and even agreed to act in their projects without pay. Brian Brookshire was twenty-five and working as a theater manager at the Vine Theatre, a bargain cinema on Hollywood Boulevard, when he met Tierney in early 1992. "I'm a movie guy, obviously," says Brookshire, today an independent filmmaker, "and I was watching American Movie Classics and they showed *Dillinger*. And then they showed *The Devil Thumbs a Ride,* and I'm like, 'Oh, my God, who is that guy?' Larry's persona in those movies is so intense, I don't know what you call that kind of acting. Just force of nature, I guess. So I'm doing my job at the theater and the guy who was in the movie I watched the night before walks by! And we just immediately became friends. He wanted to come see a movie. I'm like, 'Yeah, come on in!'

"What evolved was that he was gonna do my short film, and in exchange for that, I became his driver. I'd take him to his agent, or we'd go to lunch or to the studio where he was working on projects. And I never saw him drink once. It never was one drink, I'm sure, with him. And that's why he wouldn't drink and why he wanted to keep busy. We were going to his agent Don Gerler's office once a week to check in, to see what's next—to keep him busy, get him on a set."

Brookshire shot his movie on Super 8 film in late summer of 1992. Tierney starred in *The Route* as a dying man offered a secret to immortality by a charlatan played by Conrad Brooks (perhaps best known for his roles in Ed Wood's films). "I'd been making little Super 8 films since I was a kid," says Brookshire, "and working with Larry, a professional actor, was amazing. Having an actor of his caliber read the dialog I wrote and make it come to life, it's still one of the best things that ever happened in my life."

Brookshire's role as Tierney's driver would lead to a situation only Lawrence Tierney could engineer.

Julie Davis was twenty years old and a senior at Dartmouth College in September 1989 when she got her first look at Lawrence Tierney during a tribute to movie tough guys at the Telluride Film Festival.

"They showed *Born to Kill* and I fell in love," she says. "I didn't know what he looked like as an old man yet. I just fell in love with him. I was like, 'My God, he's the sexiest man I've ever seen in my whole life!' And then, after the screening, he got up on the stage. Now he's an old man. He did a Q&A, and he was charming and funny. I had this fascination with him."

A few years later, Davis was an aspiring filmmaker, living in Los Angeles, when she spotted Tierney at Canter's restaurant and delicatessen, the late-night haunt for rockers and showbiz types on North Fairfax Avenue. "I said, 'Oh my God, that's . . . that's Lawrence Tierney!' I went up to the table, and I said, 'Oh my God, I'm such a fan of yours.' He said, 'You loved *Reservoir Dogs,* right?' And I said, 'Oh, no, no. Not that. It was *Born to Kill.* That's one of my favorite performances, and, oh my God, you were so sexy.' I just remember he was so flattered. I started talking about all his old films, and I said to him, 'I'm a filmmaker, and I'm making a short film. Would you be interested in being in it?' And he's like, 'Yeah, here's my number. Give me a call.' And I called him."

To Davis's surprise, Tierney agreed to appear in *French Intensive,* her no-budget short film about a woman who's infatuated with her former college professor. "It was one scene, a really long dialogue scene. And he was so great: this warm, avuncular character, giving this young girl advice about taking a chance in life. It was a lot of dialogue, and he was so professional. He had all his lines memorized perfectly. He was such a star."

The young director and the old actor became friends. Davis credits Tierney with giving her confidence as she went on to direct film comedies including *Amy's Orgasm* and *I Love You, Don't Touch Me*, which prompted the *Jewish Journal* to dub her "The Female Woody Allen."

"You know, it's so funny, because he was so respectful," Davis says. "He treated me like he was my grandfather. He never made a pass at me. I mean, thank God I never came across Harvey Weinstein."

During this period, Tierney stayed busy—and showed his versatility—with guest roles on television. On an episode of the CBS late-night crime drama *Silk Stalkings*, he was a retired detective obsessed with a forty-year-old murder; on *L.A. Law*, NBC's ensemble legal drama from Steven Bochco, a creator of *Hill Street Blues*, he was a low-life career criminal and witness to a murder thirty-four years earlier.

Tierney stepped into another historic pop culture phenomenon in November: one of three competing network television movies based on the tabloid crime saga of seventeen-year-old Amy Fisher, who six months earlier shot the wife of her thirty-six-year-old lover, Joey Buttafuoco. NBC's version of the "Long Island Lolita" case, *Amy Fisher: My Story*, featured Noelle Parker as Amy and *Hill Street*'s Ed Marinaro as Buttafuoco. It was the first to air, on December 28, 1992. ABC's *The Amy Fisher Story*, starring Drew Barrymore and Anthony Denison, and the CBS attempt, *Casualties of Love: The Long Island Lolita Story*, with Alyssa Milano and Jack Scalia, aired in the same time slot on January 3, 1993. Tierney portrayed Buttafuoco's father on CBS (and helped Brookshire get his Screen Actors Guild membership by wangling him a small role). Of the three Lolita pics, critics and Nielsen viewers preferred ABC's.

The most unusual project Tierney took on in the wake of *Reservoir Dogs* was a thirty-minute film directed by Chris Gore, founder of *Film Threat*, a magazine dedicated to independent and underground films. *Red* was based on the infamous "Tube Bar tapes," recordings of prank phone calls made in the 1970s to a taproom in Jersey City, New Jersey, and answered by the bar owner, Louis "Red" Deutsch. The pranksters would ask for nonexistent patrons with punny names like Hal Jalykakik ("How'd you like a kick?"), Hugh Jass, and Al K. Holic. Deutsch would call out the names in the bar, realize he'd been pranked, and in a broken-glass gargle shout profanity-filled threats, along the lines of "I'll catch up wit' you. . . . I'll break dem bones in your feet, you'll never be able to walk for the rest a' your life!"

The recordings were passed around and bootlegged through the 1980s. Animator and cartoonist Matt Groening was a fan, and his television series *The Simpsons* began a long-running gag of Bart Simpson making similar calls to barkeep Moe Szyslak.

In Gore's short film, Tierney was, of course, Red Deutsch. The cast also featured some of Tierney's successful young filmmaker friends: Ron Zwang was a bartender; Jeff Burr, Red's wife; and "because Larry drove Chris so crazy," Joyner, the best of the Tierney impersonators, came in to dub his voice. Most of the movie consists of Tube Bar recordings over black-and-white freeze frames of Tierney at his most expressive and enraged—with the exception of a live-action fantasy sequence shot on Super 8 film, in which Red takes out his revenge on the pranksters in a bloodbath that makes *Reservoir Dogs* look tame.

In the spring of 1993, Tierney signed on to a film that was a logical, mainstream step from *Reservoir Dogs*. *Natural Born Killers* was the latest picture from adventurous, rule-breaking director Oliver Stone. Woody Harrelson and Juliette Lewis were signed to star as Mickey and Mallory, young lovers who kill her abusive father and embark on a thrill-killing spree that turns them into tabloid media stars. The script was written by Tarantino, but rewritten beyond recognition by Stone, producer Richard Rutowski, and screenwriter David Veloz. Tierney was cast as a deputy prison warden. He signed a five-week contract, at $10,000 a week, for yet another movie that promised to be a groundbreaking, cultural milestone.

He didn't make it through rehearsals.

As Tierney told it, he was going over a scene with Harrelson when actor Tom Sizemore interrupted. Sizemore, as a psychotic detective, began to ad-lib, tearing into Tierney's deputy warden. Tierney asked the director: Could he improvise? Tierney said that Stone not only gave the okay, but encouraged him. So Tierney hit back at Sizemore and gnarled out some choice insults, à la Joe Cabot.

Tierney was good—too good, it turned out. Harrelson suddenly jumped up. "You can't talk to a friend of mine like that!"

Harrelson had assumed that Tierney was insulting the actor, not the character. Tierney, as an ensemble of young actors discovered while shooting *Reservoir Dogs*, wasn't about to take any guff from a softie pothead wearing hemp pants. He told him so.

Harrelson moved closer. "You think you're a big shot?"

"What's your fucking problem?" Tierney countered.

"I don't like the way you're talking to me," Harrelson challenged, and then, according to Tierney, clenched his manicured movie star fists and moved closer. "And I'm gonna do something about it!"

Tierney stepped into range of a punch. "Yeah? What the fuck are you gonna do?" he spat. "Don't be a bullshit artist. Do it or don't do it!"

Harrelson looked at the old man, realized his own face was his fortune, and stomped out of the room. That was enough for the day. Stone told Tierney he could go home. Tierney made his exit, grumbling. Back at his apartment, he found out he'd been sent home for good. Stone had fired him! He later got a call from the Screen Actors Guild. NBK Inc., the company Stone set up for *Natural Born Killers*, reported to the union that Tierney was drunk and had threatened to punch Woody Harrelson.

Bullshit! Tierney was enraged.

Tierney didn't reach for a gun in this case, but the anger was still churning on May 1, when he arrived at the Hyatt Hotel in downtown Los Angeles for *Fangoria* magazine's annual Weekend of Horror convention. It was an opportunity to meet fans and pick up some cash by signing photos, but Tierney couldn't have been happy when he heard that Tarantino was wandering the convention—as a fan.

"Before *Pulp Fiction*, Quentin was still human," Todd Mecklem observed. "He hadn't quite risen to Asgard yet."

Tierney blew up when he got a look at the photo he was given to autograph. It depicted him with an uncharacteristic grin. "Larry said, 'I hate that fucking photo!'" Mecklem recalls with a laugh. "He liked the tough guy photos, although sometimes he'd say, 'I don't know why everybody always cast me as the tough guy.' 'Well, well, well . . . That's a tough one, Larry.'"

"Then he saw some guy who was wearing a bad Elvis costume with a big bouffant Elvis wig, and Larry said, 'What the hell's with that guy? You know, I ought to go beat him up!'"

Tierney was dissuaded with an offer of lunch.

43

Armageddon

More than a year after the Sundance premiere of *Reservoir Dogs,* Lawrence Tierney confessed that when he was working on the movie, he didn't realize its quality or significance. John Stanley from the *San Francisco Chronicle* got that out of him after *Dogs* was released as a video rental in 1993. Stanley arrived in Hollywood for a sit-down with "hot number" Tierney, "a barrel of a man with a gleaming bald head," to talk about his "triumphant comeback after years of trying to pick up a destroyed career with small parts that were sometimes good but never in films that hit big."

Stanley compared a Lawrence Tierney interview to a police interrogation with a hostile witness. The subject arrived a half hour late for the interview in a coffeehouse near Hollywood and Vine, "a look of mistrust in his eye . . . and made up of a thousand nerve endings." He spoke "mean-guy style in a gravelly voice," moving around the place in search of a cigarette, "even though he admitted that he wasn't supposed to smoke."

Tierney told the reporter that he'd considered *Dogs* to be "another robbery-type film"—until he viewed the finished work. "I realized how important it really was," he said. "It's a film that requires more than one screening. You need to see it a second or third time. The juxtaposing of scenes is confusing. If you stay with it, though, you'll realize how well-constructed it is. It's like a piece of music you have to hear many times to realize it's a classic."

Tierney said that *Reservoir Dogs* had changed his life and given him a "bright future."

"Before the film," he said, "I was a lost soul crying out loud." Then he cut the interview short, complaining that the reporter was interrupting him and claiming he had an audition for a Dennis Hopper movie.

Tarantino began filming his follow-up to *Reservoir Dogs* in Los Angeles at the end of September 1993. He was directing John Travolta and Uma Thurman on location inside a modern home on Summitridge Drive, two miles north of Sunset Boulevard in Beverly Hills, when he was faced with an unexpected and unwelcome visitor.

"I went to the set of *Pulp Fiction* with Larry," Brian Brookshire says. "Larry had me drive him. He didn't tell me where we were going. Then we see all the film trucks and Larry walks up there. I remember it didn't go the way he wanted it to go. He thought he was going to get in *Pulp Fiction*—but you should have seen Tarantino's face when he saw Larry on the set. Oh my God, it was like his world shattered for a few minutes until he could compose himself. They'd had such a run-in on *Reservoir Dogs,* I kept seeing where Tarantino said he'd never want to work with him again. But the problem with Larry is that he'd pull crazy stuff with people and then want another chance. And I think he wanted to be in another Tarantino movie because it was such a boost to his life when he got notoriety from *Reservoir Dogs.*

"It wasn't like we were kicked off, but we didn't belong there. They were seriously making a movie and we were crashing the set. I basically said, 'Larry, let's get the hell out of here.'"

And then Lawrence Tierney left Hollywood. With Michael's help, Tierney moved from his place on Hollywood Boulevard, about sixteen miles west to Venice. The second-floor apartment in an eight-unit building at 33 Brooks Avenue was a block and a half from the beachfront "boardwalk." Less than a mile down the sand from where Gwili Andre had died in obscurity, he became well-known in the neighborhood, if not for his work, then for his oversized personality. Timothy Tierney recalls accompanying his uncle to a favorite neighborhood restaurant. "They saw him coming and shut the door and put the 'closed' sign in the window—just like it was a scene from a comedy film."

Will Thimes was twenty-five and fresh out of law school when he met Tierney at his friend Frank Yankwitt's apartment at the corner of Brooks Avenue and the Ocean Front Walk. More accurately, he met Tierney halfway into the apartment. "This old bald guy, this huge old man, was trying to climb in through the window from the boardwalk, and we basically had to pull him in.

"I'm like, 'Who is this?' And Frank says, 'Larry's cool. Remember that movie *Reservoir Dogs*?' So we start chatting, and Larry tells me this story about how he got wronged by Oliver Stone on the *Natural Born Killers* set. Frank said, 'Oh, Will here's a lawyer.' And we talked for a little while, and Larry said, 'Yo, you're my lawyer, kid. Let's go get pizza.'"

❧

Tierney's seventy-fifth birthday was celebrated two days after the date, on St. Patrick's Day, 1994, at *Cult Movies* magazine's Cultmania festival at the Hollywood Moguls nightclub. There were two screenings of *Dillinger*, and Tierney's "scar" was unveiled on Hollywood Boulevard's "Walk of Shame."

Earlier in the week, Joyner had arranged for a very special present. "Quentin said some untoward things about Larry after *Reservoir Dogs* because Larry really did drive him crazy," he says. "And after all the difficulties and the blow-up, Quentin made the statement that he wished he'd hired John Ireland. That really got Larry upset. He was not a fan of John Ireland's. I don't think Quentin was aware of this, but I believe Larry had a little bit romantically to do with Joanne Dru, Ireland's wife.

"So I called Quentin the day before Larry's birthday. I told him what was going on, and that we were having a little party at a friend's apartment. I said, 'Will you please call him and reconnect?' I was with Larry the following day, and by God, he did. Quentin called him, and Larry went into a separate room. And they talked for probably twenty-five minutes. They had a long conversation, and Larry came out and said, 'He's okay, that Quentin. He's an okay guy.' That was very nice of Quentin to do that."

In the spring, Tierney filmed a brief scene with Emma Thompson for *Junior*, the movie in which Arnold Schwarzenegger played a pregnant man.

Army Archerd broke the news in his *Variety* column on July 7, 1994: "Thesp Lawrence Tierney" had filed a $2,550,000 libel suit against Oliver Stone and his NBK Inc. Tierney was demanding $2.5 million for the libel, and another $50,000 for the salary he claimed he was owed for that five-week contract for the role that went to Everett Quinton.

The complaint prepared by Will Thimes stated that Tierney's career had been damaged by untrue accusations in NBK's letter to SAG. Chief among the falsehoods: that Tierney was drunk. Tierney claimed he hadn't had a drink in over two years. The next day, the *New York Daily News* reported that Tierney claimed he'd been dry for *five* years. Both estimates strained against Michael Madsen's recollection of that pants-around-the-ankles night at the Musso & Frank Grill.

The conciliatory birthday phone call to Tierney must have softened Quentin Tarantino's attitude toward his old nemesis, because amid the *Natural Born*

Killers dispute, Tarantino was ready to hire him again on his latest film. Tarantino was one of four directors (Allison Anders, Alexandre Rockwell, and Robert Rodriguez were the others) contributing separate segments to *Four Rooms,* a black comedy anthology set in a down-at-the-heels hotel. The episodes were connected by a framing story starring Tim Roth as the hotel bellhop. "When they were building the set for *Four Rooms,* I came down and hung out with Quentin," Jeff Burr reveals. "We got to talking, and he says, 'I gotta tell you something, Jeff. We started casting this movie and there's this role for this gruff hotel night manager. And I'm talking to the other directors, and we all look at each other and I go, It's gotta be Larry. I hate to say it. I hate it for me, I hate it for all you guys, it's gotta be Larry. He's the only one who can play this role.' So Quentin decides this, all the other directors agree, and he goes to Tim Roth and says, 'Tim, it's going to be Larry next to you as the night manager.' Tim Roth goes, 'If he is in the role, I walk. I will not act in the same frame with him. I won't act in the same movie with him. I hate the guy.' So Larry did not get the part for that reason. And Quentin, because he knew I was friends with Larry, right after he told me, he goes, 'Whatever you do, don't tell Larry. Don't tell Larry! *Don't ever tell Larry!*' And you're the first person I've told."

Tierney worked in August on *Fatal Passion,* a direct-to-video movie about an "artistic serial killer," starring former fetish model Lisa Comshaw and directed by T. L. Lankford under the pseudonym Gib T. Oidi (an anagram of "big idiot"). He was a cop in *A Kiss Goodnight,* a role-reversal riff on *Fatal Attraction* (*Daily News* reviewer Phantom of the Movies called Tierney the "resilient septuagenarian thesp"), and an Italian mobster, Il Senor Marzon Consigliere, on the first episode of *Pointman,* a Prime Time Entertainment Network (soon to split into UPN and the WB) series starring his Buttafuoco, Jack Scalia. Another *Casualty of Love* connection paid off in the summer of 1995, when director John Herzfeld gave Tierney a cameo in *2 Days in the Valley,* a comedic crime thriller that was not uninfluenced by the acclaimed, game-changing *Pulp Fiction.*

Tierney entered the gamer realm that year, working with Jeff Burr on *American Hero,* an interactive movie video game designed for Atari's new Jaguar platform. "It was kind of a blue collar James Bond," Burr says. "Larry's the M figure telling Bond what his mission will be." The Jaguar was such a flop that the game was never released.

In the role that had the largest audience and cultural impact, Tierney was represented by only his voice: as guest star in the 1995 Christmas episode of the

Fox animated television series *The Simpsons*. The convicted shoplifter gave life to Don Brodka, a discount store detective (and ex-marine) who catches Bart Simpson stealing. The "Marge Be Not Proud" episode aired on December 17, 1995. The producers could compare notes with the *Seinfeld* crew. According to showrunner Josh Weinstein, the time with Tierney was "the craziest guest star experience we ever had." The old actor yelled at and intimidated show staffers, refused to read lines if he "didn't get the jokes," and although he'd been hired because of his *Reservoir Dogs* persona, insisted on reading the part in a southern accent. In the end, Tierney made use of his own distinctive style of speech. "He certainly delivered," Weinstein said, "and he's one of my favorite characters we have had (on the show)."

On the rainy afternoon of Thursday, December 28, 1995, the actor, comedian, and writer Patton Oswalt was seated near the back row of the New Beverly Cinema (the revival house on Beverly Boulevard that in 2007 would be purchased by Tarantino), watching *Citizen Kane*. About fifteen minutes into the film, he was distracted by sudden noise behind him.

"Someone was sitting down and talking to himself," he says, decades later. "Like, loud. And at first, I was kind of like, 'What the fuck, man? Don't talk during *Citizen Kane*!' I turn around, and it's Lawrence Tierney. He's just sitting there, he's wearing a white T-shirt and blue jeans. When I turned to look at him in the dark, I was like, 'Oh . . . shit.' Because his face looks like an Easter Island monolith. You can't not know what you're looking at.

"And for fifteen minutes, he's talking at the screen. 'Don't clap for that bitch, she can't sing!' 'Siddown, ya chump—' 'What are you staring at there, you fuckin'—' He was commenting on the movie as if he knew everyone in it personally—probably he did know them personally. So it's fifteen minutes into *Citizen Kane,* and for twenty minutes he just talks. 'Aggh, fuckin' look at that bitch, goddamnit!' And then this younger dude suddenly shows up behind him—I found out later that was his handler, this young guy who was driving him around—he was like, 'Larry, hey! We gotta go, man! They're waiting, we gotta go!' And so Tierney stands up, he looks up at the screen, and says, 'I ain't never seen this cocksucker. It's not half bad.' And then he leaves.

"He had just watched twenty out-of-context minutes of *Citizen Kane,* talked the whole time, and then left. And it was just perfect. It was fucking perfect. That was my Lawrence Tierney encounter. Like seeing Bigfoot."

Will Thimes was at home in Santa Monica when he picked up a phone call from Frank Yankwitt: "I just got a crazy call from Larry, and I think he might've had a stroke."

"Frank was half a block away from Larry," Thimes says. "He said, 'I'm getting ready to go over there and check on him, but start heading this way.' So I popped in my car right away and headed over there.

"Larry was conscious, displaying a lot of classic stroke symptoms. I asked Frank, 'Have you called an ambulance?' And he said, 'He won't let me.' Even after having a stroke, Larry was such an intimidating guy. He insisted no ambulance. And we couldn't tell him no, so we said, 'Let's just get him down.'"

Thimes and his friend carried Tierney to the sidewalk, intending to drive him to the hospital in Yankwitt's new car. "Larry said, 'No, no, the kid's gonna take me!' I had a beat-up old '71 Volkswagen Bug. It was not in great shape. He insisted, so it was like, 'Okay, he wants to go in my car, I guess we gotta get him over there in my car.' And we drove him to UCLA Medical Center in Santa Monica. Frank followed behind, in case my car broke down.

"Looking back on it, it's hard to believe that we just acceded to his will. We couldn't tell him, 'No, this isn't a good idea,' because we were too intimidated by this incapacitated old man."

Tierney's stroke hastened a settlement in his lawsuit against Oliver Stone. "There was a deposition after he'd had a stroke, and really he just wasn't in great shape," Thimes says. "He knew what he wanted to say, and it wasn't coming out right, and he was getting really frustrated. The other counsel and I just sat down and said, 'Let's see what we can come up with,' and we came up with something that was satisfactory to Larry. The thing that really bothered him was saying that he was drunk, because he swore up and down that he had not been drinking. And honestly, in all the time I knew him, and I hung out with him a lot of times, I don't recall ever seeing him drunk."

After the stroke, drinking was no longer an option. At seventy-six, his mobility impaired, Tierney took on more voice-over work, including the most unlikely and sensitive role of his career. He was Rick, an old homeless man, on *The Oz Kids*. The animated series derived from L. Frank Baum's *Wizard of Oz* books premiered on ABC in September 1996 and was released on home video a month later. Tierney's character is introduced in the first episode, emerging from behind a dumpster toward his shopping cart.

"When you been where I've been, and been through all I've been through, well, it's tough to believe in magic," he tells the Oz kids in a voice that's not a Red Deutsch grumble but a soft-spoken purr. The episode ends on a scene that shows Rick in more familiar Tierney territory: raising a glass in a toast to his new friends.

Casting agents didn't use Tierney's infirmity as an excuse to cross the troublesome performer off their lists. Tierney won some high-profile gigs, often receiving the same consideration given his late brother Scott Brady in his final appearances. Most of the roles did not require him to be on his feet.

He was on the Warner Bros. studio backlot in Burbank in 1996 for the third season of the hospital drama *ER*. The seventy-seven-year-old stroke survivor made his entrance strapped to a gurney being rushed into the emergency room; an eighty-nine-year-old man, "seemingly gorked"—unresponsive and requiring life support devices to function—and flatlining. For most of the episode, Tierney needed only to lie back and keep his eyes closed—until his final scene, when he sat up for a touching talk about a life well lived.

Tierney was behind a lunch counter as Frankie Balls on the CBS crime series *EZ Streets*, before returning to the site of the RKO Radio Pictures lot, whose gates he first entered in 1943. Paramount Pictures had long ago absorbed RKO but maintained some of the original buildings and, atop Stage 21 at the corner of Melrose and Gower, the RKO globe. History aside, Tierney was walking as best he could toward the future, with another place in the Star Trek universe.

Star Trek: Deep Space Nine was the third sequel to the original *Star Trek*. Devoted Trekkers know that Tierney portrayed the wealthy ruler of an interstellar empire in "Business as Usual," the eighteenth episode of season five. The Regent of Palamar was described in the script as a "lean figure" with "the humorless eyes of a True Believer . . . attired conservatively if you consider Genghis Khan conservative." Crew members who remembered Tierney from *Star Trek: The Next Generation* a decade earlier had warned against bringing back the disruptive crank, but executive producer Ira Steven Behr, like many before him, wasn't about to pass up the opportunity to meet, and work with, the legend.

Tierney arrived with his nephew Michael (who'd acted, uncredited, on *Next Generation* and *Deep Space Nine*), exhibiting obvious effects of the stroke. In a recollection on Todd Mecklem's website, Behr wrote that he was shocked to see the actor dragging a leg, with an arm hanging limply. The producer feared Tierney wouldn't make it up the stairs to the makeup department, but with Michael's assistance, the old tough guy got to the chair and was fitted with a facial prosthetic that ran from his forehead and down his nose. Tierney looked the part—perhaps not lean, but menacing and authoritative enough.

As was anticipated, Tierney was gruff and impatient from the start, and once seated on set, had a difficult time remembering his lines. He blamed the crew, the other actors, and ultimately the director. This was the first directing job for Alexander Siddig, an actor who portrayed Dr. Bashir in the series. He showed his adaptability by crouching under the table and feeding Tierney his lines.

Tierney was in even weaker condition that fall, when he shot additional scenes for an alternative version of *American Hero*. Jeff Burr had been tasked with turning the canceled video game into a linear film. "He wasn't in a wheel-chair, but the stroke definitely took its toll," Burr recalls. "In the last scene we did with him, he's on a podium with the president of the United States, played by Jeff Corey. And the last shot I do of the day, and the last shot of Larry in the project, is Larry saying, 'Congratulations, Jack' and giving him the thumbs up. So I start rolling on it, call 'action,' he does the line and I say, 'Do it again, Larry.' He does it maybe three or four times and gives the thumbs up and I just don't want to cut the camera, because in my mind, this will be the last film rolled on Larry, and I didn't want it to stop. I really thought that would be the last film rolled on him."

Principal photography began in February 1997 on *Southie*, John Shea's independent film about organized crime in South Boston. As the local mob boss, Tierney was the movie's commanding presence. In every scene but the last, he was seated.

Tierney's last work in 1997 was a cameo role in a blockbuster. *Armageddon* was producer Jerry Bruckheimer and director Michael Bay's $140 million disaster movie about a team of drilling experts, sent into space to divert a giant asteroid from a collision course with Earth. The former sandhog was cast as the invalid father of the hero, played by Bruce Willis. The pair share a tender scene, one tough guy to another, in a nursing home. Tierney is seated throughout.

Tierney initially passed on the role. "The Bruce Willis character is the toughest guy in the world. He's so tough that they put him into space to blow up an asteroid," Timothy Tierney says. "So they have to have a dad who's even tougher than he is. And who in Hollywood can you find that's tougher than Bruce Willis? Well, Larry Tierney. So they said, 'One day of work. Ten thousand dollars. It's a slam dunk scene.' And he said, 'I don't wanna do it!' They started begging and cajoling him. Larry said, 'What do I care? I'd rather just watch TV at home!'

"I happened to be at Larry's apartment the day they got a production assistant, some girl who just sounded very sweet on the phone, saying, 'Hi Larry. We sent you this script. Have you read it yet? It's just one day. It'll be so much fun.' And she got through to him! He said, 'Okay. Okay. I'll do it. All right. All right!' He couldn't disappoint this girl."

Tierney told Rick McKay that Willis "was very nice and gracious. I had a very nice time working with him. In fact, he was very quiet when we worked together." But as far as he was concerned, the role was "just a job. . . . I don't know how I am in it. I don't like to think too much or I die of chagrin when the movie finally comes out and I'm cut down to one second in it."

Tierney's instincts were spot-on. When the film premiered on June 30, 1998, his scene had been excised. According to Timothy Tierney, "he later said, 'Ah, they cut the scene from the movie 'cause I blew Bruce Willis off the screen!'"

The cutting room floor wasn't the worst place to end a career that had, against all odds, lasted as long as Tierney's. With the release of *Armageddon*, a full fifty-five years, almost to the day, from when he arrived in Hollywood, Lawrence Tierney was finished.

Except that he wasn't.

44

Dead as Dillinger

There was another young woman whom Lawrence Tierney couldn't disappoint. Elisabeth Sikes was a film student at the University of Texas at Austin. In the summer of 1997, Sikes and cinematographer Deborah Eve Lewis arrived with their gear in Tierney's new second-floor apartment at 2352 Penmar Avenue, at the corner of Venice Boulevard, about a mile from the beach. They were there to interview and profile him for a student film. After two visits, Sikes assembled *Gimme Some Larry,* a nine minute and forty-nine second documentary, mixing brief film clips and interviews with verité footage in which she attempts to corral and interview a visibly declining but still cantankerous and witty man. Among the scenes that Ron Zwang says "perfectly capture him at the time," Tierney: shirtless, imitates an ape on the Venice walk; listens to a recording of his own rap song, produced by Michael, in which he recites instructions on how to hang oneself; receives the head massage he demanded from the director, sitting back in his living room, eyes closed, his T-shirt risen above his belly, displaying the long scar from his Hell's Kitchen knifing.

Quentin Tarantino appears in the film. At a distance from his *Reservoir Dogs* experience, now an Academy Award winner for *Pulp Fiction,* he still nurses the grievance, though perhaps with the intent of making Tierney an even more towering pop culture figure. "Lawrence Tierney is probably the craziest *fuck* I've ever met in my entire life. People would say, 'Well, was he challenging to you? Was he personally challenging you?' And I go, 'No, he wasn't personally challenging me. He liked me. He's just personally challenging to the concept of making a film.'"

Michael Tierney makes reference to his father and uncles. "Larry was the oldest, the craziest, he drank the most, he fought the most, and he fucked the most. And he's the only one still alive. So you tell me which is the best way to live."

But it's Lawrence Tierney, in one of the few interview clips, who may have revealed the key to the turbulent past fifty years. "They had me so brainwashed I was gonna become a big star," he says. "So I came out here, I expected wonderful things to happen, which they told me was going to happen. When I came out here, I found there was nothing to it. Nothing was like what they promised."

(*Gimme Some Larry* was runner-up in the Documentary Short competition in the sixth annual South by Southwest Film Festival in March 1999.)

By early 1998, with a pacemaker inserted into his chest, Lawrence Tierney was no longer constantly out of breath and had less difficulty walking. He was seen on televisions across the country in a commercial for Sprint telephones. Michael Tierney, who'd been cleaning up and looking out after his uncle for over a decade (more than one of Lawrence Tierney's friends referred to Michael as "a saint"), arranged for him to move back to Hollywood, into an apartment in a renovated 1930s building at 1412 Sierra Bonita Avenue, a block south of Sunset Boulevard. On Sunday, March 19, Rick McKay attended a party in the new home, celebrating Tierney's seventy-ninth birthday. In contrast to the Venice digs, this place was "nice and clean. . . . The walls of the living room were full of memorabilia. Bronze plaques from film festivals around the country, a great poster from *Dillinger* with the caption: 'His story is written in bullets, blood, and blondes.'" All the guests were young.

One of Tierney's last public appearances took place on April 6, 1999, at the Egyptian Theatre on Hollywood Boulevard. The occasion was a screening of *Born to Kill*, as part of the American Cinematheque's film noir film festival, *Side Streets and Back Alleys*. The picture's director, eighty-four-year-old Robert Wise, was the special guest.

In the fifty-three years since he worked with Tierney on *Born to Kill*, Wise had found success and earned respect directing acclaimed films in many genres. His oeuvre included *The Day the Earth Stood Still, Somebody Up There Likes Me, I Want to Live!, The Sand Pebbles, The Andromeda Strain,* and *Star Trek: The Motion Picture*. He collected four Oscars, winning for Best Director and Best Picture for both *West Side Story* and the *Sound of Music*, and in 1998 received the American Film Institute's Lifetime Achievement Award.

Tierney showed up at the Egyptian uninvited, and unconcerned about stealing Wise's moment. According to Joyner, he held a grudge against Wise, and other directors he'd worked with early in his career, because as they rose to greater heights, "they forgot about him."

"I find it interesting that he did voice that to me," says Joyner, "because at the same time, when Gordon Douglas extended a helping hand, look how Larry reacted."

The evening's events were immortalized by film noir expert Eddie Muller in an essay (published on his website, NoirCity.com) entitled "The Big Leak." The story gathers many of the familiar contradictions and outrages that made Tierney such a fearsome, complicated figure in his final years. He barks profane orders to the young people helping him into the theater; charms a young European woman by speaking in perfect French; holds forth on the poetry of John Donne before cursing out an old rival; and while philosophizing about life's futility, suddenly throws a punch toward Muller's chin when the writer gestures too closely to his face.

Muller's story focuses on eighty-year-old Tierney's prostate issues, detailed in scenes in which he urinates in front of a crowd in the men's room, and a shocking display during the screening inside the crowded theater—a scene similar to previous incidents related by several of Tierney's friends.

"About twenty-five minutes into the picture he turns to me and he says, 'Do me a favor, get me a cup,'" Muller summarized in an interview with the Hollywood Five-O website. "I came back with the big *Prince of Egypt* plastic cup, a big soda cup. They were souvenirs because *The Prince of Egypt*, of course, had premiered at the Egyptian.

"I handed this cup to Tierney. I do not even get back in my seat when Tierney stands up, undoes his trousers, drops them to the floor and takes a monstrous piss in this cup. . . . And of course, it had to be a real quiet spot in the movie. So you could hear this torrent out loud. . . . There was a woman sitting in front of him, and I just remembered thinking, 'Come on, you know what that sound is. Please. Don't turn around.' . . . This woman turns around. And like, she's staring right at the danger zone, you know? And she's just got these huge saucer eyes. And out loud, in full voice, full projection, Tierney says, 'What the fuck are you looking at? *Ya never seen a cock before?!*'"

Muller's story, in full, stands as a tribute, reflecting the awestruck appreciation of a film noir aficionado confronted with authenticity at a time when former child actors were marketed as alpha, macho antiheroes. Lawrence Tierney, at eighty, was still a dangerous, unhinged tough guy, a lion in winter who was embarrassed but not imprisoned by his infirmities, and who quietly apologized to Muller for his lack of bladder control.

Looking toward Tierney's final scene, the "Big Leak" concluded with a suggestion for a headstone inscription: "He Did Not Go Quietly."

Dead as Dillinger

❦

Armageddon should have been Lawrence Tierney's last movie. Though his sole scene was cut from the original release, it was included in the Criterion Collection's "Director's Cut" DVD the following year. With Tierney propped in a chair in *The Godfather* shadows and Bruce Willis crouched at his side, the scene is a fitting farewell to a movie tough guy. Tierney's age and ill health are evident. Skin stretched tight across his massive head, he appears older than his years, in contrast with Willis, the smart-ass action hero and a star of Tarantino's *Pulp Fiction*. Willis is deep sea oil driller Harry Stamper; Tierney is Harry's dad, Eddie "Gramp" Stamper, a legendary driller, now a man at the end of the line: "Pills every four hours. Jello every five. Goddamn Jello. Pudding for sissies. Go ahead and laugh. Layin' around, I got dead men on my ass." Gramp asks about his granddaughter, Harry's girl, and reminds his son, "God gave us children so we'd have roses in December." It was a reference to a line from *A Window in Thrums,* the second novel from *Peter Pan* playwright, J. M. Barrie: "God gave us memory so that we might have roses in December." In a testosterone-fueled and explosion-filled popcorn flick, Tierney's "Where you see F, you see K" twist from *Ulysses* may have been more fitting, but the line worked in a scene that ends with Harry giving his father a kiss on the head. Gramp responds with an affectionate punch to the arm. "Take care of yourself, all right?" Harry says. "You too," Gramp replies.

Fewer than eighty seconds in a two-hour-and-thirty-minute picture, it was nonetheless valedictory, a farewell from one tough guy to another, leaving Lawrence Tierney to memory and the dead men forever on his ass.

But God gave Lawrence Tierney nephews to keep him active and keep him company as he dragged his bum leg around to whatever bars he could limp into, and when he couldn't get out, he'd host his young friends and fans he'd met at has-been conventions or dives to down a few drinks and watch VHS tapes of *The Hoodlum* and *The Devil Thumbs a Ride* at his apartment.

Nephew Michael Tierney, son of Tierney's late brother Edward and former youth chess champion, would add the postscript that pushed Lawrence Tierney's career into the twenty-first century.

Since the death of his father, Michael had worked in music and demolition, driven a truck, and tried to make a go of acting, resulting in a few bit parts here and there. In 1996, at thirty-one, Michael decided to make his own independent film. He'd spend the next few years achieving that goal: writing, producing, scoring, and ultimately directing and starring in *Evicted,* a black comedy that depicted, in his words, "a day in the lives of Micro, an out-of-work trash man, 'T,' who is a crippled alcoholic, and Klash, who is a seventeen-year-old homeless speed freak. Just three unambitious characters trying to survive in Hollywood."

The 16mm picture was shot over four weeks, most of it on location in Hollywood, with some desert scenes in Needles, California. Michael cast his younger cousin Terence Tierney as Micro's cousin T, who describes himself as a "drunkie." He also corralled some established actors: Shannon Elizabeth, who during postproduction became a star in *American Pie*; Terry Camilleri, who has a scene that refers to his role as Napoleon in *Bill & Ted's Excellent Adventure*; and, as Bob, Micro's elderly neighbor and adviser, his uncle Lawrence Tierney.

Evicted, which Lawrence Tierney helped finance, had its premiere at the Vogue Theatre on Hollywood Boulevard (near the Musso & Frank Grill) on December 21, 1999. It might seem the low-budget production was an unfortunate coda to his resume, but this family affair proved a more fitting send-off than his director's cut role in *Armageddon.* Tierney was filmed sitting in his actual apartment, the one seen in *Gimme Some Larry* (though decluttered, and without the *Dillinger* poster collage near the door). The lines he spoke could have been drawn from real life: "I've been down before. . . . I didn't always have a job. I got fired. I lost jobs. But I always went back and got another one. I had all kinds of jobs: lumberjack, bartender, stevedore, sandhog, ironworker. Name it, I've done everything. I'm not afraid of work." Lawrence Tierney's final scene makes the connection even more clear.

> BOB. Now get the hell out of here. I wanna wake up in peace. I
> don't have too many of these mornings left.
> MICRO. You gonna be okay, Bob?
> BOB. I think so, Micro. Be a mighty wind that blows this old oak
> over.

The mighty wind came in several blasts. In the twenty-six months Tierney had left on earth, his health deteriorated. There were at least two more strokes, and a bout with pneumonia. Michael moved him from his apartment to the Sharon Care Center, a medium-sized nursing home on West Third Street in the Beverly Grove neighborhood. At 3:15 a.m. on Tuesday, February 26, 2002, Lawrence Tierney died there. He went quietly, seventeen days shy of his eighty-third birthday.

Death was attributed to cardiac arrest due to congestive heart failure, hypertension, and a recent stroke. Michael handled the arrangements. The body was transported to the Abbott & Hast Mortuary in Silver Lake, and cremated.

After Lawrence Tierney's death was announced, the news media gave him his due. The obituary that Dennis McLellan wrote for the *Los Angeles Times* was adapted by the Associated Press and appeared in newspapers across the country and around the world.

> Lawrence Tierney, a veteran character actor and onetime B-movie leading man whose two-fisted, tough-guy image on the screen in the 1940s and 50s rivaled that of his off-screen personal life, has died. He was 82. . . . Best known for his gangster roles in an 80-film career that spanned 50 years, Tierney's most memorable credits include the title role in the 1945 B-movie classic "Dillinger" and the leader of a pack of vicious killers in Quentin Tarantino's 1992 crime drama "Reservoir Dogs." Off-screen, the actor's arrests for drunken brawls at bars and Hollywood parties took a heavy toll on his once-promising Hollywood career in the 1950s. Booze was always at the root of his misbehavior.

The 845-word obit recounted Tierney's ups and downs, and his comeback in the 1980s. The sole Hollywood figure quoted in the piece attested to the fact that when Tierney "returned to Hollywood . . . he was much better behaved." Writer-producer-director-actor Michael Tierney said, "He was still Larry for those people who knew him. He was still a tough guy, but not in jail all the time or anything like that.

"The people who knew Larry knew that wasn't all there was to Larry," he said. "He was a wacky, kind of quirky, comical guy, and a very nice man to a lot of people."

There was no big Hollywood funeral for Lawrence Tierney, not even a movie buffs' event at the Hollywood Forever cemetery. Lawrence Tierney's cremains were not interred along with his parents and brother Gerard at Holy Cross Cemetery in Culver City, nor at the National Cemetery where Eddie rested. They were given to Michael.

There was a gathering of Tierney's family and friends at Michael's Hollywood apartment on the evening of March 16. There were photos on the wall and memorabilia on display. There was much drinking and many stories told. Tierney's daughter, Elizabeth, and his other nephews stopped in.

"I went to the wake," Todd Mecklem says. "There were quite a few people. It didn't seem like all that formal of an affair. It was more like a party of his friends, and pretty relaxed." Mecklem returned to Michael Tierney a 16mm reel of *Born to Kill* that Michael's uncle had loaned him.

Evicted opened the first annual Melbourne Underground Film Festival in Melbourne, Australia, on July 20, 2000. Terry Camilleri won the festival's award for Best Sleazy Actor. The screening extended Lawrence Tierney's movie career into its seventh decade. When the film had its first official release on May 4, 2004, Lawrence Tierney's movie career officially extended into the twenty-first century.

Epilogue

"From the moment I met him until his death, he always was in rental apartments—and of course, every apartment Larry lived in looked like a bomb had gone off," C. Courtney Joyner says. "When Larry lived behind the Hollywood library in that little apartment, I was in there trying to straighten things up in the kitchen. And I go, 'Larry, what is this?' 'Oh, yeah. I've been looking for that.' It was a royalty check from the Screen Actors Guild for Larry, for like seventeen thousand dollars—and it was stuck to the bottom of a tomato soup can. Larry made a substantial amount of money in his career. I mean, he didn't die broke."

It may have been a surprise to anyone who knew Lawrence Tierney at just about any time in his turbulent adult life that he had more to show for a fifty-eight-year film and television career than a body of work, police records, lurid headlines, colorful stories, and a load of dark regrets. In fact, despite his chosen lifestyle, Lawrence Tierney did leave an estate.

"I know that there are periods in his life when he was literally homeless on the streets of New York, during the wintertime, sleeping on the sidewalk under newspaper with snow falling on him. What did he do with his money during those days? I don't know," Timothy Tierney says. "But at the end of his life, he had a reasonable amount of money. His estate was worth about a quarter million bucks. I remember Larry saying to me that he was putting it all in bonds."

Regrets? He had a few.

"He never held back on self-recrimination," Joyner says. "In his reflective times, and we certainly shared a lot of those, Larry told me straight out that drinking was just poison to him. He said every conflict he'd ever had was tied to drinking. And when we were running around Hollywood making these B-movies and making a little bit of money, Larry got concerned that *I* was drinking too much. He'd say, 'You know, you're always at Boardner's, you're always . . .' He thought *I* was dipping in too much! And I listened to him. I always listened to him.

"Unfortunately, the things that made the headlines were all the hell-raising, incredible aspects, and violence. I was certainly in a front row seat for a lot of that. But people don't talk about the other side of him, and how unbelievably smart he was. He had a lot of the classic traits of alcoholism. He couldn't stand to be alone. But he was incredibly loyal. People he had known for fifty years, if he hadn't seen them in forty-five of those years, if they called Larry or needed anything, he was right on it. And boy, he was that way with me. Always."

"He didn't have to sleep on people's couches, but he didn't want to be alone," David Del Valle says. "When he was staying with me, one of his recurring dreams was about his mother. He believed his mother committed suicide over his indiscretions. And Larry would still have nightmares about that. He would wake up in the middle of the night.

"He had all these issues, I think, because he was born with everything a man could want to have a good life. And he had a decidedly colorful life. But he caused a lot of misery, in his view."

Timothy Tierney chooses his words when asked about his uncle's legacy. "Larry was hailed as a very talented and emotionally forceful actor who turned in some great performances. So as a member of the family, I'm very pleased and proud of that. But then, when I think about Larry, I think how it's often said that genius and madness are married together. They're opposite sides of the same coin, and Larry really personified that. And that madness was not only self-destructive, but it caused a lot of destruction to other people in the family. He was a tough guy and he wasn't one to show his feelings, but he suffered just like the people around him suffered. And that's very regrettable. Now that he's gone, all the bad stuff he did, in a way, makes him more amusing to recall. It's all funny now. But it wasn't funny at the time, going through all that stuff."

In the months following Lawrence Tierney's death, Michael Tierney flew to New York City with a portion of his uncle's cremains. The nephew scattered some of the ashes around Ninth Avenue in Hell's Kitchen—near where Tierney had been gut-stabbed thirty years earlier—and crossed the bridge to Brooklyn, and the corner of Avenue S and East Thirty-Fifth Street, where he met his cousins Danny and Eddie Leahy inside the Mariners Inn bar.

"Me and my brother said, 'Can we get some ashes?'" Eddie recalls. "So we got a couple of cups and he poured some in for each of us."

Danny remembers that he held onto the ashes until a special holiday. "I think it was about a year after he died, I know for a fact that it was St. Patrick's Day, and the bar was the Mariners. I had a bag on. I was with a couple of friends."

"We were all drinking," Eddie says, "and all of a sudden, my brother Dan turned around. 'Come on, we'll go to the park. We'll spread Larry in Brooklyn!'"

Danny and his friend Kevin Murray, the quarterback from their old bar league football team, hustled out of the joint and made it as far as the sidewalk. "They had the cup, a couple of ounces of his ashes, and my brother said, 'Okay, here's to Larry!' And the winds are blowing and my brother says he threw the ashes in the air—" Eddie can't stop laughing now, "—and the ashes are coming back at 'em! The wind swept the ashes right into their faces! And my quarterback is laughing his ass off!"

"Kevin goes, 'Oh shit! I can't see, I can't see!'" Danny says. "Half went in his eyes, half went in his mouth!"

Eddie is howling with laughter. "He goes, 'Jesus Christ! *I just ate Larry Tierney!*'"

"Then we went to Kevin's brother Timmy's house, who's a retired fireman," Danny continues. "I think there was a pay-per-view fight on TV. I had the rest of the ashes and I said, 'Hey, what the hell? Let's scatter them here.' So Timmy Murray scattered the rest of the ashes right in front of his house on Stuart Street. That was the end of the line with his ashes."

Not quite.

Eddie Leahy didn't toss his portion of Lawrence Tierney's ashes. "I kept him on my dresser with my father's picture. I covered the cup with some aluminum foil and I put a crucifix on top of it—to remind Larry that God was watching. I had it on my dresser for years and years. I moved two times, and I always had it at a certain spot.

"I kept them in my house until two years ago," he says in 2021. "And then I went upstate to meet a dear old friend there. I hadn't seen her in fifty years, and I thought when I go up there to New Paltz, I'm going to bring him up to the country and maybe put him somewhere.

"We were sitting by the Wallkill River and the river was so peaceful, I turned to her and I said, 'Don't mind me, but I got my cousin in my bag.' She said, 'What are you talking about?' I said, 'I got my cousin Larry's ashes here. I was going to bury him in my parents' plot, but I don't want my father to get mad.' She started laughing. She goes, 'What do you mean?' I said, 'My father was a cop and Larry was a cop *beater*.' I showed her a picture of Lawrence

Tierney. I told her who he was. 'You know, Elaine's father from *Seinfeld, Reservoir Dogs.*' And I said, 'I'm going to put him in the river, let him be free. He'll be free.' So I crossed the bridge, went to the bank of the river, and I took the contents and I emptied them in the river.

"And I just stood there and I crossed myself and said a little prayer for him. I said, 'Larry, you're free now.'"

Acknowledgments

The writing of *Lawrence Tierney: Hollywood's Real-Life Tough Guy* relied on the recollections and reportage of many of Lawrence Tierney's contemporaries, friends, and fans. Special thanks go to Timothy Tierney, C. Courtney Joyner, David Del Valle, Scott Alexander, Todd Mecklem, and Michael Madsen, for their generosity, insight, assistance, and willingness to go that extra step to create a full picture of the man. Many thanks to Ashley Runyon, director of the University Press of Kentucky, who saw the value of this project, Screen Classics Series editor Patrick McGilligan, and the University Press team, including Victoria Robinson, Meredith Daugherty, David L. Cobb, and Janet Yoe, whose expertise improved upon it.

Alison Holloway, Jeff Abraham, Alan Bisbort, Peter Brennan, Doug Bruckner, Rick Casados, Jon Crowley, Michael Dabin, Sasha Feiler, Chris Gardner, Frank Grimes, Amy Haben, Molly Haigh, Tom Hearn, Sally Jade Kearns, Sam Kearns, Matt Lubich, Gillian McCain, Legs McNeil, Melissa Montero, Ray Richmond, Margo Tiffen, Raquel Vasquez, Danny Wolf, and Elli Wohlgelernter contributed invaluable support along the way. Among those who were generous with their time and recollections were Derek Bell, Ray Boylan, Brian Brookshire, Jeff Burr, Cornelius Byrne, Carroll Coates, Julie Davis, Cynthia Fuller, Chris Gore, AnnMarie Frisina Guertin, Will Huston, Larry Karaszewski, Terrill Lee Lankford, Daniel Leahy, Edward Leahy, Christopher LeClaire, Donald McManamon, Michael Madsen, Stephan Morrow, Patton Oswalt, Elisabeth Sikes, Will Thimes, and Ron Zwang.

Most helpful were the ones whose quotes, writings, photographs, and other works cast light on unexplored corners of Tierney's life, times, and struggles; among them Michael Tierney, Jason Alexander, Joseph B. Atkins, Ira Steven Behr, Peter Biskind, Tom Cherones, John A. Gallagher, Barry Gifford, Gabrielle Glaser, Charles Heard, David Konow, Ernest Kurtz, Rick McKay, Julia Louis-Dreyfus, Skip E. Lowe, Gregory William Mank, Alison Martino, Eddie

Muller, Cheryl Murphy, Michael Murphy, Dr. Jason A. Ney, Bill Nelson, Tim Roth, Alan K. Rode, Todd Rutt, Jerry Seinfeld, Bryan Senn, David Spaner, Gary Sweeney, Quentin Tarantino, Scott Voison, Laura Wagner, Josh Weinstein, Michael J. Welden, Mark David Welsh, and Shelley Winters.

This book would not have been published if not for the efforts and brilliance of my literary agent Lee Sobel, the first industry professional I encountered who recognized the importance of a book about Lawrence Tierney, and who in fact was attempting to get one off the ground when we connected. Lee's work with Sylvain Sylvain convinced me that he was the man for this project. His guidance, suggestions, and support proved me right.

And thanks to Larry—Lawrence Tierney—a man whose life was tragic, yet in many ways heroic, a powerful actor whom I met, and yes, drank with, shortly after the release of *Reservoir Dogs*. He was just another old guy, seated alongside me at the bar of the Formosa Cafe on Santa Monica Boulevard. I remember that Larry introduced himself, shook my hand firmly, and throughout the evening and numerous rounds, was friendly, witty, and a perfect gentleman. There were no brawls.

Source Notes

Chapter 1

Tierney family and childhood

Brooklyn in Tierney's childhood: "Valentine's City of New York: A Guide Book: Our Sister Boroughs," reprinted in "A 1920s Tourist Guide to Brooklyn," by Jen Carlson in the *Gothamist,* January 23, 2014.

Tierney family and family anecdotes: Author interviews with Timothy Tierney, February, July, October 2021; Timothy Tierney and Michael Tierney interview, *The Midnight Palace with Gary Sweeney* radio show, circa 2011; birth, census, marriage, other records, Ancestry.com.

"Everything we do goes back to our mother." Author interview with David Del Valle, May 18, 2021.

Death of Tim Crowley: Author interviews with Timothy Tierney; *The Midnight Palace* interviews with Timothy and Michael Tierney; Tim Crowley death notice, *Brooklyn Daily Eagle,* October 3, 1939.

Lawrence Hugh Tierney, chief of NY Aqueduct Police: *Herald Statesman,* Yonkers, NY, June 28, 1939, and other newspaper accounts from newspapers.com; "City to Augment Watershed Guard," *New York Times,* July 5, 1941.

Boys High School: NY Architecture website.

Boys High School curriculum: *You Never Leave Brooklyn: The Autobiography of Emanuel Celler* by Emanuel Celler, John Day Company, 1953; *Jewish Times: Voices of the American Jewish Experience* by Howard Simons, Anchor, 1990.

Tierney's hand injury, first newspaper appearance: *Herald Statesman,* Yonkers, NY, August 18, 1937; Author interviews with Timothy Tierney, February, July, October, December 2021.

Tierney enters college: "Manhattan College Lists 18 from City in Freshman Class," *Herald Statesman,* Yonkers, NY, September 21, 1937.

Tierney's athletic and work history: "The Bottle Has Kept Larry 'Dillinger' Tierney in Trouble, But Now He's Trying to Be a Good Boy," Sheilah Graham interview, syndicated column in the *Courier-Journal,* Louisville, KY, June 4, 1950.

Source Notes

Tierney's early career and "discovery"

First foray into acting: Rutgers Nielson press release, in Wood Soanes's article, "Curtain Calls: Incredible Seems the Word for Tierney," *Oakland (CA) Tribune*, February 18, 1947.

Tierney's debut in *War Wife*: *NY Daily News*, April 27, 29, May 3, 1943; *New York Times*, "Premiere Tonight for Whalen Play; Irish-American Group Will Present 'War Wife' at the Malin Studio Theatre," April 29, 1943.

Tierney as "Errol Flynn, years younger and without a yacht!": Leonard Lyons, The Lyons Den, syndicated column, *Syracuse Post-Standard*, June 9, 1949; Will Whalen death report: "Hermit Priest-Actor Found Dead in Blaze," *NY Daily News*, July 4 1949.

Tierney signs with RKO: Rutgers Nielson, in Wood Soanes's article, "Curtain Calls: Incredible Seems the Word for Tierney," *Oakland (CA) Tribune*, February 18, 1947.

Tierney at RKO

Tierney talks of signing: Lawrence Tierney interview, *Skip E. Lowe Looks at Hollywood*, Los Angeles public access television, circa 1987.

Friendship with Val Lewton at RKO: Author interviews with David Del Valle, 2021; author interview with C. Courtney Joyner, Smokehouse Restaurant, Burbank, July 16, 2021; Tierney interview with Michael and Cheryl Murphy, "The Devil Thumbs His Nose!!! To Hell and Back with Lawrence Tierney," *Psychotronic Video* magazine no. 8, Fall 1990.

"If you see Kay . . .": Author interview with Derek Bell, March 17, 2021; *Ulysses* by James Joyce, Vintage, NY, 1961; Facts about Bloomsday and Joyce's Ulysses, Interesting Literature website.

First publicity and false explanation of rejection by armed forces: "Stage Door Johnny Gets Bid to Act," *Salt Lake Tribune*, September 15, 1944.

Tierney seeks out *Dillinger* audition: Author interview with C. Courtney Joyner, March 8, 2021; Tierney interview with Michael and Cheryl Murphy, *Psychotronic Video* magazine no. 8, Fall 1990.

Chapter 2

Dillinger

Poverty Row: 1920s Film History, Filmsite, filmsite.org/20sintro.html; *Early Poverty Row Studios* by E. J. Stephens and Marc Wanamaker, Arcadia, 2014.

The King Brothers: "Kozinsky Brothers . . . super uncolossal," The Home Front by Tom Treanor, *Los Angeles Times*, November 12, 1941; Interview with Philip Yordan, *Backstory 2: Interviews with Screenwriters of the 1940s and 1950s* by Patrick McGilligan, University of California Press, 1991; *The Philip Yordan Story* by Alan K. Rode, Film Noir Foundation website.

Hays Office banning films about John Dillinger: *AFI Catalog of Motion Pictures Produced in the United States: Feature Films 1941–1950: Dillinger,* University of California Press, 1999.

Dillinger robbery scene lifted from Fritz Lang's *You Only Live Once*: Ibid, page 613.

Tierney threatening Anne Jeffreys on *Dillinger* set: "The Original Tess Trueheart: A Conversation with Anne Jeffreys," interview by Jason A. Ney, *Noir City* magazine, no. 15, Spring 2015.

Tierney seeing his image on billboard he helped erect: Walter J. Hackett, Walt in Hollywood, *Lansing (MI) State Journal,* August 5, 1945; Patricia Clary, Hollywood Film Shop, United Press, *Hobart (OK) Democrat Chief,* September 17, 1945.

Chapter 3

Dillinger premiere

Tierney credited as "Larry Tierney" in *Birthday Blues* short: Birthday Blues (1945), IMDbPro.

First review of *Dillinger*: "No. 1 entertainment for thrill-lovers," Jimmie Fidler's "pic of week," syndicated column, *Capital Times,* Madison, WI, March 22, 1945.

Tierney signed for second picture at Monogram: Sheilah Graham, Glimpses of Hollywood, syndicated column, *Atlanta Constitution,* March 28, 1945.

Dillinger world premiere in Cincinnati, OH, "An o.k. gangster picture," first review, comparison to Humphrey Bogart: "*Dillinger,* Strand," E. B. Radcliffe, *Cincinnati Enquirer,* April 7, 1945.

"*Dillinger* Opens at Victoria Theatre, NYC: At the Victoria," *New York Times,* April 26, 1945; "Melodrama of 'Dillinger' on at The Victoria," *NY Daily News,* April 26, 1945.

Sudden stardom

Dillinger NYC premiere sets box office records: "'Dillinger' Tierney Gets R. K. O. Stardom Nod," Edwin Schallert, *Los Angeles Times,* May 3, 1945.

RKO-Radio Pictures demands $35,000 to loan Tierney for second Monogram picture: "$100 'Bargain,'" Jimmie Fidler in Hollywood, syndicated column, *Sioux City (IA) Journal,* May 12, 1945.

Drinking and fighting—first incidents

Shelley Winters recalls VE-Day and her night with Tierney: chap. 10, *Shelley: Also Known as Shirley,* William Morrow, 1980.

Tierney fined for public drunkenness on May 22 and June 5, 1945: revealed in *LA Daily News* and *Los Angeles Times,* July 28, 1945.

Dillinger's spree

Dillinger inspires lawlessness: "Dillinger Film Gave Teen-Age Robbers Tips on How to Be 'More Professional,'" Associated Press story in *Louisville (KY) Courier-Journal,* July 21, 1945.

Dillinger's sister sues to stop film: "Sister Sues to Ban Movie on Dillinger," *Indianapolis Star,* July 8, 1945.

Dillinger history, family roadshow: "Dillinger Family 'Packs 'Em In,'" (photograph), *Telegraph-Forum,* Bucyrus, OH, July 31, 1934; "Dillingers Go on Spiel Tour," by Walter Dustmann, United Press staff correspondent, *Macon Chronicle Herald,* October 16, 1937.

Dillinger to gross $2.5 million on $90,000 budget: *Evening Sun,* Baltimore, MD, July 27, 1945.

Tierney's first jail sentence

Tierney arrested in "strangling condition," sentenced to 10 days in jail: *LA Daily News* and *Los Angeles Times,* July 28, 1945.

First merging of Tierney and his role as Dillinger: Jimmie Fidler in Hollywood, syndicated column, *Lancaster (PA) New Era,* August 13, 1945.

Jimmie Fidler–Errol Flynn animosity

Fidler testifies at Senate hearing: "Willkie Refuses to Attend Hearing," Paul W. Ward, *Sun,* Baltimore, MD, September 16, 1941.

Errol Flynn attacks Fidler over Senate testimony: "Fidler and Wife Draw Blood Fighting Flynn," Frederick C. Othman (United Press), *Salt Lake Tribune,* September 22, 1941; "Flynn Says No Punch Fidler Again, But He's Still Mad," Othman (United Press), *Salt Lake Tribune,* October 1, 1941.

Tierney gets more prime roles

Tierney's *Step By Step* and *Deadlier Than the Male* movies postponed for Western: "'Dillinger' Tierney to Enact Jesse James," Edwin Schallert, *Los Angeles Times,* September 15, 1945.

"Brooklyn cowboy" Tierney films *Badman's Territory*: Tierney interview with Michael and Cheryl Murphy, *Psychotronic Video* magazine no. 8, Fall 1990.

Tierney displays "enthusiasm" on set of *Step by Step*: *Step by Step* (1946) details, IMDbPro.

Tierney and *Lost Weekend* "moral": Jimmie Fidler, syndicated column, *Capital Times,* Madison, WI, November 30, 1945.

"Drinking started out as a celebratory thing": Author interview with David Del Valle, October 6, 2021.

Chapter 4

The Bundy Drive Boys

Background of John Decker and Errol Flynn's "club": *Hollywood's Hellfire Club* by Gregory William Mank with Charles Heard and Bill Nelson, Feral House, 2007.

"Mona" coming-out party and the Battle of Decker's Lawn: Ibid., chap. 19: 1946.

Diana Barrymore slaps Tierney: *Too Much, Too Soon* by Diana Barrymore and Gerold Frank, chap. 21, Henry Holt, 1957.

Battle of Decker's Lawn: "Hollywood Stars Slug It Out as Fight Ends Party," United Press report in *Battle Creek (MN) Enquirer,* January 19, 1946; "'Defending Flynn,' Says Actor in Row," International News Service report, *Pittsburgh Sun-Telegraph,* January 20, 1946.

Source Notes

Dillinger Academy Award nomination

Dillinger's "super surprise" Academy Award nomination for Best Original Screenplay: "Motion Picture Academy Selects Lists of "Bests,'" *Los Angeles Times,* January 28, 1946.

Hella Crossley incident/violence

Tierney beating of Paul de Loqueyssie over Hella Crossley: "Socking Actor Costs Tierney Fine of $600," *Valley Times,* North Hollywood CA, November 21, 1946.

Jimmie Fidler blames Hollywood: Jimmie Fidler in Hollywood, syndicated column, *Mercury,* Pottstown, PA, February 12, 1946.

Eighteenth Academy Awards

Dillinger loses, "cheated" out of Oscar: Interview with Philip Yordan, *Backstory 2: Interviews with Screenwriters of the 1940s and 1950s* by Patrick McGilligan, University of California Press, 1991.

El Mocambo arrest and sentencing

Tierney drunk arrest at Mocambo: "Film 'Dillinger' Booked on Drunk Charge," *Los Angeles Times,* March 11, 1946.

Tierney sentencing: "Lawrence Tierney Goes on Water Wagon," International News Service report, *Deseret News,* Salt Lake City, UT, March 27, 1946; "Lawrence Tierney Put on 2-Year Probation," *Green Bay (WI) Press-Gazette,* March 27, 1946.

Tierney and Alcoholics Anonymous

Alcoholics Anonymous pros and cons: *The Big Book* by Bill W., Alcoholics Anonymous World Services, 4th ed., 2002; *Not-God: History of Alcoholics Anonymous* by Ernest Kurtz, Hazelden, 1991; "The Irrationality of Alcoholics Anonymous" by Gabrielle Glaser, *Atlantic,* April 2015.

Studio campaign to overhaul reputation

Tierney stops barfight: Harrison Carroll in Hollywood, syndicated item, *Wilkes Barre (PA) Record,* April 9, 1946.

Tierney's father arrives to help son: Erskine Johnson in Hollywood, syndicated item in *Pampa (TX) Daily News,* April 14, 1946.

Tierney and Anne Jeffreys onstage with *Badman's Territory*: "Stars On Hand Tuesday to Attend Movie," *Salt Lake Tribune,* April 18, 1946; "Stars in Salt Lake for Premiere of Picture Showing," *Salt Lake Telegram,* April 22, 1946.

Tierney begins filming *Deadlier Than the Male (Born to Kill)* with Robert Wise: Dorothy Manners in Hollywood, Louella Parsons's syndicated column, *Philadelphia Inquirer,* April 20, 1946; Author interview with David Del Valle, October 6, 2021.

Brother Gerard Tierney arrives in Hollywood

Gerard Tierney gets screen test: Item, *Star Tribune,* Minneapolis, MN, July 7, 1946.

Further film work

Tierney complains he was underpaid for *Dillinger*: Hollywood Today by Sheilah Graham, syndicated item in *Asbury Park (NJ) Press,* May 15, 1946.

Tierney begins filming *The Devil Thumbs a Ride*: *Los Angeles Times,* June 26, 1946.

Step by Step opens in New York City: *New York Times* review by "T.M.P.," August 26, 1946.

Tierney begins production on *A Prison Story (San Quentin)*: "Tierney into 'Prison,'" *Variety,* August 7, 1946.

Chapter 5

Hollywood Receiving Hospital arrest and sentence

Tierney arrested for drunkenness at Hollywood Receiving Hospital: "Actor Tierney to Fight Case Periling Liberty," *Los Angeles Times,* August 20, 1946; "Lawrence Tierney Released on Bail," *Valley Times,* North Hollywood, CA, August 20, 1946.

Tierney convicted of drunkenness charge: "Court Holds Actor Tierney Was Drunk," *Los Angeles Times,* September 24, 1946.

Tierney sentenced to five days in jail: "Actor Tierney Gets Jail Term," *Los Angeles Times,* October 9, 1946; "Actor Put in Drunk Tank 5 Days to Study Alcoholics," *Pittsburgh Press,* October 9, 1946.

Jimmie Fidler commentary: syndicated column, *Durham (NC) Sun,* October 15, 1946.

Sunset Strip spree

Tierney rampage on the Sunset Strip: "Tierney Again Finds Trouble," United Press report, *Hanford (CA) Sentinel,* October 17, 1946; "Tierney Wins Brush with Law: 'Dillinger' Gets Off with Scolding," International News Service report, *Tampa Daily Times,* October 19, 1946.

Hella Crossley incident goes to court

De Loqueyssie lawsuit in court: "Try for Phone Number to Cost Tierney $600," *Los Angeles Times,* November 21, 1946.

Hella Crossley testifies that Tierney struck her dog: "Movie Tough No Lothario: He Pays $600," *Oakland Tribune,* November 21, 1946.

Tierney on East Coast

New York City sightings: Hollywood Today by Sheilah Graham, *Asbury Park (NJ) Press,* November 23, 1946; "Hollywood 'Bad Boy' Quotes Shakespeare, Bible on Dates," by Dorothy Kilgallen, Minneapolis *Star Tribune,* November 30, 1946; Little Old New York column by Ed Sullivan, *NY Daily News,* November 30, 1946.

Onstage in Boston with San Quentin: "Ex-Warden, Screen Plug-Uglies Aid 'San Quentin' Preview Here," by Marjory Adams, *Boston Globe,* December 4, 1946; "RKO-Boston 'San Quentin' Stage Show," by Marjory Adams, *Boston Globe,* December 6, 1946.

Chapter 6

East Coast tour continues

RKO publicity: "New Faces Brighten Film Fare" by Melrose Gower, syndicated item, *Salt Lake Tribune,* January 12, 1947.

Henry Sturman fight

Arrested for hotel brawl with ex-boxer: "Film Dillinger Loses Hotel Fight Decision," *NY Daily News,* January 13, 1947; "Movie Dillinger Finds He Isn't Really So Tough," *Dispatch,* Moline, IL, January 13, 1947.

Fight "witness" Silvio Domenico tries to sell testimony: "Charge of Perjury Enlivens Film Dillinger Court Drama," *NY Daily News,* January 15, 1947.

Domenico revealed as mobster: "Lombardo Puts Finger on Valenti in Evans Murder," Murder by Ray Sprigle, *Pittsburgh Post-Gazette,* April 5, 1951.

Vivi Stokes

Tierney first seen with socialite Vivi Stokes: Broadway by Dorothy Kilgallen, syndicated column item, *Pittsburgh Post-Gazette,* January 18, 1947.

Vivi Stokes background: "Things Not Jake with Jakie," Lenore Lemmon Webb, *San Francisco Examiner,* April 18, 1943; Cholly Knickerbocker Observes, syndicated column, *San Francisco Examiner,* December 29, 1947; Vivian Stokes Crespi obituary, *New York Times,* July 20, 2014.

Tierney "madly in love" with "Vivi": Louella Parsons Keeping Up with Hollywood, syndicated column, *Cumberland (MD) News,* January 28, 1947.

San Quentin tour continues

Studios share responsibility for Tierney's misdeeds: Jimmie Fidler in Hollywood, syndicated column, *Sioux City (IA) Journal,* January 21, 1947.

Tierney's *San Quentin* tour pays off: "Star's Appearance Proves Chicago 'San Quentin' Aid," *Showmen's Trade Review,* March 15, 1947.

Tierney shows bad behavior pays: Hollywood Gossip by Erskine Johnson, syndicated column, *Public Opinion,* Chambersburg, PA, January 31, 1947.

Tierney in Midwest: "Ex-Convict's Story Told in Prison Movie 'San Quentin,'" *Chicago Daily Tribune,* January 30, 1947; Let's Go Places with Arthur S. Kany, *Dayton Herald,* February 3, 1947.

Tierney gets candid in interview: "Movie Actor Tells of Battles On and Off Screen," Myles Standish, the Everyday Magazine in the *St. Louis Post-Dispatch,* February 13, 1947.

"Incidentally, Tierney is no relation of Gene Tierney": "Curtain Calls: Incredible Seems the Word for Tierney," Wood Soanes, *Oakland Tribune,* February 18, 1947.

Source Notes

Chapter 7

Midwest tour, continued

Near arrest in Baltimore: Dorothy Kilgallen, syndicated column, Minneapolis *Star Tribune*, March 3, 1947.

The Devil Thumbs a Ride opens

"Gives the movies a black eye and us a pain in the neck": "Deadhead," *The Devil Thumbs a Ride* review by Bosley Crowther, *New York Times*, March 22, 1947.

"Lawrence Tierney is at his most vicious and amoral": *The Devil Thumbs A Ride & Other Unforgettable Films* by Barry Gifford, Grove, 1988.

"I didn't like it at all . . . I thought of myself as a nice guy": "Down These Mean Streets: Lawrence Tierney interviewed by Rick McKay," *Scarlet Street* magazine, issue 29, 1998.

Tierney at opening of Alisal Theatre in Salinas, CA: "Lawrence Tierney Coming Here," *Californian*, Salinas, CA, April 9, 1947; "Will Open New Salinas Theatre," United Press report, *Santa Cruz Sentinel*, April 10, 1947; Alisal Theatre, *Cinema Treasures*.

Sentenced to county jail

Jailed on probation violation: "4 Week-Ends in Jail Decreed for Tierney," Associated Press item, *Knoxville News Sentinel*, April 17, 1947.

"He's not really a bad boy—he's just a little wild": "Hollywood Is Fond of Brooklyn's Lawrence Tierney and Pulls for Him," Jack Lait Jr., *Brooklyn Daily Eagle*, April 20, 1947.

Born to Kill opens

"A smeary tabloid tale": *Born to Kill* review by Bosley Crowther, *New York Times*, May 1, 1947.

Street fight with brother Ed

Sentenced to 90 days for brawl: "Tierney Fights Brother; Gets 90 Days in Jail," *Los Angeles Times*, May 2, 1947; "Films' Dillinger Gets 90 Days for Latest Outburst," United Press report, *Gazette*, Cedar Rapids, IA, May 2, 1947.

Tierney pictured sleeping on mattress on jailhouse floor: "Tierney Sleeps on Jailhouse Floor," United Press report, *Wilmington (CA) Daily Press Journal*, May 2, 1947.

Sentenced for fight with Ed Tierney: "Lawrence Tierney Fined $25, Given Another 90 Days," International News Service report, *Dispatch*, Moline, IL, May 10, 1947.

The Drunk Farm

Tierney transferred to Sheriff's Honor Farm: "Tierney Going to Castaic Camp," *Los Angeles Times*, May 16, 1947.

"They think . . . heroic roles can . . . turn him into a good citizen": Hedda Hopper's Hollywood, syndicated column, *Harrisburg (PA) Telegraph*, May 3, 1947.

Source Notes

"Proper place for Lawrence Tierney is a sanitarium": "Screen Drunk Needs Discipline" by Jimmie Fidler, Fidler in Hollywood, syndicated column, *Herald-News,* Passaic, NJ, May 12, 1947.

Probation violation hearing: "Actor Tierney Facing New Prospect of Jail," United Press report, *San Bernardino County Sun,* May 22, 1947.

Tierney dropped by RKO: "Lawrence Tierney off RKO Payroll" by Jimmie Fidler, syndicated column, *Herald-News,* Passaic, NJ, May 24, 1947.

Chapter 8

Tierney at Drunk Farm

Downside of celebrity status ("Shovel this shit, *Dillinger!*"): Author email exchange with Timothy Tierney, August 19, 2021.

Tierney as Alcoholics Anonymous speaker: Exclusive report in Voice of Broadway by Dorothy Kilgallen syndicated column, *Wilkes-Barre (PA) Record,* June 17, 1947.

Tierney's father pleads for son's parole: "Tierney Freed," *Los Angeles Times,* June 18, 1947; "Board Grants Pardon to Film Actor," June 18 1947; "Movie Badman Freed from County Jail," *Dayton (OH) Herald,* June 18, 1947.

Tierney walks out of prison farm, whistling: "Screen 'Bad Man' Says Drinking at End," *Albuquerque Journal,* June 19, 1947; "Tierney Free Again," wire service photo, *Circleville (OH) Herald,* June 21, 1947.

Tierney's alcoholism

Tierney's planned "Temperance Tour": Louella Parsons syndicated column, *San Francisco Examiner,* June 24, 1947; "Tierney's Proposal Ridiculous," Fidler in Hollywood by Jimmie Fidler, syndicated column, *Herald-News* (Passaic, NJ), July 9, 1947.

"Vicarious compensation for emotional frustration": "Lawrence Tierney's Big Problem," Burton Rascoe, *American Weekly, Pittsburgh Sun-Telegraph,* August 10, 1947.

Vivi Stokes comes to Tierney's aid: Hollywood on Tour by Hedda Hopper, syndicated column, *NY Daily News,* August 5, 1947.

Tierney as "good boy": Hollywood by Sheilah Graham, syndicated column in *Pittsburgh Post-Gazette,* September 9, 1947.

Incident at Mocambo: "Bar Stool Starts Row," *San Pedro News,* September 10, 1947; "Former Georgia Tech, Southern California Grid Players Battle It Out in Hollywood," *Greenville (SC) News,* September 11, 1947.

Gerard Tierney makes movie debut as "Gerard Gilbert": Films role in *The Counterfeiters,* September 1947, IMDbPro.

Tierney on outs with Vivi Stokes: Louella Parsons in Hollywood Says, syndicated column, *Scranton (PA) Tribune,* September 20, 1947.

Tierney disguised as Gargantua: "Camera Clambake," Looking at Hollywood by Hedda Hopper, syndicated column, *Chicago Tribune,* October 22, 1947; "Beauty and the Beast," photo, *Photoplay,* October 22, 1947.

Tierney opposes proposed Al Capone films: "Worried about Effect on Juveniles, Johnson's Dander Up over Capone Picture," by Erskine Johnson, syndicated column, *Springfield (MO) Press and Leader,* November 2, 1947.

RKO rehires Tierney at "reduced wage": Hollywood by Hugh Dixon, syndicated column, *Pittsburgh Post-Gazette,* November 6, 1947; Jimmie Fidler Behind The Scenes, syndicated column, *Mercury,* Pottstown, PA, December 6, 1947.

Tierney drinking on Death Valley junket: "Trip to a Silver Mine" by Lowell E. Redelings, The Hollywood Scene, *Hollywood City News,* September 23, 1947; Looking at Hollywood by Hedda Hopper, syndicated column, *Chicago Tribune,* September 25, 1947.

Confrontation with Audie Murphy: Edith Gwynn's Hollywood, syndicated column, *Cincinnati Enquirer,* November 7, 1947; "Audie Murphy, A War Hero Who Met Defeat in Hollywood," *Record,* Hackensack, NJ, June 1, 1971; Author's email exchange with Timothy Tierney, August 19, 2021.

Chapter 9

Adrift

Comparison to Errol Flynn: Hollywood by Hedda Hopper, syndicated column, *NY Daily News,* January 4, 1948.

Tierney rehired, but not cast, by RKO: Hollywood Today by Sheilah Graham, syndicated column, *Scranton Times,* January 14, 1948.

"up to gossip columnists to keep his name out there": Movieland, Its People and Products by Jimmie Fidler, syndicated column, *Post Crescent,* Zanesville, OH, January 22, 1948;

Hollywood by Harrison Carroll, syndicated column, *Evening Independent,* Massillon, OH, January 27, 1948; Louella Parsons in Hollywood, syndicated column, *Pittsburgh Sun-Telegraph,* January 28, 1948.

Fight with William Goldy

Arrested after Barney's Beanery fight: "Tierney Again in Legal Toils after Brawl," *Los Angeles Times,* February 25, 1948; "Actor Tierney in 1-Puncher," *NY Daily News,* February 25, 1948.

Assault and battery charge: "Screen Dillinger Is Having Further Fistic Troubles," International News Service report, *Muncie Evening Press,* February 25, 1948; "Tierney Surrenders to Officers after Brawl," *Valley Times,* February 25, 1948; "Actor Lawrence Tierney Arrested for Fighting," Associated Press report, *Harrisburg (PA) Evening News,* February 25, 1948; "Pleads Innocent," United Press report, *Wilmington (CA) Daily Press Journal,* March 2, 1948.

Goldy sues Tierney for $100,000: "Files Damage Suit," *Wilmington (CA) Daily Press Journal,* March 6, 1948.

Source Notes

Scott Brady

Gerard Tierney changes name to "Scott Brady": In Hollywood by Erskine Johnson, syndicated column, *Cumberland (MD) Evening Times*, March 15, 1948; "Scott Brady Makes Good in First Film," Edith Gwynn, syndicated story, *Wisconsin State Journal*, Madison, WI, March 16, 1948.

Tierney's movie career resumes

RKO announces *Bodyguard*: "Lawrence Tierney to Star in Two Pictures for R-K-O," *Valley Times*, North Hollywood, CA, March 23, 1948.

Sightings at bars and nightclubs: Broadway by Danton Walker, syndicated column, *NY Daily News*, March 23, 1948; It Happened Last Night by Earl Wilson, *Courier Post*, Camden, NJ, March 23, 1948; In Hollywood by Erskine Johnson, syndicated column, *Daily Tribune*, Wisconsin Rapids, WI, March 29, 1948.

Bodyguard production: "Fleischer Chosen to Direct Tierney in 'Bodyguard,'" *Valley Times*, North Hollywood, CA, April 2, 1948.

Rumors of drinking: "Liquor on his breath": Author interview with C. Courtney Joyner, July 16, 2021; "Lawrence Tierney Finds Drunks Do Queer Things" by Earl Wilson, syndicated column, *Miami News*, June 10, 1948.

Goldy drops lawsuit: "Bartender Withdraws Suit against Tierney," Associated Press report, *Bristol (TN) News Bulletin*, June 11, 1948.

Tierney injured on *Bodyguard* set: Jimmie Fidler, syndicated column, *Monroe (LA) News-Star*, June 30, 1948.

Chapter 10

"The Anti Tierney"

Scott Brady and *Canon City*: Author interviews with Timothy Tierney, 2021; Hollywood Today by Sheilah Graham, syndicated column, *Indianapolis Star*, July 20, 1948; "'Canon City' Star Hopes St. Jude Will Free Convict He Portrays," *Boston Globe*, July 20, 1948; "Young 'Canon City' Star Here in Off-Camera Role," Wanda Hale, *NY Daily News*, July 25, 1948.

Tierney dropped by RKO over "lost weekends": Jimmie Fidler in Hollywood, syndicated column, *Lancaster (PA) New Era*, July 6, 1948.

Tierney hires, fights with his bodyguard: Jimmie Fidler, syndicated column, *Indianapolis News*, July 29, 1948.

Santa Barbara arrest

Arrested for drunken disturbance at hotel: "Lawrence Tierney Is in Jail Again on Drunk Charge," *Californian*, Salinas, CA, August 3, 1948; "Bail Forfeited by Film Actor," *Los Angeles Times*, August 3, 1948; "Tierney 'Jugged' in Santa Barbara," *Pasadena Independent*, August 5, 1948.

"Tierney seems to be an incorrigible," Jimmie Fidler, syndicated column, *Indianapolis News*, August 11, 1948.

Tierney beaten by "old King Bourbon": Jack Koefed, *Miami Herald*, August 14, 1948.

Sympathy for Tierney's plight: In Hollywood by Sheilah Graham, syndicated column, *Tampa Times*, August 24, 1948.

Robert Mitchum arrest

Mitchum busted in marijuana raid: "Narcotics Arrest Smashes Film Career Says Mitchum," *Los Angeles Times*, September 2, 1948.

"We saved Lawrence Tierney's cell for you," news reports, *Robert Mitchum, Baby I Don't Care*, by Lee Server, St. Martin's, 2002.

RKO boss Howard Hughes cashes in on publicity: "'Rachel and Stranger' Unusual," *Los Angeles Times*, September 24, 1948; Rachel and the Stranger, *AFI Catalog of Motion Pictures Produced in the United States: Feature Films 1941–1950: Dillinger*, University of California Press, 1999.

Rita Johnson mystery

Rita Johnson injured at Chateau Marmont: "Police Probe Demanded: Rita Johnson near Death of Mystery Head Injury," INS report, *Fort Worth Star Telegram*, September 10, 1948; "Actress' Injury Probed: Rita Johnson Undergoes Surgery for Blood Clot," *Decatur Daily Review*, September 10, 1948; "Rita Johnson near Death, Mystery Blow Probed," *Miami News*, September 10, 1948; "Brain Surgery Performed," *Los Angeles Times*, September 10, 1948.

Tierney connection to Rita Johnson revealed: Hollywood by Edith Gwynn, syndicated column, *Mercury*, Pottstown, PA, October 28, 1948.

Tierney and Scott Brady proposed as *The Floyds of Oklahoma*: "Floyd Feature Proposed: Pretty Boy Floyd Narrative Maturing," Edwin Schallert, *Los Angeles Times*, September 11, 1948.

Rita Johnson emerges from coma: "Rita Johnson Breaks Coma after 16 Days," *Dothan (AL) Eagle*, September 23, 1948.

Mitchum plea: "Mitchum, 2 Others File Innocent Plea," Associated Press report, *Los Angeles Times*, September 30, 1948.

Tierney on social scene with Shelley Winters: Louella Parsons Hollywood, syndicated column, *Philadelphia Inquirer*, October 11, 1948; Hedda Hopper syndicated column, *Los Angeles Times*, October 11, 1948.

Chapter II

Tierney arrested on Catalina Island

Background on John Dillinger 1934 capture in Tucson: "Dillinger Gang Captured Here," *Arizona Daily Star*, Tucson, AZ, January 26, 1934; "Pima Bids for Dillinger Jurisdiction," *Telegraph-Forum*, Cyrus, OH, January 27, 1934; "Dillinger Captured in Tucson," Pima County Library; "Dillinger Arrested in Tucson," *Arizona Capitol Times*, January 4, 2011.

Background on jailer Andy Dobek: "Andy Dobek: A Character Study," *Arizona Daily Star,* July 2, 1944; "33 Democrats, 5 Republicans File for Pima County Offices," *Arizona Daily Star,* April 19, 1944; "Easy Street" (Dobek's street), *Arizona Daily Star.*

Catalina Island: Avalon Town, Catalina Island, David Rumsey Map Collection; History of Catalina Island, Catalina Island Company.

Tierney arrest on Catalina Island, Dobek as jailer: "Tierney in Difficulty: Film Dillinger Jailed by Original's Handler," *Los Angeles Times,* October 12, 1948; "Officer Who Jailed Tierney Arrested Dillinger," *Valley Times,* North Hollywood, CA, October 12, 1948; "Screen 'Dillinger' Arrested 9th Time," *San Francisco Examiner,* October 13, 1948.

Tierney sought for independent pictures: Remake of M, Hedda Hopper's Hollywood, syndicated column, *Star-Gazette,* Elmira, NY, October 30, 1948; *I Shot Jesse James,* Behind The Scenes In Hollywood by Harrison Carroll, syndicated column, *Daily Clintonian,* Clinton, IN, November 9, 1948.

Fidler compares Tierney to brother: Jimmie Fidler, syndicated column, *Miami Herald,* December 28, 1948.

Tierney loses *I Shot Jesse James* role: "Larry Tierney's Reputation Keeps Him Getting Role" by Erskine Johnson, syndicated column, *Daily Plainsman,* Huron, SD, December 5, 1948.

Chapter 12

Assault on taxi driver

Tierney attacks L.A. cab driver, drunk charge: "Lawrence Tierney Arrested Again," *Pomona (CA) Progress Bulletin,* January 4, 1949; "John Barleycorn Hangs Umpteenth KO on Tierney," *Akron Beacon Journal,* January 4, 1949.

Gives "OK" sign to photographers: "Lawrence Tierney Gets 'Bracelets,'" (wirephoto), *Dayton (OH) Herald,* January 4, 1949.

Judge gives him a break: "One More Chance," United Press report, *Scranton (PA) Tribune,* January 6, 1949; "Film Gangster Gets Suspended Term in Drunkenness Case," *Fresno Bee,* January 6, 1949.

Arrest costs Tierney *Inside Alcatraz* role: Louella Parsons, syndicated column, *Fresno Bee,* January 6, 1949.

Robert Mitchum trial

Mitchum trial opens: "Mitchum to Face Dope Trial Today," *NY Daily News,* January 10, 1949.

Attorney Jerry Geisler: "'Get Me Giesler!' Hollywood's First Superstar Lawyer," Steve Vaught, *Paradise Leased,* January 7, 2011; "Jerry Giesler, Superstar Lawyer, Dies at 75," *Chicago Tribune,* January 2, 1962.

Mitchum found guilty: "Robert Mitchum Found Guilty," *Los Angeles Times,* January 11, 1949.

Columnists react to Tierney and Mitchum: "Hollywood's '49 Epic—'I Was a Fugitive From a Resolution,'" by Erskine Johnson, syndicated column, *Enterprise Journal,*

McComb, MS, January 10, 1949; Jimmie Fidler in Hollywood, syndicated column, *Monroe (LA) News-Star,* January 18, 1949.

Mitchum and companions sentenced: "Mitchum Gets 60-Day Sentence," *Los Angeles Times,* February 10, 1949.

Selznick defends Mitchum: "Says Term Will Boost Mitchum: Selznick, Studio Boss, Thinks Star Will Leave Jail 'Bigger Than Ever,'" Associated Press report, *Green Bay Press-Gazette,* February 10, 1949.

Tierney and Scott Brady's film prospects

Tierney's troubles attributed to loss of Vivi Stokes: Broadway by Dorothy Kilgallen, syndicated column, *Pittsburgh Gazette,* January 19, 1949.

Tierney offered film role in Portugal: Hedda Hopper syndicated column, *Los Angeles Times,* February 8, 1949.

Jungle Storm (Kill or Be Killed) directed by Max Nossek: Louella Parsons syndicated column, *San Francisco Examiner,* February 26, 1949.

Fidler warnings about dangerous, "sick man": Jimmie Fidler in Hollywood, syndicated column, *Pasadena (CA) Independent,* February 27, 1949; *News-Star,* Monroe, LA, March 1, 1949.

Scott Brady gets seven-year deal with Universal-International: Hollywood Today by Louella Parsons, syndicated column, *Arizona Republic,* February 22, 1949.

Brady gives brother Ed a job as stand-in: Hollywood, Associated Press item, *Monrovia (CA) News-Post,* February 26, 1949.

Mitchum released from honor farm: "Robert Mitchum Was Released from Jail," Associated Press report, *Standard-Sentinel,* Stillwell, OK, March 31, 1949.

Tierney's father gets bit part in *Montana Belle:* Jimmie Fidler, syndicated column, *Lancaster (PA) New Era,* March 9, 1949.

Tierney's Portugal shoot: Hollywood Today by Sheilah Graham, syndicated column, *Indianapolis Star,* March 1, 1949.

Hedda Hopper reports Errol Flynn in Paris: Assignment Hollywood by Dorothy Manners, syndicated column, *Memphis Commercial Appeal,* Memphis, TN, May 23, 1949.

Tierney and Flynn drink at café in France: Author interview with Derek Bell, March 17, 2021.

Tierney returns to New York

Seen with hatcheck girl: It Happened One Night by Earl Wilson, syndicated column, *Courier-Post,* Camden NJ.

At Café Trouville, discussing revival of *The Last Mile:* Broadway by Danton Walker, *NY Daily News,* June 7, 1949.

Chapter 13

Disorderly conduct arrest in Weehawken, NJ

Arrested with four others after party: "Actor Tierney Arrested in Manhattan Brawl," United Press report, *Colton (CA) Courier*, June 9, 1949; "L. (Dillinger) Tierney Strikes Again," *NY Daily News*, June 10, 1949; "Actor Freed on Bail in Disorderly Conduct Case," International News Service report, *El Paso Herald Post*, June 10, 1949; "Tierney in Again, Puts Up Bail for 3 Others in Fight," International News Service report, *Courier-Post*, Camden, NJ, June 10, 1949.

Fans outside police court: "Actor Tierney Freed in Brawl," *NY Daily News*, June 14, 1949; "Free Tierney of Roughhouse Rap," International News Service report, *Long Beach (CA) Independent*, June 14, 1949.

Charge dismissed: "Tierney Acquitted in Brawl Arrest," *Los Angeles Times*, June 14, 1949.

Tierney loose in NYC

Scott Brady involvement: "Treasury Files Provide Material for Port of New York Film" by Louella Parsons, syndicated column, *Sacramento Bee*, June 15, 1949; Jimmie Fidler in Hollywood, syndicated column, *Pasadena Independent*, June 16, 1949; Hollywood Today by Sheilah Graham, syndicated column, *Indianapolis Star*, June 18, 1949.

Tierney reacts to Vivi Stokes marriage by sticking head in electric fan: Cholly Knickerbocker, syndicated column, *San Francisco Examiner*, July 19, 1949; Author visit to P. J. Clarke's saloon on Third Avenue, NYC, September 21, 2021.

Romance with Will Rogers's daughter Mary Rogers: Dorothy Kilgallen, syndicated column, *Tyler (TX) Morning Telegraph*, July 21, 1949.

Considers stay at Menninger Clinic: Hollywood by Sheilah Graham, syndicated column, *Times-Tribune*, Scranton, PA, August 3, 1949.

Tempestuous relationship with Mary Rogers: Voice of Broadway, Gossip in Gotham by Dorothy Kilgallen, syndicated column, *Wilkes-Barre Times Leader*, September 6, 1949; Hollywood by Edith Gwynn, syndicated column, *Mercury*, Pottstown, PA, September 14, 1949; Little Old New York by Ed Sullivan, *NY Daily News*, October 1, 1949; Hollywood by Erskine Johnson, syndicated column, *Bakersfield Californian*, October 11, 1949; Voice of Broadway, Broadway Bulletin by Dorothy Kilgallen, syndicated column, *News-Herald*, Franklin, PA, October 27, 1949.

Mitchum says Tierney is "very sick": Exclusive Robert Mitchum interview, Louella Parsons, syndicated column, *San Francisco Examiner*, October 30, 1949.

Tierney loses role in *Chicago Story* play: Louella Parsons syndicated column, *San Francisco Examiner*, October 31, 1949.

Acclaim for role in Newark, NJ, production of *The Last Mile*: "Lawrence Tierney Star in 'The Last Mile,'" *Montclair (NJ) Times*, November 22, 1949; In Hollywood by Louella Parsons, syndicated column, *Pittsburgh Sun-Times*, December 8, 1949.

Tierney touts movie comeback: "Lawrence Tierney Will Make Screen Comeback: Actor Returns to Hollywood for Role at Universal-International" by Louella O. Parsons, syndicated column, *San Francisco Examiner*, December 22, 1949.

Chapter 14

In and out of movie roles

Negotiations to costar with Scott Brady in *The Payoff*: "Wrong Pose," Jimmie Fidler in Hollywood, syndicated column, *Sioux City Journal*, January 17, 1950; Hollywood by Jack K. Lait, *Brooklyn Daily Eagle*, January 25, 1950; "Lawrence Tierney May Get His Break" by Sheilah Graham, syndicated column, *Spokesman Review*, Seattle, WA, February 21, 1950.

In and out of *Winchester '73*: Hollywood Today by Louella Parsons, syndicated column, *Arizona Republic*, February 21, 1950.

In and out of *Saddletramp, Tomahawk*: Hollywood by Sheilah Graham, syndicated column, *Times-Tribune*, March 14, 1950.

Films role in *The Magnificent Heel* (*Shakedown*): Louella Parsons, syndicated column, *Philadelphia Inquirer*, March 25, 1950.

Social life

Tierney among "most eligible bachelors": "Many Romeos in Hollywood" by Sheilah Graham, syndicated column, *Spokesman Review*, Seattle, WA, January 15, 1950.

Tierney's "unique explanation" for relapse: "Riding the Wagon," Jimmie Fidler in Hollywood, syndicated column, *Sioux City Journal*, March 18, 1950.

Denies fight with brother Scott Brady: Hollywood by Jack Lait Jr., *Brooklyn Eagle*, March 29, 1950.

Tierney accepts typecasting: "Lawrence Tierney Back" by Bob Thomas, Associated Press, syndicated report, *Windsor (Ontario) Star*, April 27, 1950.

Arrest at Ocean Park Arena, Santa Monica

Drunk and disorderly charge: "Lawrence Tierney in Clink Again," Associated Press report, *San Pedro News Pilot*, May 9, 1950; "Lawrence Tierney Again Is Booked as Drunk," United Press report, *Sacramento Bee*, May 9, 1950; "Tierney Goes to Jail Again, Then Gets Bail," *Los Angeles Times*, May 10, 1950.

"I plead guilty to friskiness": "'Frisky but Not Drunk,'" Associated Press report, *Argus-Leader*, Sioux Falls, SD, May 10, 1950.

Tierney as "incorrigible dipsomaniac . . . of the dangerous type": Jimmie Fidler in Hollywood, syndicated column, *Valley Morning Star*, Harlingen, TX, May 16, 1950.

Pleads guilty to drunk and disorderly charge: "Lawrence Tierney Pays $50 Fine in Beer Theft," United Press report, *Sacramento Bee*, May 25, 1950; "Actor Lawrence Tierney Is Fined for Disorderly Conduct," International News Service report, *Lubbock Morning Avalanche*, May 25, 1950.

Attempts at rehabilitation

Sympathetic press: "The Bottle Has Kept Larry 'Dillinger' Tierney in Trouble, But Now He's Trying to Be a Good Boy" by Sheilah Graham, syndicated article, *Louisville Courier-Journal*, June 4, 1950.

Source Notes

Rehired at RKO for *Best of the Badmen*: Hollywood by Sheilah Graham, syndicated column, *Times-Tribune,* Scranton, PA, August 5, 1950; Author interview with C. Courtney Joyner, March 8, 2021.

Plays Jesse James for second time in *Badmen*: "Lawrence Tierney Plays James Again," *Deseret News,* Salt Lake City, UT, August 16, 1950.

No one "rates a break less" than Tierney: In Hollywood with Jimmie Fidler, syndicated column, *Monroe (LA) Morning World,* August 6, 1950.

Ed Tierney takes acting classes: Hollywood by Sheilah Graham, syndicated column, *Pittsburgh Post-Gazette,* August 23, 1950.

Second incident at Ocean Park Arena: Hollywood by George Fisher (filling in for Edith Gwynn), syndicated column, *Mercury,* Pottstown, PA, September 25, 1950.

Shakedown opens in Los Angeles: "'Shakedown' Action Filled Crime Story," *Los Angeles Times,* September 25, 1950.

Chapter 15

Arrest with Jean Wallace

Jean Wallace background: Jean Wallace Profile, *Glamour Girls of the Silver Screen*; "Jean Wallace Pays $60 Fine for Yule Spree," International News Service report, *Long Beach Independent,* March 1, 1950; "Jean Wallace, 60, Screen Actress Known for 1940's and 50's Roles," Obituaries, *New York Times,* February 18, 1990; various articles on Jean Wallace drunk arrests, suicide attempts, custody fight.

Tierney arrested in street: "Tierney Arrested Again, This Time with Jean Wallace," United Press report, *Wilmington (DE) Daily Press,* October 14, 1950; "Tierney Once More Gets His Snoot Wet," Associated Press report, *Hutchinson (KS) Press,* October 14, 1950; "Lawrence Tierney Cited on Drunk Charge," *Los Angeles Times,* October 15, 1950.

Jean Wallace interview with Louella Parsons: "Tierney's Arrest in Bad News for Jean Wallace" by Louella Parsons, syndicated report, *San Francisco Examiner,* October 16, 1950.

The Respectful Prostitute: *The Respectful Prostitute,* play written by Jean-Paul Sartre, adapted by Eva Wolas, 1948, Internet Broadway Database; "Sartre on American Racism" from *Philosophers on Race: Critical Essays,* edited by Julie K. Ward and Tommy L. Lott, Blackwell, 2002.

Jimmie Fidler reacts to arrest: Jimmie Fidler in Hollywood, syndicated column, *Joplin (MO) Globe,* October 24, 1950.

Fighting to stay on the wagon

Tierney joins Alcoholics Anonymous: The Talk of Hollywood by Hedda Hopper, syndicated column, *Evening Sun,* Baltimore, MD, November 30, 1950; Hollywood Today by Sheilah Graham, syndicated column, *Honolulu Star Bulletin,* December 11, 1950; Broadway by Danton Walker, *NY Daily News,* December 15, 1950.

Offered stage role in *Mike McCauley*: Hollywood by Sheilah Graham, syndicated column, *Times-Tribune,* Scranton, PA, December 13, 1950.

Source Notes

Plans AA lecture tour: Broadway by Danton Walker, *NY Daily News*, December 15, 1950.

Tierney punches drunk at party: Voice of Broadway, Jottings in Pencil by Dorothy Kilgallen, syndicated column, *Republican and Herald*, Pottsville, PA, December 22, 1950.

The Hoodlum

Cast in *The Hoodlum*: Hollywood by Edith Gwynn, syndicated column, *Mercury*, Pottstown, PA, January 3, 1951.

Gets brother Ed hired as costar: Louella Parsons, syndicated column, *San Francisco Examiner*, March 16, 1951; Broadway by Danton Walker, *NY Daily News*, March 20, 1951; *The Hoodlum* (1951), IMDbPro.

Jimmie Fidler changes tune: "Friends Say Tierney Is On Wagon to Stay," Jimmie Fidler, syndicated column, *Indianapolis News*, March 7, 1951.

Three Tierney brothers are actors: Brooklyn and Broadway, Nightlife by Al Salerno, *Brooklyn Daily Eagle*, March 20, 1951.

The Greatest Show on Earth

Tierney hired for *The Greatest Show on Earth*: "Reformed Lawrence Tierney Gets Role in DeMille's Circus Epic," Louella's Movie-Go-'Round by Louella Parsons, syndicated column, *Albuquerque Journal*, April 21, 1951.

Tierney and Cecil B. DeMille: Tierney interview with Michael and Cheryl Murphy, *Psychotronic Video* magazine no. 8, Fall 1990; Author interview with David Del Valle, May 18, 2021.

Movie offers vs. violent incidents

Palm Springs nightclub fight: "Larry Tierney Wins by Punch," International News Service report, *Arizona Republic*, May 16, 1951; Backstage, In Hollywood by Erskine Johnson, syndicated column, *Johnson City (TN) Press*, June 26, 1951.

Tierney sought to play the prophet Moses: Danton Walker, syndicated column, *Philadelphia Inquirer*, June 18, 1951; "Report from Hollywood: Reviewer has field day over news of film of Moses" by Shimon Wincelberg, *Indianapolis Jewish Post*, August 10, 1951.

Santa Monica battery charge: "Tierney Faces Battery Charge," Associated Press report, *Des Moines Tribune*, June 28, 1951.

District attorney demands Tierney's surrender: "Police Hunting Actor Tierney," International News Service report, *Pasadena Independent*, June 29, 1951.

Tierney claims he wasn't John Naylor's assailant: "Lawrence Tierney Denies Beating Man," Associated Press report, *Sacramento Bee*, July 7, 1951; "Lawrence Tierney Asks Battery Trial," Associated Press report, *Valley Times*, North Hollywood, CA, July 7, 1951.

Future movie deals in jeopardy: "The Story of Mrs. Murphy," Sheilah Graham, syndicated column, *Deseret News*, Salt Lake City, UT, July 9, 1951.

Tierney to take Marlon Brando role in *Streetcar Named Desire* at El Teatro in Santa Fe: Drama by Edwin Schallert, *Los Angeles Times*, July 19, 1951.

Chapter 16

Santa Fe, NM

Tierney to take Marlon Brando role in *Streetcar Named Desire* at El Teatro in Santa Fe: Ibid., Schallert, *Los Angeles Times.*

Ann Lee and El Teatro background: "Ann Lee Does Something about Stage," Associated Press story, *Johnson City (TN) Press Chronicle,* July 9, 1951.

Tierney fired from *A Streetcar Named Desire*: "'Streetcar' Derailed: Teatro Fires Tierney; Star Fails to Appear," *Santa Fe New Mexican,* July 27, 1951; "Gets 'Pink Slip': Movie Actor Tierney Fails to Go On," Associated Press report, *El Paso Times,* July 28, 1951.

Arthur Franz replaces Tierney in *Streetcar*: "Ann Lee Fires Her Leading Man," Associated Press report, *Carlsbad (NM) Current-Argus,* July 29, 1951.

Tierney misses Naylor trial date; warrant issued: "L. A. Judge Puts Cops on 'Dillinger,'" *Los Angeles Times,* July 27, 1951; "New Mexico Trip Gets Tierney in Bad with Court," *Los Angeles Times,* July 28, 1950.

Rampage at Mayflower Café, Santa Fe: "Santa Fe police hunt for Lawrence Tierney," United Press report, *Courier Journal,* Louisville, KY, July 2, 1951; "Actor Who Played Dillinger Faces Disturbance Rap," United Press report, *Alva (OK) Review-Courier,* July 29, 1951.

Late for Naylor trial, jailed for contempt: "Actor Tierney Sent to Jail for Court Tardiness," *Los Angeles Times,* August 4, 1951; "Movie Star Sent to Jail: Lawrence Tierney Gets Five-Day Term for Contempt," Associated Press report, *News Journal,* Wilmington, DE, August 4, 1951; "Movie Tough Guy Jailed in Contempt," United Press report, *Philadelphia Inquirer,* August 4, 1951; "Jail 'Bad Boy' Actor Lawrence Tierney," International News Service report, *NY Daily News,* August 4, 1951.

Naylor trial testimony: "Actor Tierney on Trial in Beating Case," *Los Angeles Times,* August 14, 1951; "Self Defense: Threat of Knife Told by Tierney," *Los Angeles Times,* August 15, 1951; "Actor Lawrence Tierney Denies Kicking Student," United Press report, *Press Democrat,* Santa Rosa, CA, August 15, 1951; "Actor Tierney Says Knifing Fear Made Him Hit Accuser," Associated Press report, *San Francisco Examiner,* August 15, 1951.

Naylor files $30,587 civil suit against Tierney: "Actor Tierney Found Guilty in Battery Case," *Los Angeles Times,* August 16, 1951; "Actor Lawrence Tierney Convicted on Battery Count," Associated Press report, *St. Louis Post-Dispatch,* August 16, 1951.

Tierney found guilty of battery: Ibid., *Los Angeles Times, St. Louis Post-Dispatch*; "Tierney Convicted," United Press report, *Press Democrat,* Santa Rosa, CA, August 16, 1951.

"I am not guilty": "Protests Conviction: Tierney Delivers Lecture at Sentencing," *Los Angeles Times,* August 31, 1951; "Tierney Gets 90 Days in Real-Life Villainy," United Press report, *Philadelphia Inquirer,* August 31, 1951; "Lawrence Tierney Gets 90 Days on Battery Count," Associated Press report, *Panama City (FL) News-Herald,* August 31, 1951.

Tierney offered role in *The Bushwhackers*: "first time in Hollywood history that an actor with a jail term hanging over his head has been given a picture." Hollywood by Dorothy Manners, syndicated column, *San Francisco Examiner*, September 3, 1951.

Misbehavior of other Hollywood figures: "'Delinquents' Worry Hollywood," *Sydney Morning Herald*, Sydney, Australia, September 23, 1951; various contemporaneous newspaper reports.

"Movietown, U.S.A." campaign: "'Better Films' Drive Hit by Screaming Headlines" by Harold Heffernan, syndicated story, *Valley Times*, North Hollywood, CA, September 18, 1951.

Tierney wraps *The Bushwhackers*: Star Gazing by Helen Boxer, *Detroit Free Press*, September 20, 1951; *The Bushwhackers* (1951), AFI Catalog of Motion Pictures Produced in the United States (website).

"My Brother's A Screwball": Hollywood by Erskine Johnson, syndicated column, *Marshfield (WI) News-Herald*, October 4, 1951.

Death of Robert Walker: "Robt. Walker, Film Actor, Dies Unexpectedly at 32; Inhalator Squad Fails to Save His Life; Death Ascribed to Natural Causes," *Los Angeles Times*, August 29, 1951; "Actor Robert Walker Dies after Doctor's Injection," Associated Press report, *Tampa Tribune*, August 30, 1951; "The Tragedy of Robert Walker," Jim Henaghan, *Redbook* magazine, November 1951.

Chapter 17

Breakdown at St. Monica's

St. Monica Roman Catholic Church and *Going My Way*: "St. Monica Mission and History," St. Monica Catholic Community website; Review—*Going My Way*, Comedy-Drama with Bing Crosby and Barry Fitzgerald, *New York Times*, May 3, 1944; *AFI Catalog of Motion Pictures Produced in the United States: Feature Films 1941–1950: Dillinger*, University of California Press, 1999.

Police confront Tierney in church: "Actor Lawrence Tierney Captured in Church Turmoil," *Los Angeles Times*, October 9, 1951; "Actor Lawrence Tierney Found Kneeling Barefoot before Altar, Babbling Incoherently," United Press report, *El Paso Times*, October 9, 1951; "Actor Tierney Berserk Again; Captured Barefoot in Church," Associated Press report, *Windsor (Ontario) Star*, October 9, 1951.

"*They want to kill me the way they killed Robert Walker!*": "Tierney Goes Haywire at Hollywood Church; Tierney under Mental Treatment after Outburst," International News Service report, *Journal News*, White Plains, NY, October 9, 1951.

Santa Monica Police Station: "Tierney, Actor of Dillinger Role, in Psycho Ward," United Press report, *Boston Globe*, October 9, 1951.

Tierney "accepting treatment" at L.A. Neurological Institute: "Actor is Subdued," United Press report, *Californian*, Salinas, CA, October 10, 1951; "Lawrence Tierney under Treatment," *Valley Times*, North Hollywood, CA, October 10, 1951.

Jimmie Fidler on the "final tragedy": Jimmie Fidler in Hollywood, syndicated column, *Pasadena Independent*, October 23, 1951.

Source Notes

"Barefoot" bar arrest

"*I'll whip anyone in the place!*": "Actor Tierney Held as Drunk in Bar Dispute," *Los Angeles Times,* October 25, 1951; "Jailed Again, Tierney Says He's a Bum," United Press report, *Santa Fe New Mexican,* October 24, 1951; "Lawrence Tierney in Jail Again," Associated Press report, *Pomona Progress Bulletin,* October 25, 1951.

"Lack of sleep" excuse: Gadabout's Diary by Sheilah Graham, syndicated column, *Deseret News,* Salt Lake City, UT, October 27, 1951.

Judge gives Tierney a surprise break: "Actor Promises Judge to Go On Wagon; It's Six Months in Jail If He Breaks Three-Year Pledge," Associated Press report, *San Bernardino County Sun,* November 24, 1951; "Film Actor Jailed on Drinking Charge, Promises to Quit," United Press report, *Cincinnati Enquirer,* November 24, 1951.

Tierney serves three days in jail: "Tierney Promises to 'Lay Off Stuff,'" United Press report, *Wilmington (CA) Daily Press Journal,* November 24, 1951; "'Dillinger' Actor Takes Drunk Pledge," International News Service report, *Times,* Munster, IN, November 25, 1951.

Career resumes

Columnists' Christmas wishes: "Hints to Santa—from Hollywood" by Armand Archerd, syndicated column, *Terre Haute Tribune,* December 23, 1951; "Tierney has again joined AA," In Hollywood by Sheilah Graham, syndicated column, *Tampa Times,* December 26, 1951.

Fidler on "no bad publicity": "Any Publicity Will Do That's Lengthy and Lurid" by Jimmie Fidler, syndicated column, *Press Democrat,* Santa Rosa, CA, December 27, 1951.

Tierney signed by Kendall-Kirkwood Productions: Ibid., Jimmie Fidler column; "Actor Tierney on Wagon, Gets New Try with 'Indie,'" United Press story, *Pasadena Independent,* December 28, 1951.

Chapter 18

January 1957, NYC, Midwest

Radio City Music Hall premiere of *The Greatest Show on Earth*: "DeMille Puts 'Greatest Show on Earth' Film for All to See—Premiere at Music Hall," review by Bosley Crowther, *New York Times,* January 11, 1952; "The Circus Has Come to the Music Hall," *NY Daily News,* January 11, 1952; "'The Greatest Show on Earth' Now at Radio City Music Hall," *Brooklyn Daily Eagle,* January 11, 1952.

Tierney desires stay at Menninger Clinic: Broadway Grapevine, Voice of Broadway by Dorothy Kilgallen, syndicated column, *Republican and Herald,* Pottsville, PA, January 15, 1952.

The Bushwhackers promotional tour: "'Bushwhackers' 3rd rate—Even as a Western," review by May Tinee, *Chicago Tribune,* January 22, 1952; Hollywood by Edith Gwynn, syndicated column, *Mercury,* Pottstown, PA, January 25, 1952; John Lester column, *Miami News,* January 28, 1952.

Kendall-Kirkwood's Tom Neal–Barbara Payton plans: Hollywood by Erskine Johnson, syndicated column, *Kingsport Times,* March 12, 1952.

Source Notes

Naylor appeal and jail time

Tierney begins sentence while appealing Naylor verdict: "Actor Lawrence Tierney serving 90 Days in Jail," Associated Press report, *Elmira Advertiser,* March 14, 1952; "Tierney Serving 90-Day Sentence," International News Service report, *Fort Worth Star-Telegram,* March 14, 1952.

Tierney freed after seventy-four days: "Tierney out of Jail for Movie," United Press report, *Napa Valley Register,* May 12, 1952; "Lawrence Tierney Wins release in Battery Case," *Los Angeles Times,* May 13, 1952; "Judge Frees an Actor: Lawrence Tierney Released from Road Camp to Make Movie," Associated Press report, *Kansas City Times,* May 13, 1952.

The Petrified Forest stage tour

Tierney joins Franchot Tone and Betsy von Furstenberg on straw-hat circuit: "A Day in the Life of A Show Editor," Herb Rau, *Miami News,* June 4, 1952; Theatre, *NY Daily News,* June 7, 1952.

Actor Tierney compared favorably to Bogart: "Beach Debuts Summer Stock: 'The Petrified Forest,'" Herb Rau review, *Miami News,* June 10, 1952.

Betsy von Furstenberg's memories of tour: Interview with Betsy von Furstenberg, cited in "Down These Mean Streets: Lawrence Tierney interviewed by Rick McKay," *Scarlet Street* magazine, issue 29, 1998; "Lawrence Tierney," *Independent,* UK, March 1, 2002.

Jimmie Fidler criticizes Tierney from afar: Jimmie Fidler in Hollywood, syndicated column, *Monroe (LA) News-Star,* June 10, 1952; Jimmie Fidler's View of Hollywood, syndicated column, *Valley Times,* North Hollywood, CA, June 28, 1952.

Tierney's drunken behavior revealed: Interview with Betsy von Furstenberg cited in "Down These Mean Streets: Lawrence Tierney interviewed by Rick McKay," *Scarlet Street* magazine, issue 29, 1998; Bird's Eye View by Vince Bird, *Scrantonian,* October 17, 1954.

Incident at P. J. Clarke's

Tierney "socks socialite" Seward Heaton: "Tierney Brawls Again: Socks Socialite in Bar," *NY Daily News,* August 9, 1952; "Barroom Champ Defends Title" (photo), *Brooklyn Daily Eagle,* August 9, 1952; "Tierney Clips N. Y. Socialite in Bar," Associated Press report, *Valley Times,* North Hollywood, CA, August 9, 1952; "Lawrence Tierney Flattens Socialite," United Press report, *Dayton Daily News,* August 9, 1952; Author visit to P. J. Clarke's saloon on Third Avenue, NYC, September 10, 2021.

Tierney and Heaton "shake hands": Voice of Broadway, All Around Town by Dorothy Kilgallen, syndicated column, *Record-Argus,* Greenville, PA, September 4, 1952.

More Tierney scraps: Broadway Beat, Broadway by Danton Walker, *NY Daily News,* November 12, 1952; Broadway Grapevine, Voice of Broadway by Dorothy Kilgallen, syndicated column, *Republican and Herald,* Pottsville, PA, November 17, 1952; The Lyons Den by Leonard Lyons, syndicated column, *Johnson City (TN) Press Chronicle,* November 17, 1952; Celebs About Town, The Broadway Beat by Walter Winchell, syndicated column, *Miami Herald,* November 30, 1952; Off The Cuff, Voice of Broadway by Dorothy Kilgallen, syndicated column, *Fort Worth Star-Telegram,* December 3, 1952.

Affair with Betsy von Furstenberg: It Happened Last Night by Earl Wilson, syndicated column, *Honolulu Star-Bulletin;* Snapshots of Hollywood by Dorothy Manners, syndicated column, *Fort Worth Star-Telegram,* July 24, 1952; Interview with Betsy von Furstenberg cited in "Down These Mean Streets: Lawrence Tierney interviewed by Rick McKay," *Scarlet Street* magazine, issue 29, 1998.

Von Furstenberg in *Josephine:* Ibid., Rick McKay, *Scarlet Street.*

Tierney attempts to break into von Furstenberg's apartment: Ibid.

Chapter 19

"Drunk and disorderly" arrest in Santa Monica

Arrested for "making faces": "Actor Tierney Faces 14th Drunk Charge," United Press report, *Sacramento Bee,* February 11, 1953.

Sharing docket with John Agar: "Agar and Tierney in Court Again," United Press report, *Miami Herald,* February 13, 1953.

Skips bail, heads to NYC: "Warrant Issued as Lawrence Tierney Skips Court Date," *Los Angeles Times,* February 14, 1953; "Police Seek Tierney for Not Appearing in 14th Drunk Case," United Press report, *Times-Advocate,* February 14, 1953.

New York City incidents

Disturbance at Blue Angel nightclub: Broadway Bulletin Board, Voice of Broadway by Dorothy Kilgallen, syndicated column, *Republican and Herald,* Pottsville, PA, February 25, 1953.

Punches press agent at P. J. Clarke's: Broadway by Earl Wilson, syndicated column, *Winona Daily News,* March 6, 1953; "Tierney slugged Chic Farmer," Gossip in Gotham, Broadway by Dorothy Kilgallen, syndicated column, *Times Tribune,* March 7, 1953.

Related Hollywood news

Ed Tierney divorce: "Edward Tierney Sued for Divorce," *Los Angeles Times,* March 14, 1953; "Tierney Divorced by Reich-Born Actress," Associated Press report, *Green Bay (WI) Press Gazette,* April 22, 1953.

Best Picture Oscar for *The Greatest Show on Earth:* Twenty-Fifth Academy Awards, March 19, 1953; "Shirley Booth, Gary Cooper Named Top Oscar Winners, DeMille's Circus Film Gets Award," *Los Angeles Times,* March 20, 1953.

Ed Tierney changes name to "Ed Tracy": Hollywood by Edith Gwynn, syndicated column, *Mercury,* Pottstown, PA, October 10, 1953.

Incidents, arrests, trials in NYC

Reported Tierney brawls and one-punchers: Jimmie Fidler in Hollywood, syndicated column, *Sioux City (IA) Journal,* March 30, 1953; It Happened Last Night by Earl Wilson, syndicated column, *Delta Democrat,* Greenville, MS, March 31, 1953; Broadway Bulletin Board, Voice of Broadway by Dorothy Kilgallen, syndicated column, *Republican and Herald,* Pottsville, PA, June 10, 1953.

Offered role in *Black Candle*: "Lawrence Tierney Set in N. Y. Show," Hollywood Highlights by Louella Parsons, syndicated column, *Pittsburgh Sun-Telegraph,* June 13, 1953; "helping a downtrodden vagrant," Voice of Broadway by Dorothy Kilgallen, syndicated column, *Fort Worth Star-Telegram,* June 30, 1953.

Bermuda shorts "scandal": Broadway by Danton Walker, *NY Daily News,* July 21, 1953; "Everybody in a Sweat Trying to Beat the Heat," *NY Daily News,* July 28, 1953.

Arrested in "no punch" sidewalk "fight": "Actor Lawrence Tierney Squares Off with Boxer," Associated Press report, *Montgomery (AL) Advertiser,* July 26, 1953; "Lawrence Tierney Faces Court Again," United Press report, *Wisconsin State Journal,* Madison WI, July 26, 1953.

Tierney attacks pianist at Tiger Lily Lounge: "Tierney Accused Of Hitting Pianist," International News Service report, *Philadelphia Inquirer,* July 28, 1953.

Convicted and lectured by judge over sidewalk "fight": "'Tough Guy' Tierney Fined and Lectured after Fight," Associated Press report, *San Bernardino County Sun,* August 1, 1953.

Charged with "felonious assault" of pianist: "Toughie Tierney Gets $25 Tap and New Rap," *NY Daily News,* August 1, 1953.

Piano charge reduced to "simple assault": "Actor Is Paroled on Assault Rap," *NY Daily News,* August 5, 1953; "Charge against Movie Tough Guy Is Reduced," Associated Press report, *Spokesman Review,* Spokane, WA, August 5, 1953.

Jimmie Fidler weighs in, blames family: "Lawrence Tierney Seen Needing Special Care" by Jimmie Fidler, syndicated column, *Lancaster (PA) New Era,* August 11, 1953.

Tierney fights mobster's brother, "slated for slugging": It Happened Last Night by Earl Wilson, syndicated column, *Scranton (PA) Tribune,* August 5, 1953; On Broadway by Lee Mortimer, syndicated column, *Orlando Evening Star,* August 12, 1953; Ibid., Mortimer, August 14, 1953.

Acquitted in Tiger Lily Lounge assault case: "Movie Tough Guy Comes Out On Top in This Court Script," *NY Daily News,* August 18, 1953; "Actor Tierney Freed in Night Club Brawl," *Brooklyn Daily Eagle,* August 18, 1953.

Scott Brady drunk driving arrest

Scott Brady arrested on Sunset Strip: "Sip Costs $250," International News Service report, *Journal and Courier,* Lafayette, IN, October 14, 1953; "Tierney Brother Scott Brady Fined," *Valley Times,* North Hollywood, CA, October 15, 1953.

Brady begins filming *Johnny Guitar* with Joan Crawford: Hollywood by Edith Gwynn, syndicated column, *Mercury,* Pottstown, PA, October 10, 1953.

Brady a "co-escort" of Joan Crawford at Photographers' Costume Ball: Hollywood by Sheilah Graham, syndicated column, *Times Tribune,* Scranton, PA, November 21, 1953.

On the Waterfront

Tierney turns down *On the Waterfront*: *Casting Might-Have-Beens: A Film-by-Film Directory* by Ella Mell, McFarland, 2005; *On the Waterfront* (*1954*), IMDb Trivia; Author interview with David Del Valle, May 18, 2021.

Chapter 20

Tierney lies low in NYC

"Another chance": "Stars Write Santa Christmas Wishes," Armand Archerd, syndicated column, *Tyler (TX) Morning Telegraph,* December 24, 1953.

New York City sightings: "Tierney . . . wearing new shiner," It Happened Last Night by Earl Wilson, syndicated column, *Courier-Post,* Camden, NJ, December 30, 1953; "Tierney . . . playing bocce ball," Broadway by Danton Walker, *NY Daily News,* January 11, 1954; "alone at drugstore, sipping ice cream soda," Dorothy Kilgallen, syndicated column, *Muncie (IN) Evening Press,* January 18, 1954.

Tierney movies show up on television: *Kill or Be Killed,* Saturday, 4 p.m., Channel 5, This Week's Feature Films, TV Listings, *Daily News-Post,* Monrovia, CA, February 13, 1954.

Judge approves Naylor settlement: "Actor Tierney Loses $5000 in Battery Suit," *Los Angeles Times,* January 12, 1954.

Ed Tierney rape arrest

Arthur Godfrey and Julius LaRosa: "Godfrey Says He Fired Pair Because They Lost Humility," United Press report, *Shreveport (LA) Times,* October 2, 1953; "Julius LaRosa's Bookings Top $185,000 Mark," Associated Press report, *Boston Globe,* February 22, 1954; *When Television Was Young* by Ed McMahon with David Fisher, Thomas Nelson, 2007.

"Julius La Rosa Opens at Ciro's": Review of Julia La Rosa at Ciro's, *Billboard,* March 13, 1954; "Julius La Rosa Causes a Minor Traffic Jam," Associated Press report, *North Adams (MA) Transcript,* February 27, 1954.

Ed Tierney arrested for statutory rape: "Attack Charge Jails Actor Edward Tierney," *Los Angeles Times,* April 3, 1954; "Actor Seized on Morals Charge," International News Service report, *San Francisco Examiner,* April 3, 1954; "Rape Charges Filed against Actor," Associated Press report, *Long Beach (CA) Independent,* April 3, 1954; "Actor's Brother Is Held in Rape of 14-Year-Old," United Press report, *NY Daily News,* April 4, 1954.

Ed Tierney sentenced: "Edward Tierney Given Jail Term," *Los Angeles Times,* May 21, 1954; "Actor's Brother Given Three Month Sentence," International News Service report, *Albuquerque Journal,* May 21, 1954.

Scott Brady in German movie with Ed Tierney's ex-wife: *They Were So Young* (1954), IMDbPro.

Tierney stays sober and works

"On the wag" in Bermuda shorts, other sightings: Broadway by Danton Walker, *NY Daily News,* June 1, 1954; It Happened Last Night by Earl Wilson, syndicated column, *Bristol (TN) Daily Courier,* July 12, 1954; Dorothy Kilgallen, syndicated column, *Fort Worth Star-Telegram,* July 13, 1954.

Singing in the Dark: "Tierney, on wag now, returns to films," It Happened Last Night by Earl Wilson, syndicated column, *Newsday,* Nassau, Long Island, NY, May

6, 1954; Night Life by George Bourke, *Miami Herald*, September 22, 1954; *Singing in the Dark* (1956) *AFI Catalog of Feature Films: The First 100 Years*.

Television offers: Radio and television by John Lester, *York (PA) Daily Record*, December 17, 1954.

Appears in *Laura* and *Rope* on straw-hat circuit: "at Summer Theatre in Litchfield with 'Laura,'" T. W. Bridges; "touring the strawhat circuit in 'Rope,'" Harold V. Cohen, *Pittsburgh Post-Gazette*, August 6, 1954.

Man with the Golden Arm Broadway offer: "Welles, Tierney Sought for 'Arm,'" *Variety*, September 8, 1954.

Opposite Jayne Mansfield in *Girl Murdered* (*Female Jungle*): Hollywood Today by Erskine Johnson, syndicated column, *Corpus Christi (TX) Caller Times*, December 9, 1954.

Episode of *The Big Story* on NBC: "Hugh Park's Big Story: The 'Case of the County Dictator' will be dramatized on the WSB-TV Big Story program at 9," *Atlanta Constitution*, November 5, 1954.

The Steel Cage premieres on New Year's Eve: "'The Steel Cage' Due at Main Here Tuesday," *Paris (TX) News*, January 2, 1955; *The Steel Cage* (1954), IMDbPro.

Chapter 21

Affair with Gloria Vanderbilt

Gloria Vanderbilt background: "Poor Little Rich Girl: Gloria Vanderbilt Was Caught between a Neglectful Mother and an Oppressive Aunt" by Gillian Brockell, *Washington Post*, June 17, 2019; "Maestro and New Baby Son Capture Gloria's Heart," by Igor Cassini, syndicated article, *Pittsburgh Sun-Telegraph*, September 24, 1950; "Gloria Vanderbilt Dies at 95; Built a Fashion Empire," *New York Times*, June 17, 2019.

Tierney and Vanderbilt sightings in NYC: Broadway by Dorothy Kilgallen, syndicated column, *Times-Tribune*, Scranton, PA, January 13, 1955; Early Bird by Hy Gardner, *Nashville Banner*, February 1, 1955; Broadway by Danton Walker, *NY Daily News*, March 15, 1955.

Rehearsals for *Time of Your Life*: "Miracle and Me," *It Seemed Important at the Time, A Romance Memoir* by Gloria Vanderbilt, Simon & Schuster, 2004.

Tierney "drunk" at rehearsal, loses role: Ibid.

Colgate Comedy Hour incident and "break-up" with Vanderbilt: Ibid.

Tierney–Vanderbilt romance continues: "Lawrence Tierney Divides Time between 2 Favorites," Voice of Broadway by Dorothy Kilgallen, *Arizona Republic*, March 25, 1955; Sip and Sup by Frank Ross, *NY Daily News*, April 1, 1955.

"Pink elephants"

"Pink elephants": "The Colorful History and Etymology of 'Pink Elephant,'" Peter Jensen Brown, *Early Sports 'n' Pop Culture History* (blog), August 20, 2014; *The Lost Weekend* (1945), Characters, Frank Faylen as 'Bim" Nolan, IMDb.

Tierney sees "pink elephant" at circus: It Happened Last Night by Earl Wilson, syndicated column, *Scranton (PA) Tribune,* April 5, 1955; Bird's Eye View by Vince Bird, *Scrantonian Sun,* April 10, 1955.

"Dream Circus" at Madison Square Garden: "Well, Waddayaknow! The Circus Has Opened at Mad. Sq. Garden," *NY Daily News,* March 31, 1955; It Happened Last Night by Earl Wilson, syndicated column, *Scranton (PA) Tribune,* April 5, 1955.

Marilyn Monroe on pink elephant: "Even the Band Halted; Marilyn Monroe and Pink Elephant Stop Show at Circus Performance," Associated Press report, *Fort Worth Star-Telegram,* March 31, 1955.

Tierney dates "circus lass": Voice of Broadway by Dorothy Kilgallen, syndicated column, *Des Moines Register,* April 13, 1955.

Tierney's brothers

Scott Brady films *Gentlemen Prefer Brunettes*: "Jane Russell, Jeanne Crain to Star in Film with Handsome Scott Brady," Film-Flam column, *Enterprise-Journal,* McComb, MS, May 10, 1955.

Ed Tierney begins career in Germany: Ed Tracy as Captain Fox in *Heldentum nach Ladenschluß* (1955), IMDbPro; "Ed Tracy is a big star in Germany," Movie Gaddabout's Diary by Sheilah Graham, syndicated column, *Birmingham (AL) News,* December 13, 1955.

Tierney works on East Coast

Detective Story: "Tierney in *Detective Story* at Lakewood Theatre in Barnesville, PA," New Programs, *Philadelphia Inquirer,* June 12, 1955.

Judge at Miss New York pageant: "Tonight—In Person!," *NY Daily News,* July 6, 1955.

Fire Island background: "All Aboard, Shh!—For Fire Island," Rhea Talley, *Courier Journal,* Louisville, KY, July 3, 1955; Fire Island—Historical Background, State University of New York Press.

Fire island bar fight with "Shipwreck" Kelly: Voice of Broadway by Dorothy Kilgallen, syndicated column, *Mercury,* Pottstown, PA, July 27, 1955.

Chapter 22

Banished from Fire Island

1935 Banishment of Clement Levy: "Prosecutor's Pretty Secretary Traps Lothario as Purse Thief," *Brooklyn Daily Eagle,* August 18, 1936; "Stenog Got Her Man, Earns Job as Sleuth," *NY Daily News,* August 19, 1935; "Purse Snatcher 'Exiled,' Avoids Jail by Promising Not to Return to Fire Island," *New York Times,* August 19, 1935.

"Shipwreck" Kelly denies barfight with Tierney: Voice of Broadway by Dorothy Kilgallen, syndicated column, *Mercury,* Pottstown, PA, July 30, 1955.

Another bar brawl leads to Tierney's banishment: "Tierney Exiled by Fire Island," *NY Daily News,* August 13, 1955; "Actor Tierney Exiled from Entire Island," *Los Angeles*

Times, August 13, 1955; "Actor Fined, Banished in Fire Island Fight," United Press report, *Bridgeport (CT) Telegram,* August 14, 1955.

Tierney's ups and downs

Scott Brady buys story for film to star three brothers: Broadway News and Hollywood Roundup by Theresa Loeb Cone, *Oakland Tribune,* October 1, 1955.

Will Success Spoil Rock Hunter? on Broadway: "Theatre: Axelrod's Second Comedy 'Will Success Spoil Rock Hunter?' Bows," review by Brooks Atkinson, *New York Times,* October 14, 1955.

Sam Levene won't take a chance with Tierney in *The Hot Corner:* Author interview with C. Courtney Joyner, July 16, 2021; "Levene Is Signed to Baseball Play," *New York Times,* May 19, 1955; "Levene's Tale: It Might Have Been" (*Hot Corner* closes), *NY Daily News,* January 28, 1956.

Tierney loses Gloria Vanderbilt to Sidney Lumet: It Happened Last Night by Earl Wilson, syndicated column, *Austin (TX) American,* January 19, 1956.

Vanderbilt–Lumet wedding: "Gloria Vanderbilt Wed Quietly to TV Director," Associated Press report, *Atlanta Constitution,* August 28, 1956.

Reports of new Tierney bar brawls: Best of Broadway by Burt Boyar, *Philadelphia Inquirer,* February 3, 1956; Voice of Broadway by Dorothy Kilgallen, syndicated column, *Evening Herald,* Pottsville, PA, February 29, 1956.

Jayne Mansfield's Broadway success leads to distribution of *Girl Murdered* (as *Female Jungle*): "Mansfield Discoverer Plans Thriller," Drama by Edwin Schallert, *Los Angeles Times,* April 6, 1956.

Chapter 23

Tierney attacks NYPD officer Joseph Incorvaia

Slugs cop, charged with disorderly conduct: "Tierney Back in Pokey for Poking a Cop," *NY Daily News,* April 9, 1956; "Lipstick-Smeared Actor Belts Cop," *Herald-News,* Passaic, NJ, April 9, 1956.

Takes a swing at detective in stationhouse: "Tierney Aims a Right," AP wirephoto, *Argus-Leader,* Sioux Falls, SD, April 11, 1956.

Apologizes to Incorvaia in court, pleads guilty: "So Sorry, Says Sober Tierney," *NY Daily News,* April 10, 1956; "Actor Tierney Pleads Guilty in Street Row," United Press report, *Los Angeles Times,* April 10, 1956.

Tierney explores other job options

Female Jungle released: "Jayne Mansfield, Lawrence Tierney Are Starred in 'Female Jungle,'" *Owensboro (KY) Messenger-Inquirer,* June 10, 1956; *Female Jungle* (1956), IMDbPro.

Jayne Mansfield unhappy with release of *Female Jungle*: Dorothy Kilgallen, syndicated column, *Journal Herald,* Dayton, OH, June 29, 1956.

Tierney rumored about to enter monastery: Broadway by Danton Walker, *NY Daily News,* July 9, 1956.

Tierney takes job on Wall Street: It Happened Last Night by Earl Wilson, syndicated column, *Herald-Sun,* Durham, NC, July 16, 1956; "My Typewriter Talks," Jack Eigen Speaking . . . , *Chicago Tribune,* July 21, 1956.

Tierney discovered working on construction site: "Lawrence Tierney Working at Tough Job to Lose Weight" by Hy Gardner, syndicated column, *Oakland (CA) Tribune,* September 5, 1956.

Walks out of rehearsals of *The Last Mile:* Voice of Broadway by Dorothy Kilgallen, syndicated column, *Ottawa Journal,* October 18, 1956.

Drunken crash and road rage at Seventh Avenue and Fifty-Seventh Street

Arrest for drunk driving and assault: "Jail Tierney in Crash as Drunk Driver," *NY Daily News,* March 31, 1957.

No-show in court, warrants issued: "Toughie Actor Cued by Court," *NY Daily News,* April 23, 1957; "Actor Tierney Facing Arrest," United Press report, *Los Angeles Times,* April 23, 1957.

Plea deal, rejoins Alcoholics Anonymous: Show Time by Earl Wilson, syndicated column, *Richmond (VA) Times Dispatch,* May 20, 1957.

Vito Frisina and family

Leads police chase in Queens: "Larry Tierney in Dutch Again," *NY Daily News,* May 28, 1957.

Dangerous driving charge: "Tierney Faces Traffic Charges," *NY Daily News,* July 14, 1957.

Living with Vito Frisina's family in Queens: Author interviews with daughter AnnMarie Frisina Guertin, June 2021.

Struck by motorcycle, official story: "Tierney Injured by GI Motorbike," *NY Daily News,* July 29, 1957; "Motorcycle Hits Lawrence Tierney," *Los Angeles Times,* July 29, 1957; "Lawrence Tierney Struck by Motorcycle," *Orlando Sentinel,* July 29, 1957; "Motorcycle Bruises Actor Tierney in N.Y.," *Wisconsin State Journal,* Madison, WI, July 29, 1957.

Struck by motorcycle, actual story: Author interview with AnnMarie Frisina Guertin, June 8, 2021.

Romance with Georgette McDonald

Sightings and scenes: New York Confidential by Lee Mortimer, syndicated column, *Star Press,* Muncie, IN, August 4, 1957; "makes Jayne Mansfield look like a boy," The Smart Set by Cholly Knickerbocker, syndicated column, *Shamokin (PA) News-Dispatch,* October 5, 1957.

Chapter 24

Tierney's wild life

"Lawrence Tierney Tale 'Impossible for Movies,'" Dorothy Kilgallen, syndicated column, *Times-Tribune,* Scranton, PA, August 31, 1957.

Source Notes

The Eileen Keenan "burglary" incident

Breaks down Eileen Keenan's door (in search of Georgette McDonald): "Screen Dillinger Arrested Again, Now for Burglary," United Press report, *Morning News*, Wilmington, DE, August 25, 1957; "Tierney Held in Bail as Blonde Yells Cop," *NY Daily News*, August 26, 1957; "Broke into Blonde's Flat: Lawrence Tierney Again in the Soup," United Press, *Miami Herald*, August 26, 1957; "Burglary Charged: Girl Reports Star for Breaking Door," United Press report, *Charlotte (NC) Observer*, August 26, 1957.

Judge dismisses burglary case: "Actor Tierney in, out of Jam with a Blonde, Ex-Dillinger of Movies Lectured by Judge after Door-Crashing Bit," *NY Daily News*, September 22, 1957.

Keenan forced to pose with Tierney: "Eileen Keenan's expression seems wary," photo caption, "Court to Tierney: Behave," *NY Daily News*, August 30, 1957.

Public incidents with Georgette McDonald: Cholly Knickerbocker, syndicated column, *Miami Herald*, December 26, 1957.

Scott Brady and Desmond Slattery marijuana arrest

Desmond Slattery background: Author interview with Timothy Tierney, June 30, 2021; "A New Robin Hood," International News photo and report, January 20, 1951; "Desmond Slattery's Back—This Time Promoting Pet Crickets," *Ventura County (CA) Star-Free Press*, March 14, 1957; "Desmond Leaps from Monks to Crickets to Mustaches" by Paul Coates, *Los Angeles Mirror*, August 18, 1960.

Police raid 8929 Hollywood Hills Road: "Marijuana Charge: Scott Brady Says He Was 'Framed,'" *Valley Times*, North Hollywood, CA, October 19, 1957; "Actors Brady and Slattery Arrested on Dope Charge," *Ventura County Star Free Press*, October 19, 1957; Author interviews with Timothy Tierney, 2001; *Investigation Hollywood!* by Fred Otash, H. Regnery, 1976.

Brady and Slattery maintain innocence: "Charge Actor's Arrest 'Bizarre,'" *Wilmington (CA) Daily Press Journal*, October 21, 1957; "Pounding denial of narcotics charges is actor Scott Brady," photo caption, International Soundphoto, *Gallup (NM) Independent*, October 27, 1957.

Risk of "unmasking confidential informant" leads to dismissal: "Scott Brady, Slattery Cleared in Dope Case," *Los Angeles Times*, December 10, 1957; "Actor, Publicist Freed of Charges," United Press report, *Nevada State Journal*, December 12, 1957.

Chapter 25

Tierney's NYC exploits, winter 1957–spring 1958

Punches man in bar over Georgette McDonald: Cholly Knickerbocker syndicated column, *Miami Herald*, December 26, 1957.

Reports Tierney is teaching at Brooklyn drama school: The Lyons Den by Leonard Lyons, syndicated column, *Hollywood (CA) Evening Citizen News*, January 9, 1958.

Reports Tierney will wed wealthy divorcee Helen Kellogg: Voice of Broadway by Dorothy Kilgallen, syndicated column, *Star-Gazette*, Elmira, NY, February 10, 1958; Louella Parsons Talking, syndicated column, *Tipton (IN) Daily Tribune*, March 15, 1959.

Report investors want to back Tierney as private eye: The Smart Set by Cholly Knickerbocker, syndicated column, *Shamokin (PA) News Dispatch,* March 25, 1958.

Civil Air Patrol television pilot

Tierney films pilot in Florida: Interview with Sammy Petrillo by Todd Rutt, *Psychotronic Video* magazine, issue no. 11, 1992.

"New, Modern Building: Former, Present Mayor To Dedicate Theater," *Ocala (FL) Sentinel,* April 10, 1958; Best of Hollywood by Louella Parsons, syndicated column, *Philadelphia Inquirer,* April 23, 1958.

Arrested for breaking jaw of advertising man

Tierney arrested outside Hotel Astor: "'Tough Guy' Tierney in New Law Scrape," Associated Press report, *Valley Times,* North Hollywood, CA, July 24, 1958.

Tierney charged with felonious assault: "Police Land Bad Actor for Fist Play," *NY Daily News,* July 25, 1958; "Movie Actor Arraigned on Charge of Assault," *Tyler (TX) Morning Telegraph,* July 25, 1958.

Arrest doesn't affect role in *Naked City* television series: "One to Get Lost," season 1, episode 20, *Naked City* (1958–1963), IMDbPro.

West Fifty-Eighth Street brawl: New York Confidential by Kee Mortimer, *Post-Star,* Glens Falls, NY, August 6, 1958.

Sidewalk brawl with NYPD officers Louis Romano and Samuel Saipan

Bloody fight with cops outside Midtown Café: "Tierney Arrested Here: Actor Held in $3500 Bail for Brawling with Policemen," *New York Times,* October 14, 1958; "Tierney's in Again for Battling Cops," *NY Journal-American,* October 14, 1958.

Cops admit clubbing Tierney bloody: Ibid., *NY Journal American;* "Bad Actor, Bad Show" (photo), *NY Daily News,* October 15, 1958.

Tierney posed with Officer Romano: "Actor Jailed after Fight," Associated Press wirephoto, *Valley Times,* North Hollywood, CA, October 14, 1958.

Tierney goes berserk at hospital: "'Bad Actor' Tierney's Show Folded by Cops," *NY Daily News,* November 2, 1958.

Hearing: "I'm a cop hater," Ibid., *NY Daily News.*

Reveal cops broke Tierney's jaw in fight: It Happened Last Night by Earl Wilson, syndicated column, *Knoxville (TN) Journal,* October 23, 1958.

Chapter 26

Gwili Andre (Gruili A. Cross)

Gwili Andre: "The Private Life and Times of Gwili Andre," Glamour Girls of the Silver Screen (website); "Story of Gwili Andre" by Amber Grey, BellaOnline (website).

Death of Gwili Andre: "Woman Dies in Home Fire," *Los Angeles Times,* February 6, 1959.

Source Notes

"Ex-Actress Gurlie Cross Dies in Fire," *Long Beach Independent,* February 6, 1959; "Once a Top Model: Gwili Andre Cross Dies in California Fire," Associated Press report, *Kansas City (MO) Times,* February 7, 1959.

Andre, Tierney, on "Skidville Avenue": "Some Movie Greats Have Found Skidville Ave. Steep, Fast Road," Joseph L. Haas, *Nashville Banner* and *Chicago Daily News,* February 16, 1959.

Tierney turns down gangster role: "No Gangsters For Tierney," *Detroit Free Press,* February 22, 1969.

Arrested in Hollywood for drunkenness

Arrested for harassing men on Cahuenga Boulevard: "Actor Tierney Seized as Drunk," *Los Angeles Times,* May 4, 1959; "Actor Jailed Again," *York (PA) Dispatch,* May 4, 1959; "Lawrence Tierney in Trouble Again," United Press International report, *Republican and Herald,* Pottsville, PA, May 4, 1959; "Lawrence Tierney Forfeits Bail," *Los Angeles Times,* May 5, 1959.

Career contrasted with Scott Brady's

Brady stars in *Destry Rides Again* on Broadway: "Theatre: Destry Rides In," review by Brooks Atkinson, *New York Times,* April 24, 1959.

Tierney remembered in NYC: "Third Ave. Bar sports a sign: 'Lawrence Tierney Fought Here,'" It Happened Last Night by Earl Wilson, syndicated column, *Amarillo (TX) Globe-Times,* June 11, 1959.

Brady gives credit to brother Larry: "a good actor, a hell of a good brother, and I want that on the record," "Brady Takes 'Destry' In Stride," *Philadelphia Inquirer,* July 13, 1959; "My New York," Mel Heimer, *Kane (PA) Republican,* July 14, 1959.

Tierney writing *Christmas Story* script with Errol Flynn's assistant: Column item by Mike Connolly, *Daily Times,* Davenport, IA, August 3, 1959.

Scott Brady as *Shotgun Slade*: "Brady Gets Role of Flying Sleuth," *Courier-Post,* Camden, NJ, August 29, 1959.

Tierney loses role in *Lawless Years,* gains *Captain of Detectives*: Lawless: TV Off-Beat by Matt Messina, *NY Daily News*; *Captain*: Broadway by Dorothy Kilgallen, syndicated column, *Oneonta (NY) Star,* August 12, 1959.

Fisticuffs outside Hollywood High School

Fight leads to drunkenness charge: "'Tough Guy' Tierney Held as Drunk Again," United Press International report, *Oakland Tribune,* September 19, 1959; "Street Brawl Lands Actor in Hoosegow," United Press International report, *Fort Worth Star-Telegram,* September 19, 1959.

Chapter 27

The death of Errol Flynn

Errol Flynn's last days and death: "60 Years Ago, Errol Flynn's Wild Ways Ended in Vancouver," Jesse Donaldson, *Montecristo* magazine, October 4, 2019; "Errol Flynn

Dies after Heart Attack," *New York Daily News,* October 15, 1959; "Errol Flynn Dies at 50 in Vancouver," Associated Press report, *Los Angeles Times,* October 15, 1959; "Errol Flynn Dies, Medic at His Side," United Press International report, *Fort Lauderdale News,* October 15, 1959.

Incident at Beatrice Colgan's apartment

Tierney forces way into Beatrice Colgan's apartment: Author interview with Carroll Coates, June 30, 2021; "Actor Tierney Faces Fighting, Drunk Charges," Associated Press report, *Sioux City (IA) Journal,* November 19, 1959.

Tierney punches composer Carroll Coates: Ibid., Carroll Coates interview.

Charged with drunkenness, battery, and disturbing the peace: "Actor Tierney Case Continued," *Los Angeles Times,* November 10, 1969.

Tierney pleads innocent: "Tierney to Face Charges Jan. 7," *Valley Times,* North Hollywood, CA, November 24, 1959; "Actor to Face Trial: Lawrence Tierney Accused of Drunkenness," United Press International report, *York (PA) Dispatch,* November 24, 1959.

Wilshire Boulevard arrest and hospital melee

Beverly Hills drunk, fighting arrest: "Lawrence Tierney, Actor, Arrested as Drunk Again," United Press International report, *Tampa Tribune,* December 13, 1959; "Lawrence Tierney Jailed after Fight," Associated Press report, *Racine (WI) Journal Times,* December 13, 1959.

Restrained, towel in mouth, at Central Receiving Hospital: "Hush Up," Associated Press wirephoto, *Greenville (SC) News;* December 14, 1959; "Towel Used to Quiet Actor," *Progress-Bulletin,* Pomona, CA, December 14, 1959.

Sentenced on previous drunk charge: "Lawrence Tierney Receives One-Day Suspended Sentence," United Press International report, *Colton (CA) Courier,* December 14, 1959.

Death of mother, Mary Alice Tierney

Tierney admits he can't beat alcohol: Harold Heffernan Says, syndicated story, *Birmingham (AL) News,* January 1, 1960; I Heard Today in Hollywood by Harold Heffernan, syndicated story, *Edmonton (Alberta) Journal,* January 5, 1960.

Tierney pleads not guilty in Beatrice Colgan break-in: "Actor Lawrence Tierney is Arrested," *Colton (CA) Courier,* January 8, 1960.

Receives word mother has died: "Mrs. Tierney, Mother of Actors, Dies," *Los Angeles Times,* January 8, 1960; Author interviews with Timothy Tierney, 2021.

Drunk arrest following mother's death: "Nab Tierney on Drunk Count Again," *Valley Times,* North Hollywood, CA, January 8, 1960; "Actor Arrested after Mom's Death," United Press International report, *Tampa Times,* January 8, 1960; "Judge Decided against Arrest," United Press International report, *Spokane Chronicle,* January 8, 1960.

Source Notes

Mary Alice Crowley as possible suicide: "Actors' Mother Dead with Pills Nearby," Associated Press report, *Bridgeport (CT) Post,* January 8, 1960; "Actors' Kin Found Dead," Associated Press Report, *Evening Sun,* Baltimore, MD, January 8, 1960.

Family blames Tierney for mother's death: Author interviews with Timothy Tierney, C. Courtney Joyner, David Del Valle, 2021.

Fight and estrangement with brother Scott Brady: Author interviews with Timothy Tierney, June 30, July 8, October 21, 2021.

Tierney returns to New York City

Adventures in Paradise and *Man with a Camera* air on same night: Television & Radio (listings), *Fort Lauderdale News,* January 25, 1960; "Leading TV Shows Picked for Tonight," *Valley Times,* North Hollywood, CA, January 25, 1960.

Tierney rejoins Alcoholics Anonymous: It Happened Last Night by Earl Wilson, syndicated column, *Tribune,* Scranton, PA, January 28, 1960.

Hollywood "family jinx": "Being Related to a Star: Show Biz Kiss of Death?" Comments on the Passing Parade, As I See It by Harry Schreiner, *Kings County Chronicle,* Brooklyn, NY, January 28, 1960.

Celebrities' "preferential treatment" in drunk driving cases: "Leniency to Show People by the Law Stirs Furor," by Howard Heffernan, syndicated story, *Kansas City Star,* February 14, 1960.

Tierney and William Talman orgy arrest: "Guests Frolicking Nude: Prosecutor of Perry Mason Show, 7 Others Jailed in Dope Orgy," United Press International report, *Evansville (IN) Courier,* March 14, 1960; "Singer Labels Nude Party as Being 'Sociable,'" Associated Press report, *Daily Republican,* Monongahela, PA, March 15, 1960; "Talman Pleads Innocent, Loses His Job Anyway," *Arizona Daily Star,* Tucson, AZ, March 18, 1960; "Can the Good Guys Be Bad Guys Off-Screen?" *NY Daily News,* May 22, 1960.

Chapter 28

Carla Monson and Grand Macnish

Grand Macnish whisky: "Original: The Grand Macnish Story," History, Grand Macnish website.

Attempted break-in at Carla Monson's apartment: "Lawrence Tierney Jailed as Drunk," *Valley Times,* North Hollywood, CA, May 31, 1960; "'Dillinger' Jailed," United Press International report, *San Francisco Examiner,* May 31, 1960: "Actor Tierney Jailed on Woman's Plaint," United Press International report, *Atlanta Constitution,* May 31, 1960.

Drunkenness charge: "Movie Dillinger Jailed as Drunk," United Press International report, *Morning Call,* Allentown, PA, June 1, 1960; "Tierney Forfeits Drunk Charge Bail," *Daily Herald,* Provo, UT, June 2, 1960.

Sentenced for Beatrice Colgan break-in: "Lawrence Tierney Ordered to Quit Drinking by Judge," *Colton (CA) Courier,* July 29, 1960.

Unholy Alliance with Sammy Petrillo: Interview with Sammy Petrillo by Todd Rutt, *Psychotronic Video* magazine, issue no. 11, 1992.

Source Notes

Georgette McDonald marries: "Georgette McDonald is now Mrs. John Otis of the Otis Elevator clan," Walter Winchell . . . of Broadway, *NY Daily News*, October 14, 1960.

Anne Winterburn and Tierney's daughter

Relations with Anne Winterburn: "Family Tradition: Michael Tierney interviewed by Rick McKay," *Scarlet Street* magazine, issue 29, 1998; Author interviews with Timothy Tierney, 2021.

Anne Winterburn background: "Teen-Age Girls Injured as Car Plunges 30 Feet," *Los Angeles Times*, July 29, 1953; Anne Winterburn, Ancestry.com; Author interviews with Timothy Tierney, 2021.

Anne Winterburn as dancer, Miss Shellfish: Around Town with Ivan Paul, *San Francisco Examiner*, June 11, 1960; Timothy Tierney conversation with Anne's friend Cynthia Fuller, October 2021.

Drunk driving arrest with Anne Winterburn: "Deputies Nab Tierney," *Valley Times*, North Hollywood, CA, December 15, 1960; "Tough Guy Actor Nabbed: Lawrence Tierney Faces Drink Charge," United Press International report, *South (IN) Bend Tribune*, December 15, 1960; "Actor Lawrence Tierney Held on Drunk Driving Charge," United Press International report, *Oakland Tribune*, December 15, 1960; "Toughie Tierney Nabbed as Tipsy," United Press International report, *NY Daily News*, December 16, 1960.

Anne Winterburn marries Edward Tierney, raises Lawrence's daughter: "Very Chinatown": "Family Tradition: Michael Tierney interviewed by Rick McKay," *Scarlet Street* magazine, issue 29, 1998; author interviews with Timothy Tierney, 2021.

Minor roles, court appearances

Tierney pleads not guilty to drunk driving: "Lawrence Tierney Faces Drunk Trial," United Press International report, *Arizona Republic*, December 23, 1960.

Tierney role in *Peter Gunn*: Night Watch by Percy Shain, *Boston Globe*, December 27, 1960.

Tierney roles in *The Barbara Stanwyck Show*: "The Assassin" (season 1, episode 32) and "Big Jake" (season 1, episode 35), *The Barbara Stanwyck Show* (1960), IMDbPro.

"Success sickness": "'Success' Sickness of Stars: Worry on Film Roles," *Sydney Morning Herald*, Sydney, Australia, February 19, 1961.

Sentenced for drunk driving: "Lawrence Tierney's License Suspended," *Los Angeles Times*, May 5, 1961; "Tierney Pays Fine as Drunk," United Press International report, *Arizona Republic*, May 5, 1961.

"Remember Lawrence Tierney?": "When Actors and Real Life Merge" by Vernon Scott, United Press International syndicated column, *Times Colonist*, Victoria, British Columbia, May 13, 1961.

Chapter 29

Incident at Eddie Fisher–Elizabeth Taylor party

Moiseyev Dance Company: "The 1958 Tour of the Moiseyev Dance Company: A Window into American Perception" by Victoria Hallinan, Northeastern University, *Journal of History and Cultures* (1), 2012; "Soviet Troupe Due Back: Moiseyev Dancers to Come to Madison Sq. Garden in June," *New York Times,* April 24, 1958; "'Bulba'—A Song and Dance about the Potato," *San Francisco Examiner,* April 27, 1958; "Show Business 'John Dulles' Hails Exchange," Associated Press report, *Ventura County (CA) Free Press,* June 28, 1958.

Fisher–Taylor connection to Moiseyev: "Liz, Eddie Are Host to Russian Dancers: Hollywood Stars, Troupers Trade Steps at Party; Fisher Wows Reds," United Press International report, *Record,* Hackensack, NJ, June 29, 1961.

Tierney crashes party at P.J.'s: "Ho, Hum! Movie Tough Guy Is Party Crasher," Associated Press report, *News-Palladium,* Benton Harbor, MI, June 29, 1961; "Lawrence Tierney Crashes Party, Fights, Arrested," Associated Press report, *Santa Cruz (CA) Sentinel,* June 29, 1961; "Nab Tierney for Rushin' Eddie-Liz Russian Party," United Press International report, *News,* Patterson, NJ, June 29, 1961; "Tough Guy Tierney Fails Trying to Crash Liz's Party," United Press International report, *Boston Globe,* June 30, 1961.

Assault, disturbing the peace, drunkenness: "Lawrence Tierney Bails Out on Drunk Charge," Associated Press report, *Arizona Daily Star,* Tucson, AZ, June 30, 1961; "Tierney Must Answer Drunk Charge July 5," *Valley Times,* North Hollywood, CA, June 30, 1961; "Tierney Granted Continuance," United Press International report, *Tucson (AZ) Daily Citizen,* July 6, 1961.

Tierney denies political motive at P.J.'s: "Tierney Fights Cops at Party," Associated Press report, *Lancaster (PA) New Era,* June 29, 1961.

Pleads innocence, jailed for probation violation: "Jury Trial Is Asked by Lawrence Tierney," Associated Press report, *Alabama Journal,* Montgomery, AL, July 13, 1961; "Actor Tierney Gets 60-Day Sentence," United Press International report, *Boston Globe,* July 13, 1961; "Screen Dillinger Gets 60-Day Sentence," Associated Press report, *Fort Worth Star-Telegram,* July 14, 1961.

Role in *Bus Stop*: Tierney as Swede in "The Ordeal of Kevin Brooks," season 1, episode 22 of *Bus Stop,* aired ABC network, February 25, 1962, IMDbPro.

Friendship with playwright William Inge: Author interview with C. Courtney Joyner, July 16, 2021.

Role in *Follow the Sun*: Behind the Scenes in Hollywood by Harrison Carroll, syndicated column, *Wilkes-Barre (PA) Times Leader,* November 4, 1961; "Lawrence Tierney Eyes Another Comeback," Voice of Broadway by Dorothy Kilgallen, syndicated column, *Philadelphia Daily News,* November 9, 1961.

Potential role in Stanley Kramer's *Point Blank*: Dorothy Manners, syndicated column, *Record,* Hackensack, NJ, November 10, 1961.

Source Notes

Heffernan interview: "Lawrence Tierney's Struggle to Straighten Himself Out: Actor's Career Almost Ruined by Booze, He's Now on Wagon for Good," Harold Heffernan, *Boston Globe*, November 19, 1961.

Favorable review for *Follow the Sun*: Night Watch by Percy Shain, *Follow the Sun*, chap. 7, *Boston Globe*, November 27, 1961.

Chapter 30

Bowling alley incident

Battery complaint: "Actor Is Charged: Battery Complaint Latest Tierney Trouble," *York (PA) Dispatch*, December 2, 1961.

Battery charge dropped: "Bowling Brawl Charge Dropped," United Press International report, *Fort Lauderdale News*, December 14, 1961; "Lawrence Tierney Spared Court Trial," United Press International report, *Courier-Post*, Camden, NJ, December 14, 1961; "Case against Tierney Folds," United Press International report, *St. Joseph (MO) Gazette*, December 14, 1961.

Another fight outside Hollywood High

Treated at hospital jailed after fight: "Booked on plain drunk charge . . . bailed," *Valley Times*, North Hollywood, CA, December 26, 1961; "Tierney Free on Bail," *Redlands (CA) Daily Facts*, December 26, 1961.

Paired with John Agar arrests: "Famous Imbibers 'Ship' [typo, should read 'Slip'] Once Again," North American Newspaper Alliance report, *Calgary Herald*, January 8, 1962.

Storms and floods

Hollywood Hills mudslides: "L. A. Switches Signals; Prays for Rain to Stop," Associated Press report, *Cedar Rapids (IA) Gazette*, February 16, 1962.

Tierney pictured in flood: "Actor Battles Mud," Associated Press wirephoto, *Indianapolis News*, February 13, 1962.

A Child Is Waiting

Tierney comeback in *A Child Is Waiting*: Hollywood by Louella Parsons, syndicated column, *Indianapolis Star*, February 19, 1962; "Lawrence Tierney Making First Movie in Six Years" by Vernon Scott, syndicated column, *Progress Bulletin*, Pomona, CA, February 28, 1962; "Lawrence Tierney Hopeful Film Will Mark Comeback" by Dorothy Kilgallen, syndicated column, *Fort Worth Star-Telegram*, March 14, 1962.

Vow to stick with Alcoholics Anonymous: "nothing will interfere with his attendance," Hollywood by Louella Parsons, syndicated column, *Indianapolis Star*, February 19, 1962.

Seymour Cassel on Tierney and Cassavetes: *Shoot It! Hollywood Inc. and the Rising of Independent Film*, by David Spaner, Arsenal Pulp, 2011.

Judy Garland issues on set: Burt Lancaster quoted, *A Child Is Waiting*, by Jeff Stafford, Articles and Reviews, TCM.com, July 28, 2003.

Source Notes

Tierney celebrates sobriety: "Only Clink in His Future Is of Coins, Says Tierney" by Vernon Scott, syndicated column, *Press & Sun-Bulletin*, Binghamton, NY, March 5, 1962.

Scott Brady

Shotgun Slade canceled: "His 'Shotgun Slade' program hitting TV rerun trails," "Teens Have Reel-Life Father Image as Star Accepts Family's Invitation," *Atlanta Constitution*, February 7, 1962.

Brady tours with *The Best Man*: "Gore Vidal Comedy Here," *Austin (TX) American*, February 18, 1962.

More Tierney arrests

Santa Monica diner incident: "Fracas," *Long Beach (CA) Independent*, June 2, 1962; "Lawrence Tierney Drunk Trial Set," United Press International report, *Eureka Humboldt (CA) Standard*, June 2, 1962; "Tierney Forfeits $52 Bail," United Press International report, *Arizona Republic*, Phoenix, AZ, June 27, 1962.

Van Nuys warrants: "Lawrence Tierney was slated to appear," *Valley Times*, North Hollywood, CA, July 2, 1962; "Actor Asks for Jury Trial," *Los Angeles Times*, July 19, 1962.

Completes role in *Sea Hunt*: "Lloyd's Son Guest," *Valley Times*, North Hollywood, CA, July 4, 1962.

Arrests in Hollywood

Drunk in middle of Hollywood Boulevard: "Actor Tierney Is Arrested for Drunkenness," United Press International report, *Sacramento Bee*, July 21, 1962.

Fight with Dimitrios Georgopoulos: "tried to pull off a neck brace and then ripped the receiver from a telephone," "Tierney Arrested," United Press International report, *Shreveport (LA) Journal*, July 21, 1962.

Slashed in bar fight: "Actor Lands in Hospital after Brawl," *Los Angeles Citizen News*, September 28, 1962.

Edward Tierney's return

"Ed Tracy" plays Nazis on *Combat!* and *The Gallant Men*: "International 'Enemy,'" *Tampa Tribune*, January 6, 1963; Author interviews with Timothy Tierney, 2021.

Ed Tierney interview: "TV Nazis Prove Easy for Irishman," Allen Rich, TV-Radio Editor, *Valley Times*, North Hollywood, CA, October 11, 1962.

Tierney's further legal troubles

Georgopolous case dropped: "Charge Dismissed against Tierney," *Los Angeles Times*, October 17, 1962; "Tierney Cleared of Battery Charge," Associated Press report, *San Bernardino County (CA) Sun*, October 18, 1962.

Arrest for "suspicion of being drunk": "Tierney Arrested," Associated Press report, *San Bernardino County (CA) Sun*, October 20, 1962.

Chapter 31

Tierney "off the deep end" in early 1960s

Tierney vs. his brothers: Timothy Tierney and Michael Tierney interview, *The Midnight Palace with Gary Sweeney* radio show, circa 2011.

A Child Is Waiting opens: "Somebody goofed . . . drive-ins," Lively Arts by Marjory Rutherford, *Atlanta Constitution,* January 7, 1963; "'A Child Is Waiting,' Compelling Picture," On the Screen, *Baltimore Evening Sun,* January 24, 1963.

Pleads guilty to drunk charges: People in the News Today, *Valley Times,* North Hollywood, CA, January 11, 1963; Person to Person, *Honolulu Advertiser,* January 12, 1963.

Probation report: "Actor Tierney on Probation," *Valley Times,* North Hollywood, CA, February 12, 1963.

Judge gives Tierney a "break": "Tierney Arrested for Intoxication; Given Probation," Associated Press report, *Argus-Leader,* Sioux Falls, SD, February 12, 1963; "'Dillinger' Gets Break, Goes to AA," Associated Press report, *Pensacola (FL) News,* February 12, 1963.

Scott Brady scandal

Brady in *Operation Bikini*: Operation Bikini (1963), AFI Catalogue of Feature Films: The First 100 Years, 1893–1993.

Banned by NY Racing Commission: "Actor Brady, 3 Yonkers Bookies among 8 Barred from Trot Races," *Journal News,* White Plains, NY, April 2, 1963; "Actor among 8 Men Barred Permanently by N.Y Harness Racing," Associated Press report, *Rochester (NY) Democrat and Chronicle*; Author interviews with Timothy Tierney, 2021.

Assault with sugar bowl, kidnapping charges

Role in *The Alfred Hitchcock Hour*: "Show Explores Death of Cop," *Star-Gazette,* Elmira, NY, May 18, 1963.

Arrest for public intoxication, fight with counterman at Sontag Drug Store: "Actor Jailed after Fight in Drugstore," *Valley Times,* North Hollywood, CA, May 13, 1963; "Actor Booked after 'Duel' with Waiter," Associated Press report, *Fort Worth Star-Telegram,* May 13, 1963; "Assault Charged to Film 'Toughie,'" Associated Press report, *Fort Lauderdale News,* May 13, 1963; "Tierney Arrested in Row," *Pasadena (CA) Independent,* May 14, 1963; "Actor Tierney Freed on Bond," *Ventura County (CA) Star,* May 15, 1963.

"Tierney is one of the real tragedies of the movie colony": "Morals Depend On Time, Place . . . i.e. Cleopatra," Jack Kofoed, *Miami Herald,* May 19, 1963.

"Kidnapping" of Sylvia Toboas: "Kidnap Charge Filed: Tierney Held as Drunk," Associated Press report, *Chicago Tribune,* May 24, 1963.

Judge issues warrant for Tierney's arrest: "Actor Sought by LA Court," United Press International report, *Hanford (CA) Sentinel,* June 15, 1963; "Order the Arrest of Film Dillinger," United Press International report, *NY Daily News,* June 16, 1963; "Lawmen Hunt 'John Dillinger,'" United Press International report, *Miami Herald,* June 16, 1963.

Tierney runs to New York City

Friendship with Brendan Behan: Author interview with C. Courtney Joyner, July 16, 2021.

Arrest for shoving police officer: "Actor Tierney in Re-Run in with Cops," *NY Daily News*, October 18, 1963.

JFK assassination

Producer Jack I. Schwarz convicted of underage sex: "Film Producer Gets Jail in Morals Case," Associated Press report, *Fresno Bee*, November 22, 1963.

Hollywood reacts to Kennedy assassination: "Cameras Halt in Hollywood: 'Can't Continue' Film Stars Say," by Bob Thomas, Associated Press, syndicated report, *Arizona Daily Star*, Tucson, AZ, November 23, 1963; "'All Showbiz Mourns JFK': How *Variety* Covered the Aftermath of Assassination," Ted Johnson, *Variety*, November 21, 2013.

Jack LaRue's suspected heart attack: Ibid., Bob Thomas, Associated Press report.

"Tierney fined as a pusher": Headline, *NY Daily News*, December 28, 1963.

Chapter 32

Death of Lawrence Tierney Sr.

Unrecognizable Tierney outside theater: "Miracle and Me," *It Seemed Important at the Time, A Romance Memoir* by Gloria Vanderbilt, Simon & Schuster, 2004.

Lawrence H. Tierney death: "Tierney, Film Actors' Father, Dies at Age 72," *Los Angeles Times*, February 14, 1964; "Actors' Father Dies: Lawrence Tierney, Sr. Stricken at Scott Brady's Home," Associated Press report, *Kansas City Times*, February 14, 1964.

Lawrence Sr. dies in Scott Brady's arms: Author interviews with Timothy Tierney, June 30, 2021, July 8, 2021.

Arrested for choking cab driver

Assault on cabbie Jack Brass: "Actor Tierney in New Jam," *NY Daily News*, February 18, 1964; "Actor Held in Assault," Associated Press report, *Courier News*, Blytheville, AR, February 18, 1964; "Actor Tried to Choke Driver," *Sydney Morning Herald*, February 19, 1964.

Tierney gives Vito Frisina's address as his own: Author interviews with AnnMarie Frisina Guertin, June 2021.

Tierney held on bail: "Defer Tierney Hearing," *NY Daily News*, February 18, 1964; "Tierney Held in $1,500 Bail," *NY Daily News*, February 19, 1964; "Lighten Tierney Charge," *NY Daily News*, March 27, 1964.

Tierney now "beefy and florid": "Problem Actor in Trouble Again," Jack Kofoed, *Miami Herald*, May 17, 1964.

Tierney found guilty: "Actor Tierney Found Guilty in Taxi Fight," *NY Daily News*, April 21, 1964; "Actor Tierney Guilty in Cabbie Assault," New York News Service report, *Salt Lake Tribune*, Salt Lake City, UT, April 21, 1964.

Daily News interview outside courtroom: "Larry Tierney Has Court Rerun, without Commercials," *NY Daily News*, April 30, 1964.

Tierney sentenced to probation: Ibid., *NY Daily News*; "Lawrence Tierney Gets Year Suspended Term," Associated Press report, *St. Louis Post-Dispatch*, April 30, 1964.

Tierney creates more scenes

Tierney rage in apartment lobby: Hollywood Sheilah Graham, syndicated column, *Times-Tribune*, Scranton, PA, May 6, 1964.

Tierney as troublemaker, "went down like a throw rug": Author interview with Ray Boylan, September 25, 2021.

The 1964 World's Fair

World's Fair: *The 1964–1965 New York World's Fair* by Bill Cotter and Bill Young, Arcadia, 2013.

Hollywood U.S.A. pavilion: Hollywood, *Official Guide, New York World's Fair 1964/65*, Time Incorporated, 1964; Hollywood U.S.A. *1965 Official Guide, New York World's Fair*, Time Incorporated, 1964.

Tierney works at Hollywood U.S.A. pavilion: "Lawrence ('Dillinger') Tierney has landed a job at the World's Fair Hollywood Pavilion," Big City Beat by James Davis, *NY Daily News*, July 7, 1964.

Fight leads to extended jail stay

Drunken fight at Riverside Plaza Hotel: "Tierney Drops Another to Law," *NY Daily News*, August 5, 1964.

Tierney remains in jail: Broadway After Dark, *Coney Island Times*, August 28, 1964.

Chapter 33

Europe

Tierney heads to Italy: It Happened Last Night by Earl Wilson, syndicated column, *Pittsburgh Post-Gazette*, February 16, 1965.

Tierney appears in Italian *giallo*: New York Cavalcade by Louis Sobol, *Wilkes-Barre Times Leader*, April 15, 1965; Broadway by Dorothy Kilgallen, syndicated column, *Shamokin (PA) News-Dispatch*, April 19, 1965.

Assassino senza volto: "*Assassino senza volto* (*Killer Without A Face*) (1968)," *Feeding Soda Pop to the Thirsty Pigs since 2013*, Mark David Welsh film blog, March 10, 2020.

Young Dillinger: "'Young Dillinger' Right on Mark," review by Kevin Thomas, *Los Angeles Times*, June 11, 1965.

End of gossip queen era

Death of Dorothy Kilgallen: "Dorothy Kilgallen Is Found Dead in Bed at Her Home," *NY Daily News*, November 9, 1965; "Dorothy Kilgallen Death Cause Made Public," Associated Press report, *Independent-Record*, Helena, MT, November 15, 1965.

Louella Parsons retires: "Too Old, Too Ill, Louella Parsons Retires" by Bob Thomas, Associated Press, syndicated story, *Asbury Park (NJ) Press*, November 18, 1965.

Hedda Hopper dies: "Movie Writer Hedda Hopper Dies at 75," Associated Press report, *Fort Worth Star-Telegram*, February 2, 1966.

Tierney in "fatal car crash" in Europe

Tierney claims fatal crash in Steve Reeves's car, prison: Author interviews with C. Courtney Joyner, 2021; Author interviews with David De Valle, 2021.

"With Larry, I never knew what was real or invented": Author interview with Stephan Morrow, May 7, 2021.

Reeves never mentioned incident: Author's email correspondence with Christopher LeClaire, author of *Worlds to Conquer*, Reeves's authorized biography, October 21, 2021.

Tierney jailed in Europe: John Slaughter, fansite reminiscence.

Friendship with Jean-Paul Sartre: Author interview with Timothy Tierney, October 8, 2021.

Custer of the West

US columnists notice Tierney's absence: On the Town with Vic Wilmot, *Arizona Republic* (Phoenix), August 3, 1966.

Philip Yordan hires Tierney on Custer film in Spain: It Happened Last Night by Earl Wilson, syndicated column, *Tribune*, Scranton, PA, September 27, 1966; Voice of Broadway by Jack O'Brian, *Glens Falls (NY) Times*, September 30, 1966.

Shoplifting arrest in Paris

Arrested in Paris department store: Voice of Broadway by Jack O'Brian, syndicated column, *Indianapolis News*, January 26, 1967; "Suspended Term to Actor Tierney," Associated Press report, *Des Moines Tribune*, February 28, 1967; "Actor Tierney in Paris Court," United Press International report, *El Paso Herald-Post*, February 28, 1967; "Actor Tierney Fined in Paris," *Miami Herald*, March 1, 1967.

Friends recall Tierney's shoplifting habits: Author interview with AnnMarie Frisina Guertin, June 8, 2021; Author interview with C. Courtney Joyner, March 8, 2021, July 16, 2021; reminiscence by Tierney fansite administrator.

Tierney robs director Gordon Douglas: Ibid., C. Courtney Joyner interviews.

Custer of the West opens: "British Custer," publicity photo, syndicated, *News-Journal*, Mansfield, OH, December 20, 1967; "'Custer of the West' (At the Empire)," Films of the Day by Dennis Stack, *Kansas City (MO) Times*, January 27, 1968.

Tierney seeks role in *The Boston Strangler*: The Lyons Den by Leonard Lyons, *Kenosha (WI) News*, December 16, 1967.

Chapter 34

Tierney in NYC, working construction site

Columnists find Tierney at construction site: Ibid., Leonard Lyons; Sheilah Graham, syndicated column, *Valley Times*, North Hollywood, CA, December 14, 1967.

Reviews for *Custer of The West*: "'Custer of the West' Is Excellent Film," review, *Sacramento Bee*, March 3, 1968; "'Custer' Now Showing at Cooper 70," *Colorado Springs*

Gazette-Telegraph, June 29, 1968; "Custer of the West," review by Renata Adler, *New York Times,* July 4, 1968; "'Custer of the West' Plays Multiple Run," review by Kevin Thomas, *Los Angeles Times,* July 25, 1968.

Custer renamed *A Good Day for Fighting:* "Custer Still a Loser in 'Day for Fighting,'" *Boston Globe,* August 1, 1968.

Tierney representing "older generation"

"Street scene" following Martin Luther King Jr. assassination: People Will Talk, On Broadway by Walter Winchell, syndicated column, *Post-Star,* Glens Falls, NY, May 10, 1968.

"Young Dillinger" Nick Adams dies of overdose: "Actor Nick Adams Found Dead at Home; Cause Undetermined," *Los Angeles Times,* February 8, 1968; "Nick Adams, TV's 'Rebel,' Found Dead," Associated Press report, *NY Daily News,* February 8, 1968.

Silhouettes in Courage: advertisement, *Atlanta Constitution,* January 12, 1969; "NOW records 'Silhouettes in Courage,'" *Cincinnati Enquirer,* September 20, 1970.

Tierney's comments about *Bonnie and Clyde:* Inside Hollywood with Sheilah Graham, syndicated column, *News,* Paterson, NJ, June 19, 1968.

Mentions by Larry King: Larry King column, *Miami Herald,* July 2; July 11, 1968; April 27, 1969.

"Fatso" television commercial: Ibid., Larry King, July 11, 1968; Ask the Globe, *Boston Globe,* September 29, 1968.

Tierney "blimped to Orson Welles size": Voice of Broadway by Jack O'Brian, syndicated column, *Glens Falls (NY) Times,* May 26, 1969.

Tierney a "good boy again": Voice of Broadway by Jack O'Brian, syndicated column, *Republican and Herald,* Pottsville, PA, August 17, 1968.

Greenwich Village arrest

Washington Square Park and vicinity: Greenwich Village in the 1960s, Ephemeral New York; Author scouting, Washington Square Park and MacDougal Street area, May 2019, June 2021.

Arrest for attack on NBC News crew and cameraman: "Joust with TV-ers Jails Tuffy Tierney," *NY Daily News.*

Tierney and Mickey Spillane's *The Delta Factor:* Hy Gardner's Glad You Asked That!, *Daily News-Post,* Monrovia, CA, April 16, 1969.

Jake LaMotta on *The Spy:* Twice Over Lightly by Harry Missildine, *Spokesman-Review,* Spokane, WA, February 6, 1969.

Tierney and "alcoholic cancer": Hy Gardner's Glad You Asked That!, *Daily News-Post,* Monrovia, CA, April 16, 1969.

Spillane-Fellows Productions: "Spillane-Fellows Films Picks City for Home Base," *Tennessean,* Nashville, May 8, 1969.

Death of Robert Fellows: "Movie Chief, Fellows, Dies," *Tennessean,* Nashville, May 13, 1969.

Tierney "ailing in Rome": Voice of Broadway by Jack O'Brian, syndicated column, *Republican and Herald,* Pottsville, PA, May 2, 1969.

Chapter 35

1970s

Tierney "living on the streets": "Family Tradition: Michael Tierney interviewed by Rick McKay," *Scarlet Street* magazine, issue 29, 1998; author interviews with Timothy Tierney, 2021.

Loses lead role in *Joe* (public urination): John G. Avildsen, in *Film Directors on Directing,* John A. Gallagher, 1989; Lloyd Kaufman, *Screen Anarchy* in 2014.

The Last Days of Dillinger: "Winona native recreates Dillinger for TV," *Winona (MN) Daily News,* August 8, 1971.

Tierney happy as construction worker: "Former Actor Works with the Hard Hats," Voice of Broadway by Jack O'Brian, syndicated column, *Mercury,* Pottstown, PA, August 23, 1971; It Happened Last Night by Earl Wilson, syndicated column, *Courier-Post,* Camden, NJ, August 30, 1971; Voice of Broadway by Jack O'Brian, syndicated column, *Wilkes-Barre (PA) Record,* October 2, 1971.

Such Good Friends: "Tierney . . . upset a few people, including several pinched gals," Voice of Broadway by Jack O'Brian, *Springfield (MS) News-Leader,* December 6, 1971; *Such Good Friends* (1971), IMDbPro.

John Milius's *Dillinger*: "'Dillinger' Dies Again," *Fort Worth Star-Telegram,* December 7, 1972.

Tierney stabbed

Stabbed in street fight: "Lawrence Tierney Stabbed in West Side Altercation," *New York Times,* January 19, 1973; "Former Actor Stabbed on Street," Associated Press report, *Kansas City Star,* January 19, 1973; "Lawrence Tierney Stabbed in Brawl," Reuters report, *Orlando Sentinel,* January 19, 1973; "Actor Stabbed outside a Bar," United Press International report, *Daily Independent Journal,* San Rafael, CA, January 20, 1973.

Hospitalization: "Tierney Resting," *News and Observer,* Raleigh, NC, January 21, 1973; Voice of Broadway by Jack O'Brian, *Record-Argus,* Greenville, PA, March 6, 1973.

Scott Brady, "ex-star"

Scott Brady's family life in Northridge: "Yesterday's Stars Today: Scott Brady Tells It About Like It Is" by Nancy Anderson, Copley News Service syndicated feature, *Monroe (LA) News-Star,* June 5, 1973; Author interviews with Timothy Tierney, 2021.

Interview with Lawrence Tierney's nephew Tim: James M. Tate, *Cult Film Freak,* March 16, 2019.

Lawrence Tierney onstage

John Milius's *Dillinger* opens: "Movie Review: 'Dillinger' Movie Just a Shoot-em-Up," Janis Kaye, *Miami Herald,* July 3, 1973; "'Dillinger' Turns Into the Gunner," Just Between Us by Emery Wister, *Charlotte (NC) News,* July 16, 1973.

Tierney cancels appearance in production of *Gaslight*: "Charles Matlock Now Appearing in 'Gaslight,'" *Deer Park (TX) Progress,* August 23, 1973.

Plays Willy Loman's brother in *Death of a Salesman* in Philadelphia: "Remember Lawrence Tierney, who played the title role in the old movie 'Dillinger'?" Larry Fields column, *Philadelphia Daily News,* February 12, 1964.

Director George C. Scott disappears before premiere: "George C. Scott and His Mysterious Vanishing Act: Why Did He Quit? Here Are Some Clues," *Philadelphia Inquirer,* March 3, 1974.

Tierney reviewed: "Well-played: Balsam Powerful in 'Death of a Salesman,'" review by Howard A. Coffin, *Philadelphia Inquirer,* March 2, 1974.

Chapter 36

"From Stardom to Hansom"

First reports of Tierney as horse-drawn carriage driver: On the Town by Charles McHarry, *NY Daily News,* May 22, 1974; Larry Fields column, *Philadelphia Daily News,* August 28, 1974.

Competing gossip items: "Tierney opened a drama workshop," It Happened Last Night by Earl Wilson, syndicated column, *Courier-Post,* Camden, NJ, August 12, 1974; "kissing a girl's hand in front of Carnegie Hall," Voice of Broadway by Jack O'Brian, syndicated column, *Asbury Park (NJ) Press,* September 10, 1974.

Associated Press photo of Tierney and horse: "From Stardom to Hansom," *Los Angeles Times,* October 9, 1974; "'Awright You, Wanna Cab?,'" *NY Daily News,* October 10, 1974.

National attention: "Different World," *Sacramento Bee,* October 9, 1974; "Tierney Driving Hansom," People on Parade, "from Advocate wire reports," *Victoria (TX) Advocate,* October 10, 1974; "From Ham to Hansom," *La Crosse (WI) Tribune,* November 8, 1974.

Tierney as hansom cab driver: Lawrence Tierney interview, *Skip E. Lowe Looks at Hollywood,* Los Angeles public access television, circa 1987; Author phone call from Cornelius Byrne, Central Park Carriages, July 20, 2021; Author visit to Central Park Carriages stables, September 9, 2021.

"Spunky Larry still trying": Voice of Broadway by Jack O'Brian, syndicated column, *Daily Journal,* Vineland, NJ, January 28, 1975.

Movie comeback

Tierney announces role in *Abduction*: On the Town by Charles McHarry, *NY Daily News,* January 1, 1975; It Happened Last Night by Earl Wilson, *Pittsburgh Post-Gazette,* January 3, 1975.

"Black Abductor": *Black Abductor* by Harrison James, Regency, 1972.

Colorado Gold: "Western Stars Will Ride Again," *Greenville (SC) News,* February 23, 1975.

Death of Bonnie Jones

"Out the window": "Drink with Actor Tierney Ends in Leap to Her Death," *NY Daily News,* June 21, 1975.

Chapter 37

The Death of Bonnie Jones

"I think I'm going to jump": Ibid., *NY Daily News*; "Drinking Ends in Woman's Death," Metropolitan Briefs, *New York Times,* June 22, 1975; "Fall Kills Woman Partying with Tierney," United Press International report, *Atlanta Constitution,* June 22, 1975.

Reporter's details of incident, Tierney's story to police, and life-saving efforts: Ibid., *NY Daily News.*

Tierney's later mentions of incident: Author interview with Stephan Morrow, May 7, 2021; Author interview with Edward Leahy, July 9, 2021; Author interviews with Timothy Tierney, 2021.

Similarity to scene in *The Hoodlum: The Hoodlum* (1951), review by Danilo Castro, Classic Movie Hub, May 31, 2017.

"Doesn't remember": Author interview with David Del Valle, May 18, 2021.

"I got the justice": Author interview with C. Courtney Joyner, July 16, 2021; Author conversations with C. Courtney Joyner and David Del Valle, summer–fall, 2021.

Chapter 38

Tierney's renewed film career

Abduction arrives in theaters: Earl Wilson column, *Philadelphia Daily News,* October 28, 1975.

Abduction, Patty Hearst disclaimer: Untitled United Press International report, *Pocono Record,* Stroudsburg, PA, October 29, 1975; "'Abduction': Is New Flick Ripoff of Patty Hearst Tale?" by Bob Thomas, Associated Press column, *Daily Item,* Sumter, SC, November 6, 1975.

Andy Warhol's Bad: Andy Warhol's Bad (1977), IMDbPro; *Warhol* by Blake Gopnik, Ecco, 2020.

Tierney on *Bad*: "Terrible film," Tierney interview with Michael and Cheryl Murphy, *Psychotronic Video* magazine, no. 8, Fall 1990.

The Kirlian Witness: "Film: 'Kirlian Witness,' Parapsychology in SoHo," review by Vincent Canby, *New York Times,* June 14, 1979; "Talkin' 'bout My Gentrification: The Secret Life of The Kirlian Witness" by Steve Johnson, *Bright Lights Film Journal,* December 11, 2019.

Tierney as answer to question: Show Biz Quiz by Earl Wilson, syndicated column, *Indianapolis Star,* January 15, 1976; Glad You Asked That by Marilyn and Hy Gardner, syndicated column, *Sunday News and Tribune,* Jefferson City, MO, November 14, 1976.

Naked Evil: Sam Sherman interview, *Drums of Terror: Voodoo in the Cinema* by Brian Senn, Midnight Marquee, 2009; Tierney interview with Michael and Cheryl Murphy, "The Devil Thumbs His Nose!!! To Hell and Back with Lawrence Tierney," *Psychotronic Video* magazine, no. 8, Fall 1990.

Bloodrage (Never Pick Up a Stranger): Liz Smith column, *NY Daily News,* June 28, 1980.

Cassavetes casts Tierney in *One Summer Night* (*Gloria*): Pat O'Haire column, *NY Daily News,* December 21, 1979.

Gloria: "A Brilliant Film Performance," *Sacramento Bee,* November 8, 1980.

Tierney reportedly penning memoir: "Tap Tap Tap," Liz Smith, *NY Daily News,* November 29, 1979; Voice of Broadway by Jack O'Brian, *Asbury Park (NJ) Press,* February 14, 1980.

Tierney's first starring role in years

Stars in John Russo's *Midnight*: Ibid., Tierney interview with Michael and Cheryl Murphy, *Psychotronic Video*; "Horrors! Midnight Isn't Scary," *Pittsburgh Press,* September 3, 1982; *Midnight* (1982), IMDbPro.

Barry Gifford describes the "new," old Tierney: *The Devil Thumbs a Ride & Other Unforgettable Films* by Barry Gifford, Grove, 1988.

Scene stealer in *Arthur*: "Lawrence Tierney: Man in Coffee Shop, *Arthur* (1981), IMDbPro.

The Prowler: Top-billed with Farley Granger, UA Theatres ad, *Record,* Hackensack, NJ, November 25, 1981; *The Prowler* (1981), IMDbPro.

Death of *Arthur* writer-director Steve Gordon: "Steve Gordon, Screen Writer, 44," obituary, *New York Times,* November 30, 1982.

Nothing Lasts Forever: "Tom Schiller on Lost Masterpiece Nothing Lasts Forever" by Jamie Dunn, *The Skinny,* August 26, 2019.

Tierney suffers stroke: Author interviews with Timothy Tierney, 2021; Author interviews with David De Valle, May 18, August 5, 2021.

Terrible Joe Moran: "You Dirty Rat!" Liz Smith column, *NY Daily News,* September 15, 1983; Ibid., Tierney interview with Michael and Cheryl Murphy, *Psychotronic Video; Terrible Joe Moran* (1984 TV Movie), IMDbPro.

Chapter 39

Edward Tierney and brother Larry

Ed Tierney and B and T Construction: Author interviews with Timothy Tierney, 2021.

Ed Tierney's marriage and divorce from Anne Winterburn: California divorce records, 1967, 1969, 1978; Author interviews with Timothy Tierney, 2021.

Ed Tierney and chess: "Chess Champs: Being Rooked an Honor at This School," *Los Angeles Times,* April 23, 1978; "San Juan Boy Wins Title: Chess Champion at 11," *Los Angeles Times,* May 17, 1978; "In Memoriam: Ed Tierney," *Rank & File* magazine, vol. 7, no. 2, March–April 1984; Chess by Jack Peters, *Los Angeles Times,* November 20, 1983; Author interviews with Timothy Tierney, 2021.

Chess leads to Ed's sons meeting Lawrence: Timothy Tierney and Michael Tierney interview, *The Midnight Palace with Gary Sweeney* radio show, circa 2011; Author interviews with Timothy Tierney, 2021.

"Kidnapping" of Ed's sons (Tim learns he has an "Uncle Larry"): Author interviews with Timothy Tierney, 2021.

Source Notes

Scott Brady's life as "ex-star"

"Journeyman actor": Author interviews with Timothy Tierney, 2021.

Brady's many television guest spots: Scott Brady, actor, IMDbPro.

Role in *The China Syndrome*: *The China Syndrome* (1979), IMDbPro; Author interview with Timothy Tierney, July 8, October 8, 2021.

Stricken with emphysema: Author interviews with Timothy Tierney, 2021.

Brady collapses on set of *Gremlins*: Ibid., Timothy Tierney interviews; Laura Wagner interview with Joe Dante, "Happy Birthday Lawrence Tierney's Brother, Scott Brady."

Death of Edward Tierney

Edward Tierney brings high school championship chess games to the West Coast: "Call Ed Tierney," Chess by Jack Peters, *Los Angeles Times*, December 18, 1983.

Edward Tierney dies of diabetic shock: Author interviews with Timothy Tierney, 2021.

Death brings Lawrence Tierney to Scott Brady's home: Ibid., Timothy Tierney.

Tierney's threatening and embarrassing behavior at Edward's funeral: Ibid., Timothy Tierney.

Edward Tierney buried at Riverside National Cemetery: Edward Michael Tierney, Memorials, Find A Grave.

Tribute in chess magazine: "In Memoriam: Ed Tierney," *Rank & File* magazine, vol. 7, no. 2, March–April 1984.

Tierney relocates to Los Angeles

Tierney and Scott Brady go separate ways: Timothy Tierney and Michael Tierney interview, *The Midnight Palace with Gary Sweeney* radio show, circa 2011.

Tierney picks up work, with family's support: Author interviews with Tim Tierney, 2021.

Tierney cast in *Prizzi's Honor*: *Prizzi's Honor* (1985), IMDbPro.

Tierney reconnects with Brooklyn relatives: Author interview with Edward Leahy, July 9, 2021; Author interview with Daniel Leahy, July 18, 2021; Author interview with Donald McManamon, July 27, 2021.

Tierney brags of sex with Huntz Hall's wife: Author interview with Daniel Leahy, July 18, 2021; Author interview with David Del Valle, May 18, 2021.

"F those coppers": Author interview with Donald McManamon, July 27, 2021.

Silver Bullet: *Silver Bullet* (1985), IMDbPro; Author interview with C. Courtney Joyner, March 8, 2021; Ibid., McManamon interview.

Death of Scott Brady

Scott Brady in *Whiz Kids*: *Whiz Kids*, "Altair," season 1, episode 17, IMDbPro; "Altair" episode, YouTube.

Scott Brady dies of pulmonary fibrosis: "Actor Scott Brady Dies at 60," *Los Angeles Times*, April 17, 1985; "Movie Tough Guy Scott Brady Dies: Ruggedly Handsome Star of Westerns Was 60," *Los Angeles Times*, April 18, 1985; "Scott Brady, Actor, is Dead;

Appeared in Films and on TV," Associated Press report, *New York Times,* April 18, 1985; "Actor Scott Brady, 60, Once Hollywood's No. 1 bachelor," Herald wire services, *Miami Herald,* April 18, 1985.

Eddie Leahy accompanies Tierney to brother's wake: Author interview with Edward Leahy, July 9, 2021.

Tierney urinates outside funeral home, smashes Michael's guitar: Ibid., Edward Leahy; Author interview with Timothy Tierney, June 30, July 8, 2021.

Chapter 40

Tierney's new generation of fans and friends

Young fans: Author interview with Todd Mecklem, May 28, 2021; Author interview with David Del Valle, May 18, August 5, 2021.

C. Courtney Joyner and friends meet Tierney for first time: Author interviews and correspondence with C. Courtney Joyner, 2021; Author interview with Will Huston, June 14, 2021; Author interview with Ron Zwang, July 1, 2021; Author interview with Jeff Burr, March 7, 2022.

Tierney's adult relationship with daughter: Ibid., C. Courtney Joyner; Author interviews with Timothy Tierney, 2021; Author interviews with David De Valle, 2021.

Tierney's relationship with nephew Michael: "Family Tradition: Michael Tierney interviewed by Rick McKay," *Scarlet Street* magazine, issue 29, 1998; Timothy Tierney and Michael Tierney interview, *The Midnight Palace with Gary Sweeney* radio show, circa 2011; Author interviews with Timothy Tierney, 2021; Author interviews with C. Courtney Joyner, 2021; Author interview with Derek Bell, March 17, 2021; Author interview with Will Thimes, May 16, 2021.

Murphy's Law: Author interview with C. Courtney Joyner, March 8, 2021; *Murphy's Law* (1986), IMDbPro.

Tierney speaks at Tyrone Power tribute: "27 Years Later: Fans Gather to Remember Tyrone Power," by Patt Morrison, *Los Angeles Times,* November 26, 1985.

Scott Alexander and Larry Karaszewski meet Tierney: Author interview with Scott Alexander and Larry Karaszewski, May 14, 2021; Author correspondence with Scott Alexander, May 2021.

From a Whisper to a Scream: Author interview with C. Courtney Joyner, March 8, 2021; Author interview with David Del Valle, May 18, August 5, 2021.

Tierney in *Tough Guys Don't Dance*: Author interview with Stephan Morrow, May 7, 2021; Tierney interview with Michael and Cheryl Murphy, *Psychotronic Video* magazine, no. 8, Fall 1990; "Film Review: Tough Guys Don't Dance," *Variety,* May 20, 1987; By Mitchell Smyth; "Norman Mailer 'Tough' Enough?" *NY Daily News,* September 20, 1987; "Mailer's Mind's Eye," *Vancouver (British Columbia) Sun,* October 10, 1987.

Tierney in final scene of *Hill Street Blues*: "'Hill Street' Finale: It's Time to Go," *Chicago Tribune,* May 12, 1987; *Hill Street Blues* (1981–1987), "It Ain't Over Till It's Over," season 7, episode 22, aired May 12, 1987, IMDbPro.

Pilot Derek Bell meets Tierney, takes him flying, other stories: Author interview with Derek Bell, March 17, 2021.

Tierney television work: Lawrence Tierney, IMDbPro.

Star Trek: The Next Generation: Lawrence Tierney as Cyrus Redblock in "The Big Goodbye," IMDb; "Holodeck," *Star Trek: The Next Generation Technical Manual* by Rick Sternbach and Michael Okuda, Pocket Books, 1991.

"Heck, I threw away about seven careers through drink": "'Dillinger' has finally wised up," Mitchell Smyth, *Toronto Star,* December 6, 1987.

Tierney's last hurrah; brawl and bar crawl: Author interview with C. Courtney Joyner, March 8, 2021.

Jimmie Fidler dies: "Jimmie Fidler, 89, Hollywood Columnist," obituary, *New York Times,* August 12, 1988.

Platinum Violin Case award: "Ball Brings out Furs, Sequins, Stars of Prohibition Hollywood," *Los Angeles Times,* September 14, 1988.

Cast in *Dillinger* television movie: Lawrence Tierney as Sheriff Sarber, *Dillinger* (1991), IMDbPro; "Say Murderer Escaped from Indiana Prison: Jesse Sarber Killed by Gunman, Who Frees Noted Prisoner; John Dillinger is Taken from Jail," *Dayton (OH) Daily News,* October 13, 1933.

City of Hope "one of the best acting jobs": Author interview with C. Courtney Joyner, July 16, 2021.

Tarantino and John Sayles's *Lady in Red* script: *Once Upon a Time in Hollywood: A Novel* by Quentin Tarantino, Harper Perennial, 2021.

Problem Child 2 audition: Author interview with Scott Alexander and Larry Karaszewski, May 14, 2021; Author correspondence with Scott Alexander, May 2021.

"The Jacket" episode of *Seinfeld*: Author interviews with C. Courtney Joyner, 2021; Author interviews with David Del Valle, 2021; Julia Louis-Dreyfus, Jason Alexander, *Seinfeld*: "Inside Look: The Jacket," *Seinfeld: The Complete Series,* DVD set.

More on Tierney's kleptomania: Ibid., C. Courtney Joyner, David Del Valle.

Chapter 41

Quentin Tarantino

Tarantino assumed Tierney was dead: Author interview with C. Courtney Joyner, March 8, 2021.

Tarantino meets Tierney: Ibid., C. Courtney Joyner; Author interviews with Ron Zwang, July 1, November 9, 2021.

Lawrence Bender rejects advice in hiring Tierney: Author interview with Will Huston, June 14, 2021

Reservoir Dogs

Michael Madsen on Tierney: Author interview with Michael Madsen, June 17, 2021; Michael Madsen interview, "One Big Teddy Bear: A Tribute to Lawrence Tierney," *Reservoir Dogs* 10th Anniversary Special Limited Edition DVD, 2002.

Filming of *Reservoir Dogs*: Ibid., Michael Madsen interview; Author interview with C. Courtney Joyner, March 8, 2021; "One Big Teddy Bear: A Tribute to Lawrence Tierney," *Reservoir Dogs* 10th Anniversary Special Limited Edition DVD, 2002.

"Tierney was a complete lunatic...needed to be sedated": "Why Quentin Tarantino wants to be the Next Howard Hawks," *Guardian*, January 12, 2010.

Tierney scene outside Musso & Frank Grill: Author interview with Michael Madsen, June 17, 2021; Michael Madsen, Tim Roth interviews, "One Big Teddy Bear: A Tribute to Lawrence Tierney," *Reservoir Dogs* 10th Anniversary Special Limited Edition DVD, 2002.

Tierney upbraids Madsen during "naming" scene: *Reservoir Dogs* (1992); Author interview with Michael Madsen, June 17, 2021.

Tierney and Tarantino fight on *Reservoir Dogs* set: Author interviews with C. Courtney Joyner, 2021; Author interview with Michael Madsen, June 17, 2021; Quentin Tarantino, Michael Madsen, Tim Roth interviews, "One Big Teddy Bear: A Tribute to Lawrence Tierney," *Reservoir Dogs* 10th Anniversary Special Limited Edition DVD, 2002.

Tierney shoots at nephew Michael: Author interview with Timothy Tierney, June 30, 2021; Author interviews with C. Courtney Joyner, 2021; Author interview with Will Huston, June 14, 2021; Author interview with Michael Madsen, June 17, 2021; Author interview with Ron Zwang, July 1, 2021; Don Gerler interview cited in "Down These Mean Streets: Lawrence Tierney interviewed by Rick McKay," *Scarlet Street* magazine, issue 29, 1998; Los Angeles Superior Court view, State Records of the United States.

Sentence for shooting: Ibid., State Records of the United States; Author interview with Stephan Morrow, May 7, 2021.

Edward Bunker on first time he met Tierney: Edward Bunker interview, "One Big Teddy Bear: A Tribute to Lawrence Tierney," *Reservoir Dogs* 10th Anniversary Special Limited Edition DVD, 2002.

Chris Penn lawn furniture anecdotes: Chris Penn interview, "One Big Teddy Bear: A Tribute to Lawrence Tierney," *Reservoir Dogs* 10th Anniversary Special Limited Edition DVD, 2002; Michael Madsen interview, "One Big Teddy Bear: A Tribute to Lawrence Tierney," *Reservoir Dogs* 10th Anniversary Special Limited Edition DVD, 2002; Author interview with Michael Madsen, June 17, 2021.

Reservoir Dogs premieres at Sundance festival: "Sundance Snowballs into a Big, Cozy Film Fest" by Kenneth Turan, *Los Angeles Times*, January 24, 1992; "Film Review: Reservoir Dogs," *Variety*, January 26, 1992; "Not Enough Bite in 'Reservoir Dogs,'" by Roger Ebert, syndicated review, *Sacramento Bee*, October 30, 1992; *Down and Dirty Pictures: Miramax, Sundance and the Rise of Independent Film* by Peter Biskind, Simon & Schuster, 2004.

Chapter 42

Post *Reservoir Dogs*

Tierney's face: interview, "One Big Teddy Bear: A Tribute to Lawrence Tierney," *Reservoir Dogs* 10th Anniversary Special Limited Edition DVD, 2002.

Eddie Presley: Author correspondence with Jeff Burr, May 2021; Author interview with Will Huston, June 16, 2021; Author interview with Jeff Burr, March 7, 2022;

Eddie Presley (1992), IMDbPro; *Eddie Presley* Two-Disc Special Edition DVD, Tempe Video, 2004.

Tarantino and Duane Whitaker commiserate about Tierney: *Character Kings 2: Hollywood's Familiar Faces Discuss the Art & Business of Acting,* by Scott Voisin, Bear-Manor Media, 2016. "Tierney's Tyranny," Eleven-minute special feature, *Eddie Presley* Two-Disc Special Edition DVD, Tempe Video, 2004.

Tierney well-educated, well-read: Author interview with C. Courtney Joyner, July 16, 2021; Author interviews with David Del Valle, 2021; Author interviews with Timothy Tierney, 2021.

Tierney's prostate issues: Author interview with David Del Valle, May 18, 2021.

Tierney's hijinks: Author interview with Scott Alexander and Larry Karaszewski, May 14, 2021; Author correspondence with Scott Alexander, May 2021; Author interviews with David Del Valle, 2021; Author interviews with Timothy Tierney, 2021.

Tierney with a drag queen at Cornel Wilde's party: Author interview with David Del Valle, May 18, 2021; "Dillinger and the Drag Queen," David Del Valle, The Del Valle Archives, July 3, 2013.

Tierney as annoyance to young friends: Author interview with Ron Zwang, July 1, 2021; Author interviews with David Del Valle, May 15, 2021.

Tierney's friends from "old days": Author interviews with C. Courtney Joyner, 2021; email correspondence from C. Courtney Joyner, October 24, 2021.

Brian Brookshire and *The Route*

Brookshire meets Tierney: Author interview with Brian Brookshire, July 22, 2022.

Tierney films *The Route*: Ibid., Brookshire interview; Conrad Brooks, *Conrad Talks Hollywood: A Scott Shaw Zen Documentary,* Light Source Films; *The Route* (1993), IMDbPro.

Julie Davis and *French Intensive*

Tierney at 1989 Telluride Film Festival: Author interview with Julie Davis, June 16, 2021; "Better-Than-Average Crop at Telluride," Jay Carr, *Boston Globe,* September 6, 1989; "Surprises and Disappointments Mark Telluride Film Festival" by Roger Ebert, syndicated column, *Salt Lake Tribune,* September 8, 1989.

Tierney films role in *French Intensive*: Ibid., Julie Davis interview; *French Intensive* (1994), IMDbPro.

"Female Woody Allen": "The Female Woody Allen," Harry Medved, *Jewish Journal,* February 26, 1998.

"He treated me like a grandfather": Author interview with Julie Davis, June 16, 2021.

Television work

Silk Stalkings: *Silk Stalkings* (1991) (TV series), IMDbPro.

Amy Fisher–Joey Buttafuoco television movies: "Television Movies about Amy Fisher Score Big," Associated Press report, *La Crosse (WI) Tribune,* January 6, 1993.

Red

Tube Bar tapes: "The Legend of the Tube Bar," The Legendary Tube Bar Recordings, by Mike Walsh, The Tube Bar Homepage, missionCREEP.

Filming *Red*: Author interview with C. Courtney Joyner, July 16, 2021; Author interview with Ron Zwang, July 1, 2021; *Red* (1993), IMDbPro; *Red* (DVD) *Film Threat*, October 1, 2004.

Natural Born Killers

Fight with Woody Harrelson: Ibid., C. Courtney Joyner interview; Author interview with Will Thimes, May 16, 2021; "Thesp Sues Stone over 'Killer' Canning," Army Archerd, *Variety*, July 7, 1994; "Tough Guys Do Sue," George Rush, *NY Daily News*, July 8, 1994.

Weekend of Horrors convention: Author interview with Todd Mecklem, May 28, 2021; "Horror Weekend," *San Bernardino County Sun*, April 30, 1993.

Chapter 43

Final decade

Tierney interviewed in coffee shop: "'Dogs' Lifts '40s Tough Guy out of Dumps: Actor Tierney's Attitude Doesn't Match New Success," John Stanley, *San Francisco Chronicle*, June 20, 1993.

Tierney crashes Beverly Hills house location of *Pulp Fiction*: Author interview with Brian Brookshire, July 22, 2022.

Tierney moves to Venice, CA: Author interviews with Timothy Tierney, 2021; Author interview with Will Thimes, May 16, 2021; "Down These Mean Streets: Lawrence Tierney interviewed by Rick McKay" and "Family Tradition: Michael Tierney interviewed by Rick McKay," *Scarlet Street* magazine, issue 29, 1998; Author scout of Tierney home locations, May–June 2021.

Will Thimes meets Tierney, becomes his lawyer: Ibid., Will Thimes interview.

Tierney's birthday at Hollywood Moguls nightclub: "Cult Film Fest Offers the Best of the Worst," *Los Angeles Times*, February 26, 1994.

Tarantino makes up with Tierney: Author interview with C. Courtney Joyner, July 16, 2021, and related email correspondence.

Junior: Tierney as Mover in *Junior* (1994), IMDbPro; "Pregnant Arnold as Preposterous as It Sounds: 'Junior' Saved by Brilliant Thompson," *Santa Fe New Mexican*, December 9, 1994.

Natural Born Killers lawsuit: Author interview with Will Thimes, May 16, 2021; "Thesp Sues Stone over 'Killer' Canning," Army Archerd, *Variety*, July 7, 1994.

More film and television roles

Tierney considered for *Four Rooms*: Author interview with Jeff Burr, March 7, 2022.

As "Don Brodka" in "Marge Be Not Proud" episode: *The Simpsons*, "Marge Be Not Proud," season 7, episode 11, IMDbPro.

Tierney as "craziest guest star experience": Josh Weinstein, "*The Simpsons,* season 7 DVD commentary for the episode 'Marge Be Not Proud,'" 20th Century Fox 2005; "The Simpsons Writer Marks 25 Years of Episode with Crazy Behind-the-Scenes Story of Cameo Star," Cydney Yeates, *Metro,* December 18, 2020.

Patton Oswalt sees Tierney in New Beverly Cinema: Author interview with Patton Oswalt, July 19, 2021.

Tierney suffers stroke, refuses ambulance: Author interview with Will Thimes, May 16, 2021.

Voice of Rick in *Oz Kids: Who Stole Santa and Christmas in Oz,* 1996, IMDbPro.

ER: Tierney as Jack Johnson in "Don't Ask Don't Tell," *ER,* season 3, episode 3, aired October 19, 1996, IMDbPro.

Star Trek: Deep Space Nine: Tierney as Regent of Palamar in "Business as Usual," *Star Trek: Deep Space Nine,* season 5, episode 18, IMDbPro; Ira Steven Behr, executive producer, recollection on Todd Mecklem's Lawrence Tierney Tribute Page.

American Hero, "I thought it would be the last film rolled on Larry": Author interview with Jeff Burr, March 7, 2022.

Role in *Southie* (also seated): *Southie* (1998), IMDbPro.

Filming cameo in *Armageddon*: Author interviews with Timothy Tierney, 2021; "Down These Mean Streets: Lawrence Tierney interviewed by Rick McKay," *Scarlet Street* magazine, issue 29, 1998; Tierney as Gramp Stamper (uncredited) in *Armageddon* (1998), IMDbPro; *Armageddon,* Alternate Versions, Criterion's two-DVD "including scene between Harry Stamper and his father (played by Lawrence Tierney)," IMDbPro.

Chapter 44

Gimme Some Larry

Gimme Some Larry: *Gimme Some Larry* DVD; Phone message from Elisabeth Sikes, August 12, 2021; Author interview with Ron Zwang, July 1, 2021; SXSW Film Festival winners, Documentary Short, Runner-up: "Gimme Some Larry" (Elisabeth Sikes), *Austin American-Statesman,* March 1999; Short Cuts, *Austin Chronicle,* May 7, 1999; "Down These Mean Streets: Lawrence Tierney interviewed by Rick McKay," *Scarlet Street* magazine, issue 29, 1998.

"They had me brainwashed": *Gimme Some Larry* DVD.

Michael moves Tierney back to Hollywood: Author interviews with Timothy Tierney, 2021; "Down These Mean Streets: Lawrence Tierney interviewed by Rick McKay," *Scarlet Street* magazine, issue 29, 1998.

Born to Kill screening: "The Big Leak," Eddie Muller, 1999, NoirCity.com; Muller interview, *Hollywood Five-O,* Fall 2002; author interview with C. Courtney Joyner, July 16, 2021.

Armageddon Director's Cut released: *Armageddon* (The Criterion Collection), Touchstone Pictures, 2008.

Evicted: *Evicted,* MovieLink, Blockbuster Productions; "Family Tradition: Michael Tierney interviewed by Rick McKay," *Scarlet Street* magazine, issue 29, 1998; author interviews with Timothy Tierney, 2021; *Evicted* (1999), IMDbPro.

Tierney's death in Sharon Medical Center: Author interviews with Timothy Tierney, 2001; Author interviews with C. Courtney Joyner, 2021; Lawrence Tierney certificate of death, Registrar-Recorder, County of Los Angeles, State of California, VitalChek.

Media coverage of death: "Lawrence Tierney, 82; Actor Was Real-Life Tough Guy," *Los Angeles Times,* February 28, 2002; "Lawrence Tierney, 82, Actor Known for Tough Guy Roles," Associated Press report, *New York Times,* March 1, 2002; Lawrence Tierney, *(UK) Independent,* March 1, 2002.

Tierney's wake: Ibid., Timothy Tierney interviews; Ibid., C. Courtney Joyner interviews; Author interview with Todd Mecklem, May 28, 2021.

Evicted's first official release: *Evicted* (1999) DVD release, May 4, 2004, IMDbPro.

Epilogue

Lawrence Tierney's legacy

Tierney's legacy: Author interview with C. Courtney Joyner, July 16, 2021.

Tierney's estate: Author interview with Timothy Tierney, October 8, 2021.

Tierney's legacy: Author interviews with Timothy Tierney, 2021; Author interview with David Del Valle, October 6, 2021.

Lawrence Tierney's cremains

Michael Tierney takes ashes to New York City: Author interviews with Timothy Tierney, 2021; Author interview with Daniel Leahy, July 18, 2021; Author interview with Edward Leahy, July 9, 2021, phone calls and correspondence, July, August 2021.

Cousin Danny Leahy scatters ashes outside Brooklyn bar: Ibid., Daniel Leahy interview; Ibid., Edward Leahy interviews, calls and correspondence.

Eddie Leahy saves portion of cremains, pours them in Wallkill River: Ibid., Edward Leahy interviews, calls and correspondence.

Index

Index

Index

Index

Index

Screen Classics

Screen Classics is a series of critical biographies, film histories, and analytical studies focusing on neglected filmmakers and important screen artists and subjects, from the era of silent cinema through the golden age of Hollywood to the international generation of today. Books in the Screen Classics series are intended for scholars and general readers alike. The contributing authors are established figures in their respective fields. This series also serves the purpose of advancing scholarship on film personalities and themes with ties to Kentucky.

Series Editor
Patrick McGilligan

Books in the Series

Olivia de Havilland: Lady Triumphant
　　Victoria Amador
Mae Murray: The Girl with the Bee-Stung Lips
　　Michael G. Ankerich
Harry Dean Stanton: Hollywood's Zen Rebel
　　Joseph B. Atkins
Hedy Lamarr: The Most Beautiful Woman in Film
　　Ruth Barton
Rex Ingram: Visionary Director of the Silent Screen
　　Ruth Barton
Conversations with Classic Film Stars: Interviews from Hollywood's Golden Era
　　James Bawden and Ron Miller
Conversations with Legendary Television Stars: Interviews from the First Fifty Years
　　James Bawden and Ron Miller
You Ain't Heard Nothin' Yet: Interviews with Stars from Hollywood's Golden Era
　　James Bawden and Ron Miller
Charles Boyer: The French Lover
　　John Baxter
Von Sternberg
　　John Baxter
Hitchcock's Partner in Suspense: The Life of Screenwriter Charles Bennett
　　Charles Bennett, edited by John Charles Bennett
Hitchcock and the Censors
　　John Billheimer
A Uniquely American Epic: Intimacy and Action, Tenderness and Violence in Sam Peckinpah's The Wild Bunch
　　Edited by Michael Bliss
My Life in Focus: A Photographer's Journey with Elizabeth Taylor and the Hollywood Jet Set
　　Gianni Bozzacchi with Joey Tayler